Nature Wars

Studies in Environmental Anthropology and Ethnobiology

General Editor: **Roy Ellen**, FBA
Emeritus Professor of Anthropology and Human Ecology, University of Kent at Canterbury
Interest in environmental anthropology has grown steadily in recent years, reflecting national and international concern about the environment and developing research priorities. This major international series, which continues a series first published by Harwood and Routledge, is a vehicle for publishing up-to-date monographs and edited works on particular issues, themes, places or peoples which focus on the interrelationship between society, culture and environment. Relevant areas include human ecology, the perception and representation of the environment, ethno-ecological knowledge, the human dimension of biodiversity conservation and the ethnography of environmental problems. While the underlying ethos of the series will be anthropological, the approach is interdisciplinary.

Recent volumes:

Volume 27
Nature Wars
Essays around a Contested Concept
Roy Ellen

Volume 26
Ecological Nostalgias
Memory, Affect and Creativity in Times of
Ecological Upheavals
Edited by Olivia Angé and David Berliner

Volume 25
Birds of Passage
Hunting and Conservation in Malta
Mark-Anthony Falzon

Volume 24
At Home on the Waves
Human Habitation of the Sea from the Mesolithic
to Today
Edited by Tanya J. King and Gary Robinson

Volume 23
Edges, Fringes, Frontiers
Integral Ecology, Indigenous Knowledge and
Sustainability in Guyana
Thomas B. Henfrey

Volume 22
Indigeneity and the Sacred
Indigenous Revival and the Conservation of
Sacred Natural Sites in the Americas
Edited by Fausto Sarmiento and Sarah Hitchner

Volume 21
Trees, Knots, and Outriggers
Environmental Knowledge in the Northeast Kula
Ring
Frederick H. Damon

Volume 20
Beyond the Lens of Conservation
Malagasy and Swiss Imaginations of One Another
Eva Keller

Volume 19
Sustainable Development
An Appraisal from the Gulf Region
Edited by Paul Sillitoe

Volume 18
Things Fall Apart?
The Political Ecology of Forest Governance in
Southern Nigeria
Pauline von Hellermann

For a full volume listing, please see the series page on our website:
http://berghahnbooks.com/series/environmental-anthropology-and-ethnobiology

Nature Wars

Essays around a Contested Concept

Roy Ellen

berghahn
NEW YORK · OXFORD
www.berghahnbooks.com

First published in 2021 by
Berghahn Books
www.berghahnbooks.com

© 2021, 2026 Roy Ellen
First paperback edition published in 2026

All rights reserved. Except for the quotation of short passages for the purposes of criticism and review, no part of this book may be reproduced in any form or by any means, electronic or mechanical, including photocopying, recording, or any information storage and retrieval system now known or to be invented, without written permission of the publisher.

Library of Congress Cataloging-in-Publication Data

Names: Ellen, R. F., 1947– author.
Title: Nature wars : essays around a contested concept / Roy Ellen.
Description: New York : Berghahn Books, 2021. | Series: Studies in environmental anthropology and ethnobiology; volume 27 | Includes bibliographical references and index.
Identifiers: LCCN 2020017772 (print) | LCCN 2020017773 (ebook) | ISBN 9781789208979 (hardcover) | ISBN 9781789208986 (ebook)
Subjects: LCSH: Nature—Effect of human beings on. | Ethnoscience. | Ethnoscience—Indonesia. | Philosophical anthropology. | Ethnoecology.
Classification: LCC GF75 .E48 2021 (print) | LCC GF75 (ebook) | DDC 304.2—dc23
LC record available at https://lccn.loc.gov/2020017772
LC ebook record available at https://lccn.loc.gov/2020017773

British Library Cataloguing in Publication Data

A catalogue record for this book is available from the British Library

EU GPSR Authorized Representative

LOGOS EUROPE, 9 rue Nicolas Poussin, 17000, LA ROCHELLE, France
Email: Contact@logoseurope.eu

ISBN 978-1-78920-897-9 hardback
ISBN 978-1-83695-688-4 paperback
ISBN 978-1-80758-576-1 epub
ISBN 978-1-78920-898-6 web pdf

https://doi.org/10.3167/9781789208979

Contents

List of Illustrations	vi
Preface	ix
Acknowledgements	xii
Note on Orthography	xiv
Introduction. Nature Beyond the 'Ontological Turn'	1
Chapter 1. What Black Elk Left Unsaid	28
Chapter 2. Comparative Natures in Melanesia	40
Chapter 3. Political Contingency, Historical Ecology and the Renegotiation of Nature	53
Appendix: The Consequences of Deforestation – A Nuaulu Text from Rouhua Seram 1994	72
Chapter 4. Indigenous Environmental Knowledge and Its Transformations	76
Chapter 5. From Ethno-science to Science	103
Chapter 6. Local and Scientific Understandings of Forest Diversity	135
Chapter 7. Why Aren't the Nuaulu Like the Matsigenka?	161
Chapter 8. Roots, Shoots and Leaves: The Art of Weeding	183
Chapter 9. Tools, Agency and the Category of 'Living Things'	199
Chapter 10. Is There a Role for Ontologies in Understanding Plant Knowledge Systems?	224
References	244
Index	277

Illustrations

Figures

1.1.	A banner publicising the Green Collective, which 'seeks to facilitate the growth of a green movement through nonviolence, creative action and networking'.	33
3.1.	Three frames from a videotape recorded on 8 March 1990 and discussed in this chapter. Komisi Soumori (*ia onate* Soumori and 'kepala kampung') addresses the world.	69
5.1.	Mezzotint of Linnaeus in Lapp costume; Dunkerton, from a painting by M. Hoffman.	108
5.2.	Print of Linnaeus outside his tent, the Frontispiece to the *Flora Lapponica*, published in 1737.	109
5.3.	Spermatozoa as depicted in different seventeenth-century images: *a, b* and *c* are from Antony van Leeuwenhoek's drawings of dog spermatozoa (1679), *d* is Hartsoeker's homunculus in a human spermatazoan (1694), and *e, f* and *g* are human spermatozoa from Francois Plantades (Delenpatius), respectively showing intact cell, and broken to show the homunculi.	110
5.4.	Early illustrations of the crustacean *Squilla mantis* and the nymphs of *Irona renardi*, including (6) and (9) taken from Valentijn (2002–2003 [1726]), following Rumphius.	111
5.5.	Illustration from R.J. Thornton, *Temple of Flora*, Volume II, 1807, showing Aesculapius, Flora, Ceres and Cupid paying homage to a bust of Linnaeus.	125
6.1.	Species numbers in relation to plot size for various forest composition studies in the Moluccas.	141
6.2.	Looking eastwards along the Nua valley towards Mount Binaiya from Notone Hatae on the trans-Seram highway; midway between the south coast and Sawai on the north coast, but on the southern watershed.	145

6.3.	Plot 8. Riparian forest at Sokonana, north of the Ruatan river.	147
6.4.	Upland forest with *Agathis dammara*, near plot 9 (Rohnesi), west of trans-Seram highway near Wae Sune Maraputi.	152
6.5.	*Canarium hirsutum* below the old village site of Amatene (plot 11).	153
7.1.	Plot 11. Amatene: old village site, northwest of Upa estuary.	169
7.2.	Plot 7. Part of *sin wesie* Peinisa (protected forest) at Mon Sanae.	173
8.1.	Power grip (a) and precision grip (b).	190
8.2.	The default weeding action (in a Kentish country garden).	191
8.3.	The institutional context of learning how to garden in the contemporary UK.	197
9.1.	Series of **asunaete**: cuscus (*Phalanger*) skewers planted as an offering to ancestral spirits.	203
9.2.	*Aha*, Nuaulu sago-processing apparatus.	204
9.3.	Treadle-operated coconut grater, Rouhua village, Seram.	206
9.4.	Tobelo taxonomy of 'biotic forms' based on semantic componential analysis.	209
9.5.	Edmund Leach's (1964) version of the English classification of nature.	210
9.6.	American English tool taxonomy.	213
10.1.	One of a set of 77 medical paintings copied in the time of the Thirteenth Dalai Lama in the 1920s for the training of physicians in Buryiatia.	239

Maps

3.1.	South Seram, showing former and current Nuaulu settlements and plot locations mentioned in Chapters 3, 6 and 7, as of 1996.	55
6.1.	Seram in the context of the eastern Indonesian archipelago, showing places mentioned in the text. Line A represents Wallace's Line of faunal balance, Line B is Weber's Line, and Line C is the western boundary of the Australo-Pacific region.	139

| 6.2. | South Seram, showing superimposed official forestry categories. | 149 |

Tables

6.1.	Basic data on location and description of plots.	140
6.2.	Summary of selected 1996 plot data: levels of identification.	142
6.3.	Family frequencies for individual trees in 1996 plots.	144
6.4.	Summary of plot data: floristics and forest structure.	146
6.5.	Forest types distinguished by Pattimura University Agricultural Faculty survey team and utilised by Glatzel (1992).	150
7.1.	Summary of selected 1996 plot data: selected and aggregated uses.	175
7.2.	General characteristics of Nuaulu forest patch categories based on 1996 plot data.	176

Preface

The title of this book is both deliberately provocative and deliberately ambiguous. An obvious allusion for many will be to recent controversies in the politics of the environment, and indeed it is partly about this. However, these episodes in our recent and current history cannot be understood except in relation to parallel academic controversies of equal ferocity (though less open to public view) concerning 'nature' as an idea, both as apparent in public discourse and in science, between the sciences, and in philosophy and the humanities. Organised around contentious issues, debates and discussions concerning the various ways in which the concept of nature has been used, abused, endlessly deconstructed and reclaimed, as reflected in anthropological, scientific and similar writing over the last several decades, this volume comprises eleven chapters, nine of which have been previously published, plus two that have not.

All the chapters were originally conceived as self-standing presentations, essays or articles, but of those pieces previously published I have made a few alterations to the text. These include shortening titles, editing passages where contemporaneous references and allusions would now look dated, absorbing plates into a continuous series of figures, deleting (and instead cross-referencing) figures that appear in more than one original publication, and updating figures and tables where new data have become available, such as revised plant nomenclature. These and other small alterations help to bring all the chapters in line with the overarching themes, so as better to connect the subject matter. In some cases this has involved removing text that – while appropriate in the original – in the present context has become redundant. I have also taken the opportunity to make a few corrections. Most of the chapters have – I think – stood the test of time. Only Chapter 1 retains a slightly dated feel to it, published as it was as a more popular intervention in discussions about traditional peoples and Green politics at a time when events were fast moving and later to develop much more.

The chapters appear in the chronological order of their publication or first public appearance. Year of first publication helps to explain factual information (such as population figures, other numerical data that have since altered, spans of time or political events) that now might seem dated, provides further context, and in some cases indicates how the debates have changed over time; but of course in not every case is order of publication an accurate marker of when they were actually written, or when the research was undertaken. Finally, much of the Introduction, Chapters 2, 4 and 10, which were first written as contributions to collected works, afterwords or as commentaries, have a particular narrative structure, and necessarily refer to other contributions in the collections of which they are part. In republishing them here, a certain amount of judicious editing has been required, including, for example, adding full references to the other published chapters commented on, or in some cases referring the reader to oral presentations that were not published as part of the collection. The details of publication history and the circumstances of production of individual chapters are as follows.

The larger part of the Introduction was originally written for a proposed Italian collection of essays on the 'ontological turn', which did not materialize. It appears here for the first time, though several passages in the final two sections have previously appeared in Ellen (2016), here Chapter 10. Chapter 1 is a slightly modified version of a public lecture delivered at the University of Durham in November 1985. It was first offered to *The Ecologist* under its then editor Edward Goldsmith, where it was rejected as being not in keeping with the ethos of the magazine. It was subsequently published in 1986 in *Anthropology Today* as 'What Black Elk Left Unsaid: On the Illusory Images of Green Primitivism'.

Chapter 2 started life as an invited commentary for a session at the 1996 American Anthropological Association conference held in San Francisco, and was published in 1998 as 'Comparative Natures in Melanesia: An External Perspective', in a special issue of *Social Analysis* edited by Sandra Bamford.

Chapter 3 was presented at a conference held at Dalhousie University in Halifax, Nova Scotia in 1995, organised by Tania Li. A condensed version was published in the conference report, and the definitive version in 1999, as 'Forest Knowledge, Forest Transformation: Political Contingency, Historical Ecology and the Renegotiation of Nature in Central Seram', in *Transforming the Indonesian Uplands: Marginality, Power and Production*, edited by Tania Li.

Chapter 4 first made an appearance as a prospectus and summary prepared for a workshop held at the University of Kent in 1997. The version reproduced here was published in 2000 with Holly Harris as the 'Introduction' to *Indigenous Environmental Knowledge and Its Transformations: Critical Anthropological Perspectives*, edited by myself, Peter Parkes and Alan Bicker. However, a partial prequel appeared in 1997, also co-authored with Holly Harris, as 'Concepts of Indigenous Knowledge in Scientific and Development Studies Literature: A Critical Assessment', *APFT Working*

Papers, No. 2, 15 pp, and in part in 1999 as 'Embeddedness of Indigenous Environmental Knowledge', in *Cultural and Spiritual Values of Biodiversity*, edited by D. Posey (United Nations Environmental Programme; London: Intermediate Technology Publications, pp. 180–84), and in 2003 as 'Indigenous Environmental Knowledge, the History of Science and the Discourse of Development', in *Nature Knowledge: Ethnoscience, Cognition and Utility*, edited by G. Sanga and G. Ortalli (Oxford: Berghahn Books, pp. 297–300).

Chapter 5 was presented at a meeting of the British Association's Festival of Science held in Salford in 2003, in a session organised by Paul Sillitoe. It was subsequently published in 2004 as 'From Ethno-science to Science, or "What the Indigenous Knowledge Debate Tells Us About How Scientists Define Their Project"', in a special issue of the *Journal of Cognition and Culture* devoted to 'Studies in Cognitive Anthropology of Science'.

Chapters 6 and 7 are linked, as they are two iterations and elaborations of a paper delivered at the Eighth International Congress of Ethnobiology held in Addis Ababa in 2002, as 'Local Knowledge and Categorisation of Forest Diversity Among the Nuaulu of Seram, Eastern Indonesia'. Chapter 6 was published in 2007 as 'Plots, Typologies and Ethnoecology: Local and Scientific Understandings of Forest Diversity on Seram', in *Global vs Local Knowledge*, edited by Paul Sillitoe; and Chapter 7 in 2010 as 'Why Aren't the Nuaulu Like the Matsigenka? Knowledge and Categorization of Forest Diversity on Seram, Eastern Indonesia', in *Landscape Ethnoecology: Concepts of Biotic and Physical Space*, edited by Leslie Main Johnson and Eugene Hunn.

Chapter 8 was prepared for a conference on 'The Anthropology of Hands' that took place on 24–26 June 2015 to mark the fiftieth anniversary celebrations of the University of Kent. An earlier version of Chapter 9 was given at the colloquium 'Des Êtres Vivants et des Artefacts' held in April 2014 at the Musée du Quai Branly in Paris, and published in 2016 as 'Tools, Agency and the Category of "Living Things"', in *Des Êtres Vivants et des Artefacts, Paris* (Les Actes de colloques en ligne du musée du quai Branly), available at http://actesbranly.revues.org/655. A revised version was published in *Classification from Antiquity to Modern Times: Sources, Methods, and Theories from an Interdisciplinary Perspective*, edited by Tanja Pommerening and Walter Bisang, the outcome of a German Research Training Workshop held at the University of Mainz in 2014.

Chapter 10 was presented in 2014 at a conference held in Oxford under the auspices of the Oxford Centre for Research in the Humanities, and published in 2016 as 'Is There a Role for Ontologies in Understanding Plant Knowledge Systems?', in a special issue of the *Journal of Ethnobiology* entitled 'Botanical Ontologies'.

Roy Ellen
Crockshard Farmhouse, Wingham

Acknowledgements

All the chapters, though to differing extents, draw upon my own fieldwork in Indonesia. Research in the Nuaulu area of Seram (1970–2015) has been sponsored by the Indonesian Institute of Sciences (LIPI: Lembaga llmu Pengetahuan Indonesia) and more recently also by Pattimura University, and the Maluku Study Centre attached to the University in Ambon. Financial support between 1969 and 1992 came from a combination of the former UK Social Science Research Council, the London-Cornell Project for East and Southeast Asian Studies, the Central Research Fund of the University of London, the Galton Foundation and the Hayter Travel Awards Scheme. Most recently, directly and substantially, it relies on the support of ESRC (Economic and Social Research Council) grant R000 236082 for work on 'Deforestation and forest knowledge in south central Seram, eastern Indonesia' during 1996. Additionally, for this work I need to acknowledge the support of Professor Hermien Soselisa and Dr Rosemary Bolton in Ambon, the Indonesian National Herbarium in Bogor, and in particular Dr Johannis Mogea and Professor Johan Iskandar of the Institute of Ecology, Padjadjaran University, Bandung. The fieldwork reported here was undertaken mainly in 1996, but also draws on long-term fieldwork conducted between 1969 and 1971, and for shorter periods in 1973, 1975, 1981, 1986 and 1992. As ever, I rely on the continuing and enthusiastic involvement and support of Nuaulu friends and co-researchers. In Canterbury I am grateful for the advice of Helen Newing. Christine Eagle and Lesley Farr helped with the maps, plot diagrams and the development of the ethnobotanical database, while Simon Platten and Amy Warren have assisted with data processing. Christie Allan, Emily Brennan and Margaret Florey kindly permitted me to refer to their unpublished material, while the final editing and preparation of the revised manuscript has benefitted from the assistance of Mercy Morris and receipt of a Leverhulme Trust Emeritus Fellowship (EM-2018-057\6, 2018-20).

In connection with individual chapters I would like to thank the following: Riccardo Vergnani and Andrea Zuppi (Introduction); Bob Foley and the 'History of Man and the Environment' group at Durham (Chapter 1); Sandra Bamford, Paul Sillitoe, Christin Kocher-Schmid and European

Commission D-G 8, Avenir des Peuples des Foret Tropicales (APFT) (Chapter 2); Tania Li, Rosemary Bolton of the Summer Institute of Linguistics in Ambon, and an anonymised Nuaulu author, for permission to reproduce the text presented as an appendix, ESRC grants R000 23 3028 and R000 23 6082 (Chapter 3); Holly Harris, Peter Parkes, Alan Bicker and the Asia Committee of the European Science Foundation under the auspices of the East-West Environmental Linkages consortium (Chapter 4); Christophe Heintz (Chapter 5); ESRC grant RES-000-22-1106 and the British Academy (Chapter 6); Leslie Main Johnson, Brien Meilleur and ESRC grant (R000 23 3088) for work on 'The Ecology and Ethnobiology of Human-Rainforest Interaction in Brunei: A Dusun Case Study' (Chapter 7); Simon Platten, Rachel Kaleta, Nikki Goward and Leverhulme Trust grant 5/00 236/N, 'The ethnobotany of British homegardens: diversity, knowledge and exchange' (Chapter 8); and Walter Bisang, Tanja Pommerening, Laura Rival, Perig Pitrou, Ludovic Coupaye, Adam Miklosi, Garry Marvin, Joachim Kadereit and Jochen Althoff (Chapter 9). Finally, in connection with Chapter 10, I need to thank Cathy Cantwell, Will McClatchey, Theresa Miller and Emily Brennan; and the Royal Botanic Gardens Kew and the Indonesian National Herbarium in Bogor for palm identification.

Note on Orthography

Nuaulu terms appear here in bold italics and mostly follow the phonology and spelling adopted by Rosemary Bolton and Hunanatu Matoke in the 2005 edition of their dictionary (*Kamus Sou Naune – Sou Manai, Bahasa Indonesia – Nuaulu*; Badan Pemberdayaan Masyarakat Propinisi Maluku and SIL International Cabang Malaulu). All other local terms are placed in single inverted commas, while italics are used for scientific biological nomenclature.

INTRODUCTION

Nature Beyond the 'Ontological Turn'

> I'll tell you all my ideas about Looking-glass House. First, there's the room you can see through the glass – that's just the same as our drawing room, only the things go the other way . . . the books are something like our books only the words go the wrong way . . . she began looking about, and noticed that what could be seen from the old room was quite common and uninteresting, but that all the rest was as different as possible.
> —Lewis Carroll, *Through the Looking-Glass*

Beyond 'The End of Nature' and 'Post-nature'

I have called this collection of essays – perhaps provocatively – 'Nature Wars'. The phrase is also deliberately ambiguously polyvalent, the warring factions in the various disputes being sometimes eco-warriors, sometimes indigenous peoples defending their patrimony, sometimes official guardians of various vested interests and status quos, and on the other hand academic anthropologists and scientists plying their trades by disagreeing how best to portray and dissect how people perceive and engage with their material and biological worlds. 'Nature wars' suggests episodes and phenomena, as diverse and as historically separated as Agent Orange despoliation, industrial deforestation, atmospheric pollution, GM pharmacopeias, angst over appropriate clinical interventions to redefine gender, micro-plastic contamination of marine life, and our attempts to combat them, through the socio-economic institutions and processes that make them possible, whether neoliberal global capitalisation, the blind and remorseless central planning of the old Soviet Union or the People's Republic of China, or remorseless consumer demand and globalisation fuelled by social media and other modern communications. The hyperbole is, I believe, justified: the issues involved are very real for many individuals and globally and collectively transformative. People fight over resources and material advances that redefine nature, but equally find that the conceptual tools at their disposal are inadequate for the purpose, sometimes illusory mirages or at best transient and precarious – if convenient – props. Alice walked through the looking glass only to look back to find that what was on the other side was no more real than it seemed when she was there. There is a tension between the necessity to operate with nature-like concepts and the recognition that at every stage of enaction, these same concepts are compromised by their embeddedness in particular social situations.

An intellectual engagement with the concept of 'nature' has been seemingly at the centre of debates in anthropology (and especially anthropologies of the environment) forever. This should be no surprise as explication of the concept seems to address the very essence of what it means to be human, in the sense of 'our nature' and what is 'natural', and in its problematic semantic contrast with 'culture' and 'society'. Since the 1960s, however, there has been a heightened awareness of some special implications of its deployment, as the world has self-consciously addressed issues of environmental degradation and biodiversity loss. A naive definition of what nature might be – a fixed mechanistic thing, phenomenon or quality, or merely a backdrop for important events – soon led to attempts to deconstruct it and show its intrinsic socialness, including its gendered dimensions, together with cultural interpretations that varied between different populations and languages, and between contexts within the same culture, and meanings that slipped away as soon as some firm grasp was apparently attained. Those who talked about nature as if it were a real thing, unreflectively, and not in a nuanced or ironic way, were often associated with a natural science vision of the world, or a vision unduly influenced by simplistic scientific generalisations.

Part of the issue was always the scale at which the concept was employed, for what might be acceptably described as nature at one level can be shown to be nature-social entanglement of a very intricate kind when you dig deeper (e.g. Howell 2011). Ethnography, whether of scientific practices in laboratories or of anthropological field sites in specific locations, is subversive precisely because it puts back all the social and cultural connective tissue into the process through which scientists and others actually test hypotheses and gather data that had earlier been stripped out in the simplifying knowledge-making process that produces the scripts that others consume, such as scientific papers and communications. Indeed, in its most recent iteration in the context of the so-called 'ontological turn' (about which more later), nature disappears altogether. Nature is problematic not only because it can be viewed both from an outside looking in and from an inside looking out (Ingold 1993), but also because it is simultaneously held to be something out there that we study – something beyond our own apparatus for studying it – and yet compromised by the fact that we can never escape the influence of ideology and culture in defining it.

Many anthropologists have followed Bill McKibben (1989) in announcing 'the end of nature'. McKibben had in mind a very material nature increasingly inseparable from human controls or the consequences of human cultural actions, and was less concerned with whether or not it was a conceptual necessity. By contrast, for Latour (2009: 2) the critique of nature : social dualism and the repeated demonstration of how nature more generally is always culturally constructed 'destroys the nature of nature as an operating concept covering the globe'. Kirsten Hastrup (2011: 1) seems to think we are fortunately no longer saddled with the handicap of dualism and that the battle against it has been won; all that is necessary now is to routinise a new critical anthropology of 'nature-cultures' and celebrate the true 'deep-seated entanglements of natural and social' . . . 'beyond the dualism'. Indeed, she shares Descola's (1996: 99) optimism that the concept of nature will somehow go away once its ontological shortcomings have been asserted. I beg to differ.

While nature is often discussed as an abstract analytic category in works such as this, it impinges on our ordinary experiential lives in more specific contexts, such as through biogeographic categories that are thought to typify it (such as forest or 'jungle', themselves no less culturally compromised). But in debating the dualistic reinforcement of the concept, it is important not to conflate or elide 'nature : society' contrasts with 'nature : culture', 'nature : nurture', 'human : environment' or 'nature : human' contrasts. These are not always implying similar contrasts. We can agree with Anna Tsing (2011: 27) that the concept of sociality does not distinguish humans from non-humans, and that, of course, species other than humans display sociality, both between members of the same species and between species. Indeed, students of animal behaviour have long written sympathetically about animal social relations – long before the advent of evolutionary psychology or sociobiology – and therefore society and nature are not always or necessarily opposed in these senses. But while it is tempting and legitimate to contest and undermine dichotomies of many kinds, there are good intellectual and practical reasons why we find ourselves reinventing and relying on them (Kopnina 2016).

The concept of nature is much more complex and interesting than simply another socially constructed idea, everywhere integral to social life, and everywhere malleable and ductile. It is interesting partly because as a concept it is so resilient despite the critique. It is such a useful concept that it does not seem to go away. In responding to the 'end of nature' consensus, there are four powerful arguments. The first is a revisionist argument – that those seeking its demise have over-simplified and caricatured past scholarship and science; the second is the argument that received notions of the concept of 'nature' were key to the rise of global science and for this reason necessary; the third is the argument deriving from the rhetorical power of the concept in everyday and ideological discourse; and the fourth is the cognitivist argument claiming, despite the ambiguities and the social framing and cultural variation, that there do indeed exist underlying cognitive predispositions which encourage 'nature-like' concepts.

The first argument in defence of the concept of nature is that for rhetorical effect, and paradoxically to emphasise a dualism between their own monism and previous conceptions of nature, those arguing against nature : human dualisms have tended to draw the difference between their own position and those of their predecessors far too starkly, downplaying or ignoring previous attempts to recognise and get round the problems posed by dualist conceptions. Thus, when it comes to the 'co-constitution' of species, we should note that biologists have long worked with the concept of co-evolution as an underlying system dynamic, and developed sophisticated models of ecological dynamics which emphasise intricate interdependencies reflected in Darwin's description of 'an entangled bank'. The ecological anthropology model as it developed in the 1960s and 1970s, with the centrality it accorded to the concept of adaptation, did not – as some have suggested (e.g. Hastrup 2011) – somehow foster a simplistic binary concept of nature-culture. This is a very shallow reading of a complex history. Such a criticism might have been more accurately directed at the older Stewardian model that the smart young systems-oriented ecological anthropologists such as Roy Rappaport and Pete Vayda overtly rejected (Vayda and Rappaport 1968). The new systems approach was certainly borrowed from biology, but broke down the binary division between nature and culture by emphasising the connection and co-constitution of elements within both, and accepted that nature had been much modified by culture. Moreover, the kind of feedback relationships identified by Rappaport (1968) in his work in turn fostered the highly productive historical ecology paradigm that developed through the efforts of such researchers as Bill Balée (e.g. Balée 1989) and Carole Crumley (1994), the ideas of whom served to entrench this critique. Likewise, we find here the precursors of a raft of bio-cultural approaches within the environmental humanities and anthropology, which in turn have undermined further more conventional ideas of where 'nature' might lie.

The second argument in defence of nature derives from the observation that since the emergence of science as an idea in European natural philosophy from the sixteenth century onwards, nature has been constructed as the object of scrutiny, necessary at every turn in framing an issue to be investigated, but always contingent and temporary, falling away to reveal a new nature once the superficiality and inadequacy of the first has been revealed. The very fact that we argue about the concept of nature is testament to the fact that while in all systems of folk knowledge nature-like concepts are a flexible ill-defined idea, in Western philosophy there have been repeated attempts to control and define it to serve the purposes of the emergent sciences (Pálsson 2018). Fair enough, but in the formal histories of 'nature' and in the emerging critique, perhaps too much emphasis has been placed on etymology, which can be dangerous, and ultimately pointless. Concepts of nature have always adjusted to current and specific realities, whether scientific or social.

The third argument in defence of nature is well articulated by Rayner and Heyward (2014: 125), who object to the calls to abandon the concept of nature on the grounds that it is an 'indispensable rhetorical tool'. Their example is the science and politics surrounding global climate change. All societies, they argue, invoke nature in moral discourse, even if they have no word for it, since as an idea it has such 'coercive power'. Although we might be advised to refrain from deploying appeals to nature as a standard for political action, the idea is so thoroughly entrenched that dispensing with it is just unrealistic. As Latour (2008) puts it, matters of concern are generally instrumental in the constitution of fact, as we shall see later in this introduction and elsewhere in the book.

Finally, precisely because nature-like concepts have become such a powerful conceptual prop everywhere in working out how the world works and in pursuing symbolic political ends, it might be thought that this is in itself evidence for something even more fundamental in terms of how humans apprehend and make sense of their environment. I have previously (e.g. Ellen 1996a, 1996d) argued for the existence of a small number of cognitive imperatives underpinning the ways in which all peoples shape their world, and will return to these ideas below. I contend that it is possible to accept that nature is constantly being defined and redefined and yet still be something 'real' and not illusory. Rather than announcing the 'end of nature', it might be more realistic to explore how people 'redefine' – or even better 'reconfigure' nature-like semantic spaces to deal with new socio-environmental situations.

In this book I use the trope of nature to bring together a number of essays I have written since 1986, essays that explore the tensions between nature as a subject of investigation and as an analytic and symbolic concept. It attempts to engage with the different ways in which we use the word or its cognates, and illustrates some of the irresolvable and resolvable problems encountered when we use the word at the interface of different discourses: across the many discourses of science, in the specific literature of anthropology, and the non-specialist popular and folk usages across cultures and in ordinary 'common-sense' language.

Defining Our Terms of Reference

The larger part of this introductory essay has its origins in an invitation to write an afterword to accompany a collection of seven indicative and influential papers published over the last ten years on what is sometimes called the 'ontological turn', at least as this applies in anthropology. This was a daunting commission given the enormous body of existing commentary on the subject and its seemingly exponential growth, almost in equal measure by authors inspired or exasperated by it. What I offer here, therefore, is no more than a partial review of a few issues as they relate to ethnographic practice, comparative anthropology and anthropological generalisation, from an anthropologist who has taken a professional long-term interest in how one people (the Nuaulu of eastern Indonesia) apprehend and conceptualise other species and entities which comprise their world.

A 'turn' in the present context might be understood to be a movement in general intellectual practice, somewhat short of a paradigm shift, signalling a general change in direction, and with a rather loosely defined focus. This is a bit like the way in which the term concept metaphor has been used in circumstances where we would not wish to imply something as explicit and thought-through as a theory (Ellen 2010b). When this particular use of 'turn' began is unclear, but it seems to have emerged (at least in anthropology) with those currents of interpretivism that followed the decline in the influence of structuralism. By contrast, the term 'ontology' has good philosophical precedents, but some divergent meanings. Here are just a few definitions from anthropologists writing on the subject (see also Kohn 2015). For Descola (2005b: 8) it is 'the main framework through which people perceive and interpret reality'. For Carrithers (in Carrithers et al. 2010: 160) it is 'a set of propositions urging a particular viewpoint on reality'. For Scott (2013: 859) it is 'the investigation and theorization of diverse experiences and understandings of the nature of being'. For Pina-Cabral (2014) it is no less than 'worldview' or perhaps 'cosmology'. Rather differently, in computer and information science, an ontology is what formally represents knowledge as a set of concepts within a domain, using a shared vocabulary to denote the types, properties and interrelationships of those concepts. In yet other texts, a large part of its intention is covered by the phrase 'a framework for thinking'. But if this is so, then it comes close to Clifford Geertz's (e.g. 1973) 'webs of significance', which was of course his pithy definition of culture. And it might be relevant to note also that the word 'ontology' is not mentioned at all in a key paper by Vilaça (2002) considered widely to be central to the debate. So, the fact that there are many ways of defining it suggests one reason why ontology is causing so much trouble. For the time being, I prefer to remain agnostic as to which definition, if any, is the most persuasive.

The chronological order of original publication of the papers examined here is as follows: Ingold (1995, revised 2000), Vilaça (2002), Viveiros de Castro (2004a), Descola (2005b), Kohn (2007), Pedersen (2007) and Holbraad (2008). But this sequence is slightly misleading if we are interested in the dissemination and development of ideas. Thus, the revised version of Ingold's 'A Circumpolar Night's Dream' was able to benefit from fast-moving developments in several areas between 1995 and 2000, while the piece by Descola draws on work going back to 1992 at least, and Vilaça takes his cue very much from what Viveiros de Castro was already saying in the 1990s. Moreover, the last three in this list – Kohn, Pedersen and Holbraad – are clearly separated from the rest, providing a distinctive, and possibly more self-conscious second wave of reflection. Between them, these selected authors draw on the work of a number of key thinkers, among whom Michel Foucault, Marilyn Strathern, Gilles Deleuze, Félix Guattari, Bruno Latour, Jakob von Uexküll and Martin Heidegger are perhaps the most important for understanding what has motivated and validated their standpoints. In this commentary I want to draw out certain themes as these have emerged, more or less chronologically, in the literature, and which are reflected in this selection. What is loosely called the ontological turn loosely connects a number of semi-detached debates: the deconstruction of nature, the notion of ontology itself, animism, perspectivism, the meaning of 'life', human exceptionalism, the new materialities, and recursivity, all part of the fall-out from the perceived collapse of the major hegemonic paradigms during the 1970s.[1]

It also needs to be noted that many of the strongest proponents of the ontological turn work in particular parts of the world, partly – we must assume – because the problems that they seek to address are most acutely posed in the ethnography of these places. Of the present group of papers, four discuss work in Amazonia, one Native North America, one Mongolia and one Cuba. Among them, perspectivist worldviews are prominently associated with Amazonia. However, there is a danger here that we might slip into a kind of typological thinking based on geography, overemphasising difference rhetorically to make some general point. I am suspicious of any claim that the cultures of certain parts of the world said to display 'radical alterity' thereby require a completely different scientific mind-set to understand them (Ellen 1998c [Chapter 2 in this volume]; see also Laidlaw 2012).

The Deconstruction of Nature

The group of ideas that are the focus of work described as the 'ontological turn' have their roots firmly situated in some very old and venerable debates in anthropology and philosophy (some of which I return to below), but the contemporary discourse, judging from patterns of citation and reference, begins to emerge with the culture/nature debates of the 1970s onwards. It is no coincidence that in the human sciences – and especially in anthropology – the rise of the concept of ontology has been especially connected with ways of apprehending the natural world embedded in nature-culture dualism, the idea of the social construction of nature, and recognition that not all peoples everywhere or in different contexts of engagement define nature in the same way, if at all. Ontology, after all, is often understood as being about the nature of being, and the nature of different beings.

The deconstruction of nature literature begins with the critique of materialism in ecological anthropology: that nature 'out there' is elusive in empirical terms, both because it is constantly being reworked through human action on the world (culture), and because despite a shared evolved cognitive framework (the extent and influence of which is contested) different people see the world in different ways, through various 'cultural constructions' and local culturally-inflected experiences of ecology. But at the same time that the meaning of 'nature out there' was being questioned, Lévi-Strauss's notion of 'nature in there' was also being interrogated. Lévi-Strauss had never had much to say – except implicitly – about nature as an analytical construct underpinning realist science, but he was part of a long philosophical tradition attached to naturalism as a paradigm (Leach 1965, 1970). This is one reason why he was content to assume that the nature-culture distinction was intrinsic to the working of the human mind, even if it was difficult to find words in other languages that conveyed precisely the same meanings as seemed evident in a naturalist sense of nature.

The deconstruction of nature debate begins by demonstrating that the received Western concept of nature does not exist in many cultures, and in the Western tradition is anyway historically situated, with its precise intent in the present depending on social positioning. In other words, its definition is relational. Indeed, Escobar (e.g. 2017) and many earlier writers have argued that the contemporary divide between nature and culture and between modern and non-modern is historically co-emergent and co-sustaining, a product of the discovery of 'science' in the Western tradition. These issues were debated in a number of influential texts throughout the 1980s and 1990s (e.g. McCormack and Strathern 1980; Descola and Pálsson 1996; Ellen and Fukui 1996; Roepstorff, Bubant and Kull 2003). While some were content to defend the critique as a relativist victory, others acknowledged that while there was cultural variation in how nature was constructed, there remained considerable evidence for underlying shared commonalities. Such views tended to come from cognitive anthropology and ethnobiology. Thus, the tradition rooted in ethnoscience could demonstrate a pan-cultural body of concepts for making sense of biological diversity and organising it through language. These data supported the existence of a shared notion of something like 'nature'. Ellen (1996a, 1996d), for example, suggested that one way of modelling the diversity of natures was through a tripartite scheme of essence, thinginess and otherness: all cultures attributing essential inner qualities to people and things that we might call their 'nature'; all cultures having a notion of natural kind or natural 'things', including a basic species-like concept, that provides a means of modelling the relationship between organisms based on different degrees and kinds of resemblance; and all cultures organising their world in terms of distinctions between the human self and some less-than-human other (e.g. village : forest, land : sea). Inevitably, these notions interconnect and present themselves to ethnographers as different kinds of representation of nature. Others went still further and made claims for an evolved taxonomic framework underpinning all cultural variations in the classification of biodiversity (Atran 1990), even proposing the existence of a separate natural history module in the mind (Mithen 1996).

Strikingly, though perhaps not surprisingly, those approaching the perception of the natural world from cognitive science and psychology tend to see all human populations operating with a single ontology (e.g. Atran 1990), though there are differences in the claims made for that ontology. Thus, Susan Carey (1985) sees human children early attributing human-like life essence to all living organisms, while Frank Keil (1979) emphasises the evidence for the opposite – the domain specificity of living things. Others have argued for a reinvention of the nature-culture distinction as a cognitive universal based on experimental and ethnographic data (Astuti 2001), and for domain mutualism in general as a necessary means of representing or 'thinking through' anything in the mind. This is because nature (that which is non-human) cannot be understood except through the metaphors of the social (that which is human), and the social through the metaphors of the natural. It is characteristic of that body of work that I am here discussing that it seeks to 'get beyond these sorts of dualisms and the mixtures that often serve as their resolution' (Kohn 2007: 5), such as Latour's 'nature-cultures' (Franklin 2003). However, despite its internal contradictions, 'nature' as a concept does appear to have been remarkably resilient in both science and everyday discourse over the last two decades of what we have now come to call the Anthropocene. Indeed, the defiant claim that 'its foreseeable demise . . . will . . . close a long chapter of our own history' (Descola 1996: 98) now seems rather premature. To say that the concept of nature in this sense is resilient is, of course, not the same as assuming that the facts evinced through the naturalist paradigm are out there unadorned and uninfluenced by how we perceive them, or always independent of the contexts in which they are used, and of the instruments employed to measure them. We might say that they are Latourian 'factishes'. But when different conceptions of nature come into contact, or are compared, there is, as Blaser (2009) might say, an 'appearance of an agreement', of a unified environment, a single reality 'out there', achieved despite multiple and different performances.

Making Sense of One Ontology: Irving Hallowell on the Ojibwa

Tim Ingold has probably done more than anyone to revive interest in the work of Hallowell (1960), who explicitly develops the notion of ontology in relation to his Ojibwa ethnography. Hallowell's data are rich and grounded in a secure fluency of the language, which makes it ideal for Ingold's sustained meditation, and the demands he makes of it. As an account of the perspectives on the world of a non-Western people it was path-breaking in its time, but the kinds of observations he makes are now commonplace in many ethnographic accounts. Many of the issues raised by proponents of the ontological turn find an appearance in Hallowell's work, so there is some sense in examining it first as an exemplary text.

For a start, Hallowell shows how persons in the Ojibwa world can take on a great variety of forms, and how powerful humans can change into non-humans and back again, and how for Ojibwa the sun is also perceived as a person in an 'other-than-human' class, not intrinsically a natural object to which person-attributes are later attached but a person because it is so experienced. Hallowell also says that Ojibwa do not experience stones as animate as such, but that the animate stone is less a living thing than 'alive', which depends on the relational context in which it is placed. For Ojibwa (and for Ingold 2000b), therefore, life is not a property of objects, but 'a condition of being'. Like other similar traditional peoples, Ojibwa acquire knowledge by moving around, which tends to yield personal rather than propositional knowledge, in which 'the self exists in an ongoing engagement with the environment', employing a 'poetics of dwelling rather than science' (Ingold 2000b: 100), where the self is relational rather than in the head.

But in the hands of Ingold, the Ojibwa ethnography, and perhaps Hallowell's handling of it, raises lots of other questions. Thus, if knowledge is purely relational, non-propositional and not 'in the head', what happens in those moments of knowledge transfer between individuals where a previous personal context cannot be entirely shared? I think we can reasonably presume that there must be some cognitive mechanism for moving from the personal-episodic to the shared-semantic. Similarly, Mary Black (1969), who worked with Ojibwa during the 1960s, claims that Ojibwa classification is therefore 'anti-taxonomic', that it is impossible to find a neat classification of the kind beloved of ethnoscience. Ojibwa metaphysics certainly pose a challenge to our own ontological certainties, but as some of the cases examined here indicate, they are by no means unique in this. I cannot think of any people that do not treat some animals as both persons (and therefore by implication possessing souls) and things, or for whom persons can be both human and non-human, if not universally or simultaneously, then in different contexts as pragmatically required.

Ontologies as Comparative Schemata: Descola

In anthropology the ontological turn is particularly associated with the work of Philippe Descola (e.g. 2005b), who distinguishes animist, totemic, analogical and naturalist ontologies. For Des Fitzgerald (2013), Descola offers us 'a grand project in the old style', one that flirts with a dangerous sociological holism, if not explicitly with mechanistic determinism. Although in his work Descola was initially responding to the special difficulties he faced in accounting for Amazonian perceptions of the world that seemed inherently positional, relational and unstable, by the time he elaborated his distinctions he had been, as we have seen, working around the problem of nature as a cross-cultural and analytic category for some time. Provoked by the difficulties of accounting for his own fieldwork data through existing tools, he came to see these differences as essentially ontological. Having established that the construction of nature varied between cultural groups, he attempted to find different types of ontology that might explain regularities in the cross-cultural data and develop it into a model that could be applied cross-culturally and comparatively. For Descola (2005b: 3), 'rather than experiencing the duality of nature/culture we all experience physicality and intentionality', which combine in different ways in totemism, animism, analogism and naturalism. Thus, Descola establishes four types of ontology, 'which provide anchoring points for socio-cosmic forms of aggregation and conceptions of self and other'.

Descola's first two types are *totemism* and *animism*. If for Lévi-Strauss totemism was a universal classificatory device employing discontinuities between natural kinds to map social relations, then animism employs social experience to map the relations between humans and natural objects. However, Descola argues that this inversion is too neat, and does not do justice at least to Amazonian cosmologies. Rather than deriving ontological properties from relational processes, he suggests the reverse, that social realities are subordinate to ontological realities. Descola's third ontology is *analogism*, in which all entities are 'fragmented into a multiplicity of essences, forms and substances, and then re-combined' (2005b: 7), and his fourth is *naturalism*, the idea that there is a single unifying nature and many cultures, an idea that emerged as a coherent ontology in its usually known cultural form in Europe and North America between the seventeenth and nineteenth centuries, and is approximately coterminous with 'science'.

For Descola, the four modes of identification are not mutually exclusive, 'but one of them is always dominant at a specific time and place' providing 'the main framework through which they perceive and interpret reality' (2005b: 8). These modes are sufficiently dominant to be correlated with distinctive social patterns: egalitarian in the case of totemism, egalitarian and mono-specific in the case of animism, hierarchised and segmented in the case of analogism (Descola 2005b: 12–13). These Descola sees as 'alternative schemata of practice' with a characteristic geographic distribution.

The problem with Descola's formulation is – in common with other often quasi-relativist positions – that in setting up totemism, animism, analogism and naturalism as separate and ideal types, he has nevertheless (and paradoxically) had to adopt a meta-naturalist position in order to provide a basis for comparing different ontologies in the first place. In other words, he has had to make the comparison between all four, by accepting the priority of one – naturalism.

A second problem, though by no means restricted to Descola, is found in the claim 'that the major part of humankind has not, until very recently, made stark distinctions between what is natural and what is social' (2005b: 9). This is an idea that I have already broached and recognised above. However, the claim does tend to downplay significantly the findings of much cognitive anthropology of the biological world (e.g. in the work of Brent Berlin and Scott Atran), which strongly supports shared modes of cognising plants and animals that cut across social boundaries, allowing generalisation and communication between cultures. This is not to deny that all cultural groups organise their experience of the natural world in culturally specific ways.

Descola's quadripartite distinction is a helpful way of identifying contrasting ways of organising knowledge about the world, but we might doubt that the variation can be restricted to four, that the ontologies are as distinct as he claims, that they map as easily on to geographic discontinuities as he suggests, or correlate as simply with other features of social organisation. How does one draw the boundary between one ontology and another? If we have difficulty in identifying basic units for comparison in terms of observable and verifiable practice (e.g. residence patterns), how much more difficult is it going to be with ways of thinking? So, when we look at actual cases it is clear that all four ontologies can in principle – as among the Nuaulu – co-exist within the same society, different underlying assumptions emerging as contexts vary.

If we understand ontology in terms of the logical relations and cosmological assumptions underpinning a particular discourse or set of practices, there is also ambiguity in the way specific philosophical themes are nested within broader cultural traditions. So, how does something called 'Western' ontology relate, say, to Cartesian or Kantian ontology? There are plainly major differences in terms of epistemology and basic working assumptions between scientific disciplines and between theoretical strands within the same discipline, which in other respects might be said to share aspects of a single overarching ontology. Moreover, in terms of the convenient binaries we like to invent, we might ask whether 'Western ontology' is constructed in the same way as other ontologies we distinguish on quasi geo-cultural grounds when we reify cultures and speak of – say – 'Nuaulu ontology' or 'Ojibwa ontology'.

All peoples rely upon ontologies, but problems arise when we seek to taxonomise and reify them, treat them as culturally discrete entities that can be subjected to empirical 'ontography' (Holbraad 2008; Pedersen 2007: 154). Indeed, the suggestion that many cultural populations have recourse to 'polyontologies' (Scott 2013) suggests that ontological types are not a particularly robust means of distinguishing between cultural groups. While we need clarity in our concepts, the delineation of bounded ontological types is possibly only achievable in philosophical texts rather than in the complex patterns generated in ethnographic data.

Perspectivisms, Local and Global

If animism is the attribution of sentient life and agency to other organisms and objects, then perspectivism is the claim that those organisms have views on the world, and that humans can in certain circumstances access these. The idea is implicit in Descola's notion of animism, in which different animal species are claimed to have the same type of interiority but a different physicality, which determines their worldview and induces contrasted perspectives on the world. This is said to be especially evident in the positional quality of some Amerindian cosmologies. For Viveiros de Castro (2004a: 5–6), the existence of such viewpoints reveals a kind of human cosmology or 'cosmo-praxis' in which there is one shared cross-species culture but many natures, in which what one species sees as one thing another sees as something different: for example, what jaguars see as manioc beer humans see as blood, where jaguars see a muddy salt-lick humans see a ceremonial house. Some peoples claim to see themselves from the perspective of a jaguar. Such worldviews inherently presuppose a comparison of ways in which different kinds of body '"naturally" experience the world as an affectual multiplicity'. Perspectivism, therefore, 'supposes a constant epistemology and variable ontologies' (Viveiros de Castro 2004a: 6–7), while 'what is literal and what is metaphoric shifts' (Kohn 2007: 12), depending on the perspective adopted.

Pedersen (2007) takes Viveiros de Castro's notion of many natures or multi-naturalism as a starting point in his analysis of shamanic practice among Dahad Mongolian pastoralists. Pedersen (2007: 158) explains how Dahad divide the world into a multiplicity of 'ontologically discrete' bodies (notably humans and game animals) that share the same invisible intentionality and capacity to have body-specific perspectives. But Pedersen takes this further and shows how artefacts too take on the appearance and perspective on non-human entities. Thus, if a man is to be a good wolf hunter, he must make a wolf 'Ongon', and when a shaman puts on a costume he is transformed into a multi-natural entity. Both Ongon and costume allow each person to see itself from the viewpoint of the other (Pedersen 2007: 160) and builds capacity to personify as many disparate relations as possible. The 'perspectival traffic' in Dahad shamanism, therefore, hinges on a shaman's ability – using the materiality of art objects as vehicles – to transgress the human/non-human divide and to personify multiple social worlds that are otherwise hidden.

Thus far, Viveiros de Castro's insights are illuminating. The problems lie, as in so many anthropological theories, when claims are made for their generalisation, first to a regional level, and then to a pan-cultural level, and finally in the claims about what a perspectivist account might tell us about anthropology as a theoretical practice. Thus, although there is 'an Amazonian preoccupation with inhabiting the points of view of our non-human selves' (Kohn 2007), it is not present in all Amerindian societies. On the opposite side of the world, Nuaulu readily provide mythic accounts of soul-bearing (especially totemic) animals, which replicate the institutions of human society, including the distinctive Patalima-Patasiwa divisions of the wider Moluccan world, while they also use such knowledge when interrogating animal spirits and explaining the interiority of other species, for example when hunting. However, I do not think that they are thereby claiming that different species have essentially different worldviews, but rather that they in fact share the same basic worldview as people.

The Meaning of Life, Living Organisms and Persons

Another theme running through studies utilising the concept of ontology is what we might call the anthropology of life. One route into this is through Ingold's (2000b: 89) discussion of why we call plants and animals 'living things' and yet call humans 'human beings', and whether 'an organism is a thing or a being'. He suggests that if life is tantamount to 'being then an organism is a material way of being alive' (Ingold 2000b: 96). Such considerations about what it might be that makes something alive or animate have revitalised our thinking about animism.

Kohn (2007) too argues for an anthropology of life, but also for an expanded ethnography beyond the human. Like Pedersen, he follows Viveiros de Castro (2004a) in arguing for the importance of recognising the perspectives of other species that engage with humans, and adopts multi-natural perspectivism as a 'way of understanding relations [that] allows people to account for the distinctive qualities that characterize different kinds of beings' (Kohn 2007: 7). But while Viveiros de Castro is apparently content to accept that non-human perspectives are ultimately part of a particular human ontology, Kohn argues that the objective 'worldviews' of non-human species must be taken into account in explaining the terms of their engagement with humans. His point is that how we know and interact with other species has implications for anthropology, since how other species represent us influences the kinds of encounters we have. Our world is defined by how we get caught up in the interpretative worlds of other species with which we interact. His approach to this is through embodied and emergentist understanding of a semiosis beyond (but including) language of the kind promoted by Terrence Deacon (e.g. 1997), for whom representation, intention and basic signing processes appear wherever there is life, even the most elementary. Since both humans and non-humans perceive and represent their surroundings, 'how other selves represent us can come to matter vitally' (Kohn 2007: 7). Kohn explores this by examining upper Amazonian Runa 'dog-human becomings', how Runa address dogs, how dogs have penetrated Runa social worlds in their understanding of human communication, and how different communicative modes emerge to protect people against the dangers of 'blurred ontological boundaries'.

Recursiveness: Specific Alterities and General Ontologies

A number of recent studies taking inspiration from the ontological turn stress the centrality of recursiveness – either directly or by implication – in anthropological interpretation. Kohn, in his grappling with Runa understandings of dog perspectives on the world, achieves this by using it as a springboard for discussing cross-species semiosis in a naturalist sense. However, it is Holbraad (2008: s106) who addresses the issue most directly in examining the notion of 'prueba' (proof) used by practitioners of Afro-Cuban religion in Havana 'as a lever for transforming' notions of evidence in anthropology as a scientific and scholarly practice. Following Viveiros de Castro, but like many others before him, he suggests that what makes the people we study interesting is the mutual misunderstanding that leads us to question and revise initial assumptions and conceptualisations. This might entail, for example, our willingness to ask 'what is a spirit' rather than 'how do Cubans think of spirits' (Holbraad 2008: s101). In the hands of Viveiros de Castro (2004a: 3), the study of societies where perspectivism underpins worldviews is that it also tells us something about anthropology as a subject: that it is a 'hybrid ... the result of a recursive imbrication in Western anthropological discourses', rooted in modern 'multiculturalist and uni-naturalist ontology'.

The ideas at stake here address two perennial issues in anthropology: that other people often think in different ways from the observing investigator, and given that this is so, how we can best investigate them. Much conceptual development in anthropology is in effect 'recursive'; indeed, for Viveiros de Castro (2004a: 4) this is 'anthropology's defining problem'. While such a claim might be said to confuse the 'translative' project of ethnographic fieldwork with anthropology as it has emerged historically as a diverse and encompassing subject admitting many legitimate perspectives, it is certainly a fundamental and recurrent problem. Anthropologists have repeatedly refined their critical comparative apparatus by borrowing and modifying concepts such as 'totem' and 'taboo', by using the emic to fortify the etic. When a Zande woman notes termites eating through the piles of a granary, does she move away because she fears the working out of physical and biological laws, or witchcraft, or both? When Holbraad (2008: s102) says 'that a [Cuban] house is occupied by spirits [this] is not to describe an existing state of affairs, but rather ... [brings] such a state of affairs about', he is pointing to an idea widely found in the literature on spirit causation. When Nuer say that twins are birds, or cucumbers are oxen, or when a Catholic priest claims that a blessed wafer *is* the body of Christ, how are we to interpret this? These are all problems of understanding that arise with any cross-cultural comparison. What is helpful about such examples is that they allow us to stand back and reflect on (often arbitrary) 'common sense' WEIRD (Western, Educated, Industrialised, Rich, and Democratic) assumptions (Henrich, Heine and Norenzayan 2010) and to work things through using recursiveness.

The ontological movement within anthropology, therefore, shows a clear intellectual pedigree with previous attempts to explain startling disjunctions between worldviews, that goes back at least to James Frazer in the British tradition, and as typified by the classic posing of questions pertaining to 'belief', 'metaphor' and 'alterity' in the classical ethnographies of the mid twentieth century. As we have seen, there are several examples of such conundrums in literature reviewed here: Holbraad's meditation on Afro-Cuban pruebas, Kohn's on Runa claims about dog communication, Hallowell's assertion that the Ojibwa treat the sun as a person. Vilaça covers the same intellectual ground, but starts instead from Lucien Lévy-Bruhl's observation that some peoples reckon that a child born to a woman is not necessarily human, but could be an animal. Vilaça's solution to this problem is that the observing ethnographer accept that biological and social consubstantiality are constantly being produced through acts of sharing, in which the intimacy and physical reality of shared domestic life is equivalent to the social universe.

However, the problem with ontologists is not that they recommend that we take seriously various counter-intuitive chunks of ethnography, but rather their preoccupation with the exceptional rather than with the ordinary, the claim that a special 'revelatory moment' can somehow define, or is more important than the ordinary. Chua (2015: 645) has recently shown how dramatising 'uncommon occurrences' normalises alterity at the expense of a balanced analysis of everyday otherness with which most ethnographers engage. Why are only certain things 'taken seriously' and why should we accept that ontologists do a 'better job of thinking through ethnography'? For Chua (2015: 645), the danger of such recursive strategies is that they progressively distance 'certain singular ethnographic encounters or episodes from the wider relations of interaction in which events are embedded'. Such encounters become a privileged 'conceptual trampoline' (Vigh and Sausdal 2014: 62), focusing on certain kinds of informant and excluding others. Like most ethnographers, Chua was confronted with a very mixed set of viewpoints in a time of rapid social change for the Bidayuh, the people with whom she worked in Malaysian Borneo.

But, rather than assuming a fundamental incommensurability between 'Bidayuh thought' and the interpretive frame of the ethnographer, she recognises that anthropological knowledge is continually co-produced by ethnographers and their research subjects in a variety of ways.

It is precisely because (assuming a basic linguistic competence) we are able to understand much of what is going on within more or less the same ontological frame that such episodes on which ontologists focus can be reified. Ontologists overstate and overinterpret 'the agency and aptitude of the ethnographer', conferring a degree of unaccountability and invulnerability that is separated from and inconsistent with the 'messy reality' of fieldwork. As Chua (2015: 655) notes, 'politics and methodological constraints of ethnography does not feature highly on ontological agendas', which are more about theoretical experimentation and a grand programme to reinvent anthropology. In such a context, the reflective concerns of the ontologist do not seem to have much bearing on the real-world concerns of the people who have them, except where there is an explicit focus on how ontologies are articulated in moments of conflict (see below).

The Paradox of Naturalism

The imperative of the ontological turn has been to challenge the conventional Western concept of nature on the grounds that it is internally problematic and that other peoples do not share it, indeed to such an extent that ontological differences make translation between one and the other difficult, if not impossible. And yet there is a paradox here, for the very demonstration that there are many natures requires accepting some kind of meta-ontology for the purpose of making the comparison, and in practice this baseline is that set of conceptual assumptions, and epistemological and methodological practices, that we all share as anthropologists. It seems that we can only understand other ontologies anthropologically, can only recognise that different societies and contexts generate different underlying ontologies, if we do this from our own shared baseline for ontological translation. Thus, the diagram in Ingold's (2000b) figure 6.1 depends on an assumption that his readers share a dualistic ontological difference, while Scott (2013: 862) is happy to draw up an entire table of binaries contrasting naturalist and non-Western ontologies, without commenting on the irony of so doing. The more we understand about how the symbolic potential of humans might have evolved from a phylogenetically dispersed semiosis (pace Deacon 1997), and the more we understand about the relationship between analogue and digital processes in the brain, the more it seems likely that Lévi-Strauss was correct after all in his assertion of a central role for binary distinction in establishing and reinforcing meaning in language.

Anthropologists and scholars have long been aware of the 'ontological paradox', which to put it another way is that their etic framework is another anthropologist's emic framework (for example, the ethnographer at work in a forensic anthropology laboratory). Ingold (2000b: 90) pursues the conundrum: 'to be human . . . to exist as a knowing subject – is . . . to be a person', but is a scientist a person or an organism? How can we be both in nature (the world) and outside it (as scientists)? This is an enduring and ultimately irresolvable puzzle at one level of contemplation, but in practice anthropologists and other scientists and scholars have found a way round it in a kind of naturalism. We cannot, of course, know the world by 'taking ourselves out of it'; a brain with no sensory perceptors cannot think as it has nothing to think about, just as a line has no length until it is measured. The act of thinking is determined by what there is to think about, or as Kohn (2007: 5) might put it, 'the analytical object becomes isomorphic with the analytics'. We can accept that what scientists do requires suspending a certain kind of inferential logic, and is no more than a convenient set of conventions; but these conventions have worked sufficiently well for them to continue to be used as a reliable basis for communication in a professional context, and to underpin otherwise life-threatening engineering and medical assumptions. There must be limits to the notion that we are victims of our organs of perception, for if not how have we effectively adapted to the hazards of the biological world that we inhabit, including how we understand animals as part of a wider semiotic community? In anthropology, such an approach is consistent with the approach of those who argue for a 'middling' or 'critical' realism that is prepared to accept the shared conventions of ethnographic practice (e.g. Herzfeld 1997: 165; Morris 1997; Zeitlyn and Just 2014).

The naturalism we associate with science is a complex cultural phenomenon and set of practices that have been exported and embraced by a global scholarly community. But this is only possible because versions of a naturalist ontology exist everywhere, which help ordinary folk cope with the data input and social interaction of everyday life. There is plenty of evidence to show that humans can simultaneously operate using multiple and cross-cutting frameworks for thinking. The fact that we cannot understand the natural world – whether as scientists or ethnographic subjects – without making recourse to the cultural content of our everyday lives, does not prevent us from understanding that we can transcend cultural differences. For science and folk science to work, there needs to be a framework of assumptions about how the world is constructed and how human actors relate to that world. Such a framework often corresponds to what we conventionally call 'nature', although anthropologists tend to disagree on the extent to which 'common sense' naturalist and cosmic ontologies are logically and operationally separate in the lives of ordinary people (Atran 1990: 268, 286–87, 290).

This framework does not have to be everywhere constructed in the same way or need to be universally the same, only sufficiently robust to serve as a shared point of investigative departure. Newtonian physics does not provide a perfect explanation of what we now know about the properties of the universe, but it does serve as a practical basis for technology. Likewise, the Micronesian *etak* system of navigation employs a set of conventions rooted in a partly imaginary cosmos, a convenient fiction that allows real-world and real-time assumptions related to navigational practice that are sufficiently correct most of the time to be considered reliable (Chapter 5 in the present volume).

Speaking, Listening, Reading and Writing Ontology

Inferences about ontological difference have a complex relationship with language. While it is possible that some languages may complicate certain ontological positions due to the absence of compliant semantic and morpho-syntactic resources, and while some features may reveal themselves through non-linguistic indicators, we can only really infer ontological difference by hearing people talk about their experiences. But the use of a different language (e.g. Runa trans-species pidgins) is not evidence in itself of ontological difference, neither are grammatical differences in Ojibwa. That there is a distinction between animate and inanimate nouns may be no different from the role of male and feminine forms in other languages that do not have semantic consequences, or grammatically embedded forms of classifier that while they may once have served a semantic purpose have become inert.

But it is not only the intrinsic relationship between language structure and ontological difference that has become a matter for examination, but – to speak recursively – the language of the ontological turn itself. Chua (2015: 657) has noted how many 'ontologically-inflected monographs' also contain rich ethnography irrespective of their meta-theoretical prescriptions, but the challenge for beginner and sceptic alike is the theoretically dense and occasionally convoluted and obfuscating language in which the debate is conducted, where, for example, something 'counterinvents the equivocation it enables' (Viveiros de Castro 2004a: 15), or where 'the anthropocene . . . is . . . an opportunity for pluriversal worldings' (de la Cadena and Blaser 2018: 14). Moreover, there are sometimes doubts as to why the term 'ontological' is used at all. If we remove the word in a phrase (as in 'ontological division', or 'ontologically separate'), frequently nothing changes in an argument. The word ontology has been embraced with a quasi-religious passion in some quarters, and used where it need not be. While difficult subjects cannot be addressed without the difficulty being reflected in the language used, ontologists often test the endurance of readers like myself, who are left with an impression of gratuitous playfulness for stylistic effect. Where style results in obfuscation and rhetoric obscures an argument, we should be concerned. On such occasions, it might be useful to have a guidebook or an 'app' of the kind Alfred Gell (1999: 29) offers in his teasing engagement with the sometimes challenging prose of Marilyn Strathern, to warn the easily impressed to avoid 'citation for effect rather than sense'.

The Present Collection

Here I have introduced the themes of the book as a whole, by reviewing the apparently persistent (and some might say pernicious) problem posed by the concept of nature, a concept that much recent work in anthropology – most saliently that characterised by the phrase 'the ontological turn' – has sought to dispense with, but which stubbornly does not seem to go away. I argue that this is because it is too useful a concept in the context of current concerns about environmental change, has a necessary function in how science has developed and continues to operate, and is anyway rooted in certain pan-human cognitive imperatives that shape the ways all humans see and engage with the world.

Chapter 1 picks up on the observation that some prominent adherents to Green causes during the growth period of environmentalist movement between the 1960s and 1980s often saw in traditional small-scale societies a vision of ecological reverence and sustainability lost in the West, and then runs with it. Where such populations are small, the demands they make on the environment around them are often slight, and the frugal use of resources permits a kind of ecological sustainability. However, this is an idea that has subsequently developed further and become a handy form of self-identification for traditional peoples in their political struggles. I show that as a generalisation the claim is weak, without denying that many peoples have knowledge of the environment that was often previously denied them by outsiders, and which we need to recognise and respect.

Chapter 2 focuses on some work from Melanesia conducted before 1998, but it could have been about virtually any apparently coherent ethnographic area. It explores the idea of the plurality and unstable character of ideas about nature looked at in the context of a region where we might expect a degree of homogeneity. In reviewing accounts of nature concepts in New Guinea, I develop points of contrast and similarity with how Nuaulu living on the western boundary of Melanesia, but still in a biogeographic zone that is recognisably southwest Pacific and dominated by tropical forest, conceptualise their relations with the material world around them.

Chapter 3 addresses how Nuaulu conceptions of nature were changing during the 1980s, as they became increasingly concerned and politically active about threats to their traditional resource base, as it became increasingly eroded by transmigration resettlement on the one hand and logging incursions on the other. It was in some respects the sequel to an earlier paper (Ellen 1993b) that portrayed a more passive view of Nuaulu engagement with forest resources and authorities, as this existed in the early 1970s. I report how conflict has occurred in the Ruatan transmigration area leading to the imprisonment of Nuaulu, but how Nuaulu were also able to successfully defend some land claims in the courts, and in their representations to outsiders have become increasingly articulate about the threats posed to their environment. The chapter argues that as material and social change has taken place, so Nuaulu have renegotiated their conception of forest, what it means in their lives, and are strongly motivated to articulate its uses for them. The main question the chapter seeks to answer is why, given their traditional knowledge of the market and deliberate modification and destruction of forest, and former resistance to ecological thinking, Nuaulu now appear to be engaged in environmentalist rhetoric that we would recognise as such. Though historically prior, the account evokes other recent discussions relating to the contestation of nature in a variety of settings (e.g. Blaser 2013). The chapter reminds us that we have to be attentive to the power relation between different knowledges (Blaser 2009; Escobar 2017) – political ontologies if you must – and that concepts of nature shaped by interactions between local people, states and non-governmental organisations engaged in environmentalist programmes become governmentally-compliant, what Agrawal (2005) – adapting Foucault's notion of governmentality – has called 'environmentality', that is 'environmentalised' by government (though see Cepek 2011).

Chapter 4 was originally co-written with Holly Harris as an introduction to the book *Indigenous Environmental Knowledge and Its Transformations*. It explores the concept of indigenous knowledge that was becoming increasingly widely employed in development studies, environment conservation programmes, and in the political rhetoric of international funding agencies, non-governmental organisations and national governments by the beginning of the twenty-first century, and partly arises from the kind of politics broached in Chapter 1. During this period, 'indigenous knowledge' was being increasingly adopted as an insurgent claim of indigenous minorities and regional movements throughout the developing world. The book that it introduced was among the first concerted critical examinations of the uses and abuses of the concept from an anthropological perspective. It interrogated the idea of indigenous knowledge and its specific applications within the localised contexts of particular Asian societies and regional cultures, such as the problems of translation and mistranslation of traditional practices and representations of resource management, the match and mismatch of practical reasoning in indigenous subsistence regimens and their depiction by outsiders, and the developmental and political consequences of contemporary ethnic and regional claims rooted in an ideology of 'traditional' indigenous knowledge.

Chapter 5 begins by examining the response of the organised scientific community to the claims of the indigenous knowledge lobby, and with some observations on the dichotomy between science and traditional technical knowledge. It reiterates the view that the potency of the distinction arises from a fusion of the general human cognitive impulse to simplify the processes by which we understand the world, reinforced by the socially driven need of science to maintain an effective boundary around the practices in which scientists engage. The chapter goes on to argue that the existence of these two epistemological meta-categories obscures the presence of different ways of securing predictive knowledge of the material world, each of which is characterised by a distinctive configuration of cognitive and technical features, and which in several ways cut across the usual dualism between science and traditional knowledge. The argument is illustrated using examples from the history of biology and the ethnography of ethnobiological knowledge. It engages critically with insights drawn from cognitive psychology, the philosophy and sociology of science, and cognitive anthropology, as well as with scientists' own descriptions of what distinguishes the mental operations in which they engage.

Chapters 6 and 7 belong together, and indeed overlap. Both examine 'official', scientific and political aspects of the classification of secondary biodiversity through what James Scott (1998) calls the 'administrative ordering of nature', in relation to Nuaulu understandings of forest diversity. That local peoples have a profound knowledge of forest diversity is now hardly doubted, but what light can this shed on the problems faced by scientists and others in describing it, and how can we account for discrepancies in the lexicalisation of knowledge for people living in ecologically very similar environments? Chapter 6 attempts to answer this question by reporting on a study that compared local knowledge elicited from

Nuaulu informants concerning eleven 0.5-hectare plots in ecologically varied kinds of vegetation cover. The differences between the plots reflect altitude, geomorphology and anthropic influences, and the objective was to measure the extent to which knowledge varies according to different kinds of forest, geographic area and between informants, and why. The analysis demonstrates a high ability to name trees consistently, irrespective of locality and ecology; a high degree of shared knowledge between male informants; and the extent to which Nuaulu understanding of forest diversity and patterning matches recent ecological modelling in rainforest science as a complex mosaic.

Chapter 7 begins with the observation that available data on the folk classification of forest habitats and biotopes globally suggest significant variation in the extent to which recognition of compositional diversity translates into complex, fixed and labelled categories for different types. Although there are some early references to the importance of establishing ethnoecological categories for the Asian tropics, the pioneer work on this subject was conducted in the Amazon, and has since extended elsewhere. Dependable data for island Southeast Asia are sparse, but what evidence there is suggests relatively limited labelling of forest types. By contrast, a number of researchers working in the Amazon region have recently reported folk classifications of forest evidently more terminologically refined and extensive than the Southeast Asian ethnography suggests. The chapter uses the same dataset introduced in Chapter 6 to show how Nuaulu eschew the detailed lexically-coded habitat classifications reported for some Amazonian peoples in favour of a less lexically-fixed but no less knowledgeable approach. An attempt is made to specify a general model which accounts for how Nuaulu perceive and represent different kinds of forest, which addresses the general propositions that (a) not all knowledge, everywhere, is equally lexicalised, (b) that ecological and subsistence differences influence the extent to which people categorise and lexicalise, and (c) that models based on the structure of folk taxonomies generated in studies of folk systematics bias our methodologies when studying ethnoecological categories.

Chapter 8 changes tack completely, to examine one of the main themes of the British Homegardens Project that preoccupied me, some colleagues and several cohorts of Kent ethnobotany students during the mid 2000s: how gardening skills and knowledge are transmitted inter-generationally in the modern world. While it is recognised that print and electronic media are an important element in the late twentieth-century growth of UK recreational gardening, an underlying hypothesis has been that because gardening is ultimately a practical bodily skill it must be acquired through direct physical activity and interaction between skilled and less skilled gardeners. Contemporary anthropological literature has much to say about knowledge and skill transmission, but mainly in relation to either abstract bodies of knowledge (e.g. plant name recognition) or in relation to craft activity, that is 'making'. Weeding is a synaesthetic process in which the hand mediates a relationship between plant and body. It involves the mastery of various types of manual dexterity and tool manipulation, the coordination between tactile skills, visual competence and the other senses in relation to acquired background knowledge. However, these are not necessarily the same as those employed in making things. I conclude that from an evolutionary point of view, weeding is a secondary cultural adaptation of a general foraging facility that involves the same cognitive and manipulative skills and which must have evolved early in human history.

Chapter 9 is an intervention in the revived debate on animism, which – as this introduction notes – has come to occupy a special place in the comparative study of how life and nature are conceptualised. The chapter reminds us how humans and other animals attribute the qualities of living matter and agency to what we call tools and other cultural objects. In both cases a paradox may arise when autonomy is attributed to the object at the same time that it is recognised that its life-like characteristics are motivated by human actions. The chapter shows how Nuaulu describe many kinds of object as having qualities we might otherwise reserve for biological organisms. Nuaulu also distinguish entities that have many of the qualities of life but which ordinarily have no corporeal existence (spirits). While all cultural objects are potentially regarded in this way, in practice some objects are more alive and have more agency than others. I argue that part of the problem with existing anthropological treatments of the category 'living things' is that they are either logical extrapolations through polythetic extension or based on formal taxonomic deduction/induction (ethnoscience). Using examples of meat skewers, outboard motors, coconut graters and sago-processing devices, together with certain 'peripheral' forms of biological life, I demonstrate how Nuaulu ideas of what is animate and agentive are always fuzzy and contingent, and that by combining data from different kinds of ethnographic context, using different elicitation procedures, a more complex picture emerges.

Finally, Chapter 10 brings us back to the vexed question raised by the ontological turn, and offers a critical examination in relation to ethnobotany. Competing definitions and problems are first assessed for recent work in anthropology and the history of science. This is followed by a review of seven areas of current ethnobotanical investigation where there are disjunctions of approach that could arguably be said to be ontological: post-Linnean taxonomic orthodoxy versus local plant classification, pre-Linnean natural history versus science, phytopharmaceutical orthodoxy versus medical anthropology, museum practice versus lived practice, ecological versus phylogenetic explanation, plant movement versus knowledge movement, and shifts in understanding contingent on membership of different intra-cultural domains. In the light of these examples, a threefold meta-conceptual distinction is suggested: between cultural domains (distinguishing knowledge and practice on the grounds of content), epistemes (distinguishing knowledge in terms of the methods and approaches used to acquire it), and ontologies in the strict sense (defined in terms of underlying logical relations and cosmological assumptions).

Conclusion

Despite Sahlins' (2013) view that ontologism really does represent a paradigm shift, the big 'utopian' claim (Bessire and Bond 2014: 449) that it is a fundamental reinvention of anthropology necessary for the whole subject to move forward is probably unsustainable. Like several previous 'turns' in the past, it will no doubt prove to have been a refreshing diversion, 'an unmoored form of speculative futurism' (Bessire and Bond 2014: 441) that has reinvigorated our sense of 'wonder' (Scott 2013), and a series of analytically subversive meditations that has helped refine approaches that are broadly and inevitably framed by a naturalist and realist ontology. Its claim (by implication) to be the only approach that 'takes ethnography seriously' cannot itself be taken seriously (Chua 2015: 643). Nevertheless, I have over the last few years relaxed my resistance to the apparently irresistible tide of the ontological turn, as those around me all seem to think that an argument has to ontologise just about everything. While acknowledging that there is an important debate going on (in fact several important debates), what I think many are trying to say is often what scholars and scientists have been grappling with for a long time, only using different conceptual baggage. And in apparently offering pretty much a 'theory of everything' when it comes to the Anthropocene, some are in danger of stretching the credibility of their arguments.

If, as Henare, Holbraad and Wastell (2007: 27) suggest, 'there are as many ontologies as there are things to think through', then the concept of ontology might be considered entirely superfluous. Much of what is so described can often be expressed through other forms of radical conceptual disjuncture. We can refer to contrasting paradigms, perspectives, frameworks for thinking, worldviews, schemata, cosmologies and epistemologies. While I accept that these notions are not necessarily identical, and in some instances express important and subtle distinctions that we need to respect, according to the definitions and usages of many they are virtually interchangeable, while the meaning of ontology in some quarters itself has become woolly and inconsistent in its application, and virtually devoid of precise meaning (Woolgar and Lezaun 2013). Someone needs to issue a danger warning, to advise that the term be used sparingly, lest we risk over-complexifying our analyses and undermining its productivity altogether. As even Viveiros de Castro (2004b: 484) puts it, simply producing increasingly 'richer ontologies' is not the answer. It may well be that lived ontologies are not preformed things that determine all else at all, but rather emergent and changeable processes for making sense of experience that our current modes of analysis just find convenient to reify. In this set of essays I attempt to further engage with the sometimes muddled thinking surrounding our use of the word 'nature' – through discussions of indigenous knowledge of the environment, science, concepts of 'life', knowledge acquisition, and ontology – in order to better anchor our analyses and understanding.

Note

1. The list of authorities referred to here is inevitably partial and many other recent works speak quite directly to the central concerns raised by this volume, and specifically issues articulated through the larger 'ontological turn'; for example the writings of Marisol de la Cadena (especially de la Cadena 2015, but see Blaser [e.g. 2009, 2013]), which relate to a broader intellectual project framed around Arturo Escobar's work on relationality and the 'pluriverse' (e.g. Escobar 2017; see also de la Cadena and Blaser 2018), works explicitly articulated around environmental conflicts and disputes.

CHAPTER 1

What Black Elk Left Unsaid

Many will be familiar with those twin traditions in Western thought that simultaneously idolise and savage the primitive.[1] The balance of these paradoxical views (which appear in a variety of cultural guises) has, however, never been perfect. While images of a noble savagery appear in popular literature and philosophy, the historical record proclaims unambiguously that the prevailing attitude towards so-called primitive peoples has been as objects of contempt and ridicule. In the nineteenth century, despite a Laocoonian 'struggle with the conflicting theories presented by the literary tradition on the one hand and contemporary reporters and scientists on the other', as illustrated in the work of, say, Rider Haggard, 'the pristine goodness of primitive life' was eventually submerged by the ideological fetish of 'progress' (Street 1975: 7–8).

There is a modern ecological transformation of the first tradition – based upon assumptions about the proper 'natural' order of original human society. It is there in our visions of Ecotopia, of Walden, and finds its more extreme expression in the 'ecopsychic mission' of contemporary neo-pagans (Roszak 1978: 40), in the notion of the primordial mother earth Gaia, metaphorical or otherwise, in the spirituality of green politics (Capra and Spretnak 1984: 545), and in a 'biospheric egalitarianism' which seriously debates the rights of rocks and viruses (Sylvan 1985: 7). Such notions at once sustain and spring from a mystical philosophical ecology that finds its contemporary impulse in modern scientific ecology. The connection is well made in the 'rhapsodic intellect' of that most persuasive of commentators, Theodore Roszak, for whom 'ecology does not systematize by mathematical generalization or materialist reductionism, but by the almost sensuous intuiting of natural harmonies' (1972: 400).

This appeal to nature is hardly new, and all ideologies seek to legitimate or subvert a particular state of affairs through comparisons with the natural order. In the Judaeo-Christian tradition it is found twice in the stories of Eden, and then again in the story of the Flood. On each occasion a perfect and harmonious creation is destroyed by human evil. Among the ancients, Tacitus contrasts the decadence of Roman culture with the unspoiled values of Barbarian society. Roszak's words, which I have just quoted, are (after all) in the romantic tradition of English literature. The theme is echoed in the Marxist concept of 'primitive communism' and other degenerative theologies of the origin of human sociality. Anthropologists too are not immune from this poetic infection, as the work of Carlos Castaneda and the sometimes-millenarian enthusiasm for a revolutionary anthropological ecology (Anderson 1973) admirably demonstrate. As an apologia for the existing state of affairs it is discernible in the way capitalism appeals to the natural order of things through the rhetoric of the New Right and the socio-biologists or the old-style social Darwinists, or in the soft-sell of the Cheltenham and Gloucester Building Society advertisement which, by projecting images of lovable wild animals caring for their young, drives home the message that saving for retirement is the most 'natural' thing in the world. The myth is that primitive societies, shorn of the artifice of civilisation, are in harmony with their environment through the wisdom of their folkways and that it is only the foolishness and wickedness of modern society that has rejected this. We are persuaded that somehow, 'life nearer to nature is more virtuous and "real" than in the superficial urban environment that man creates for himself' (Street 1975: 120).

In all this the purported words of the American Indian sage Black Elk have become a canonical text, and Native American culture the epitome of ecological good sense. Neihardt's *Black Elk Speaks* (1972 [1932]) became something of a cult book during the early days of the environmentalist counter-culture in the 1960s. It stands for, if you like, that vision of Native Americans that holds them to be entirely fraternal in their relations with nature. What Black Elk left unsaid, of course, was that such views are not necessarily incompatible with purposeful activities that appear to run against prevailing folk wisdom. In the separate fictional reality of Ernest Callenbach's *Ecotopia*, we are told that citizens feel 'sentimental about Indians', do not feel 'separate from their technology' and 'evidently feel a little as the Indians must have felt; that the horse and tepee and bow and arrow all sprang, like the human being, from the womb of nature . . . they treat materials in the same spirit of respect, comradeship . . . what matters most is the aspiration to live in balance with nature: "walk lightly on the land", treat the earth as a mother' (Callenbach 1978: 29, 47).

In the politicisation of indigenous peoples, even the protagonists themselves, no doubt perfectly sincerely, can be persuaded to believe this, but the evidence is not good. Occasionally the practice of traditional peoples comes into conflict with that of modern environmentalists, and this poses a real problem. A particular case is of the aboriginal Indian and Inuit sealers and fur-trappers of Greenland, Canada and Alaska (as represented through the organisation Indigenous Survival International) versus Greenpeace. A spokesperson at the time made clear that with hunting the only viable means of earning a living in such territories, the urban-based soya-bean philosophies of Greenpeace were a luxury that they could ill afford. Such philosophies could only be understood as the product of people who had lost touch with nature for some centuries, but who now through their ill-thought-out campaigning were condemning 'our people' to slow genocide. Greenpeace conceded a temporary defeat (*The Guardian*, 4–5 October 1985). There are many other similar examples that could be cited.

This whole opposition between nature and culture, by which humanity is assigned to one or the other, and where each in turn reigns ideologically supreme or serves a particular legitimating purpose, is omnipresent, and is itself a product of the human mind. Different societies, and different ages, reinvent Nature in their own image, sometimes benignly, sometimes with hostility, but rarely with indifference.

Here I wish to examine the reality of one myth, that concerning the ecological wisdom of native peoples. There are two versions. The first is that such populations, through their collective wisdom, consummate skill and empathy with the natural order, know how to, and do, conserve resources in ways we have lost. The second is the more sophisticated anthropological version that says that the practices of traditional peoples are functionally adapted through cybernetic loops and homeostasis. Now these assertions are based on two major and unexamined assumptions: that we know what *kind* of society we have in mind when speaking of 'primitive' or 'traditional', and that whatever kind of society it is, it is characterised by an extraordinary degree of geographical isolation. Let us take the second of these assumptions first since it is that most easily disposed of.

It is undeniably true that human societies were once more isolated from one another than they have been over the last 100 years or so. It is such isolation that has been largely responsible for processes of genetic, linguistic and cultural differentiation. On the other hand, it is most unlikely that any human population has ever been completely isolated, and many of those societies which we routinely call 'primitive', 'tribal', 'traditional' or whatever have been part of wider – often global – systems of exchange for many millennia. Typically, they have represented the outliers of a world system, or of regional economic systems, acting as the advanced guard of that system in its assault on the more peripheral environments. Thus, the trade in bird-of-paradise feathers is centuries – possibly millennia – old, feathers which eventually ended up in fashionable milliners in Paris or

London having embarked on their journey on the end of a hunter's arrow in the remoter parts of New Guinea.

We next have to decide what kinds of real-world societies are being referred to in such summaries. The notion of primitive humankind in harmony with nature is historically associated with the idea of primitive 'man' being part of nature. This idea is based on a distinct evolutionist assumption: primitive peoples are still part of nature, and therefore adjusted to natural cycles in ways in which animals are assumed to be. We find this echoed in Germanic conceptions of 'Naturvolker' or Kropotkin's 'life in a state of nature'. Viewed this way, 'the natural order of the close-knit community' (Cotgrove 1982: 5) corresponds to Tonnies' notion of 'Gemeinschaft'. It is an alternative environmental paradigm, in which the prime virtues become decentralisation, smallness of scale, communality, flexibility and a benign construction of nature (Kluckhohn and Strodtbeck 1961). However, the word 'primitive', apart from being pejorative in its implication of mental and moral inadequacy, what John Lubbock described, in the crude and naive racist language of his time, as 'the inactivity of the savage intellect', is additionally useless because it still begs the questions as to what kind of structure such societies have. Those who use it in common parlance do so rhetorically and ideologically to refer to cultures whose customs are seen as inferior or barbaric, Shakespeare's 'most savage and unnatural'. In the past it has often been applied to societies whose structure and mode of production has varied from hunting bands to complex traditional states with bureaucracies and a high division of labour. In other words, it has not a shred of scientific validity.

The societies which are being invoked are presumably not peasantries, where famine, inequality and violence are ubiquitous, even if such cultures have often produced philosophical doctrines of which the spiritual environmentalists would approve. We can thus dispose of the fashionable belief that oriental ideologies, such as Zen Buddhism or Taoism, are somehow a spiritual bulwark against pollution, erosion, deforestation and environmental wreckage (Anderson 1969: 273). Neither are the societies referred to as 'tribal' in the usual sense that this word is used by anthropologists. One widely shared view is that tribal societies are those that are functionally generalised while structurally decentralised. If we accept this definition then tribal organisation is found among peoples who obtain their food through a wide range of technologies: hunting, forest agriculture, nomadic pastoralism, fishing, gathering and intensive agriculture. In this sense the Ifugao of northern Luzon, with their high population densities and technically sophisticated agricultural terraces, are every bit as much 'tribal' as the Tasaday of Mindanao who allegedly have no means of catching animals other than with their bare hands. What those who project such societies as paragons of ecological virtue appear to be referring to are certain populations which are small in size and politically un-centralised, and which do not obviously modify their environment in any radical way. And so, by a process of progressive elimination of social types, we are left with foraging peoples as the archetypal primitives. Among these, as I have already said, the Native American is paramount. However, the cut-off point is by no means clear. For example, Native Americans were not only hunters and gatherers, but pastoralists and horticulturalists as well. Some also had complex social hierarchies. One rather nice paradox that the ignorance of the environmental movement has thrown up is the selection of totem poles as a symbol of ecological wisdom of Native Americans. The difficulty with this is that the totem pole, though seen as the archetypal artefact of all Native Americans, is in fact restricted to a group of peoples of the Pacific northwest coasts, such as the Haida and Kwakiutl, who are best known in the ethnographic literature for the institution of potlatch, festivals in which in its extreme form enormous surpluses of food, clothing and money were actually destroyed publicly, in an apparently maniacal way, in order to affirm positions of clan status. Ruth Benedict called this kind of culture 'Dionysian' to contrast it with those other North American Indian peoples who have more equipoise in their relations with nature, such as those of the Great Plains. Their altogether more 'Apollonian' attitudes are well summed up in the following passage, which must surely be typical of the reasons why Native American culture holds such a special place in the mythology of the modern green movement:

> a hunted animal is propitiated, one apologises to it, explaining that it is being killed only because of great need – one never kills more than is needed and every part of the animal must be used; similarly, only the number of plants needed is picked; the first plant of the type sought is never picked, an offering is placed before it and others sought. (Rapoport 1969: 70)

But the Indians of the Great Plains, as they are popularly imagined, did not exist before the coming of the White man.

Also drawn in to the definition of the archetypal primitive are some peoples engaged in agriculture, and pastoralists. So, it seems that it is no easier to define the *kind* of culture that enshrines such wisdom than it is to define those other nebulous and pernicious cultural entities such as 'Western civilisation'. However, let us assume – at least for the moment – that we share a covert understanding of what is meant by an 'ecologically wise society'. Do such societies fare any better than their more complex counterparts?

The problem is that far from such societies being universally 'in harmony' with nature, they are often cruelly the victims of it, as with the peoples of the Sahel (e.g. Swift 1977) and among the Karimojong and other peoples of the arid zone of East Africa. Small populations with minimal technologies may also, themselves, be perpetrators of environmental havoc (Ellen 1982: 22–23). The Plains Indians, whose tepee – along with the totem pole of the Haida – has become one of the cult symbols among one sect of the green movement (Figure 1.1), were in part responsible for widespread deforestation and the near elimination of the North American bison.[2] In the New Guinea highlands vast areas of grassland have been produced through over-cultivation. Turnbull (1961: 92) tells us how, despite Mbuti respect and veneration of the forest, they are prepared to burn it to drive out game. To those who say 'yes, but much of this environmental de-stabilisation arises precisely because they have contact with the outside world', I would remind them that neither forest destruction nor hunting to extinction are restricted to the modern era. There is evidence that the Pleistocene megafauna as a whole in Europe became extinct in the main through over-hunting, and the temperate forest of Europe was decimated by early farmers living at low population densities in non-stratified societies using simple technologies. Today, presented with such peoples

Figure 1.1. A banner publicising the Green Collective, which 'seeks to facilitate the growth of a green movement through nonviolence, creative action and networking'. Banner artist: John Clarke (Jonny Brush). Photographer: Cheryl Waterhouse. Published as a colour postcard; reproduced here courtesy of David Taylor; see https://green-history.uk/component/search/?searchword=Green%20Collective&searchphrase=all&Itemid=101.

face to face we would regard them as the very epitome of the primitive living with nature. Indeed, they were so regarded by the Ancients.

So, the environmental spirituality of the Sioux went hand in hand with a rapaciously carnivorous diet, in much the same way as Hindu vegetarianism is found in a society with extreme poverty and environmental imbalance. I say this not to make some jibe against the inconsistencies in the worldviews of a certain section of the green movement, but to hammer home the point that no one human culture has the monopoly on environmental wisdom, and that it seems unlikely that we could ever escape some of the more profound dilemmas of human social life.

The potency of the myth of primitive environmental wisdom persists. It does so for three interconnected reasons: firstly, because particular societies do, indeed, have ideologies and cosmologies which stress environmental harmony; secondly, because at particular times anthropologists and others have appeared to describe societies which have something approaching an ecologically self-sustaining economy; and, thirdly, because many find it attractive to use the Darwinian concept of 'adaptation' to explain why societies should have achieved such a favourable accommodation.

First, ideology and cosmology are a bad guide to real life. Ideologies often diverge markedly from what actually happens in practice. Even the existence in some societies of techniques *designed* to conserve resources do not always have the desired effect. Those societies that are so routinely held up as models of good environmental management have rarely been studied by scholars particularly interested in their ecology. Often, the environmental balance which it is implied they maintained has become only a matter for historical enquiry, and therefore not readily accessible. Moreover, such a worldview is by no means the monopoly of such societies. I have already mentioned the Hindu, Buddhist and Taoist peasantries. In addition, for every ecological remark of the Black Elk variety, it is possible to find its measure in British folklore, and Judaeo-Christianity includes plenty of sound ecology. There is the Franciscan tradition of the virtue of humility – not merely for the individual but for humankind as a species – and the Provencal Cabbala of Western Judaism with its metapsychotic elements. Christianity inherited from Judaism a striking story of creation in which, by gradual stages, a loving and all-powerful God creates light and darkness, the heavenly bodies, the earth and all its living organisms and gives humanity stewardship overall. And although the Baconian creed that scientific knowledge is coterminous with technological power over nature became widespread from about 1850 (White 1969), even by the end of the preceding century 'a growing number of people had come to find man's ascendancy over nature increasingly abhorrent to their moral and aesthetic sensibilities' (Thomas 1983: 300). While religion and belief may stress harmonious relations with nature, this does not prevent 'wholesale ecosystem damage due to pure economic necessity, in explicit, self-admitted violation of their norms and knowledge of final effect' (Anderson 1969: 273–74). In short, because you speak to nature as if it has a soul does not make you immune to its more malevolent forces.

Second, it is true that populations have been described which as a whole appear in harmony with the environment. The difficulty is that there are seldom opportunities to study such societies over the long term to see whether or not first appearances are at all vindicated. It used to be the privilege of social anthropologists to be able to formulate theories of society unburdened by the intrusion of history, on the basis of the rather quaint and questionable assumption that the kind of societies which they studied did not have histories, and if they did then these were anyway inaccessible because of the absence of writing. The assumption no longer holds, but in the late 1960s there was an echo of such arrogance in the world of human ecology. Some societies, particularly in the remoter parts of New Guinea, were claimed to be in an environmental equilibrium that their cultural institutions were responsible for regulating, after the fashion of a thermostat on a fridge. Of those populations that have been subjected to detailed scrutiny, first appearances have – I am afraid – often transpired to be deceptive.

Third, adaptation is a notorious weasel word. All individuals, collectivities and populations adapt to their environment through a combination of conscious manipulation and structural determination, but this is a dynamic process, and adaptation is never perfect. If by 'adaptation' we have in mind the development of certain social institutions to maintain a particular environmental state, then we are on especially shaky ground. And, anyway, 'societies', because they are second-order abstractions which have no existence 'out there', cannot in any sense be the empirical units of adaptation. Roy Rappaport (1984) in his justifiably influential monograph on the Tsembaga Maring people of Papua New Guinea argued that an elaborate ritual cycle called the 'kaiko' is an adaptation through which their environment is regulated by periodically reducing the pressure on resources and readjusting clan territories. Now, even if it can be shown that the ritual cycle has the effects that Rappaport claimed it had, of preventing environmental mayhem, it is difficult to demonstrate how this came about, and why we should consider it to be an adaptation. Now, I do not want to appear entirely negative. It is undeniably true that some societies do not degrade their environment in any obvious way, but this is a matter of *appearances* and as much the consequence of, as an adaptation to, a particular social organisation, demographic structure and pattern of subsistence. There are a number of reasons why such societies appear successful.

Firstly, they are small, and therefore have very little impact on the environment anyway. This is not the result of population planning designed to minimise environmental damage. It is either the consequence of a particular lifestyle, or it is the result of a population policy to achieve other ends. In such societies, infant mortality, stillbirths and miscarriages are common, and life expectancy and the effective reproductive life of women short. In nomadic and sedentary societies alike, spacing children is important, and practices such as abortion and infanticide frequent. Nancy Howell (1976) has reported that the !Kung San of Botswana have a very low natural fertility, which is neither due to foetal wastage, infanticide nor to methods of artificial birth control. Rather, low fertility is to be explained in terms of a high incidence of venereal disease, poor nutritional status and chronic seasonal calorie insufficiency (Truswell and Hansen 1976). It could be said, therefore, that it is the *inability* to have more children that prevents overpopulation, not some conscious decision.

In many small-scale societies size alone is a sufficient condition to prevent the more dire environmental hazards, as long as they are not in competition with other populations for the same resources. They need pay no heed to environmentalist doctrines. It is not, of course, size alone that is critical here, but size in relation to a particular kind of ecological system. Thus, Nuaulu hunters on the Indonesian island of Seram often seem to have a vandalistic attitude to the rainforest that any self-respecting Friend of the Earth would find positively obscene. As they walk along well-trodden forest paths they quite deliberately hack away at lianas, tree trunks and other vegetation, for no other reason than it gives them pleasure. But the scale of this destruction is so minute compared with the forest as a whole, the rate of regrowth so rapid, that any amount of wilfulness on the part of Nuaulu travellers is of negligible effect. Thus, many people, such as the Mbuti of the Ituri forest, described by Colin Turnbull (1961), are able to maintain harmonious relations with their environment despite their practices. Given a particular population density they would have to work very hard indeed to cause any ecologically significant damage. Although Marshall Sahlins (1968) did not put it quite this way when he coined the phrase 'the original affluent society', it is the privilege of not having to be worried about the consequences for subsistence of prodigal or wanton environmental excesses that makes people like the Mbuti, though not the San, 'affluent'.

The second reason why such populations manage is that they generally have 'broad spectrum' subsistence strategies. That is, they are not entirely dependent on one, or a few resources, and if one resource begins to decline, they can switch to another. If the Nuaulu yam harvest fails, there is always sago; if pig meat is not available, they can turn to marsupials. On the other hand, if the rice crop fails in rural Java or Maasai cattle in Tanzania succumb to bovine sleeping sickness, famine prevails. To take another example. The difference between modern logging and all earlier patterns of extraction from the rainforests of Seram, Indonesia (where the Nuaulu live) is that the latter involves, for the most part, a gradual denudation of primary growth and the selective (but not exhaustive) extraction of a variety of species to cater for a wide range of essentially local uses. Modern methods involve either the selective extraction of just a few species to exhaustion, or the total destruction of the forest in a short period to cater for a narrow range of non-local uses. Specialisation leads to system instability, by reducing the number of alternative pathways achieving the same end. Such duplication is wasteful in terms of conventional economic criteria, but ensures greater system resilience and flexible response.

The third reason why certain small-scale societies appear to be ecologically sound is because of their degree of isolation from other systems, a factor dependent on their population level. Such system closure was no doubt a common feature of early hominids, as they migrated, became isolated and diversified. No existing human population is completely closed off from its neighbours, and it is this that makes homeostatic arguments so difficult to apply to human societies. Complete isolation is an existence only viable if a population is able to maintain a self-sufficient economy. If you cannot, you either die out or exchange. In this respect human social organisation is very different from that of other animals, giving profundity to the otherwise seemingly trivial observation that human cultural evolution is predicated on exchange and is no more than so many elaborations and transformations of that basic idea. So, the key general ecological trend in human history and evolution is the breakdown of local self-sufficiency, due to internal and external factors, and the various cultural responses to cope with this. Without exchange, there is no incentive to over-produce; in fact, the opposite is the case, and it is this that contributes towards a sustainable economy.

It follows that the greater the degree of isolation, the more effective is control over land, and therefore of the position of the human population in the ecosystem. This does not mean that people actively seek to regulate, or that their cultures are adapted to do so. I have already argued against this. It is simply that isolation and low population are properties of a system that has the mechanical effect of making regulation easier and more probable. Such populations have regulatory autonomy denied to those populations that are components of more inclusive and hierarchical systems. And those systems of which small, relatively isolated non-differentiated human populations are part hinder cultural innovation and diffusion, resulting in a slow rate of change, reinforcing all the characteristics I have so far mentioned. This makes destabilisation resulting from rapid change likely.

Fourth and finally, the kind of human populations I have been speaking of tend to invest in environmental resources only in short-term cycles. The degree to which they modify their environments is, therefore, for the most part, partial and temporary. This promotes greater ecological efficiency, though not necessarily any greater economic efficiency in the terms we might employ to measure it.

Thus, it is less the conscious wisdom or the superior mental abilities of such societies, or even some superbly adjusted system that has evolved over the millennia, which leads to the maintenance of a state of environmental relations which we describe as 'balanced', so much as the consequences of a particular demographic, social structural, subsistence and ecological complex. Alter any of these variables and the situation might look very different. Although such populations, through their particular mode of subsistence, have a more direct and greater semantic and practical collective contact with their environment than the average person from the industrialised world, which often leads to both an extraordinary encyclopaedic knowledge of their environment and understanding of its properties, no one human society has privileged access to 'knowledge' of how best to manage environmental relations in the abstract.

When the words of Black Elk are taken from their original complex cultural context to make a particular environmentalist point, we must understand that that statement has now become part of the discourse of modern politics in a context far removed from that in which it was first spoken. In itself it tells us little of the environmental attitudes of members of small-scale societies, let alone of the degree of success with which they manage their environment. Many political Greens have accepted that they are attempting to build a rational society that has never existed – which itself does not make it any less desirable. But others, not all of whom can be consigned to the mystical fringes, still operate with profoundly false assumptions about the ecological character of pre-industrial societies, assumptions which continue to underpin their prescriptions for present-day political action. Even if their romantic vision of environmental serendipity were true, the cultural and social legacy of centuries of urban and industrial life makes it virtually impossible to simply regress and devolve. We are hopelessly post-industrial. The kind of semantic contact we in the West have with the environment is that which comes from a long cultural tradition which has relentlessly moved away from any simple relationship with nature and has in fact come to dominate it. There are many ecological lessons to be learned from an understanding of the structure of small-scale societies, but they are not necessarily those which some influential Green gurus have drawn attention to, or would approve of.

Notes

First published in *Anthropology Today* (1986: 2 (6 December): 8–12) as 'What Black Elk Left Unsaid: On the Illusory Images of Green Primitivism'. Reproduced courtesy of Wiley and the Royal Anthropological Institute.

1. A kindly reviewer has pointed out that this chapter has a rather dated feel to it, and I agree. It was written before the main growth in writing on traditional environmental knowledge, and before this had become a major part of the self-conscious identity of many traditional peoples themselves. In hindsight, some of the claims might today seem to require qualification. However, rather than fix the chapter in a way that would take into account the developments of the last thirty years, I have decided to leave it as a 'period piece' which retains a valid take-home message.
2. In the light of more recent discussion, and perhaps even at the time the chapter was written, this claim is controversial, but see, for example, Hämäläinen (2008: 294–99). In the long term, the near extinction of the North American bison was mainly the result of commercial hunting, the impact of introduced bovine diseases, habitat destruction as the frontier advanced, the growth of the railroad network, and politically motivated US army culls during the Indian Wars, but the introduction of guns and horses into Native American hunting technology also played a part.

CHAPTER 2

Comparative Natures in Melanesia

Introduction

Sandra Bamford (1998b) notes that Melanesianists have not attended sufficiently to the ways in which human identities are shaped by interactions with the physical world. She also observes that there has been little sustained discussion aimed at investigating commonalities and differences in this regard. No doubt some ethnographers will protest that there are distinguished exceptions to this view, but one of the considerable merits of the special issue of *Social Analysis* (Bamford 1998a) that she has edited is that it has begun to redress the imbalance. In this commentary I try to bring some of the themes together, through the perspective of someone who has an interest in human conceptions of the natural world generally, and more specifically someone who has undertaken field research in a neighbouring region (eastern Indonesia) where the environment is essentially the same, but where history has conspired to construct cultural particulars rather differently.

The Bamford collection deals with a number of themes that bear on issues of sociality and the environment. It would be possible to group them in a number of alternative and radically cross-cutting ways, and no doubt different readers will be drawn to contrasting unifying features. Jimmy Weiner (1998) notes that the chapters appear to divide between those asserting a profound distinction between the domains of nature and human action on the part of the peoples they describe, and those that do not. Although we are in danger here of presupposing just what 'nature' is, this is a convenient working distinction with which I concur, though I am not sure I would draw the line in quite the same place. For me, perhaps because I come to the contributions with a preconceived agenda, generated by a particular research experience and familiarity with a particular literature, the following themes are salient: the mutual embeddedness of social life and the physical world (both the naturalisation of society and the socialisation – including the engendering – of nature); the relationship between anthropogenic process, local history and landscape; acoustical dimensions of the environment; and the linkage between concepts of nature and recent social and environmental change. None of these themes are mutually exclusive. Here, I shall first summarise the arguments, and then review them from a comparative perspective, both within Melanesia, in relation to the similar and emerging literature for eastern Indonesia, and in the context of general debates about underlying tendencies in the ways in which socialised humans engage with the natural world. I conclude that we must avoid reading 'the cultural construction of nature' in too glib, superficial, or uni-dimensional a way, and recognise that it is possible to identify unifying pan-human features at the level of common cognitive process, and at the level of widely distributed shared representations and cultural imagery. At the same time, we must accept that in individual cases concepts of nature and their polythetic cognates serve many – sometimes conflicting – purposes which we can seldom hope to reconcile, but which paradoxically reflect the common resonances of a richly complex notion and its transformations.

Themes in Melanesian Constructions of Nature

The Mutual Embeddedness of Physical and Social Worlds

Anthropologists working in New Guinea have long commented on the close link between indigenous social forms and cultural representations of the physical environment, and a number of chapters in the Bamford volume show how particular bits of the physical world are used metaphorically for, or are consubstantial with, social relations. For example, Bamford herself (1998c) deals with the equivalences established amongst Kamea between the growth of trees and the growth of social relationships; and Fajans (1998) too, speaking of the Baining of New Britain, deals with the transformative resemblance between natural and social products, how making gardens moves nature into social and cultural spaces, and how parental adoption and exchanging food metamorphoses children from natural to social beings. Thus, when Baining sell logging rights, the complaint against the loggers is not just that they destroy physical objects or natural resources, but that they destroy things that have a social life as well and which are the products of Baining labour. Damon (1998) explores another aspect of the mutual embeddedness of the natural and the social, the case of Muyuw anthropomorphisation and personification of trees, particularly the culturally salient genus *Calophyllum*. Bamford (1998c) deals with gender in the landscape, though what is surprising about this set of papers as a whole – especially given that Melanesia is well known in the general anthropological literature for its marked gender distinctions, and given the seminal work of Marilyn Strathern (1980) and Gillison (1980), and its prominence in discussions of the category 'nature' – is that gender features so slightly in overall concerns. Bamford's point about the Kamea, however, is one which we might expect to find resonances with elsewhere, namely that women do not appear to become part of – are not 'inscripted' in – the humanised landscape in any significant way.

Nature and Landscape as Anthropogenic Phenomena

In Melanesia, as in other parts of the tropical world, it is now widely recognised that human populations have often played a crucial role over some thousands of years in modifying and maintaining the environment. In other words, what we call nature is to a considerable extent anthropogenic. Sometimes this is recognised in human conceptualisations, sometimes it is not; and what is the product of social and cultural processes is often doggedly treated as independent of human inputs. In the Bamford collection, both Damon (1998) on Muyuw and Wagner (1998) on the Daribi grasslands are concerned with forest as an anthropogenic entity, reminding us of the considerable effort invested in transforming or sustaining parts of nature. According to Weiner (1998), Foi trees are more 'mobile' and less 'rooted' than the humans who move and uproot them. On Vanuatu, as described by Rodman (1998), the process of beginning to use land, then contesting it and abandoning it for a long time, inevitably creates an ambiguous area in terms of conventional nature/culture distinctions, and even where the growth of bush might be thought to have obliterated the traces of human occupation, the memories of former occupancy still exercise a powerful presence.

Thus, we have a grouping of the papers which illustrate how local histories are mapped onto, interact with, or are an intrinsic part of landscapes (as in Kirsch's presentation on Ok Tedi Yonggom at the original conference session),[1] how the identities of people are embedded in the landscape (Bamford on the Kamea), and on how space or forest is used to map time (Wagner on the Daribi, and Bamford on the Kamea).[2] Elsewhere, names of things and of people are an integral part of the environment; objects, places and names provide a collective conceptual scheme. Rodman shows for Vanuatu how labelled trees are used to convey time depth: how trees thrive but buildings do not, and therefore are considered to be the best landmarks to evoke history, in a sense contra Foi. In Vanuatu, 'dark bush' – what we might loosely gloss as 'wilderness', as well as domesticated landscapes – are seen as being inherently social. All salient sites in the bush are reported in terms of official government categories as 'historic', 'traditional' or 'cultural', only the cultural being specifically 'indigenous'. In this latter respect it appears that 'cultural' parallels the older concept of 'custom'.

Sound as a Sensory Coordinate

Schieffelin in his conference presentation (and very much echoing Feld, e.g. 1996) on the Kaluli argues that people in dense tropical forest are primarily oriented around the auditory and oral mode. The same theme has been taken up by Gell for the Umeda. For Gell (1995: 235), landscape contexts are keyed to sound symbolism at a very basic level, and the forest environment in particular prioritises the auditory sense to the extent that it even promotes phonological iconicity in language. Hearing, and iconic language, it is argued, is a relatively intimate, concrete and tactile sense, whereas language generally is abstract and arbitrary.

The Consequences of Recent Social, Economic and Environmental Change

One of the reasons why many contemporary scholars have so much difficulty with the idea that certain recurrent cognitive coordinates underlie concepts of nature is that such concepts measurably alter in response to social, economic and environmental change. Most of the papers in the Bamford collection engage with modifications in the conceptualisation of nature and sociality as a result of recent events. Kirsch (2001) in his conference presentation, for example, notes that Ok Tedi accounts of the past have become more chronological and less spatial. Elsewhere (as with the Rauto of New Britain described by Maschio in his presentation), there has been an increased separation of biography from place, through a discourse of custom, nationalism and modernisation. Robbins, in his conference paper, tells us that the Urapmin have a strong desire for a mine, in the same way that many other Papua New Guinea people have a desire to sell timber. Telefomin, as described by Jorgensen (1998), impose intimate meanings on a new landscape of mining. As we know from some of the comparative case material from outside of Melanesia (e.g. Ellen 1993a, 1999a), the fulfilment of such desires for economic gain transforms local understandings of nature, commoditising and de-socialising it. Although scholars no longer understand nature in any objective sense as being outside society, or society outside nature, it is possible to identify instances of social and environmental change leading to the perception that nature has been 'externalised', reified as something apart, as people cease to engage with it other than recreationally or as 'wilderness'. We see this in the developed North (Thomas 1983), and increasingly it is happening in the developing South (Ellen and Bernstein 1994).

Rodman (1998) shows how while colonial planters on Vanuatu managed to create history by distancing themselves from the colony, local people still experience the same artefacts as biographical signs in the landscape. In terms of official categories on Vanuatu, history contrasts with culture, and we seem to find a consequently greater separation of time from space, with a new emphasis on differences between humans and nature. A couple of papers (Wagner 1998, on the Daribi, and Robbins's presentation on Urapmin) imply a link between cargo cults and their associated concepts of time and environmental degradation,[3] although it is necessary to acknowledge that most places where cargo cults have been important are without such degradation. Changes in concepts of nature do occur without changes in the objective local environment. The Urapmin, says Robbins, have been moved into the 'bush' by the encroaching new mental landscape. Similarly, Biersack in her presentation reports the role of increasing travel on changing views of nature, while in Vanuatu, what newly arrived Europeans classified as empty spaces (including 'dark bush'), with the implication of denial of previous 'ownership', were in fact indigenous places; no physical modification here, just different perceptions of the same thing.

Cognitive versus Social Theories of Nature

It is rare to find analyses of commonalities for Melanesian societies in regard to concepts of nature in the existing literature, mainly I think because regional ethnographers have not been interested, partly because the extent and continuous character of variation has made comparison difficult, and also because of the general tendency towards the particularistic account. Such reluctance to engage in systematic and rigorous regional comparison is striking when compared, say, with Amazonia or eastern Indonesia. It is almost as if the early attempts to force Melanesian ethnography into pre-existing comparative frameworks have been so problematic and devastatingly critiqued (e.g. Barnes 1962; see also Sillitoe 1979; Strathern 1992a) that this has undermined the ethos of comparative work. Researchers have been wary of seeking generalisations above the level of the local for fear of repeating earlier straitjacketing errors. While not wishing to deny evident ethnographic and regional difference, such reluctance has been turned by some into a convenient but unexamined virtue which stresses how New Guinea is like no other part of the world, which at times – usually at the anecdotal level – comes dangerously close to a form of primordial essentialism. One can see a reflection of such assumptions and attitudes in the extreme deconstructionism exhibited in publications on nature and society.

I agree with Damon (1998) that the nature-culture distinction is now so over-critiqued that it has blunted our appreciation of complexities of non-western understandings and blinded us to the similarities and overlapping multiple usages that exist. I would add that the over-critique has also prevented the emergence of a serious and sustained comparative analysis of different constructions of nature, and simplistically avoided the identification of underlying cognitive coordinates. The absence of such interest has been fertile ground for accounts that tend to debunk traditional dualist conceptions of nature and culture, which endorse the extreme cultural subjectivisation of nature (e.g. MacCormack 1980; Strathern 1980), and which in themselves make comparison difficult. For if no part of what we call nature is *'sui generis'*, then what is it that we are comparing? If nature can be anything or everything, what can we grasp in order to compare varying conceptualisations of the world? If, indeed, social life is lived in a world where the distinction between reified nature and culture has no significance, then one possibility is to attempt to break down the unworkable abstractions into some plausible component parts.

There are compelling methodological, logical, ethnographic and psychological grounds for accepting the existence of some underlying universal cognitive coordinates for what is conventionally recognised as nature in the Western tradition.

On methodological grounds alone, there are immense difficulties in denying the existence of something conceptually cognate with nature. Thus, despite the attempts of many to downplay the relevance of the nature-culture distinction, writers still routinely imply its existence. It is an inescapable device for describing scientifically and comparatively how humans engage in the world. What intrigues me is the casuistry which people employ, having deconstructed the culture-nature opposition, to account for the world effectively without reverting to it. Time and time again, synonyms and literary tropes are employed which appear to distance ourselves from the opposition, but which simply resurrect it in a different form. Thus, we get the 'non-human environment' and the 'physical world'. To say, for example, that Kamea women do not become part of the 'humanised landscape' suggests that there is a *'non*-humanised' landscape somewhere, even though its existence may be simply virtual, rhetorical or polemical. I have discussed further the logical tautology we can get into when describing the world without resorting to nature-like elsewhere (Ellen 1996a).

As a scientific idea, some version of nature must be more than a mere arbitrary construction evolved in Western society: it has deep cognitive roots which – in a sense – make science itself, and any systematic description and understanding of the world, possible. It is evident in the organisation of what is now called intuitive physics and natural history knowledge; and is reflected in what Lévi-Strauss called totemic thought underpinned by a classification which systematically distinguishes the social with reference to natural particulars. It can be inferred also from the often complex folk-ecological distinctions which people make and label, as between different types of habitat, vegetation, topography and so on (e.g. Hyndman 1982; Sillitoe 1996), for such distinctions imply that they are *part of* some generic (if linguistically covert) phenomenon or entity. And, of course, the differences that are made in European languages between, say, types of vegetation and types of topography often merge in Melanesian classifications, also suggesting some overarching conceptual apparatus. None of this makes nature-like concepts in all societies identical, or versions of a simple and single unified concept. Moreover, an idealisation or reification that seeks to be an aggregation or distillation of *all* natures will forever be chimerical. Our particular cultural constructions of nature alter depending on time, what it is we are perceiving and what we seek to emphasise, not only between but within cultures; but this should not detract from the search for themes which underlie all versions.

For example, I have suggested elsewhere (Ellen 1996a, 1996d) that one solution to this problem is to identify a tripartite cognitive geometry of thingification, otherness and essence. The ability and tendency of all human minds to organise knowledge of the natural world in terms of discrete generic entities at a 'basic' level, and to aggregate and disaggregate such entities (thingification), as well as the tendency to attribute to such categories essential qualities, finds support in recent work on natural history intelligence drawing on the insights and evidence of both cognitive psychology and ethnobiology (e.g. Atran 1998). Moreover, one does not have to accept the general universalist-evolutionist position as found, for example, in the early work of Brent Berlin (e.g. Berlin, Breedlove and Raven 1973) to subscribe to such a view. The evidence for the recognition of a pan-human cognitively-rooted essence-based concept of natural kind is rather compelling. The same can be said for the existence of certain cross-culturally stable prototypical phenomenal forms, such as 'plant' or 'animal' (of which humans themselves have ambiguous membership), though these are not routinely translated into labelled categories. Interestingly, the New Guinea ethnography has contributed towards our understanding of the underlying imperatives and cultural organisation of natural history intelligence in an important body of work, most obviously that authored by Bulmer (1970, 1974a, 1974b; see also bibliography in A. Bulmer 1991: 46–47) but also, amongst others, Glick (1964), Diamond (1966), Dwyer (1976), Healey (1978–79), Hays (1983) and Kocher-Schmid (1991). It is strange, however, that relatively little attention has been paid to the connection between this body of work and current writing on concepts of nature. Thus, while we might agree that conceptions of nature are not merely the outcome of some pan-human cultural logic or universal classification for engaging with the world, they are at the very least heavily constrained by the cognitive requirements to concretise bits of nature, distinguish the extended self from the other and attribute to parts of the world essential qualities. It is therefore no wonder that conceptions of nature are intrinsically about identity, both of the human self and of the collectivity.

We can see in the papers gathered in the Bamford collection all three of these elements, but the one which is most developed is the idea of nature as other. Thus, in Fajans' (1998) account of the Baining we find nature as forest, nature as raw material, together with a 'bush':'place' (social space) opposition. While Fajans argues that for the Baining nature is not an essentialised category – natural places (e.g. forest) being conceptualised more as a source of materials to be transformed into social products – Jorgensen (1998) is very emphatic that Telefomin *abiip* (village) and *sep* (surrounding bush) reflect a strong and enduring opposition between human and natural worlds. It is in this context, when we think of nature as other or as background, that its similarity with the cognate concepts of land, environment and landscape becomes apparent. As with nature, so with landscape, we are constantly forced, by the analytical power of the subject-object, material-mental dualism, to distinguish physical from conceptual (or perceptual), un-reflexive from reflexive, the inevitable outcomes of ecological cycles from active human planning. In each case the distinction is between foreground actuality and background posteriority: place versus space, inside versus outside, image versus representation (Hirsch 1995: 4).

Now, of course, we are all well aware of the intrinsic, if variably, anthropic character of most physical environments, and in cognitive, cultural and sensory terms we are inclined to see all as being in a state of flux: landscape, nature and environment as all being processual, contingent and historical (Hirsch 1995: 5). But the idea of nature, environment and landscape all being processual is allied to the idea that conceptions of time are closely connected with conceptions of nature, that people have space-time conceptions rather than separate conceptions of space and time. Indeed, the metaphors we use to speak of time are often spatial and those we use to speak of space often chronological and durational. However, just as it is unwise and simplistic to dismiss underlying cognitive processes at work in our conceptions of nature by asserting that nature is intrinsically 'socially constructed', so we would be wise not to dismiss the evidence suggesting that one of the things which makes us human in evolutionary terms is the development of an abstract historical sense. Carrithers (1990: 199) calls this narrativity, 'the propensity to cognise not merely immediate relations between oneself and another, but also many-sided human interactions carried out over a considerable period', though we should not confuse this with a particular lived conception of time. Of course, the expression of time and the mnemonics of history will be different for people who have different systems of production, for people with, say, relatively discrete corporate descent groups, such as the Lio (e.g. Howell 1992), as opposed to a system where descent is unimportant (such as the Kamea). In some cases, the prospect of locating the social and cultural underpinnings of history is truly daunting, as with the Daribi, for whom all things appear to be in a constant state of anarchical flux. And it is this rather extreme example which may provide some clue as to why it has been correspondingly difficult to locate clearly articulated conceptions of nature in Melanesia more generally.

Maluku and Melanesia Compared

What is striking about the themes that run through the papers collected here is that none of the points made are uniquely Melanesian. Thus, we can look to the work of Rival (1998) on the imagery of trees and social development and relationships for many parts of the world and find the same patterns in Melanesia (see, e.g., Bonnemere 1998). Damon (1998) reminds us of the common presence of plant and growth symbolism in the Austronesian world (but also into the Papuan-speaking parts of Melanesia as well), of the significance of the base and tip dichotomy, of metaphors of root, shoot and trunk (e.g. on the Iatmul, Coiffier 1994: 575; on the Yopno, Schmid and Kocher-Schmid 1992). Similarly, transformative resemblances between natural and social products are a recurrent theme in the eastern Indonesian ethnographic literature (e.g. Fox 1971, 1980; Traube 1986; Grimes 1993), while the mapping of social time onto the landscape is classically explored by Condominas (Mnong-Gar) in *Nous Avons Mangé la Forêt* (1954). 'Mutual embeddedness' also describes well the relationship between Nuaulu social life in south Seram, Maluku, and their environment: landscape is important in the ongoing negotiation of identity and relationships, as well as reflecting the social past in the present. Nuaulu name all features of the landscape, and patches of secondary regrowth (especially old village sites) bear the imprint of human activity, and are a record of human movement over time. Landscape, therefore, is – to echo Bamford (1998b) – implicated in the very definition of human sociality: the very name Nua-ulu means 'the upstream of the Nua river', and unlike many ethnonyms this is a name with which the Nuaulu themselves fully identify. Moreover, the production of humans and the environment is part of an integrated totality, household and garden sharing a common principle and linked reproductively, while fruit and other useful trees are personalised and thus provide a link to past generations. I do not believe that for the Nuaulu there is any less 'animation/humanisation' of the environment than we find in Melanesia, yet this does not appear to have prevented in any way the emergence of a strongly dichotomous notion of nature : culture difference (Ellen 1996a, 1996b; cf. Valeri 1990), arguably more salient in symbolic classifications than we find in Melanesia. Similarly, the Kamea myth of people emerging from different parts of a tree bears an uncanny resemblance to a Nuaulu myth of origin, except that in the Nuaulu case the plant is a bamboo. For the Nuaulu no less than for the Kamea, myth establishes the generative potential of the landscape, and a close relationship with the environment. In short, the environment everywhere is imbued with social significance, the landscape coterminus with the parameters of human sociality. Given such observations, how might we begin to identify anything which might constitute a *distinctively* Melanesian construction of nature?

One point of departure might be the objective distinctiveness of the ecology of Melanesia and the modes of subsistence that it can sustain. We also need to ask whether particular kinds of mapping of history might be linked to particular extractive technologies. Thus, do modes of subsistence in which sago extraction, swiddening and intensive cultivation respectively predominate tend to sustain different conceptions of the natural world, and therefore different identities? The answer to this question would appear to be in the affirmative. It has been noted by others that vegetative (usually root) and seed cultures tend to run parallel with different conceptions of the natural world: the first in which the natural and the social are less markedly drawn and participatory, the second in which there are stronger distinctions between the natural and the cultural, the wild and the tamed (Haudricourt 1962, 1964; Coursey 1978; Ellen 1999a). Similarly, a gradient can be established between the polar opposites of incipient and intensive agriculture: as humans increasingly dominate the productive process, as forest decreases and landscape is modified, so a stronger contrast appears to be drawn between the natural and the cultural. Consistent with this line of argument is the widely asserted observation that amongst hunting and gathering peoples the natural and the social are even less evident than amongst cultivators of vegetatively reproducing crops, and in New Guinea we might extend this to what Guddemi (1992) calls 'hunter-horticulturalists'. Amongst cultivators we might also identify a significant point of transition in people's constructions of nature, identity and sociality when land as an abstracted entity, and certainly as a commodity, becomes more important than the things that grow on it. The fact that alienation and commoditisation of land have been widely resisted in Melanesia may go some way towards explaining the absence of sharp nature-culture distinctions. One attempt to examine comparatively how conceptions of nature vary in Melanesia according to subsistence is provided by Dwyer (1996), though it should be noted that the different contrasts which I have drawn – the one based on vegetative versus seed propagation, the other based on a gradient of intensification – need not necessarily correlate. Where they do not (as amongst the Wola [Sillitoe 1996], and other New Guinea highland intensive cultivators of sweet potato), we might well expect different symbolic patterns from where they do (as in intensive lowland rice agriculture in Java).

This present Melanesian collection deals mainly with peoples whose primary point of natural reference is forest. Given that the experience of tropical rainforest is everywhere pretty much the same, except for local biogeographic variations, it is implausible to expect that Melanesian sensory construction will be very different from elsewhere. Except perhaps for some of the more exotic imagery, Nuaulu auditory sensitisation to the rainforest environment and the translation of this into useful knowledge and a 'forest aesthetic' is not obviously different from that of the Kaluli (Feld 1996). This is why I am slightly sceptical of – and have difficulties with – the special readings of the role of sound which are currently fashionable. No doubt sound is more important technically in realising subsistence objectives and in symbolically organising the Melanesian natural world where forest is the dominant habitat, and we must accept that the normal sensory modality for language is hearing. Indeed, when the forest disappears, this is reflected in the disappearance of a peculiar soundscape, as Kirsch (2001) claims for the Ok Tedi. But sound cannot replace completely the visual sense, which must remain privileged. Neither can social identities easily be constructed from a soundscape, and I would add that although New Guinea provides ample illustration of the importance of vocalisations in identifying frogs and birds, we have yet to find a systematic classification of plants based on the sounds that they make. If you are interacting with something intimately, then there will generally be multiple ways of registering difference and complexity, a propensity to easily translate into and interrelate qualities of one sensory modality to another (synaesthesia), and no need for abstract categories restricted to a single sense dimension. Languages in forest habitats certainly do seem to privilege audition and olfaction and de-emphasise vision, but vision still co-dominates in cultural spaces, and even where traditions of painting and sculpture are absent, dancing and costume complement sophisticated oral arts. The cultural world, on the whole, is experienced at close range, where vision predominates as the means of registering difference (Gell 1995: 237, 239, 245).

Once we have exhausted the possible ways in which different kinds of environment, subsistence regime and cultigen might influence the representation of nature, we can turn, not to intrinsic cultural difference, but to a consideration of sociological variation. In Maluku, for example, it is much easier to discern bounded cultural groups and clans on the ground than it is in Melanesia, and this is reflected in ethno-sociological consciousness; in this sense society as a bounded abstraction might be said to exist. By comparison, in Melanesia stable groups and stable hierarchy are notoriously difficult to identify (despite some significant differences between highlands and islands, and between east and west), and there appears to be an all-pervading fluidity which comes close to mocking the holistic models of classical sociology. Instead, 'the characteristic Melanesian idea is that the individual person embodies a world of social relations ... which can be ... picked apart and reconstructed', while individual 'Melanesians do not imagine that their experience can be organised by an overarching framework – "society" – embracing all the persons with whom they interact' (Kuper 1992: 10, on Strathern 1992b; but see also Sillitoe 1979). So, if, as Descola (1992) says, humans model their relationships with nature on how they treat the other, we can well ask with Bamford what happens when otherness is subject to renegotiation, when social life has such a constantly emergent, revisionary quality. The Kamea and Daribi worlds, by contrast with those of the Nuaulu and Huaulu, are characterised by their seamlessness.

Conclusion

The non-human world is certainly not inert, nature and culture are not separate domains of existence, and there is no vast chasm between nature and culture. Over the last decade or more, there have been many exultations to reach 'beyond' static nature : culture dualisms, and repeated attacks on Cartesian dualism as a universal model for understanding the world. In social anthropology – and as echoed by Bamford – there is a clear movement away from the Lévi-Straussian use of nature as simply a metaphorical and analogical language to talk about cultural distinctions, in favour of an emphasis on metonymy (Descola 1992: 111). We are now preoccupied much more with homologies between the way we address nature and the way we address social others, replacing – as it were – simple co-evolving metaphors with cognitive simultaneity and consubstantiality. However, the relationship between humans and the world around them is always ambiguous, and this is why humans in certain contexts seek to enforce cognitive separation. As in processes of category formation generally, the human mind latches onto certain perceptual prompts and attempts to make sense of them through simplification, comparison and generalisation. Concepts of nature as we apprehend them are just one particularly abstract outcome of this process, underpinned by the cognitive forces of which I have spoken. Given that this is the case, despite the imperative to separate material from mental, visible from invisible, human from non-human, personal space from far space, it is bizarre to think that there will only be one homogeneous and consistent concept of nature in any particular culture. We can discern plural natures in the casuistry of all peoples, each serving different (perhaps contrasting) purposes. It is true that nature is not a 'basic category' – it can be endlessly reworked culturally and socially to achieve particular ends, and is always characterised by immanence and emergence, as, for example, the boundary between subject and object shifts (cf. Hirsch 1995: 6), and as content and metaphorical linkages change. It is precisely this vagueness – as Roy Rappaport (1971b) taught us – which gives such categories and labels their rhetorical and moral force.

Notes

First published in 1998 as 'Comparative Natures in Melanesia: An External Perspective', in a special issue of *Social Analysis* (42 (3), 143–58) on 'Identity, Nature and Culture: Sociality and Environment in Melanesia', edited by Sandra Bamford. Reproduced courtesy of Berghahn Journals.

1. For a revised version of this, see Kirsch 2001.
2. In this respect, the Daribi and Urapmin compare with the Huli, Duna, Oksapmin and other peoples of the Southern Highlands, who believe that environmental changes (such as volcanic ash falls) indicate that the Earth is losing its fertility and that people are at moral risk (Brutti 1997; Morgan 1997; Strathern and Stewart 1997).
3. But see, e.g., Coiffier 1994: 702 ff; Kocher-Schmid 1991: 44–47, 1997; Schmid and Kocher-Schmid 1992: 44.

Chapter 3

Political Contingency, Historical Ecology and the Renegotiation of Nature

Since the mid 1980s, Nuaulu living on the edge of lowland rainforest[1] in central Seram, Maluku, have become increasingly active in countering threats to their traditional resource base. This latter has been dramatically eroded, mainly through government-sponsored settlement and logging. Nuaulu have successfully defended land claims in the courts, there have been violent incidents at a nearby transmigration area leading to their imprisonment, and in their representations to outsiders they have become articulate about the damage done to their environment. However, Nuaulu have a long history of interaction with 'the outside world', of forest modification and participation in the market. They were politically engaged as early as the Dutch wars of the late seventeenth century and have been indirectly, and more recently directly, subject to the oscillations and economic fall-out of the spice trade ever since. The 1970s and 1980s have seen the expansion of cash-cropping, together with accelerated rates of land sale and forest extraction.[2]

I shall argue in this chapter that as different material and social changes take place, so Nuaulu have renegotiated their conceptual relationship with the forest. In particular, I seek to ask why, given an apparent historic readiness to accept environmental change, they have now adopted a rhetoric that we would recognise as 'environmentalist'. I claim that part of the explanation is that older, local forms of knowledge that underpin subsistence strategies are qualitatively different from knowledge of macro-level processes – 'environmental consciousness' in the abstract – which only comes with a widening of political and ecological horizons.

The Nuaulu in the World System

The patterns of ecological change which have accompanied Nuaulu interaction with the rainforest cannot be understood properly except in relation to the history of contact (direct and indirect) between the forest peoples of Seram and various groups of outsiders: the rulers and subjects of various traditional coastal polities; the Dutch East India Company, its heirs and successors; various agencies of the colonial Dutch government, and thereafter of the government of an independent Indonesia (local district officers, police, military, and the personnel of assorted provincial-level departments); and finally traders and settlers of diverse ethnic origins, but predominantly Chinese, Butonese and Ambonese.

The details of the early phase of the movement of biological species in and out of Seram (Ellen 1993c) is not relevant to the specific argument put forward in this chapter, but that it happened is a part of the general background picture. Thus, the circulation of valuables, upon which the reproduction of Nuaulu social structure became effectively dependent over several hundreds of years (Ellen 1988a), was based on articles traded in from the Asian mainland (porcelain from China and elsewhere, and cloth from India) and from other parts of the archipelago (including textiles from Timor and Java); and what we know of the dynamics of the regional Moluccan system suggests contact which goes back much further than this, and which must have involved the export of forest products.

The most important single factor affecting Moluccan forests during the early period was the rise in the international demand for spices, which by the early sixteenth century had led to the spread of production from the northern to the central Moluccan islands. Expansion and fluctuation in growing clove in particular from this time onwards (Ellen 1985, 1987: 39–41) played a crucial role – both directly and indirectly – in the lives of inland and coastal peoples alike. Although there is no evidence that the Nuaulu planted cloves or collected wild cloves for sale until the twentieth century, they did have an identifiable role in relations with politically significant trading polities and Europeans as early as the Dutch wars of the late seventeenth century, as we know from the VOC archives and from the *Landbeschrijving* of Rumphius (Ellen 1988a: 118, 132n2). We have a remarkably clear idea of the general location of their settlements in the mountains of central Seram from this time to the end of the nineteenth century through oral histories, corroborated by surface archaeology, botanical evidence and eighteenth-century maps (Ellen 1978, 2018a: figure 2.1). By the end of the nineteenth century, most Nuaulu clans had relocated around Sepa on the south coast (Map 3.1), largely as a result of Dutch pressure, though they have continued an essentially highland, interior-oriented

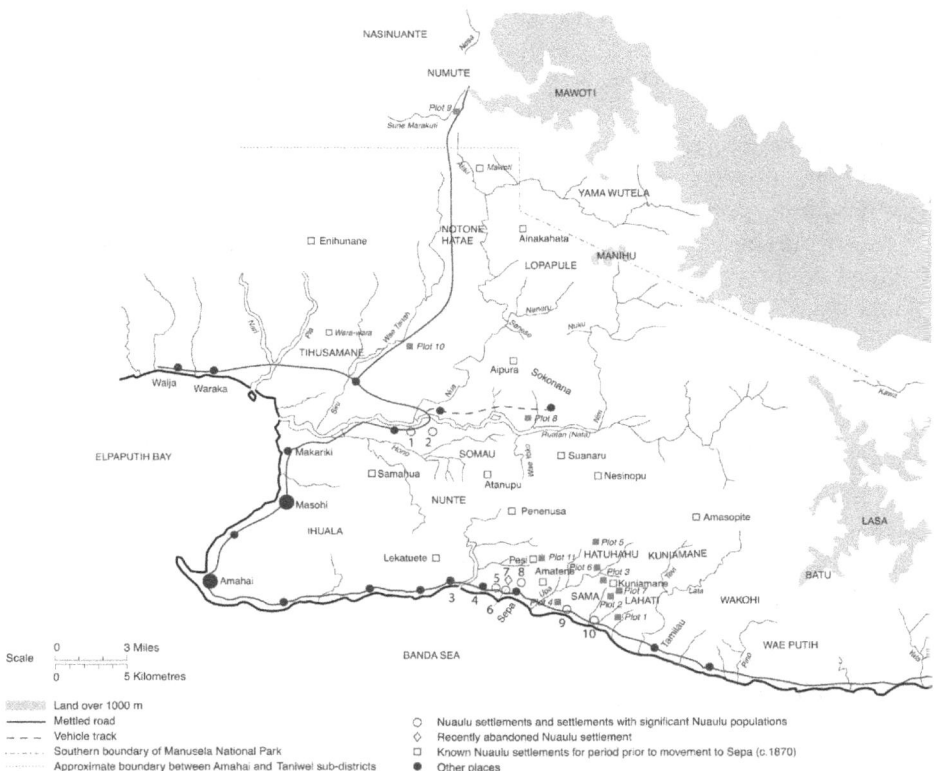

Map 3.1. South Seram, showing former and current Nuaulu settlements and plot locations mentioned in Chapters 6 and 7, as of 1996. Map 6.1 shows area in relation to Seram as a whole. The numbered settlements are as follows (Nuaulu settlements in *italics*): 1, *Simalouw* (Kilo 9); 2, *Tahena Ukuna* (Kilo 12, after 2012 absorbed into *Nuanea*); 3, Hatuheno; 4, Nuelitetu; 5, *Bunara*; 6, *Watane*; 7, *Aihisuru*; 8, *Hahualan*; 9, *Rouhua*; 10, *Moni*. Map created by the author.

way of life down to the present, relying on historic zones of extraction. In the eyes of official agents of the present Indonesian government, other coastal peoples, and in terms of their own self-definition, they have never ceased being uplanders and people of the forests.

During the twentieth century there has been renewed clearance, on Seram as a whole, for clove, nutmeg and other tree crops, such as coconut, cacao and coffee. The 1970s and 1980s saw an expansion of market participation and cash-cropping (of clove, nutmeg and copra in particular), the planting of fast-growing pulp trees, together with accelerated rates of land sale and forest extraction. This has mainly taken place through logging and in-migration, first spontaneous and then official. Forest is being destroyed through unplanned slash and burn cultivation by non-indigenous pioneer settlers, and by the expansion of transmigration settlements into surrounding areas. There is no doubt that rapid forest clearance of this kind is damaging, and that long-standing swiddening practices which modify the forest, increase its genetic diversity and usefulness, and permit extraction on a sustainable basis, are being eroded by technological innovation, population pressure and market forces. Local populations are encouraged by government to deliberately cut mature forest for cash crops, and commercial estate plantations are spreading widely. Logging is a particularly serious threat in the area where the Manusela National Park meets the Samal transmigration zone. Here and elsewhere, so-called 'selective' logging of *Shorea selanica* has led to water shortages, serious gully erosion and soil compaction. It has undermined existing forest ecology, resulting in more open canopy structures, *Macaranga* dominance, a greater proportion of dead wood, and herbaceous and *Imperata* invasions. In terms of fauna, there has been an obvious reduction in game animals. These effects have been systematically inventoried in the Wahai area by Ian Darwin Edwards (1993: 9, 11), but it is instructive to compare his description with that provided in the Nuaulu text discussed later, and which is appended to this chapter. However, it has been transmigration and its various knock-on effects that – more than anything else – have been responsible for forest transformation.

Nuaulu Responses to Intrusion since 1970

The phasing and character of indigenous responses to the kinds of change I have highlighted have depended very much on local perceptions of government policy and on the ways in which law and policy are interpreted by officials and translated into action. It is now widely acknowledged, for example, that the Basic Agrarian Law of 1960 and the Basic Forestry Law of 1967 are fundamentally contradictory and overlapping, and are viewed differently by different government departments and in different situations. Sometimes they are used to defend the rights of indigenous peoples, but more often they override '*adat*', legitimating the confiscation of land, and criminalising those local inhabitants who insist on asserting long-established rights of use (Colchester 1993: 75; Hurst 1990; MacAndrews 1986; Moniaga 1991; SKEPHI 1992; SKEPHI and Kiddell-Monroe 1993; Zerner 1990). Where there are doubts, national interest is invariably placed above local interests (Hardjono 1991: 9). Up until recently, Nuaulu have been beneficiaries of an, on the whole, advantageous interpretation of the law (Ellen 1993a), though as I go on to explain, this may now be changing.

During the period covered by my own fieldwork, the Nuaulu population has continued to grow dramatically: from 496 in 1971 to an estimated 1,256 in 1990. This has led to greater pressure on existing land, intensified by competition along the south Seram littoral with people from traditional non-Nuaulu villages, and due to unplanned immigration, mainly of Butonese. Growth along the south coast has been facilitated by the extension of a metalled road during the early 1980s. At about the same time, the government began to establish transmigration settlements along the Ruatan valley (Map 3.1).

The overtures by provincial government authorities to the Nuaulu with respect to these developments were, at least initially, benign and paternalistic. In part they have been guided by the special administrative status of the Nuaulu as *'masyarakat terasing'* (an Indonesian term for 'marginalised communities' now generally regarded as pejorative: Koentjaraningrat 1993: 9–16; Persoon 1994: 65–67). Thus, local government officers (*'camat'*, *'bupati'*) have recognised uncut forest in the vicinity of transmigration settlements as 'belonging' to the Nuaulu, following the widely held view of many non-Nuaulu inhabitants of south Seram. They then encouraged them to move into one of the new transmigration zone settlements along the Ruatan river, at Simalouw (Map 3.1), an area which abutted sago swamps long claimed and utilised by Nuaulu. Although by 1990 only the villages of Watane and Aihisuru had moved permanently from their earlier locations on the south coast (about a quarter to a third of all Nuaulu households), many Nuaulu established temporary dwellings, used the improved transport facilities to reach ancestral sago areas, and began to cut land for cash crop plantations. Moreover, two clans (Matoke-hanaie and Sounaue-ainakahata) moved even further inland, out of the original transmigration zone altogether to a place called Tahena Ukuna. Many Nuaulu saw these shifts as a return to traditional land, and for outsiders it confirmed Nuaulu status as upland forest peoples rather than lowland and coastal. Although Nuaulu had been located around the Muslim coastal domain of Sepa for the best part of one hundred years, and subject to the tutelage of its raja, their self-image and the image of them held by non-Nuaulu had never been otherwise. Moreover, implicit government recognition of Nuaulu preferential rights to over one-and-a-half thousand square kilometres enabled them to sell land in the Ruatan area to other incomers. This unusually positive approach was reflected in a successfully defended land claim in the courts at Masohi, the capital of Kabupaten Maluku Tengah.

The practical consequences of all this were alleviation of the growing pressure on Nuaulu land generally, and an opportunity to sell land along the more crowded south coast, most of which was sold to the inhabitants of Sepa itself and to incoming Butonese. This latter land, mainly old garden land and secondary forest, was a mixture of land gifted by the raja of Sepa since the late nineteenth century, and land further inland which had always been regarded as Nuaulu. As I have argued elsewhere (Ellen 1993a), altogether, this created a rarely reported situation whereby an indigenous forest people appeared to be endorsing further forest destruction (both in the interior and along the south coast) by themselves and by others, for short-term gain.

Nuaulu cash incomes certainly increased through sale of land and trade with immigrants. Moreover, the practices that accompanied this were not dramatically contrary to any locally asserted principles of indigenous ecological wisdom. However, there has recently been increased conflict with other autochthonous villages over rights to land, disenchantment with the effects of logging, and, since 1990, serious conflict with settlers resulting in convictions for the murders of two Saparuan migrants being brought against three residents of Rouhua. This incident was widely reported in the local press, who made much of the manner of death (decapitation), and of removal of the heads back to the village and their burial near a *'rumah adat' (custom house)*. The episode has understandably been viewed by some government officials and other observers as a reversion to head hunting, or confirmation that it had never ceased, though the protagonists themselves strenuously deny such interpretations. Whatever the case, this narrative amply highlights the fundamental ambiguity in the concept 'masyarakat terasing', seemingly indicating both the vulnerability of a people so labelled, their need of special protection and advancement by the state, as well as their primitive threatening character, which the state must subject and change. Either way, Nuaulu are frequently viewed as prime candidates for *'pembangunan'* (development) in its moral and ideological sense (Grzimek 1991: 263–83). Moreover, recent events reinforce a particularly pejorative local Ambonese stereotype of interior peoples as *'Alifuru' (savages)*, and have made it easier for the government to explicitly expropriate territory when the occasion arises.

How the Nuaulu Have Changed Their Environment

Conventional Western conceptions of nature are usually of some unaltered other, of wilderness; and conventional views of traditional peoples living on forest margins or biotopes, of tribes benignly extracting from an essentially pristine ecosystem. Such a view is, of course, now wholly unacceptable and there is mounting evidence of the ways in which humans dependent on forest actively change it. Much tropical lowland rainforest – in Indonesia as elsewhere – is the product of many generations of selective human interaction and modification (deliberate and inadvertent), optimising its usefulness and enhancing biodiversity. The outcome is a co-evolutionary process to which human populations are crucial. Indeed, particular patterns of forest extraction and modification are often seen as integral to its sustainable future. For some authorities, the evidence for intentional rather than serendipitous human influence is so compelling as to invite the description of 'managed' forest (Clay 1988; Schmink, Redford and Padoch 1992: 7–8).

The empirical work supporting these claims comes mainly from the Amazon (e.g. Balée 1992, 1994; Posey 1988; Prance et al. 1987), but there is emerging evidence that it also applies to large parts of Malaysia and the Western Indonesian archipelago (Aumeeruddy and Bakels 1994; Dove 1983; Maloney 1993; Peluso and Padoch 1996; Rambo 1979). My own work, supported by recent botanical research, suggests that it is no less true for the forests of Seram, which have long been a focus of subsistence extraction, and where human agency has had decisive consequences for ecology. This has been largely through the long-term impact of small-scale forest-fallow swiddening and the extraction of palm sago over many hundreds of years (Ellen 1988a), but also through the introduction and hunting of deer, selective logging and collection for exchange in more recent centuries (Ellen 1985: 563). Since sago is a frequent reason for venturing into forest beyond the limits of the most distant gardens, and since it illustrates so well the kind of co-evolutionary relationship I have just been discussing, it is helpful to say a bit more about it here.

Sago (*Metroxylon sagu*) is currently extracted by Nuaulu both from extensive swamp forest reserves along major rivers and from planted groves much nearer to settlements. Certain swamp forest zones, such as at Somau, appear to have been continuously important for several hundred years, though smaller patches in the vicinity of the south coast villages may be the artefacts of more recent settlement histories. Smaller inland sago groves have been abandoned since coming to the coast, or are extracted from only occasionally.

Nuaulu manipulate vegetative reproduction of sago by replanting and protecting suckers from recently cut palms, selecting suckers from some palms rather than others, and transferring root stocks to village groves. The result is an interchange of genetic material between cultivated and 'non-cultivated' areas, even though there is no particular evidence of domestication through selective planting of seeds. Although most reproduction of sago palms in the lowland riverine forest areas of Seram occurs quite independently of human interference, in certain areas human involvement is highly significant, and the contemporary phenotypes of Southeast Asian sago palms are best seen as the outcome of a long-term process of human–plant interaction. Indeed, the historic spread of *Metroxylon* from its assumed centres of dispersal in New Guinea or Maluku suggests very strongly anthropogenic factors. Ecologically, the heavy reliance placed by Nuaulu and other indigenous peoples of Seram on sago has, over some hundreds of years, reduced the necessity to cut forest for swiddens. This has an important bearing on Nuaulu changing conceptions of their environment, as we shall see.

The distribution of many other useful trees throughout the lowland forests of Seram reflects patterns of human modification, and serves as a convenient botanical indicator of settlement histories. Many are certain or probable domesticates and semi-domesticates. One of the most culturally salient of these is the *'kenari' (Canarium)*. This is found so widely in lowland areas, and in particular configurations, that its distribution must almost certainly be explained as a consequence of human interference, both motivated and inadvertent (Ian Edwards, personal communication). 'Kenari' provides nuts rich in protein and essential oils, which are an important ingredient in local diet, but which for the Nuaulu also have a salient symbolic role, the precise character of which I shall return to later.[3]

Nuaulu practices of swidden cultivation and movement have, over several centuries, altered the character of forest vegetation in measurable ways: increasing the proportion of useful species, increasing the numbers of stands of particular useful species, decreasing the proportion of easily extracted timber trees against those which are resistant to extraction, creating patches of culturally productive forest in more accessible areas, and creating dense groves of fruit trees in old village sites. Many of the trees nowadays found in areas otherwise not obviously modified by humans represent species introduced historically, and even prehistorically, for their useful timber, fruits and other properties (Ellen 1985). Indeed, approximately 78 per cent of the 319 or more forest trees identified by the Nuaulu have particular human uses that make them potentially subject to manipulation through forms of protection and selective extraction. No wonder, then, that the distinctions between mature forest, different kinds and degrees of secondary regrowth and grove land are often difficult to establish. Although the contribution of non-agricultural activities, narrowly defined, to overall Nuaulu energy expenditure and production is not to be under-estimated, and by comparison with other Indonesian swiddening peoples is rather high, my earlier contrast (Ellen 1975) between 'domesticated' and 'non-domesticated' resources was, in retrospect, drawn too starkly.

Renegotiating Nature

My main argument in this chapter is that as different material and social changes have occurred – changes that have accelerated since the 1980s – so Nuaulu have renegotiated their relationship with the forest, and with 'nature' more generally. How people conceptualise nature depends on how they use it, how they transform it, and how, in so doing, they invest knowledge in different parts of it. I have argued in another paper (Ellen 1996d) that concepts of nature have underlying pan-human cognitive roots, all people appearing to derive them from imperatives to identify 'things' in their field of perception, situate these in terms of a calculus of self and other, and identify in discrete bits and aggregations essential inner properties. However, identifying these commonalities is not to deny that such concepts are everywhere ambiguous, intrinsically moral in character and a *condition* of knowledge (Strathern 1992a: 194). Nature is not a *basic* category in the sense specified by Pascal Boyer (1993), and means different – often contradictory – things in different contexts. It is constantly being reworked as people respond to new social and environmental situations (Croll and Parkin 1992: 16), and provides in the guise of something all-encompassing what I have elsewhere (Ellen 1986c: 24) called a 'theory of selective representations'. Ambiguity itself, as Bloch (1974) has pointed out, can be socially useful. In the Nuaulu case there is an evident underlying tension between an oppositional calculus of forest and 'village' or 'house', and a non-oppositional calculus that draws much more on the lived experience of particular strategies of subsistence that unite what we loosely call nature and culture. Such an ambivalent conception of nature is wholly consistent with the difficulties faced in classifying the Nuaulu mode of subsistence according to conventional anthropological criteria (Ellen 1988a).

Before examining how these different concepts and their relative balance might be the outcome of a particular sequence of past events, and before highlighting contemporary patterns of change, it is necessary to sketch out in general terms the substance of the two apparently competing models or orientations. I do so on the basis of ethnographic data acquired by me at various times between 1970 and 1990. Since it is so obviously central, I start with the Nuaulu category of forest.

The Nuaulu use the term *wesie* to refer to forest of most kinds, but the term belies a complex categorical construction. Nuaulu relate to different parts of the forest – indeed to different species – in different ways. This mode of interaction is inimical to a concept of forest as some kind of void or homogeneous entity, and certain parts require different responses and evince different conceptualisations. Some bits of forest are protected, others destroyed without thought. Forest is never experienced as homogeneous, but is much more of a combination (rather than a *mixture*) of different biotopes and patches. As such it well reflects the complex historical ecology that I referred to at the beginning of this chapter. With its emphasis on human acculturation, it fits comfortably into a non-oppositional model of the kind we more usually associate with hunting and gathering peoples (Ingold 1996).

On the other hand, the generic term *wesie* exists, and is linked into general symbolic schemes such that it stands for some kind of conceptual exterior, a natural other. In some significant respects it is rather like the received twentieth-century English *concept* of nature. Although subject to degrees of effective control through practical and supernatural mastery, *wesie* is associated with essential qualities of danger and otherness, and opposed to an unmarked category of 'culture', most palpably evident in – but certainly not restricted to – the category *numa*, 'house' (alternatively *niane*, 'village'). As such it is intricately linked with gender imagery (cf. Valeri 1990). This forest : house : : nature : culture : : female : male logic is evident in a whole raft of rituals, and in the symbolic organisation of space. In some ways it is not what we might expect given Nuaulu lived subsistence, with its heavy reliance on extracting forest resources, where gardening is traditionally rudimentary, swiddening practised on a forest-fallow basis, where regenerated growth supplies many 'forest' resources over the longer term, and where consequently there is a definite blurring of anthropogenic and other forest.

The two somewhat contradictory models we find with respect to forest are repeated at the level of interactions with specific parts of nature. Thus, Nuaulu are (and have been continuously so for many centuries) primarily vegetative rather than seed propagators, and most of their starchy garden crops are roots and tubers (taro, cassava, yam, *Xanthosoma*). Such agricultural regimes are widely associated in the ethnographic literature with notions of continuity between nature and culture, in contrast to seed propagators who tend to emphasise a sudden transition between nature and culture (Coursey 1978; Haudricourt 1962, 1964). In particular, Nuaulu place great practical and symbolic emphasis on sago palm starch extraction, and as we have seen, this species is ambiguously wild and domesticated. Such a view is reinforced by the highly reliable character of palm starch as a staple, with a stable output subject to little fluctuation, lack of economically significant pests (Flach 1976) and considerable potential as a food reserve. In these ways, not only does sago contrast with grain domesticates, but it is superior to tubers such as yams and taro, and is, therefore, an even better symbol of the continuity between nature and culture.

Given that many forest trees show evidence of human manipulation, occur simultaneously in cultivated and uncultivated areas, and provide long-term supplies of particular resources without continuous human attention and susceptibility to hazard, they too reinforce the applicability of the non-oppositional model. However, 'trees' are only homogeneous as a category if we ruthlessly simplify it to some common cognitive morphotype (woody, foliaceous, rigid). Different modes of extraction, *use* and characteristics involve different relationships with people, different social profiles and potential symbolic values. This often leads to classificatory patterns which appear to cut across conventional logics, and which are almost provocatively ambiguous. I have already indicated that two extremely important sources of food – the sago palm and the 'kenari' tree – are ambiguous in terms of the forest : village (house) logic, and in terms of the unlabelled 'nature/wild' and 'culture/tame' categories of which forest and house are, respectively, the most dominant expression. Both species show evidence of protodomestication, insipient cultivation, and their distribution is heavily affected by human *use*, despite the fact that they are for the most part culturally 'of the forest' and reproduce without much human interference. The problem is accentuated by the symbolic complementarity of the two: sago is the everyday starch staple and the product of – almost always – male labour, while 'kenari' is collected for special festive occasions, when it is combined with sago by females to make *maea* (Ellen and Goward 1984: 32). Thus, in certain contexts sago and 'kenari' are linked together in opposition to products of the garden; in others they are contrasted in terms of an implicit gender distinction. Similarly, in the sphere of interaction with forest animals, I have been able to demonstrate how a single ritual associated with killing *(asunaete)* can simultaneously reflect a perspective which stresses the unity of all living things, and one which stresses human opposition through killing [see Chapter 9 here; also Ellen 1996d: 116–18; cf. Karim 1981: 188]. Nature, I repeat, is not a basic category in the sense that it has a rooted perceptual salience, but though it may be symbolically deployed in radically different ways, it is still able to convey notions of logical primacy.

In developing a model which will help us understand how social and ecological changes have influenced Nuaulu conceptions and representations of forest and nature, we also need to recognise that in almost every instance this will have been motivated by an alteration in the character and intensity of relationships with non-Nuaulu, and how the Nuaulu deal with this socially. As I have indicated, ecological change has almost always been a consequence of exogenous factors: whether this involves the introduction of new species, outside appropriation of endemic resources or clearance of forest for extraction, or agriculture. But whenever there is an environmental interface of this kind, there is also a cultural and social one. Transfer of new cultigens is not just about the movement of genetic material, but of cultural knowledge as well, knowledge which always carries a social burden. Contact with outsiders, in particular, seldom involves actors operating on equal terms, and the relationship is always mediated by considerations of power and control. For their part, the Nuaulu repeatedly represent changes of all kinds in terms of the interplay of principles of opposition and continuity, complementarity and hierarchy,[4] symbolic schemes as opposed to practical experiences, outside influence versus persisting tradition. To show how this might work, we can, I think, provisionally identify four historical periods which are likely to have been associated with somewhat different conceptualisations of the natural world: pre-European contact; the VOC and early colonial period until about 1880; 1880 to 1980; and 1980 to the present.

From what we can reconstruct of pre-European Nuaulu social organisation, clans appear to have occupied separate dispersed settlements and had considerable autonomy, entering into loose alliances only for the purpose of intermittent political negotiation and to manage hostilities with outsiders. Thus, that subsistence placed less stress on gardening than became the case later on was wholly in keeping with what we know of political arrangements. We might, therefore, expect here a concept of nature which focuses much more on the symbolic logic of vegetative propagation and the systematic harvesting of forest trees, and which involves a less oppositional conception of *wesie*. Moving around in the forest is not conducive, after all, to developing an enduring opposition with it. Historically, we know gardening on Seram to be very underdeveloped, and even at the present time gardens are relatively unimportant in many areas, while in describing Nuaulu subsistence the distinction between 'gathering' and 'cultivation' is very fuzzy (Ellen 1988a: 117, 119, 123, 126–27). There is no new evidence, as yet, ethnobotanical or archaeological (Stark and Latinis 1992), to suggest that horticulture amongst the native peoples of Seram was once more important than it is now (c.f. Balée 1992), except the general ethnological observation that pioneer migrant Austronesian speakers, their linguistic if not directly genetic precursors, depended on domesticates, including – in all probability – seed cultigens (Blust 1976; Bellwood 1978: 141).

The new embeddedness in the world system which developed from the sixteenth century onwards opened up new pan-Pacific links, cut out intermediary connections, and intensified exchange with Oriental, Asiatic and European centres. It also had immediate economic consequences in terms of spice production, and longer-term implications for subsistence ecology. With the introduction of maize, cassava, *Xanthosoma* and sweet potato, reliable garden yields increased, making these cultigens competitive with sago in their reliability and superior in the effort required to harvest them. This appears to have led to a greater dependence on gardens (Ellen 1988a: 123). Almost all the new garden crops were vegetatively propagated roots or tubers, therefore sustaining a pre-existing conceptualisation of reproductive process and its metaphoric transformations; but they were also the harbingers of a longer-term process of decentring sago from people's conceptions of nature. Although sago is still culturally salient for the Nuaulu, amongst many present-day peoples of the central Moluccas sago (an indigenous crop) is nutritionally crucial but widely seen as inferior to (imported) rice. The same crops, because they decreased dependency on sago and other forest resources, encouraged greater emphasis on the symbolic opposition between gardens and forest. Increasing attention to cash-cropping, which both required high yield cultigens to offset the reduction of time and land available for subsistence extraction, and which provided opportunities to purchase – for example – rice, further accentuated this division.

The next major change came when the peripheral areas of Seram were formally drawn into the administrative system of the Dutch East Indies in the 1880s. From this time onwards, environmental and social distinctions that had hitherto been implicit became underscored by administrative fiat. We have seen that from at least the late seventeenth century, the Nuaulu have had a distinct political identity in the eyes of outsiders. They had identifiable leaders, and were drawn into various alliances, always including Sepa. Indeed, this long history of interaction has made Nuaulu ultra-sensitive to questions of identity vis-à-vis other cultural groups, even though that identity has not always been reflected in any degree of permanent political centralisation. Formal incorporation into the Dutch administrative system, however, required that this identity and arrangement of traditional alliances of mutual advantage be regularised (Ellen 1988c: 118–19), both for administrative convenience and to provide the Nuaulu themselves with an effective channel of political communication. It is not therefore surprising that, at the time when the Nuaulu clans were relocating around Sepa, when Sepa was – in Dutch eyes – becoming administratively responsible for Nuaulu '*rust, orde en belasting*' *(peace, order and taxes)*, there emerges a line of Nuaulu *rajas*. This, in turn, changes the terms of the oppositional relationship between Nuaulu and Sepa into a more hierarchical one. Clans begin to lose some of their autonomy, even though the line of rajas effectively terminated after only a few generations. And ever since, the question of a Nuaulu raja and his possible reinstatement has been an issue that has periodically become the subject of heated debate, most recently at the time of the establishment of the Nuaulu presence at Simalouw. The same necessity for formal mechanisms to communicate with the holders of administrative power in Sepa, Amahai, Masohi, Amboina or Jakarta is reflected in Nuaulu involvement in rituals of the Indonesian state (Ellen 1988c).

Nuaulu movement to the coast meant a shift from a pattern of dispersed clan-hamlets and swiddens to concentrated multi-clan villages with large connected areas of garden land. This, in turn, led to a reconceptualisation of the forest : village (house) boundary, contrasting owned land (*wasi*) with unowned forest (*wesie*), and gardens (*nisi*) with uncleared forest (*wesie*); the first distinction juridical, the second technical. The changes in Nuaulu social relations of land use which accompanied this (Ellen 1977b, 1993a) – land sale, cash-cropping, individualisation, permanent occupancy – emphasised still further a view of the natural world in which dualistic and contrastive properties predominated, even though sago continued to dominate their lives as their most important source of carbohydrate and as a cultural symbol.

So, it is at least plausible that the apparent contradiction between oppositional and non-oppositional models, the one more concordant with external relations of exchange, the other with internal subsistence experience, is a dialectical function of a particular transitional history. It might also be connected with the historic emphasis on exchange of valuables for forest products (see above, and Ellen 1988a), and the influence and internalisation of Austronesian symbolic schemes otherwise more amenable to seed cultivation. Whatever the case, the balance is tipping in favour of an emergent, more oppositional, reified concept of 'forest/nature'. Amongst the coastal peoples of Seram (such as the inhabitants of Sepa), the enduring perception of the Nuaulu has been as a forest people – the opposite of themselves. Forest is a much stronger exteriority for coastal Muslims than it has traditionally been for animist Nuaulu, but it is towards this view that the Nuaulu are now progressing. Similarly, the Dutch colonial government, and thereafter the Indonesian government, created forest as a strong official category, establishing bureaucracies to manage it, a component in a wider state administrative division of labour that encouraged implicit linkages between the geographical designation of forest and the social category '*masyarakat terasing*'.

Moreover, as forest has been reduced in extent, so its representation as some kind of ether in which humans are suspended has been transformed into a much more restricted environmental category, as just one ever-diminishing part of a wider non-afforested dwelling space. Not only does the small size of Moluccan islands make the forest more vulnerable physically, but also, as forest disappears, so it is reconceived as a fundamentally limited, rather than limitless, good. Thus, both material experience of environmental change and the necessity to participate in a state level of discourse are reifying Nuaulu concepts of forest, just as environmental degradation and the ecological movement have done in the West. In order to protect their own lives, Nuaulu find themselves adopting the discourse of officialdom and national politics, responding to agendas dictated by the state. From a history of commitment to environmental change, they have now adopted a rhetoric that we would recognise as broadly 'environmentalist'.

New Rhetorics and Rapid Social Change

What I have in mind by this new Nuaulu conception of nature and its relation to a more reflexive, globally situated understanding of their own identity is well exemplified by two empirical cases: the first is a video recording (cassette 90-2, 8-3-90) which I was asked to make by the people of Rouhua in 1990 and which was prompted by Nuaulu concerns of state non-recognition of their religion; the second is a text recorded and transcribed in 1994 by Rosemary Bolton addressed as a personal appeal to me.

The first – the video recording – consists of three parts, all of which refer to performances that occurred on 8 March 1990. The first is a formal address given by Komisi Soumori (the 'kepala kampung' and most senior secular clan head). It is an impassioned assertion of the legitimacy of Nuaulu core beliefs, showing how many Nuaulu believe their cultural identity to be, quite literally, 'rooted' in land, forest and sago. The spoken words and the visual imagery used (and this would be well understood by the local Nuaulu witnessing the event) evoke – though not explicitly – widely shared mythologies of origin. All this is unashamedly broadcast to an outside, unseen audience. What is significant about the event is in part its presentation: it is given in Nuaulu, because to speak of such things – the domain of the ancestors – in any other language is to deny Nuauluness, but also because Komisi is *most* comfortable in Nuaulu. But the oratorical style and the physical props – for example the rostrum – indicate the acceptance that discourse should assume formats appropriate to engagement with the state (Figure 3.1), and a notion that it is possible to communicate with an unseen audience, not indirectly through a human mediator, but directly employing an electronic medium to which they have only recently had access. The second part is a short dramatic performance by adolescents about discrimination against Nuaulu customs and religion at school and in the labour market. This is conducted entirely in terms of the kind of performance rhetoric which is, again, associated with government institutions, and which is, appropriately, spoken in Indonesian – the language of the state. Paradoxically, such conventions (and the education through which they are acquired) inevitably result in the further attrition of Nuaulu distinctiveness as perceived by non-Nuaulu, and perhaps the eventual disappearance of certain cultural markers that were once salient. This is, of course, not to rule out the likelihood that Nuaulu 'cultural identity' is anyway in transformation, subject to continual renegotiation, and might emerge as strong as ever, but in a slightly different guise. The third part of the video recording is a speech by the *'kepala pemuda', the spokesperson for the youth of the village*, Sonohue Soumori, again in Indonesian, which pulls the various themes together. Such reflections can also be cast in a more traditional idiom, such as the **kepata arariranae** (a ritual verse form associated with male–female tug-of-war) and the **kapata Sepa** (a ritual verse form associated with workplace routines and domestic relaxation), though on this occasion they were not.

The transcribed text, the English language version of which is provided here as an appendix, is a rather different kind of document. It was dictated by a long-standing acquaintance to Rosemary Bolton, and is separated in time from the 1990 performance by the harrowing events of 1993 in the Ruatan transmigration area, to which I have already referred. These events are structurally significant in Nuaulu representations of themselves because an attempt to defend legitimate interests resulted in defeat. The rugged independence and assertiveness so typical of the 1970s and 1980s, and so well exemplified in the 1990 videotaped events, has – it would seem – been replaced by a new quiescence and passivity: 'we are quiet and obeying them' (section 5). From a position in which Nuaulu saw themselves negotiating *with* the Indonesian state, they are now simply citizens *of* that same state. There is an acceptance that events are no longer under their own control, that they can no longer take them or leave them. As it happens, Nuaulu have a history of accommodating certain kinds of pragmatic change. This may explain their cultural survival, when most other groups of tribal animists on Seram have all but disappeared. But Nuaulu now claim not to want anything to do with the outside agents of change: government or logging companies. There is a realisation that the government does not keep its promises (section 7).

We can also see from this text how it is that the rapidity of environmental change has forced the Nuaulu to redefine their relationship with the natural world, to see connections between microclimatic change, deforestation and erosion, and game depletion; between land clearance, river

Political Contingency, Historical Ecology and the Renegotiation of Nature | 69

Figure 3.1. Three frames from a videotape recorded on 8 March 1990 and discussed in this chapter. Komisi Soumori (*ia onate* Soumori and 'kepala kampung') addresses the world. His props include a young clove seedling and sago palm. Note the makeshift rostrum behind which he stands. Screenshots by the author.

flow, impacting caused by logging vehicles, and fish depletion. We can see in it how Nuaulu now identify their forest as a whole as a commodity, something that has exchange value, when previously it was inalienable. We find an equation between big trees and profit (sections 5 and 6), and governmental prohibition on sale. To begin with, Nuaulu accepted the advantages brought by the lumber companies: vehicles used the tracks and kept them clear, the tracks and trucks facilitated hunting (sections 1 and 2). We also find recognition that replacement of large trees is on a time scale that is beyond the use of Nuaulu, that sustainable use has been superseded by something which Nuaulu would never seek to sustain (section 6), that old secondary forest, based on the cutting of patches and individual trees (Ellen 1985), has been replaced by wholesale clearance, which results in quite different patterns of regeneration, including more noxious vegetation (e.g. thorns). And the blame for these changes is placed quite squarely at the feet of logging companies and the state.

So, recent Nuaulu reworking of their conceptions and responses to those things which we designate as 'nature' show that the patronage of various government departments, levels of organisation, and types of parastatal agency, as well as official categories, are no less central to an understanding of what is going on at the forest frontier than they are for lowland agrarian processes (cf. Hart 1989: 31). 'Bringing the state into the analysis ... entails understanding how power struggles at different levels of society are connected with one another and related to access to and control over resources' (Hart 1989: 48). As the forest frontier reproduces the inequalities of the wider state and its economically dominant groups, and as short-term production for use arises and is sustained by production for exchange (Gudeman 1988: 216), as Nuaulu move from being semi-independent 'tribesmen', relying on sago and non-domesticated forest resources, to being dependent peasant farmers, increasingly reliant on introduced cultigens and cash crops, so their conceptions of nature reflect this. There is, in an important sense, an ecological, economic and conceptual continuity between forest modification and farming, and redefining forest extraction as a kind of farming may help us appreciate its similarities with the agrarian process.

In the Nuaulu case, intensification of subsistence agriculture, cash-cropping, forest extraction, commercial logging and transmigration combine to threaten an existing relationship with the forest. But Nuaulu attitudes have always been tactical, depending on their perceived material interests, and it is therefore not surprising that their conceptualisations of nature should mirror this. Their initial response to forest destruction and consequent land settlement reflected perceived advantages in terms of a traditional model of forest interaction, based on *implicit* notions of sustainability of reproductive cycles of tree growth and animal populations. When this logic failed, complacency was replaced by uncertainty and bewilderment, eventually translating into hostility and decisive actions to defend their subsistence interests. Punitive actions taken by the state in response to this have engendered further uncertainty and bewilderment.

Conclusion

What I have tried to demonstrate in this chapter is that there is a connection between shifting Nuaulu constructions and representations of nature (particularly of environmental change), their social identity and the way they interact with the outside world.

There is nothing intrinsically problematic about environmental change for the Nuaulu. As we have seen, their cultural history is full of it. There is no overarching 'ecocosmology' or 'cosmovision' that rules it to be culturally illegitimate. Indeed, during the early phase of transmigration and logging in the 1980s it was regarded wholly positively. What we need to recognise, however, is that there are different kinds of environmental change. The crucial distinctions here are between change that you can control, and change that is outside your control (and more specifically, is controlled by outsiders); and between change which is readily recognised as bearing unacceptable detrimental risks and that which is not so recognised. In terms of both distinctions it is the *scale* of change that provokes direct or delayed political responses and conceptual rejigging. The older, local, embedded forms of knowledge that underpin Nuaulu subsistence strategies are qualitatively different from knowledge of higher-order processes, 'environmental consciousness' in the abstract, which only comes with a widening of political and ecological horizons to a national and global level. In some ways this process is similar to how articulate Nuaulu have come to reconceptualise their ritual practice as '*agama*' (religion), and their distinct way of life as '*kebudayaan* (culture); 'agama', 'kebudayaan', '*lingkungan hidup*' (living space, milieu, environment) are in Indonesian officialese secondary abstractions of a comparable order. Forest, they now understand, is subject to pressures of in-migration, expropriation and economic exploitation in many places other than their own.

This quasi-global[5] consciousness is no better symbolised than by the arrival of electronic means of communication in Nuaulu villages, first radio and then television. Television has not only enabled Nuaulu to keep in touch with the world by watching English league soccer matches and Thomas Cup badminton, but – and this is the reflexive twist – to watch David Attenborough eulogise tropical rainforest in its death throes. Despite a long history of interaction with outsiders of various origins, changing patterns of environmental modification, patterns of subsistence and the conceptual modulation of these things, it is the major changes associated with cultural globalisation that have forced a really radical response from them. It could be said that the aggressive individualism of the 1980s, the selling of land and market engagement represented both the end of an old small-scale conception of nature in which resources and forest are infinite, and the beginning of a new conception of participation in an open global ecology of limited goods. The changes, therefore, are a response to a different problematic, to a different social and political agenda, rather than a rejection of environmental change itself or an a priori endorsement of ecological holism. Nuaulu constructions of environment are changing to accommodate a new *level* of discourse, and it is no coincidence that those who currently complain that their schooled children are unable to obtain appropriate employment in the Indonesian state because they are told that the doctrine of *Pancasila* is an impediment, also – though paradoxically – adopt an environmentalist rhetoric which seeks to keep the state from their land.

Appendix: The Consequences of Deforestation – A Nuaulu Text from Rouhua, Seram 1994

1. About we Nuaulu people. Our own government here in Indonesia allowed large lumber companies to come here looking for timber. Like **onia** [Malay '*kayu meranti*', *Shorea* spp.]. So they levelled the tops of mountains, digging them all up. At the heads of rivers they cut down **punara** [*Octomeles sumatrana*] trees, they cut down **onia** along the edges of rivers, vehicles levelled and filled in the heads of rivers. While they lived here it was still good. We got around well because they were working.
2. Vehicles went up and down the roads so they were clear. Or if we went hunting we rode on their vehicles with them. But when they went home, our roads were covered up, trees started to grow on them and then we couldn't travel about well because when it rained landslides covered the roads. Game animals moved far away as did cuscus. Land slid into the rivers because they cut down the big trees along the edges of the rivers.
3. Therefore we are really suffering because we have to go around the roads. Before they came here we knew when it was rainy season and when it was dry season. But when they levelled our lands and rivers here in our forest it wasn't the same when it rained and when it was

sunny. It was sunny all the time so land slid into all the rivers. Therefore we do not feed good because it is no longer like before.
4. Before, the rivers flowed well and the sun shone well so they looked good to us. But now that the vehicles levelled them so much the fish in the rivers and the game animals in the forest have moved far away. They electrocuted all the fish in the rivers so there are no more fish. So where can we look for our food? Even if we look for our food in rivers that are far away we do not find any fish. We do not find any game animals. The deer have moved far away.
5. Therefore we want to ask for money to cover the price of our forest but the government in Masohi and Amahai forbid us from doing so. So we are quiet and are obeying them. But because of our village and forest we are suffering. We suffer when it is so difficult to go to our forest and look for our food because they levelled all the rivers. They levelled all the mountains. The rivers do not flow well. It is difficult to find game animals. Therefore, we do not feel well about this.
6. They destroyed the lands and rivers. They took away all the big trees. They sold them and made a profit but they did not give any of it to us. Therefore the Nuaulu elders do not want anything to do with them because they did not think of us. We let them take the wood because they said that they would plant new trees to replace those they cut down. But when will those trees grow? They will never grow like the trees before. How will they grow like those big trees? And when will they plant the trees to replace them? It will be a long time before those little trees are big.
7. Therefore the elders do not want anything to do with them because the lumber companies came here making things difficult for us with our forest. Our lands and rivers are no good at all. They have been gone a long time like the Filipinos. When we go to the river Lata Nuaulu or Lata Tamilou we have to cut the thorns that have grown with our machetes until we are almost dead because they block the path. If it rains just a little there are landslides cutting off the path and then we have to go far around them before we can find a straight path. Therefore, we are suffering a lot just because of this.
8. Therefore if there is any help or any word that can be given here in Indonesia that would help the officials here in Indonesia. Help quickly so that they will not agree that all our lands, rivers, and trees be taken. So the heads of rivers would not be levelled so we cannot eat well or find food well.
9. We people find our food in the forest. There are a lot of Nuaulu people who do not fish well so they look for food in the forest. This is just us Nuaulu people. Other people look for food and have a lot of peo-

ple who fish but there are only a few of us who fish. Therefore these people look for food but do not find it. We are all dead from hunger [hyperbole]. Before the lumber companies came we got around well. We found food well because the deer slept nearby, pigs lived nearby, and cassowaries lived nearby. But when they levelled and destroyed these animals' places and caves they ran away. So it is very hard for the Nuaulu people to find food because they chased away all the pigs and deer so that they are now far away.
10. Therefore if Roy (Ellen) can find a little help and wants to talk to the officials here in Indonesia I ask that he help us a little so that they do not come here and work again. We do not want them to because we are already suffering a lot. That is all.

[Text recorded and translated by Rosemary Bolton, 1994.]

Notes

First published 1999, as 'Forest Knowledge, Forest Transformation: Political Contingency, Historical Ecology and the Renegotiation of Nature in Central Seram', in *Transforming the Indonesian Uplands: Marginality, Power and Production*, edited by Tania Li (Amsterdam: Harwood, pp. 131–57). Reproduced courtesy of Harwood and Taylor & Francis.
1. Lowland is used here to refer to a forest type generally dominated by the dipterocarp *Shorea selanica*, in contrast to the montane vegetation of higher altitudes. In fact, the lowland forest of Seram covers, on the whole, hilly country and may extend to an altitude of some 1,000 metres.
2. The original version of this chapter was written as a stand-alone piece, not requiring additional background material, but in the context of the present volume readers may find the ecological and ethnographic data included in Chapters 6 and 7 relevant.
3. Another striking case of human management of forest trees (though not one which I have observed in the Nuaulu area) is reported by Soedjito, Suyanto and Sulaeman (1986) for higher altitude forests in west Seram. Here, seedlings of the resin-producing *Agathis dammara*, important as a source of cash, are systematically planted to replace older, less productive trees.
4. Nuaulu symbolically represent their relations with outsiders, dialectically, in two ways: in terms of relations of complementarity, and in terms of hierarchy. The first is exemplified in the relationship between most local clans, in '*pela*' partnerships (that is between individuals linked through historical blood siblinghoods between villages) and through common membership of the '*patalima*' grouping (Valeri 1989). The second is reflected in their relations with Sepa and the Indonesian state. Here they manage to assert, simultaneously, a mythic superiority (usually expressed in the conventional older-younger sibling metaphor) and a pragmatic political submissiveness. The articulation

Political Contingency, Historical Ecology and the Renegotiation of Nature | 75

of the two principles, however, is on their terms. They insist that they are prepared to accept the benefits of a good raja, but equally prepared to withdraw into their own autonomy when it suits them.

5. I use the term 'quasi-global' to avoid any accusation that Nuaulu consciously conceive of themselves as global actors and consumers in the sense that has entered the consciousness of many in the West. It would be more accurate to say that they have become increasingly conscious of the degree of connectedness between their lives and those in remote places with whom they share common experiences (such as televised football matches) and material products (such as cassette players).

CHAPTER 4

Indigenous Environmental Knowledge and Its Transformations

With Holly Harris

Introduction

This chapter does not seek to demonstrate the superiority, or even the complementarity, of local knowledge compared with dominant global scientific knowledge in particular instances. Neither does it attempt to provide further empirical documentation of indigenous knowledge for its own sake, or of its applications in development and scientific contexts. Neither does it seek to enter into any polemical discourse suggesting the converse. It is assumed that most readers will already be persuaded that indigenous environmental knowledge (hereafter IK)[1] can hardly be ignored in development contexts and that it is an essential ingredient in any pragmatic development strategy, especially those which claim to achieve a degree of sustainability, as well as having applications in industry and commerce. And yet, equally, we suspect, most of us will also accept that the claims made for the environmental wisdom of native peoples have sometimes been misjudged and naive, replacing denial with effusive blanket endorsement and presenting an 'ecological Eden' to counter some European or other exemplary 'world we have lost' [Chapter 1 in this volume].

Here our aim is different: to examine dispassionately yet critically the status of, and claims made for, IK in the rhetoric and practice of different academic disciplines, at different times and in different political situations, ranging through environmental movements, states, NGOs and local indigenist activism. We are particularly concerned to focus on the *transfer* of ideas between these groups and contexts. In short, we take it for granted that IK is useful in particular contexts, but seek to go beyond such demonstrations and statements of the obvious to ask what role it plays in green arguments and scientific and political discourse more generally. Our intention is to focus on several issues and themes: (1) the extent to which IK is still a significant category within Western patterns of production and consumption and the extent to which the development of professional science and technology have undermined or obscured it; (2) the relationship between the great indigenous traditions (such as Ayurvedic medicine) and the local myriad little folk traditions; (3) the way IK is constantly changing, being produced as well as reproduced, discovered as well as lost; (4) the often contradictory and changing scientific and moral attitudes towards IK which are linked to a history in which Western science has by turns absorbed local knowledge (both non-Western and folk European) into its own and rejected it as inferior, only to rediscover its practical benefits; and (5) competing definitions and conceptions of IK in the context of contemporary theory and practice in development and conservation. In this last respect, we place particular emphasis on how IK has been recorded and represented. We take the view that the distinction indigenous : non-indigenous has many highly specific regional and historical connotations which are not always appropriate to other ethnographic contexts. This makes comparative generalisations difficult. Some, indeed, argue that the term 'indigenous' forces us into an oppositional logic of 'us and them', while others assert that the category of IK is wholly compromised by the hegemonic opposition of the privileged *us* to the subordinated *them* and is therefore morally objectionable as well as being practically useless. We try to explain how it has become possible to articulate these positions, given the way in which IK studies have developed, without necessarily agreeing with the more extreme formulations.

Indigenousness as Applied to Knowledge: A Provisional Model

What is meant by 'indigenous knowledge' is by no means clear, and part of the purpose of this chapter is to draw attention to the variety of terminologies, definitions and cognate concepts through their geographical, local-global and various historic and disciplinary refractions. The words we use are not insignificant, since whether we speak of 'indigenous knowledge' (IK), 'indigenous technical knowledge' (ITK), 'ethnoecology', 'local knowledge', 'folk knowledge', 'traditional knowledge', 'traditional environmental (or ecological) knowledge' (TEK), 'people's science' or 'rural people's knowledge' says something about the direction from which we approach the subject and the assumptions we make about it.[2] However, these terms are often used interchangeably, and there is arguably enough overlap between their meanings to recognise the existence of a shared intersubjective understanding, some 'epistemic community' which permits a sufficient degree of common-sense engagement to allow that they refer to the same focal semantic space. However, if we are to move beyond the level of describing particular empirical bodies of such knowledge and their applications, we cannot proceed far without a more rigorous attempt to deconstruct the subject.

Part of the problem is what we mean by 'indigenous'. Those to whom we attribute indigenous knowledge must be indigenous people, and yet the terminological difficulties we confront in saying as much uncover a veritable semantic, legal, political and cultural minefield. For Posey (1996: 7), indigenous people are 'Indigenous and local communities embodying traditional lifestyles', a formulation which indicates the inevitable immanence of tautology. Moreover, it is impossible to use 'indigenous' in a morally neutral or apolitical way. Peoples identify themselves as indigenous to establish rights and to protect their interests, NGOs are established to support them, and government departments to administer them. We have Survival International, Cultural Survival, the International Work Group for Indigenous Affairs (IWGIA), periodical publications with titles such as *Indigenous Affairs* and *The Indigenous World*, which 'support indigenous people in their struggle against oppression', and so on. At the same time, governments claim that peoples so labelled are no more or less indigenous than other minorities or majorities under their jurisdiction. This, for example, is the very clear view of the Indonesian government. Although it may be convenient to seek a technical definition of indigenousness in terms of prior occupancy, length of occupancy, a capacity to remain unchanged or whatever, such matters are seldom politically neutral. Measuring indigenousness is not an exact science (see, for example, Barnes 1995; Gray 1995; Kingsbury 1995).

Given its conflicting, ambiguous and strong moral load, 'indigenous' might seem the least useful way to describe a particular kind of knowledge. 'Native' and 'aboriginal' have similar connotations; 'tribal' is too restrictive and confuses a political condition with a distinct kind of knowledge; 'folk' and 'traditional' are less morally loaded, though 'folk' still has rather quaint associations in some quarters. 'Local' has the merit of sounding more neutral, but fails adequately to indicate key qualitative differences in the character of knowledge usually alluded to, while being in danger of becoming coyly euphemistic. Of them all, despite its implications of anachronism and long-term cultural stasis, 'traditional' seems to have more credibility and is among the most common ways of describing a particular kind of anthropological other. Like the alternatives, it derives its meanings from variations on the modernity–traditional dualism, which we have quite rightly learned to treat with suspicion.

We shall return to some of the problems associated with this dualism as applied to knowledge below, where we outline a more critical approach to the distinctive features attributed to indigenous or traditional knowledge. At this stage, however, it is convenient to have some standard by which to operationalise a few arguments, and to this end we can at least provisionally list some of the more commonly asserted characteristics of IK:

1. IK is local: it is rooted to a particular place and set of experiences, and generated by people living in those places. The corollary of this is that transferring that knowledge to other places runs the risk of, quite literally, dislocating it. Thus, the salience and significance of the same series of, let us say, plant species for a particular indigenous people compared with global science is likely to be very different, as their taxonomic and utilitarian linkages are, on the one hand, local, culture-specific and restricted, and on the other, global, culturally decontextualised and extensive.

2. IK is orally transmitted, or transmitted through imitation and demonstration. The corollary is that writing it down changes some of its fundamental properties. Writing, of course, also makes it more portable and permanent, reinforcing the dislocation referred to in 1. The latter transformation is in evidence every time the affinities between ethnobiological categories are rendered as abstract taxonomic trees.

3. IK is the consequence of practical engagement in everyday life and is constantly reinforced by experience, trial and error, and deliberate experiment. This experience is characteristically the product of many generations of intelligent reasoning, and since its failure has immediate consequences for the lives of its practitioners its success is very often a good measure of Darwinian fitness. It is, as Hunn (1993: 13; cf. Chambers 1983: 91) neatly puts it, 'tested in the rigorous laboratory of survival'.

4. 1 and 3 support a further general observation, that IK tends to be empirical and empirico-hypothetical knowledge rather than theoretical knowledge in the strict sense. To some extent its non-literate oral character – as well as, in many cases, its embeddedness in the non-verbally articulated interstices of everyday technical practice and the memory that informs this – hinders the kind of organisation necessary for the development of true theoretical knowledge.

5. Repetition is a defining characteristic of tradition (Hobsbawm and Ranger 1983), even when new knowledge is added. Repetition (re-

dundancy) aids retention and reinforces ideas; it is also partly a consequence of 1 and 2.
6. Tradition is 'a fluid and transforming agent with no real end' when applied to knowledge; negotiation is a central concept (Hunn 1993: 13). IK is, therefore, constantly changing, being produced as well as reproduced, discovered as well as lost, though it is often represented as being somehow static.
7. IK is characteristically shared to a much greater degree than other forms of knowledge, including global science. This is why it is sometimes called 'people's science', an appellation that also arises from its generation in contexts of everyday production. However, its distribution is still segmentary, that is, socially differentiated (Hobart 1993: 13). It is usually asymmetrically distributed within a population, by gender and age, for example, and preserved through distribution in the memories of different individuals. Specialists may exist by virtue of experience, but also by virtue of ritual or political authority.
8. Although IK may be focused on particular individuals and may achieve a degree of coherence in rituals and other symbolic constructs, its distribution is always fragmentary: it does not exist in its totality in any one place or individual. Indeed, to a considerable extent it is devolved not from individual to individual at all, but in the practices and interactions in which people themselves engage.
9. Despite claims for the existence of underlying culture-wide (indeed universal) abstract classifications of the biological world based on non-functional criteria (see, e.g., Atran 1990; Berlin 1992), where IK is at its densest its organisation is essentially functional, denotative know-how geared to practical response and performance (Lyotard 1979).
10. IK is characteristically holistic, integrative and situated within broader cultural traditions; separating the technical from the non-technical, the rational from the non-rational is problematic (Scoones and Thompson 1994: 18).

Using this rather crude checklist of characteristics, we are now in a position to examine a number of substantive areas of critical relevance. The first is what IK and its various semantic cognates might mean in the context of Western traditions of knowledge, what they might mean in the context of non-Western (particularly Asiatic) traditions of knowledge, and what its impact has been on the development of those traditions we call science.

Indigenous Knowledge at Home in the West

The West often assumes that it has no IK that is relevant, in the sense of folk knowledge, that it once existed but has now disappeared, and that somehow science and technology have become its indigenous knowledge. Certainly, there is plenty of evidence that the existence of, for example, codified pharmacopoeias such as the *De Materia Medica* of Dioscorides displaced local knowledge and oral tradition extensively in Europe and the Mediterranean, but un-codified knowledge persisted and gradually filtered into organised texts, as the number of modern remedies of European folk origin manifestly attests to (Cotton 1996: 10–11).

But Western folk knowledge (non-professional, experimental, uncodified, *ad hoc*, often orally transmitted) is arguably just as important as it ever has been, though different, informed by science where appropriate and located in different contexts (gardening, dog breeding, bee keeping etc.): the folk are no less creative. Moreover, in parts of Europe urbane folk actively seek out the authoritative knowledge still regarded as being present in their own peasant traditions, as in truffle hunting, geese rearing or the preservation of rare breeds of sheep. This is splendidly illustrated in the work of people like Raymond Pujol (e.g. Lecuyer and Pujol 1975) in France. Peasant or rural knowledge becomes, in this context, the peculiar product of Europe's own inner indigenous other. Interestingly, and paralleling a development we shall examine later for indigenous knowledge elsewhere, such European folk traditions have in the last forty years or so been reified, reinvented, celebrated and commoditised, as demonstrated in the contemporary cultural significance of living folk museums, craft fairs and such like. One of the ironies of this is that these folk traditions have become highly codified. But the double irony, as we shall see, is that the process of codifying folk knowledge into organised scholarly knowledge has ever been thus.

In mediaeval and early modern Europe, proto-scientific knowledge of plants and animals superseded folk knowledge through classification, analysis, comparison, dissemination (usually through books and formal learning) and thus generalisation. The process was not sudden: for a long time, common experience, oral tradition, personal experience and learned authority contributed to the aphoristic knowledge or received wisdom upon which organised specialised knowledge, particularly medical knowledge, depended (Wear 1995: 158–59); and knowing where unorganised folk knowledge, professionally restricted organised knowledge and proper scientific knowledge began and ended is not at all easy. In such proto-scientific technological practices, it is significant that elements of discrete knowledge do not usually disclose how they were arrived at. In other words, their epistemic origins are hidden. Sometimes they are of European folk origin, but especially from the sixteenth century onwards they incorporated medicines of Asian and American origin. It was this anonymity that helped define an emergent scientific practice in opposition to folk knowledge. Even after scientific discourse and practice had become distinct, methodologically self-conscious and discriminating, it continued to draw on practical folk experience. Darwin, for example, depended extensively on the knowledge of pigeon fanciers in working out the details of natural selection (Desmond and Moore 1991: 425–30; Secord 1981, 1985). Indeed, more generally we can see that modern natural history arose through a combination of such indigenous expertise and field studies (Zimmermann 1995: 312), and field studies themselves often drew heavily in turn on the knowledge of local experts. Some have argued that the phylogenetic taxonomies of contemporary post-Linnaean biology are based on a European folk template (Atran 1990; Ellen 1979; Knight 1981). Others have gone further by claiming that the European folk scheme and that of modern biology are no more than variants on a single cognitive arrangement of living kinds to which all humans are predisposed through natural selection (Atran 1990; Boster 1996).

What we now recognise as scientific knowledge of the natural world was, therefore, constituted during the eighteenth and nineteenth centuries in a way which absorbed such pre-existing local folk knowledge as was absorbable and, ultimately, confined what was not to oblivion. The latter was at best of antiquarian interest, at worst denied any existence as a meaningful and credible set of practices, precisely because of the inability of the new paradigm to absorb it. Part of this residue re-emerged as recognised folk knowledge in the late twentieth century and has been subjected to the kind of cultural revival we have already referred to. The rest, unlabelled and unloved, continues as that vast body of tacit knowledge which is necessary to operationalise book and theoretical knowledge and which continues to inform the practical engagement of ordinary skilled people: the informal un-codified knowledge of house workers, of Durrenberger and Pálsson's (1986; also Pálsson 1994; Pálsson and Durrenberger 1982) Icelandic fishing boat skippers, or of any number of skilled professionals who take their cue from real life situations unmediated by books. Unfortunately, nowadays the economic pressures of publishing and the demand for useful information are leading us to the further codification of the hitherto un-codified, of the '1001 handy household hints' and 'tips from the greenhouse' variety, thus giving the appearance of moving even further from the realm of IK.

Impact of Asian Folk Knowledge on the Development of Western Scientific Traditions

As we have seen, much Western science and technology emanates from indigenous European folk knowledge (e.g. herbal cures), but from the earliest times ideas and practices were flowing into Europe from other parts of the world and vice versa. By the later middle ages, however, and the beginnings of modern European global expansion, there emerged a self-consciousness about the desirability of obtaining new knowledge. We can see this process at work by examining some recent scholarship relating to European scientific interests in India and Indonesia.

As early as the sixteenth century, travellers were being advised to observe indigenous practices and to collect material with a view to extending European *materia medica*. For example, Garcia da Orta, a Portuguese physician living in Goa, provides us with a description of plants of the East that formed the basis of medicines available in Europe and Portuguese colonies, and from which they could be extracted. Da Orta relied on personal medical experience, fieldwork and indigenous knowledge, and initially depended on Arabic sources, thus reflecting the centre of gravity of the international trade in *materia medica*. Da Orta's *Colóquios dos simples e drogas he cousas medicinais da India*, published in Goa in 1563, was translated into Latin in 1567 by Charles d'Ecluse (Clusius), who went on to establish the *Hortus Medicus* in Vienna and, in 1593, the Leiden botanical gardens.[3] In turn, Jacob Bondt relied heavily on the *Colóquios* for his pioneering book on tropical medicine, *De Medicina Indorum*, published in Leiden in 1642.[4] The decline of Portuguese power in Goa and the establishment of the Dutch in Cochin was marked in botanical terms by the *Hortus Indicus Malabaricus*, initiated by Hendrik van Rheede tot Drakenstein (1636–91) in response to the medicinal needs of the Dutch East India Company.[5] We can thus see a remarkable chain linking Indian medical ethnobotany, compilations of Middle Eastern and south Asian knowledge organised on essentially non-European precepts, Portuguese and Dutch political interests, and the formative period of modern scientific botany and pharmacology.[6] But this is only the beginning.

What makes this story of knowledge transformation of particular interest here is that in both the *Colóquios* of da Orta and the *Hortus* of van Rheede, contemporary Hippocratic emphases on accuracy and efficiency tended to privilege strongly local medical and biological knowledge, leading to effective discrimination against older classical texts and systems of cognition in natural history. Because van Rheede, in particular, was unable to rely on any pre-existing European template for south Asian plant knowledge, Grove argues that he was largely responsible for elevating Ezhava knowledge above that of the dominant Ayurvedic schemes, with the aim of acquiring the highest-quality indigenous expertise. The Ezhavas were a lowly Shudra caste whose traditional occupation was toddy-tapping, but many were also Ayurvedic physicians who were highly regarded. As Brahmans were forced to rely on their low-caste servants for detailed field knowledge of plants, it made sense for van Rheede to bypass academic Brahman knowledge (Grove 1996: 136–37n52). He thus went through the same process of rejecting Arabic classification and nomenclature and European knowledge as da Orta, in favour of a more rigorous adherence to local systems. It should be said, however, that an interpretation privileging Ezhava is not supported by the work of Zimmerman (1989; personal communication).

The perfection of European printing, the establishment of botanical gardens, global networks of information and *materia medica* transfer, together with the increasing professionalisation of natural history, facilitated the diffusion and dominance of Indian medico-botanical knowledge and epistemological hegemony, and imposed an Indic technical logic on subsequent European texts concerning south Asian botany. These retain the essentially indigenous structure of the *Colóquios* and the *Hortus*, thereby transforming European botanical science through contact with south Asian methodologies of classification, rather than the other way round. But given the long history of mutual knowledge transfer going back to ancient times, any division between European and Asian botanical systems might be construed as arbitrary (Grove 1996: 127–28).

We can see a similar, though, in terms of the epidemiology of ideas, less complex process in the work and influence of George Rumphius. Rumphius was a German naturalist employed by the Dutch East India Company who lived in Amboina between 1653 and 1702, where he systematically recorded the natural history of not only the islands immediately surrounding Amboina, but, through the organisms provided him, island Southeast Asia in general. In doing this he relied heavily on local assistants and their knowledge. His most important work, on plants, was published posthumously as the *Herbarium Amboinense*. What is remarkable about this work is not just its importance in listing many species hitherto unknown in European botanical descriptions, but its heavy reliance on native descriptions of plant ecology, growth patterns and habits, as well as the extent to which its author relied on Malay and other local folk classifications and terms to provide a meaningful and comprehensive account (Beekman 1981; Peeters 1979). However, compared with van Rheede's work on western India, rather than interference from or rejection of classical Javanese and other politically dominant schemes, we find instead a reliance on Malay (essentially a new language at that time in the Moluccas) as a linguistic filter for indigenous ideas and knowledge. In turn, Linnaeus, in particular in 1740, fully adopted the Indian classification and affinities in establishing 240 entirely new species, and to a lesser extent relied on the Ambonese and Malay classifications and descriptions provided by Rumphius.

The influence of the *Herbarium Amboinense* and the *Hortus Malabaricus* immediately established Holland as the centre of tropical botany, and French, English and Dutch naturalists employed by respective East India companies, following Dutch methods, were instructed to collect as much indigenous knowledge as possible (Grove 1996: 140–41). Their influence on the canonical Linnaean texts meant that subsequent authorities came to depend on essentially Asian organising frameworks, as with Roxburgh, Buchanan-Hamilton and Hooker in India (ibid.: 139) and Burman, Blume, Henschel and Radermacher in Indonesia. But more than this, the 'seeds of modern conservationism developed as an integral part of the European encounter with the tropics and with local classifications and interpretations of the natural world and its symbolism' (Grove 1995: 3).

During the nineteenth and twentieth centuries, local knowledge was increasingly systematically tapped and codified. Such routinisation resulted in the publication of scientific accounts of new species and revisions of classifications that, ironically, depended upon a set of diagnostic and classificatory practices which, though represented as Western science, had been derived from earlier codifications of indigenous knowledge. Numerous encyclopaedic inventories began to appear, such as George Watt's *Dictionary of the Economic Products of India* (1889–96) and Burkill's (1935) similar encyclopaedia on Malaya inspired by the work of Watt, which had all the hallmarks of the scholarly arm of imperialism. Thus, the European relationship with local Asian knowledge was, paradoxically, to acknowledge it through scholarly and technical appropriation and yet somehow to deny it by reordering it in cultural schemes which link it to an explanatory system that is proclaimed as Western. While on a personal level, scientists may have acknowledged the contributions of their local informants, on the professional level the cultural influences which those same informants represented were mute.[7]

Indigenous Knowledge Marginalised

If, in the context of late European colonial scientific fieldwork in Asia, traditional knowledge was evident but mute, with the inexorable rise of modernity it became a kind of ignorance (Hunn 1993: 13). Tradition was something to be overcome, to be subverted rather than encouraged, its legitimacy questioned. Several generations of top-down development experts and organisations engaged in resource extraction and management in the underdeveloped world either deliberately avoided IK on the grounds that their own models were superior, or simply never realised that it might be a resource to be tapped. For some fifty years or more, the dominant model of development has been based on useful knowledge generated in laboratories, research stations and universities, and only then transferred to ignorant peasants (Chambers and Richards 1995: xiii). Such attitudes are now very much on record thanks to the work of, for example, Paul Richards (e.g. 1985). But not only has IK been grossly undervalued by Western-trained scientific managers in terms of its potential practical applications, when it was at last absorbed into scientific solutions it was curiously insufficiently real to merit any certain legal status or protection from the battery of patents and copyrights which give value and ownership to Western scholarly knowledge and expertise. Even when the knowledge was clearly being utilised, it was often re-described in ways which eliminated any credit to those who had brought it to the attention of science in the first place. This point is made by Harris (1996: 11, following Shiva and Holla-Bhar 1993), in her discussion of 'neem' (*Azadirachta indica*):

> Whether or not the chemical properties assumed to provide the active substance for cure have been identified by the communities does not appear relevant. Rather, it appeared that the method used by these western firms, and their ability to synthetically reproduce the compounds, was perceived as the true science and consequently, deserving of patent. Because the knowledge held by the local populations is commonly shared, it is deemed 'obvious' and traditional, folk knowledge as opposed to modern, scientific, specialist knowledge. Not only does this distinction seem arbitrary, it also implies certain institutionally based criteria where laboratory professionals practice recognized science, while indigenous lay peoples are seen to possess folk knowledge.

The inherent ethnocentrism and elitism of late twentieth-century global science, therefore, has made it difficult for scientists themselves to accept that the folk have any knowledge of worth (Johannes 1989: ix), a culture of denial which has been justified by a methodological reductionism and evaluative process which systematically renders such knowledge unscientific. This view is reinforced by perceptions that traditional peoples often adopted wasteful, even delinquent patterns of resource extraction, as classically exemplified in the literature on shifting cultivation (e.g. Dove 1983) and that when subsistence practices were evidently damaging, this was a matter of preference or conscious indifference rather than poverty.

The Rediscovery and Reinvention of Indigenous Knowledge

Since about the mid 1960s the process of marginalising IK as outlined above has been put into reverse and is indeed accelerating to a remarkable (some would say alarming) degree. There are both romantic and practical reasons for this.

The romantic reasons have their immediate political renaissance in the 1960s counter-culture [Chapter 1], with the notion that traditional, indigenous or primitive peoples are in some kind of idyllic harmony with nature. Such a view was initially prompted by a crisis in the modernist project of science and technology, in terms of both the increasing remoteness and arcane character of science, its perceived arrogance and negative technological outcomes, and its inability to explain much about the world which ordinary people sought explanations for. As has been suggested on various occasions (Budiansky 1995: 3n7, 251, quoting Kaufman, quoting Chesson), it amounted to 'good poetry' but 'bad science'. Others have gone even further and questioned the poetry. What this often involved was the selective remodelling of Asian and other exotic traditions to suit the aesthetic needs of Western environmentalist rhetoric drawn from an intellectual pedigree which favoured idealised native images. Conklin and Graham (1995: 697) put it this way:

> Contemporary visions of transcultural eco-solidarity differ in that native peoples are treated not as peripheral members whose inclusion requires shedding their own traditions but as paradigmatic exemplars of the community's core values.

In this new vision, indigenous peoples are given central focus *because of* rather than *in spite of* their cultural differences. But, as Conklin and Graham point out, this perception and consequent alliance between indigenous peoples and science is a fragile one, based upon an assumed ideal of (indigenous) realities which contrasts with realities for the local people themselves. Such assumptions are in danger of leading to 'cross-cultural misperceptions and strategic misrepresentations' (1995: 696). Reconstitution in an Asian context has often involved both the great and the little traditions (the scholarly and the tribal), often failing to distinguish between the two and confusing ideal symbolic representations with hard-headed empirical practice. It is not altogether surprising, therefore, that this muddle has confirmed some scientists in their worst prejudices and led to the inevitable backlash summed up in phrases such as 'the environmentalist myth' (see, for example, Diamond 1986; cf. Johannes 1987).

Nevertheless, with the discarding of the more fanciful portrayals of the wisdom of traditional peoples, a more practical approach has emerged. This has been encouraged by anthropologists and other development professionals eager to make IK palatable to technocratic consumers, and by technocrats themselves already predisposed to see a role for IK. Its dissemination has been part of a rhetoric extolling the virtues of participation, empowerment, bottom up and farmer first. Some measure of the institutionalisation of this version of IK (and in this version abbreviations of the IK and TEK variety are *de rigeur*) is the number of networking organisations and research units (see Warren, Slikkerveer and Brokensha 1995: xv–xviii, 426–516). One of the difficulties with this approach, however, has been that categorisation of IK effectively becomes 'a direct consequence of the limited parameters of western development/scientific theories which rely upon an ordered conceptual framework from which and in which to work'. As Hobart (1993: 16) observes:

> there is an unbridgeable, but largely unappreciated gap between the neat rationality of development agencies' representations, which imagine the world as ordered and manageable, and the actualities of situated social practices.

As a consequence, we seem to end up with a theory that misrepresents the context in which certain knowledges occur and are experienced. Hobart has pointed to the limitations of development and scientific knowledge in that they ignore or undervalue contexts. Decontextualisation is necessarily implied by the uncritical placing of local knowledge systems under the umbrella concept of indigenous knowledge, and the unique and important knowledge of specific local groups becomes subject to the same limitations and criticisms that we make on behalf of Western science and development theories. Moreover, the tendency to define indigenous knowledge in relation to Western knowledge is problematic in that it raises Western science to a level of reference, ignoring the fact that all systems are culture-bound and thereby excluding Western knowledge itself from investigation. This restricts analysis of indigenous systems by narrowing the parameters of understanding through the imposition of Western categories. Fairhead and Leach (1994: 75) draw attention to this problem, particularly regarding the tendency to isolate bits of knowledge which are fitted into a 'mirror set of ethno-disciplines' for the purposes of analysis and documentation. By examining local knowledge in relation to scientific disciplinary distinctions, they are pointing out how this can lead to the construction of certain aspects of local knowledge as important, while excluding or ignoring other areas and possibilities of knowledge that do not fall within the selective criteria of Western science. Moreover, they argue that this risks overlooking broadly-held understandings of agroecological knowledge and social relations. So, for example, research and extension agents examining Kouranko farmers' tree-management practices in Guinea fail to take into account farmers' tree-related knowledge, which involves knowledge and management of crops, water and vegetation succession, as well as the ecological and socio-economic conditions which influence them. By failing to include the broader constitutive processes surrounding Kouranko tree management, extension workers risk obscuring and decontextualising local knowledge, thus jeopardising the potential this may have for development on specific and general levels.

Thus, in this depleted vision, IK becomes a major concept within development discourse, a convenient abstraction, consisting of bite-sized chunks of information that can be slotted into Western paradigms, fragmented, decontextualised, a kind of quick fix, if not a panacea. Such approaches are in danger of repeating the same problems of simplification and over-generalisation that Richards and Hobart identify as major limitations in development theory, and in science applied to development 'ignoring specific and local experience in favour of a generalizable and universal solution' (Harris 1996: 14). Moreover, IK has become further reified in the hands of NGOs that in the last few decades have become significant knowledge-making institutions – and within the universalising discourse of environmentalism. Because environmentalist and indigenous NGOs are now an influential moral and social force, stimulating public awareness, acting as whistle-blowers and watch-dogs, and moving from the role of critics to offering policy proposals to governments, and since they often use the rhetoric of science, they have gained enormous authority (Yearly 1996: 134). This process has evidently yielded politically advantageous results in terms of projecting a more positive image of IK.

In some important respects, the way development professionals have contextualised and scientised IK, by codifying it and rejecting the cultural context, has simply repeated what has happened in previous scientific encounters with traditional knowledge. And similarly, once IK is absorbed, it is difficult to know where to draw the boundaries between it and science. As we have already seen, changing the boundaries is often sufficient to redefine something as science, as what defines it is to a considerable extent determined by who practises it and the institutional context in which the practices take place. However, the danger of turning local knowledge into global knowledge is that 'at the empirical level all IK is relative and parochial; no two societies perceive or act upon the environment in the same ways. Science, by comparison, is a system of knowledge in rapid flux that seeks universal rather than local understanding' (Hunn 1993: 13). It is precisely the local embeddedness of IK that has made it successful.

Recording Indigenous Knowledge

In the introduction to *The Cultural Dimension of Development*, Warren, Slikkerveer and Brokensha (1995: xvii) express what is at present central to the indigenous knowledge enterprise – the focus on documenting and recording indigenous systems in order that they be 'systematically deposited and stored for use by development practitioners'. However, when we consider the ways in which indigenous knowledge is perceived and defined, the idea of a project to centralise and store this knowledge appears to be a contradiction in terms. Thus, how is it possible to organise something for practical purposes that is inherently 'manifold, discontinuous and dispersed' (Scoones and Thompson 1994: 19)? This is where its ambiguity as a concept is perhaps most evident. On the one hand, it is described as above, with the authors arguing against the assumption that indigenous knowledge is an 'easily definable stock of knowledge ready for extraction and incorporation'. On the other hand, despite this warning against erroneous assimilation and interpretation, Warren, Slikkerveer and Brokensha observe that the priority of regional and international indigenous resource centres is currently the codification and documentation of this knowledge for general use. A similar stress is found in an editorial for the *Indigenous Knowledge and Development Monitor* (vol. 113, 1993), which states:

> Knowledge produced by universities and research institutes around the world is gathered, documented and disseminated in a coherent and systematic way. The same should be done with community-based, local or indigenous knowledge [which] should be included alongside the more usual scientific knowledge.

This is clearly an agenda for indigenous knowledge, despite the widespread recognition of it being embedded in a web of meaning and influence. In his criticism of the Western–indigenous dichotomy, Agrawal (1995: 5) deals succinctly with this contradiction and its implications:

> If indigenous knowledge is inherently scattered and local in character, and gains its vitality from being deeply implicated in people's lives, then the attempt to essentialize, isolate, archive and transfer such knowledge can only seem contradictory. If western science is to be condemned for being non-responsive to local demands, and divorced from people's lives, then centralized storage and management of indigenous knowledge lays itself open to the same criticism.

Not only is this a concern to be addressed within a theory of indigenous knowledge, particularly for its implications in development projects – which makes it vulnerable to the same set of limitations that scientific theory possesses – it is also necessary to consider just what is being recorded and documented. For example, it is not clear whether 'local', when it defines indigenous knowledge, signifies that knowledge which is peculiar to a particular group of people, and if so, how it is to be utilised by other groups who must equally possess their own specific knowledge.

Richards' analysis (1993: 62) of knowledge as performance challenges the very idea of practices being grounded in indigenous knowledge, suggesting rather that the range of skills and strategies employed by farmers extends beyond simple applied knowledge into a 'set of improvisational capacities called forth by the needs of the moment'. He posits a theory of performance that challenges the assumption that cultivation practices are evidence of a fixed stock of knowledge from which techniques are drawn. Rather, by drawing on the analogy of musicians who rehearse many times for a performance but who adapt and draw on their own resource skills when needed at a particular moment, he suggests that farmers likewise adjust and adapt their techniques and skills according to the needs that arise at a particular time. He illustrates what he means by performance knowledge, and the difficulties this presents for the recording of these practices for use elsewhere, or even in the same location the following year, with an example of Hausa intercropping plants in northern Nigeria. He observes how Hausa farmers make a series of adjustments to drought by planting and replanting different seed mixes until germination is secured or until available resources are exhausted. The resulting cropping pattern is not, he argues, a necessarily predetermined design; rather:

> each mixture is a historical record of what happened to a specific farmer on a specific piece of land in a specific year. It is not the outcome of a prior body of 'indigenous technical knowledge' in which farmers are figuring out variations on a local theory of inter-species ecological complementarity. (Ibid.: 67)

His point has important methodological implications too, highlighting the dangers of misplaced abstraction whereby development practitioners create a complete theory based on assumed and observed practices. Now, this idea seriously challenges the notion of a material stock of indigenous knowledge which can be analysed and extracted for use in any context, even its own context, which, as Richards suggests, is constantly changing and intrinsically interactive. This is not to say that nothing is analysable or useful beyond its own boundaries, but rather that it perhaps makes better sense to recognise knowledge as grounded in multiple domains, logics and epistemologies. Richards' point is useful in calling attention to the range of skills and practices which a group collectively or individually may manipulate within their particular locations, thus making pertinent the local or peculiar knowledge generated within a particular cultural context. Furthermore, as Agrawal (1995: 5) suggests, it may be far more productive to move away from the 'sterile dichotomy between indigenous and western' which idealises and obscures knowledge and practices, disempowering peoples and systems through artificially constrictive frameworks.

Codifying and documenting indigenous knowledge systems could be a worthwhile endeavour if it were not for the tendency to present such systems as models or blueprints for general use, and under the broad reified heading 'indigenous knowledge'. As such people's knowledge and the different ways in which they use, expand and manage take on a static semblance, it increasingly resembles earlier anthropological accounts of culture as timeless, non-dynamic, bounded systems. *The Cultural Dimension of Development* (Warren, Slikkerveer and Brokensha 1995) provides some evidence of this. Chapter 1 of this book reads like a manual for development workers and even bio-prospecting agents, with an interest in the value and use of ethnobotanical resources. Without contextual analysis, Alcorn (1995: 7) lists the kinds of resources that can be mined from ethnobotanical knowledge: principles, facts, technologies, crops, farming systems, strategies, and information on local constraints and opportunities. She continues:

> Traditional farmers have developed *packages of practices* for tropical forested lands, arid lands, steep lands, swamp lands and other marginal lands ... Most of these systems renew fertility, control erosion, and maintain biodiversity through fallowing ... these systems integrate useful wild plants into their management regime. (Ibid., italics added)

What are useful plants? Useful to whom? By presenting these systems as packages of practices, all agency and creative, dynamic potential is drained, reducing local knowledge to some sort of commodity, secured and easily transferable from its locality to somewhere else. The implication that people are not agents but actors simply reacting to a set of established prompts is strongly apparent, especially when Alcorn (1995: 6) advises us that:

> farmers do not describe the details of their traditional farming activities well. It is necessary to try to learn to farm as they do, learn the decisions that are made, to learn exactly what they are doing, and thereby, discover the wisdom held in their methods.

This is a far cry from the dynamic, living systems that indigenous knowledge is purported to be and which are advocated as the key to future development. Moreover, these kinds of analysis present little more than decontextualised inventories of people's knowledge, providing documents for, rather than about, people. From an anthropological perspective, such contributions are inadequate because they ignore the social and cultural context in which knowledge is generated and put to practical use. Fairhead and Leach (1994) make a similar point when they observe the ways in which specific utilisation patterns are separated into isolated parts for the purposes of scientific analysis. Research and extension workers thus isolate knowledge into studies of geographical differences, specific crop species and their uses, particular practices – agro-forestry, hunting, fishing and so on – disregarding the entirety of circumstances which surround these practices. While we are not suggesting that Alcorn herself is guilty of depersonalising and immobilising local knowledge systems (she provides references to more detailed documentation of farming systems), the outcome of such a general analysis nevertheless suggests the existence of a definable body of knowledge *independent* of the contexts in which it arises. One of the problems with this approach is that it removes people's agency, facilitating the appropriation by non-local agents of these practices and techniques, only to be imposed as top-down development. Not only does this defeat the objectives of participatory development and local empowerment which an IK-oriented theory expounds, it also establishes and legitimates itself in the same way as previous Western-centred development theories have done, thereby presenting neither an effective nor a radical alternative to the present development crisis. Furthermore, as local knowledge is analysed and documented for use, it undergoes changes that necessarily result from the specific orientations, strategies and agendas of those using it, as well as the transformations that inevitably occur through translation.

Hobart (1993: 14) underlines some of the potential problems for agency that can occur when knowledge is collected, codified and decontextualised using an example from Croll's (1993) study of the post-revolutionary period in China. He notes how people's agency was diffused and depersonalised by attributing knowledge to 'the masses' in a government attempt to reverse the idea of a vision of knowledge stemming from the elite and educated. He describes the result:

> As problems inevitably emerged in putting this reworked and decontextualized knowledge into practice, local populations came progressively to be defined as backward and ignorant ... they became presented not as agents but as objects to be changed.

Similarly, Zerner (1994) discusses the introduction of an awards scheme by the Indonesian government for villages who observe idealised *sasi* customs in the central Moluccan Islands. *Sasi* are ritualised arrangements for controlling access to natural resources on a temporal and spatial basis, including closed seasons for particular species – often those of commercial value – enforced through traditional sanctions. Zerner (1994: 1104) notes that the effect of this is to put villages in the public eye and under the direction of local officials who are now able to get villagers to make changes regarding the management of their resources. In the same way, support groups and NGOs have been set up to observe and ensure that *sasi* law is adhered to. Village councils, for example, now have to submit annual reports to the provincial Environmental Studies Centre at Pattimura University. It is not within the scope of this chapter to examine in depth the political implications of the reorientation in development towards indigenous people and their knowledge and practice. It is, nevertheless, an important issue that has a direct bearing on the indigenous people themselves and needs to be considered carefully for the future of indigenous knowledge in development projects. As it stands, indigenous knowledge emphasises the personal, the specific and the contextual. To some extent, we would suggest that it too is in danger of becoming a depersonalised, objectivised concept, which, if used as a top-down approach to development, may inevitably lose its agency and efficacy once a new trend is established. Should this happen, it is doubtful whether Western images of tribal indigenous peoples who require Western aid will change, thereby guaranteeing a continued role within development enterprises. Much depends on the many indigenous groups and alliances that are active in advocating political rights for and over indigenous knowledge.

The Construction of Indigenous Knowledge in Contemporary Contexts

So far, the conceptualisations of IK that we have offered have been implicitly those of Western (or Western-trained) professionals, even if they do claim to be acting with the authority, and in the interests, of indigenous peoples. However, the status of such knowledge from the point of view of indigenous peoples themselves or from their non-Western compatriots and political leaders may be rather different. In Asia, for example, what counts as indigenous knowledge is certainly more problematic than it is for those operating from the West.

Thus, for Western and non-Western elites alike, IK variously refers to some great tradition (e.g. Ayurvedic medicine), or more often to myriad little local traditions. The great Asian scholarly ways of knowing were a combination of epistemic and gnostic knowledge, dependent respectively on an agreed shared authority and the personal authority of a practitioner. They were often grounded in written texts and resembled the European scholarly traditions already discussed. Galenic, Chinese and Ayurvedic traditions of medicine differed from each other, but each had scholarship in common: 'the foundational knowledge of each could only be acquired by careful study under teachers relying on ancient texts' (Bates 1995: back cover). Where the great and little traditions merge is unclear, and as in the European case there is historical evidence to suggest, for example, that the great Asian herbalist traditions have been systematically absorbing and then replacing local folk knowledge. Indeed, traditional Chinese medicine is increasingly influenced by the work of medical scientisers who seek to produce a body of internally consistent, uncontested and impersonal knowledge that can be called Chinese medicine (Farquhar 1995: 273n27). Thus, we see here something very reminiscent of the codifying and simplifying processes that accompanied the incorporation of European folk knowledge into the early modern scholarly traditions.

In the modern period, Asian reliance on indigenous knowledge has been a combination of economic necessity and tradition. Many Asian scientists, decision-makers and administrators have frequently internalised an essentially Western model in rejecting IK as backward and as something which has to be replaced. Others have always recognised the efficacy of some kinds of IK but seen it as strictly complementary knowledge, which has little to do with science-driven development. In recent years, however, the state sector and NGOs in many countries have moved from colonial hegemonic denial towards the positive acceptance of the utility of local knowledge in medicine and sustainable development, partly for political and partly for economic reasons. IK is being rediscovered and reinvented. A classic example is the *sasi* institution of the central Moluccan Islands of eastern Indonesia, to which we have already referred. These arrangements for ritually protecting resources by imposing prohibitions on harvesting at a critical period in the growth or reproduction of the resource, which in many areas had become moribund by the 1980s, experienced a revival through endorsement by NGOs, were integrated into national development plans, celebrated at a national level in the discourse on development – linking ancestral culture with historic resistance to Dutch depredations on resources – and redefined as people's science, as a form of resource management and conservation that was wholly positive (Zerner 1994: 1101–4). We might take this argument still further, and show how rapidly changing representations, productions and reproductions of *sasi* raise interesting issues about what happens to knowledge once it becomes institutionalised, codified and packaged – perhaps disseminated globally through electronic media – and thereafter applied outside its original context.

Explicit and full recognition – in developing countries and in the West – together with the rights that are deemed to accompany this, has only come with the failure of top-down approaches. This has been associated with the quest for appropriate and cheap technologies for development and with the rise of ethnobotany in the pharmaceutical industry, at a time when the environmental movement has become morally committed to the notion of indigenous environmental wisdom. No wonder then that at this precise historical moment, when IK (through the assertion of intellectual property rights) and the rights of indigenous peoples in more general terms are higher on the political agenda than they have ever been before, 'indigenous' as a label is being reclaimed by the protagonists themselves in pursuance of their own interests. Distinct native peoples, though less so in Asia than in, say, the Americas, have seen indigenous knowledge as part of their own cultural identity and as a very concrete and politically appropriate way of asserting it. Part of the reason for this is that, although the guardians of such knowledge are traditionally oriented individuals and groups, those who wish to document it are from westernised elites or other outsiders. A very important relationship of unequal power is thus articulated (Healey 1993).

States and NGOs have both sought to protect indigenous rights to such knowledge, and this has given rise to a whole set of new issues in merging the philosophies, legal traditions and discourses of the West and the rest of the world. In some cases, cross-fertilisation of different local traditions and the reification of tribal or folk knowledge has occurred. Third World/Global South politicians, scientists and others have had to work out for themselves how indigenous or traditional knowledge is to be defined and whether its existence is altogether to be welcomed. When it becomes a means by which to flag problematic local minorities making political and cultural claims against a government, it is clearly threatening; if it can be defined in a more nationally inclusive way and commoditised, it is a resource to be exploited.

Most of the contributions that appeared in *Indigenous Environmental Knowledge and Its Transformations* (Ellen, Parkes and Bicker 2000) addressed issues raised in this section: indigenous knowledge as a present social reality articulated through the voices of governments, NGOs, scientists, ordinary citizens and those who claim it for their own. Posey (2000), who situates IK in the context of the property rights debate and who summarises the complex international legal and political setting in which other themes explored here must be understood, also provides a useful clarification of the distinction between the knowledge of indigenous peoples and indigenous knowledge. Osseweijer (2000) demonstrates the importance of nuancing what we mean by indigenous or local in anthropological appeals for the importance of stressing local knowledge and reminds us that specialist knowledge may – almost by definition – be accompanied by generalist ignorance: the IK which she demonstrates is a necessary precondition for both economic productivity and effective marine conservation of 'trepang' (sea cucumbers) in the Aru islands of eastern Indonesia is not only that of the indigenous extractors and producers, but also the knowledge which non-indigenous traders have of the 'trepang' from a distribution and consumption angle. Indeed, these knowledges are dialogically related, to the extent that indigeneity (local Aruese or local Chinese) becomes a questionable label for their practical distinction.

Sundar (2000) also critiques the assumption within development discourse that IK is an easily identifiable body of knowledge which can be instituted as development practice, drawing attention to the differences between local knowledge and IK as represented in government programmes. Baviskar (2000) considers the various claims made for IK by locals, NGOs and government departments in the context of Indian eco-development and the implications of this for our understanding of tradition, locality and indigenousness. Similarly, Li (2000) analyses the field of power surrounding the concept of indigenous environmental knowledge in Indonesia and the circumstances in which it may or may not serve as a vehicle to enhance claims to resources. She does this by first examining the often contradictory position taken on IK by different agencies within the Indonesian government and the deployment of the concept by NGOs in relationship to the state and donors. This then provides the context for an analysis of the processes, both politico-historic and local-global, which provide one Indonesian group with an opportunity to articulate an identity through IK, while another must remain inarticulate. The position in non-colonised developed Asian states such as Japan is understandably different, with a less clear historic denigration of the traditional past. Nevertheless, John Knight (2000), examining Japanese attitudes to their own indigenous (upland) other with respect to the rediscovery of specific traditional knowledge of the forest and hunting, is able to explore rhetorical indigenisation as part of an upland cultural revival.

A number of researchers have concerned themselves with the ways in which official and native attitudes to IK change depending on the ruling development ideology, scientific evaluations and concatenation of political circumstances. Masipiqueña, Persoon and Snelder (2000), for example, illustrate shifting attitudes by state authorities to the role of fire in resource management in the Philippines. Dove (2000) further explores the repackaging issues by tracking the successful transfer of rubber production and management practices from its original Brazilian environment to Southeast Asia, suggesting advantages in leaving behind the cultural baggage of American folk knowledge and relying on the flexible innovative knowledge of the receiving local populations. Parkes (2000) too examines conditions of miscommunication in the representation of IK in his account of the Kalasha of northern Pakistan, but in this case the miscommunication is intentional, or at least habitually instilled through historical circumstances of enclavement. He also notes the unintended and adverse political consequences of this for minority enclaves. Brosius (2000) examines the rhetoric of an international environmental campaign in support of the Penan of East Malaysia against the activities of logging companies, especially the ways in which Western environmentalists have constructed Penan environmental knowledge and used and transformed (his own) ethnographic accounts in the generation of appropriate – largely obscurantist and essentialist – rhetorical images, images which have been recycled to the Penan themselves as part of a self-definition which they find it politically expedient to project. The recycling of distorted images of knowledge is increasingly evident as information moves between different players in environmentalist debates, from local peoples, through the green lens of NGOs and other organisations, and back to local peoples. It is part of the process by which groups such as the Kayapó and Penan become icons for the international environmentalist movement.

The End of Indigenous Knowledge?

We began this chapter with a list of distinctive features of what, for the sake of convenience, we have called IK. However, IK is increasingly being criticised for its lack of organising themes, and whatever characteristics might be used to carve out a meaningful intellectual space, the cognate terms we use and concepts against which they are matched suffer from several major epistemological weaknesses. One of these concerns the question of context and the relationship between IK and culture in its generality. A second is the extent to which IK involves practices and patterns of thought which might be described as comparable to science. A third is that it implies the existence of some overarching comparator, what we might call Universal Reason (or science), which is always ontologically privileged. These issues are all closely related to one another, but the emphasis in each case is slightly different. Our purpose here is not to attempt a resolution of the problems so much as to highlight them as questions for further debate.

In our discussion of the effects of recording and codifying indigenous knowledge, we have drawn attention to the problem of decontextualisation, in particular the separation of such knowledge from its human agents and from the situations in which it is produced, reproduced, transformed and (presumably) is at its most effective. It is important, however, to question the extent to which something called IK can ever be successfully decoupled from the wider cultural context. Despite programmatic rhetorics to the effect that considering 'the cultural dimension' of knowledge is important, in a collection such as the eponymous *The Cultural Dimension of Development* (Warren, Slikkerveer and Brokensha 1995), many examples provided appear to have little to do with the cultural contexts in which they occur. The result is an ambiguous representation of IK as indigenous science, rational knowledge or empirical knowledge. Current literature on IK presents it as largely separate from the cultures in which it originates. At best, reference is made to certain ritual and symbolic factors which should be considered, but any consideration of whether and how indigenous knowledge and culture might differ is ignored. In this way, IK is almost placed *outside* culture. Thus, in their analysis of farmer experimentation in the Andes, Rhoades and Bebbington (1995: 298) present local knowledge as a sort of free-floating quasi-science-based elaboration of individual creativity. In an effort to liberate small-scale farmers from previous assumptions that presented them as passive and culture-bound, the authors are concerned to show that farmer knowledge is as much a science as that of laboratory scientists and to separate what is useful from what is not. This approach has the effect of redefining what is useful in a somewhat narrow and technocentric way, externalising culture (separating it from what good farmers do) and recasting it as an impediment to successful development. Such experimental techniques are no less cultural than anything else farmers may do or believe.[8] The failure to take into account the co-existence and interconnections between both empirically and symbolically motivated criteria within any system of knowledge inevitably leads to limited understandings and perhaps even fundamental failures of understanding about how IK operates and how it is situationally successful.

Indigenous knowledge has been categorised by outside interests stemming from environmental and socio-economic influences that have more to do with the popular perceptions of others than with what others have themselves made clear. In this sense, the word 'indigenous' becomes relevant and necessary to separate an observer from an observable other. Also, this neat categorisation can be seen as a direct consequence of the limited parameters of Western development or scientific theories, which rely on an ordered conceptual framework from which and in which to work. We also need to ask if it is possible to define effectively the shifting boundaries between science and folk knowledge, whether the distinction is in any way helpful, and whether there is a difference between folk knowledge and folk science. On the one hand, there is a sense in which both traditional and Western knowledge are anchored in their own particular socio-economic milieu: they are all indigenous to a particular context. This is reflected in the failure of scientific solutions due to ignorance concerning particular cultural circumstances (Agrawal 1995: 5). But is there just good and bad science, or is science qualitatively different in its underlying cognitive organisation? Is it all applied common sense, the only difference being that one is practised by the folk and the other by professionals, in other words an outcome of some division of intellectual labour? Alternatively, is folk knowledge hopelessly embedded in particular symbolic patterns of thought, while *real* science is a distinctive kind of uncommon sense, driven by a logic which often results in demonstrating its counter-intuitive character (Wolpert 1992)? Such an approach constructs science as reductive, generalisable, universalist, disinterested, open, cumulative and reliant on an explicit methodology legitimated by the generation of results. If *so*, to what extent can we say that science ever existed in Asiatic traditions prior to Western borrowings – a position that many commentators would find quite indefensible in the light of the revolution in our understanding of Asian science initiated by Joseph Needham (see, for example, Staal 1993)? At this point, of course, the trail leads us into the familiar anthropological thicket of the rationality and relativism debate (Hollis and Lukes 1982; Horton and Finnegan 1973; Overing 1985; Wilson 1970), of 'the great cognitive divide', and the highly charged confrontations between defenders of a philosophically narrow definition of how science works, the more broad-minded pragmatists and cultural studies theorists.

Arguments about the existence of an overarching comparator in the constitution of the subject matter of IK parallel those disaggregating the concept of nature (Ingold 1992). If recognising separate local cultural constructions *of nature* necessarily implies the existence of NATURE as a philosophical point of departure from which particular cultural deviations might be measured (Ellen 1996a), the same applies to the recognition of local knowledges. This should not surprise us, since the cultural construction of nature is the necessary condition for establishing knowledge (Strathern 1992a: 194). Each indigenous knowledge is necessarily locally situated and the emanation of a particular worldview (it parallels 'perceived nature'). Now, in this model, there may be many indigenous knowledges (Ingold 1997), each of which accesses *the real world* to various degrees of imperfection and subjectiveness. From these partial, imperfect knowledges can be distilled 'universal reason' by eliminating what is incorrect, subjective, vague or local through the application of agreed tests of authoritative validation. Thus, universal reason is a superior understanding of the real world. An alternative view, that of post-modernism, cultural studies and certain versions of the sociology of science, is one of extreme relativism, claiming that indigenous knowledge and science are epistemologically equivalent and equal. Our position is slightly different:

that a baseline of universal reason exists and that in all traditions it is driven by shared human economic needs and cognitive processes, but also that they are activated and expressed in different cultural contexts.

A final problem we must face is what some recent writers have called 'time-space compression'. What, for example, does the implicit distinction between West and 'other' – used throughout this chapter – encode? More particularly, global–local distinctions are now blurring and we are told that we inhabit a world of transcultural discourse (Milton 1996: 170). However sloppy some of us may find the conceptual apparatus that is being offered to cope with these issues, they do directly address the question as to whether it is still possible to regard local knowledges as something discrete, even less pristine, or whether we are trapped by the representations of such in global (Western) media and their reformulation by indigenous people who learn it from, and who raise their consciousness of it through, Western sources. Should we continue to try to separate local knowledge from global knowledge on the assumption that one or other is superior in a particular context, or should we give preference to the mixture of local and global which most indigenous peoples now rely on? It is this blurring which results in neologisms such as 'glocal' (Robertson 1996) and a new analytical emphasis on how people shift the geographical context of their knowledge (Strathern 1995). For Vitebsky (1995: 183), the problem is encapsulated in the historical simultaneity of shamanism expiring on the tundra just at that moment that it is taken up by new agents in the West. Can indigenous knowledge survive such appropriations? However, we believe that IK, in the sense of tacit, intuitive, experiential, informal, un-codified knowledge, will always be necessary and will always be generated, since, however much we come to rely on literate knowledge that has authority, the validation of technical experts and knowledge that is systematically available, there will always be an interface between this kind of expert knowledge and real-world situations. It will always have to be translated and adapted to local situations and will still depend on what individuals know and reconfigure independently of formal and book knowledge. Indigenous knowledge is dead. Long live indigenous knowledge.

Notes

First published in 2000 as the 'Introduction' to *Indigenous Environmental Knowledge and Its Transformations: Critical Anthropological Perspectives*, edited by Roy Ellen, Peter Parkes and Alan Bicker (Amsterdam: Harwood, pp. 1–3). Reproduced courtesy of Harwood and Taylor & Francis.

1. In this context it is perhaps important to stress that by IK we have in mind local *environmental* knowledge (knowledge of plants, animals, soils and other natural components) with *practical* applications, rather than the more encompassing sense of IK associated with environmental philosophies or worldviews, or even ITK (indigenous technical knowledge) in its wider sense. However, we accept that such practical, technical and empirical knowledge is characteristically embedded in, linked to and informed by *these* broader understandings.
2. On definitions, see also Berkes 1992; Chambers 1983: 82–83; Johnson 1992: 4; Warren, Slikkerveer and Brokensha 1995.
3. Published in English as *Colloquies on the Simples and Drugs of India by Garcia da Orta*, transl. Sir Clements Markham (London: Henry Southern, 1913).
4. See *An account of the diseases, natural history and medicine of the East Indies, translated from the Latin of James Bontius, Physician to the Dutch settlement at Batavia, to which are added annotations by a physician* (London: T. Noteman, 1769).
5. *Continans Regioni Malabarici apud Indos celeberrimos omnus generis Plantas rariores*, 12 vols (Amsterdam, 1678–93).
6. Most of the details presented in this paragraph are derived from Grove (1996: 125–34), but see also the important work of Zimmerman (1989).
7. One cannot avoid noting the comparison here between nineteenth-century field science and modernist (functionalist) anthropology in *the* tradition of Malinowski.
8. The difficulties of separating rational empirical knowledge from religious, moral or symbolic knowledge are well illustrated in an analysis by Lemonnier (1993) of Ankave-Anga eel-trapping.

CHAPTER 5

From Ethno-science to Science

The History of 'Indigenous Knowledge'

The surge of interest in indigenous knowledge during the eighties and nineties of the twentieth century produced, in its turn, a counter offensive from some scientists concerned at the kinds of claims that proponents of indigenous knowledge were making, an attempt by others to reconcile traditional knowledge and science, and to distinguish both from pseudo-science.[1] Many otherwise pragmatic individuals were wary of endorsing the utility of 'indigenous' knowledge because this seemed to question their own credentials as scientists and professionals. Similarly, some scientists detected an embedded anti-scientific tradition, historically rooted in certain formulations of cultural relativism, and most recently evident in its post-modernist guise. The more extreme versions of this position, it is often said, undermine the possibility of objective science, and go against our common-sense experience that enough science works sufficiently well to allow us to rely on the predictions upon which medicine and engineering depend. This overcharged interchange has been dubbed the 'science wars' (Anderson 2000). In retrospect, both sides were making some outrageous claims, and for the most part there is now a large degree of consensus. I do not wish to revisit this ground here, merely to register its existence. Nor do I wish to return to the terminological squabbles which have confused the issue, or to provide further endorsement of the value of indigenous knowledge. The important thing is to note the terms, conditions and timing of the debate. For over much the same period other scientists have been embroiled in a parallel and equally acrimonious debate with cultural theorists, sociologists and historians of science, intent, as it was seen, on undermining the objectivity and value-neutrality of science. Some, it is asserted, sought to rewrite the great scientific breakthroughs in ways which the authors would claim improved on older, ideological, revisionist and selective presentist histories of science, histories which had airbrushed out the inconvenient non-scientific context and presented us with representations of the minds and achievements of great scientists which suited the present-day high priests and guardians of scientific method. At a distance, the potency of the sterile dichotomies being drawn here arises from a fusion of a general human cognitive impulse to simplify the processes by which we understand the world – reinforced by the socially driven need of science to maintain an effective boundary (Nader 1996: xii–xiv, 3–4) around the practices which scientists engage in – and of the West's mission to preserve its cultural pre-eminence. I wish to suggest that the opposition of science and indigenous knowledge (which in the minds of the more extreme protagonists becomes one between science and superstition) is yet another manifestation of what anthropologists have called 'the great cognitive divide'. Even though the opposition between primitive and civilised thought has fallen under the weight of the evidence, and its surrogates (most recently that between literacy and orality) have similarly been shown to be problematic (Frake 1983), the apparent need to divide the world into just two ways of thinking persists.

The existence of two epistemological meta-categories – let us call them for the time being science and indigenous knowledge – unfortunately obscures the evident presence of many different ways of securing predictive knowledge of the material world, each of which is characterised by a distinctive configuration of cognitive and technical features, and which in several dimensions cut across the usual dualism between science and indigenous knowledge. In this chapter I try to look at science as a cognitive anthropologist might look at a local ethno-science. My examples will be largely, though not exclusively, drawn from natural history and biology, on the grounds that this is my own area of specialist knowledge, and I shall attempt to relate this to the historical emergence of global, transmodern, scientific biology, with its formative phase in Western cultural history between 1600 and 1900. I shall first examine theories of science, in relation to its actual practice, and consider the proposals of those who see science as different only in degree from wider cognitive practices, to varying extents constrained by neurophysiology, either distinctively human or shared with other higher organisms. This deconstruction of the uniqueness of science inevitably means that it becomes ever more difficult to distinguish and label the practices in which those we call scientists engage. I shall examine the meta-category of science in relation to the historical generation of its antonym (indigenous, local, traditional, intuitive, ordinary, knowledge), and in the light of all the deconstruction try to characterise the combination of cognitive, technical and social practices which help us maintain modern global science as a social and cultural entity distinct from the many cross-cutting ethno-sciences.

Diversity in Biological Knowledge Traditions
Indigenous Knowledge

Indigenous or traditional knowledge emerged as a generic category quite late, during the second half of the twentieth century [Chapter 4 in this volume]. In the seventeenth and eighteenth centuries, European naturalists and medical practitioners readily assimilated knowledge from newly colonised or contacted people, and it was only really with the rise of the development industry in the twentieth century that such knowledge, having been at first mute and then actively rejected, was subsequently rediscovered and celebrated. From about the mid 1960s the tendency to marginalise local biological knowledges had begun to be put into reverse, prompted by a combination of romantic idealism and pragmatism. Attempts were made to make it more like science, to reduce it to a codified, packageable commodity, secure and easily transferable from one place to another. And, once ethnobiological knowledge had been drawn within the orbit of modern science and its origins forgotten, it became difficult to know where to place the boundary between the two. Indeed, changing the boundaries was often sufficient to redefine something as science, as what defines it as such was to a considerable extent determined by those who practised it, and in what institutional context the practices took place. We can see a parallel here between the scientist and the artist under high modernism and post-modernism, where it is less the substantive materiality of the creation which is crucial than the context and who does the creating.

Another way of highlighting the absurdity of the category 'indigenous knowledge' or 'traditional knowledge' as applied to biology is to define it as what is left once 'biological science' has been subtracted. Looked at this way, 'indigenous knowledge' is just like the multitude of manifestations of 'the other', what is left when we take ourselves out. As a single all-encompassing notion it is nonsense, as terminologies, definitions and cognate concepts vary throughout their geographical, local-global and various historic and disciplinary refractions. There are many indigenous biological knowledges, each accessing the real world to various degrees of imperfection and subjectiveness. These diverse biological knowledges, for well over sixty thousand years, have constituted the main body of our adaptive knowledge as a species. Some are part of specialised scholarly textual traditions (which I shall return to shortly), but those outside such traditions have been represented as sharing a number of broad common characteristics [Chapter 4 in this volume]. They are rooted in particular places and sets of experiences; are generated by people living in those places; are mostly orally transmitted or transmitted through imitation and demonstration; are a consequence of practical engagement in everyday life constantly reinforced by experience and error; and are the product of generations of intelligent reasoning. They are empirical in character, orality to some extent constraining the kind of organisation necessary for the development of abstract theoretical knowledge. The redundancy which they embody aids retention and reinforces ideas; they are fluid and the outcome of continuous negotiation, constantly changing, being produced as well as reproduced, discovered as well as lost; though often represented as static. They are characteristically shared to a much greater degree than global biological science, but are still socially clustered within a population, by gender and age for example, and preserved through distribution in the memories of different individuals. Specialists may exist by virtue of experience, but also by virtue of ritual or political authority. Although knowledge may be the prerogative of particular individuals and may achieve a degree of coherence in rituals and other symbolic constructs, it does not exist in its totality in any one place or individual, devolved not in individuals at all, but in the practices and interactions in which people themselves engage. Such knowledges are characteristically situated within broader cultural traditions, so that separating the technical from the non-technical, the rational from the non-rational, is problematic.

Scholarly Ways of Knowing

By comparison, the great 'scholarly ways of knowing', or what Dunbar (1995b: 36) rather derogatorily calls 'cookbook science', come midway between these essentially local folk knowledges and biological science. They combine knowledge dependent on an agreed shared authority with that of the personal authority of a practitioner. They are often grounded in written texts, and resemble the European scholarly traditions. Galenic, Tibetan, Chinese and Ayurvedic traditions of medicine differ from each other, but each have a notion of scholarship in common (see, e.g., Bates 1995). Where the scholarly and local folk traditions merge is unclear, and as in the European case there is historical evidence to suggest, for example, that the great Asian herbalist systems have been systematically absorbing and then replacing local folk knowledge. We see here something very reminiscent of the codifying and simplifying processes which accompanied the incorporation of European folk knowledge into the early modern scholarly traditions. These 'folk' traditions have themselves become highly codified. During mediaeval and early modern Europe, proto-scientific knowledge of plants and animals superseded folk knowledge by classification, analysis, comparison, dissemination (usually through books and formal learning) and thus generalisation. The process was not sudden: for a long time common experience, oral tradition, personal experience and learned authority contributed to the 'received wisdom' upon which organised specialist knowledge, particularly medical knowledge, depended; and delineating the boundaries between uncodified folk knowledge, professionally restricted organised knowledge, and proper scientific knowledge is not always easy. Some have argued that the phylogenetic taxonomies of contemporary post-Linnean biology are based on a European folk template (Ellen 1979; Atran 1990), and some have gone even further by claiming that the European folk scheme and that which emerged in nineteenth-century professional natural history are no more than variants on a single cognitive arrangement to which all humans are predisposed through natural selection (Atran 1998; Boster 1996).

Proto-scientific and Scientific Knowledge

A similar process in terms of the epidemiology of ideas was at work in the way non-European folk and scholarly traditions were absorbed into science, and simultaneously employed – at least in the early modern period – to legitimate it. I have, for example, already discussed in Chapter 4 the work and influence of the Dutch East India Company naturalist George Rumphius, while Grove (1996) has provided us with the parallel case of Garcia da Orta in relation to Hendrik van Rheede. Their work resulted in the publication of scientific accounts of new species and revisions of taxonomies which, ironically, depended upon a set of diagnostic and classificatory practices which, though represented as 'Western science', had been derived from earlier codifications of indigenous knowledge. Rumphius and other scholars of their time also sought to confer authority on their work and writing by appealing to the wisdom of local peoples. Linnaeus, for example, self-consciously drew on the traditions of the Lapps in order to promote his scientific work, to the extent that he had his portrait painted wearing Lapp costume, even though – and revealingly – the details of the clothing are ethnographically questionable (Figures 5.1 and 5.2).[2] Seeing Linnaeus dressed as a Lapp in early eighteenth-century Sweden conveyed much the same impression and authority as the proverbial photograph of the anthropologist's tent in the context of ethnographic writing (Clifford 1986: 1–2).

Rumphius and Linnaeus make an interesting comparison because their lives and work fall around the temporal boundary between what Foucault (1970: 127–28) has called the natural history and biology epistemes, or what we might call a Foucauldian moment or transition, when traditional knowledge or scholastic knowledge becomes science. Rumphius had no pretensions to be a 'scientist' and no understanding of what this might

108 | Nature Wars

Figure 5.1. Mezzotint of Linnaeus in Lapp costume; Dunkerton, from a painting by M. Hoffman. Reproduced by permission of the Linnean Society, London.

Figure 5.2. Print of Linnaeus outside his tent, the Frontispiece to the *Flora Lapponica*, published in 1737. Reproduced by permission of the Linnean Society of London.

have meant in contemporary terms; and otherwise performed successfully as a Company historian and naturalist. Linnaeus, by contrast, and certainly the later Linnaeus, was more self-consciously operating within a scientific paradigm, controlling a network of acolytes who contributed to his wider comparative project. But on either side of the epistemic divide, those who would call themselves scientists often had no problem in underpinning their scientific observation with ideas and perceptions which today we would consign to the realm of the non-scientific: Rumphius, like his infinitely more famous contemporary, Isaac Newton (e.g. Dobbs 1975), believed in magical 'ancient wisdom', astrology, the spontaneous generation of living matter, species transformation and the idea of the homunculus (Figure 5.3). This latter notion, whereby the discovery of the spermatozoan through microscopy is combined with an imaginative folk embryology which places the pre-formed human actually within the head of the spermatozoan, finds an interesting echo in the anthropomorphic faces which Rumphius's plagiarist and follower, François Valentijn, placed on the heads of nymphs of the arthropod *Irona renardi* observed under a magnifying glass (Figure 5.4).

During the nineteenth and twentieth centuries, local knowledge was increasingly tapped and codified. Such practices became so routinised that once absorbed into 'scientific' solutions local biological knowledge disappeared from view, separated from its symbolic underpinnings, and insufficiently 'real' to merit any certain legal status or protection in the same ways which gave value and ownership to Western scholarly knowledge and expertise. Even when the knowledge was clearly being utilised,

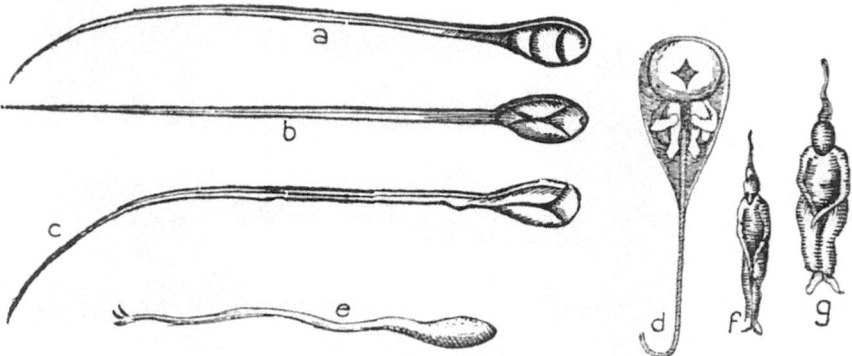

Figure 5.3. Spermatozoa as depicted in different seventeenth-century images: *a*, *b* and *c* are from Antony van Leeuwenhoek's drawings of dog spermatozoa (1679), *d* is Hartsoeker's homunculus in a human spermatazoan (1694), and *e*, *f* and *g* are human spermatozoa from Francois Plantades (Delenpatius), respectively showing intact cell, and broken to show the homunculi (all from Singer 1959: 507).

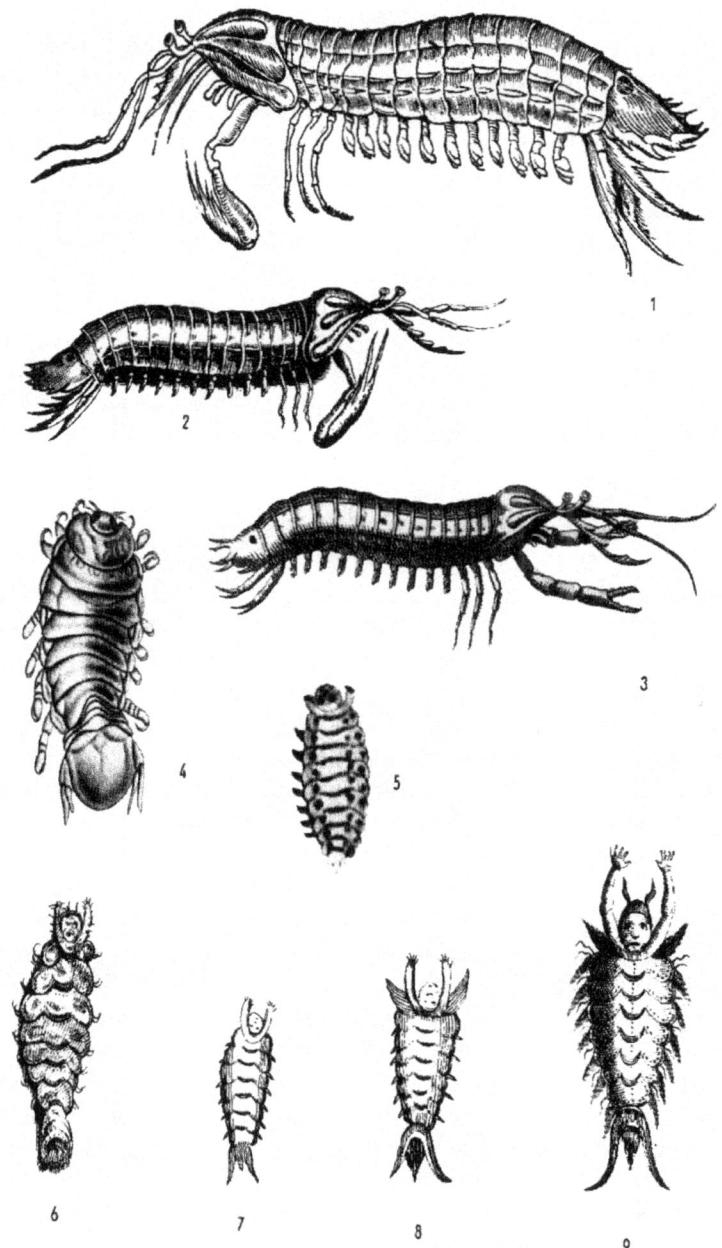

Figure 5.4. Early illustrations of the crustacea *Squilla mantis* and the nymphs of *Irona renardi*, including (6) and (9) taken from Valentijn (2002–2003 [1726]), following Rumphius. Source: Plate 11, *Rumphius Memorial Volume* (de Wit 1959).

it was often re-described in ways which eliminated any credit to those who had brought it to the attention of science in the first place. With the reification of the modernist project of science-driven progress during the middle part of the twentieth century, the traditional became widely accepted as irrelevant, and indigenous knowledge was used much more selectively, being virtually abandoned for several decades in certain fields, such as pharmacology. Under high modernism, science becomes the superior *a priori* standard by which all truths, including those derived from traditional teachings, are measured, validated and valued (Pfaffenberger 1992; Turnbull 2000). Thus, the boundaries between science, scholarly knowledge and folk knowledge, as these terms apply to biological phenomena, are constantly shifting, and the distinctions themselves are not always helpful. All knowledges are anchored in their own particular socio-economic milieu; all are indigenous to a particular context (Agrawal 1995: 5).

Theories of Science

The ways in which science has been hitherto theorised are broadly of two kinds. The first, what we might call traditional philosophy of science, is characterised by idealistic or programmatic theories (which take their cue from assertions about how good science should be conducted). The second kind of theory varies somewhat, but includes cognitive theories, emphasising the empirical character of scientific thought (either as a species of everyday cogni tion or as a special kind of thought); theories which focus on the empirical analyses of laboratory practice (which emphasise what scientists do, say and how they interact in working relations); and cultural theories, either those which scientists construct for themselves about their conduct, or those derived from outside observers. These latter emphasise science as a combination of shared norms and values, cognitive and technical practices. The data which sustain all of these are of four kinds: historical studies of prominent scientists, ethnographic studies of the conduct of contemporary science, ethnographic studies of indigenous knowledge, and psychological studies of science as a kind of thought.

Programmatic theories which emphasise ideal and formal methodology (laws, falsification and objectivity) have become increasingly difficult to defend and largely abandoned. Although some philosophers of science and scientists themselves do so, most who seriously reflect upon the subject rarely seek to defend them in their pristine form (Oatley 1996: 131). The archetypically austere Popperian account still has surprising currency in some quarters, but is now much critiqued in the world of philosophy of science itself. Such a view is often linked to the idea of science as the 'real' or 'absolute' truth, as a repository of 'facts', 'out there', waiting to be discovered by great individual minds rather than being the outcome of interactions in intersubjective space (ibid.: 126, 133–34). Rather, the new consensus is that 'philosophers have grossly overestimated the way in which science is actually done' (Dunbar 1995b: 78), and that 'we get trapped by the ideals of science when we insist on an exclusive role for well-formed computation, verifiability, and truth conditionality' (Bruner 1996: 100). The real 'multi-layered' world of science, it is observed, involves contradictions in actual practice and radically different kinds of theory, where some 'operate programmatically and others [are] more concerned with the details'. Whereas the programme may function after the fashion of a Kuhnian paradigm (a framework theory), subsidiary hypotheses are formulated and tested according to neo-Popperian criteria (Dunbar 1995b: 23). In a sense, theoretical and empirical observations represent two parallel worlds with different internal rules, which feed into and reinforce one another, a view which is essentially that of Lakatos and of Carl Hempel's hypothetico-deductive model (ibid.: 25). This accords with the notion that science is a methodological prescription rather than a particular body of theory, a method for finding out about the world (ibid.: 32). Nevertheless, most scientists continue to define their project as the search for truth, accurate data about the world, and in terms of theories and hypotheses that model this search (e.g. Wolpert 1992; see Oatley 1996: 133–34), and for this reason tend to imagine that their thinking is special, despite the fact that cognitive psychologists using these very methods find it difficult to locate its specialness. For Bruner (1996: 103), there can be no one model of cognition or of the mind, and we should 'avoid theories of meaning-making tied exclusively to the needs of science' for which no reductionist theory will ever do proper justice. Indeed, simple, formal definitions of what science is are always going to be problematic because they end up excluding practices and kinds of knowledge which are, in common-sense terms, integral to how science works. Science is not consistently 'rational, objective and produced according to the canons of scientific method', but is rather 'messy, contingent, unplanned and arational', a polythetic practice and conditional 'assemblage' of local knowledges (Turnbull 2000: 6, 14).

Despite such an emerging consensus, there is rear-guard resistance to the abandonment of programmatic theories. This is in part fuelled by prevailing popular conceptions of science as narrow, compartmentalising, technical, esoteric, accessible and relevant only to specially trained experts. But resistance is also encouraged by the perceived excesses of the cultural constructionists (the likes of Hacking, Lakatos, Kuhn and Feyerabend) who, it is asserted, insist on trying to show that science is 'nothing more than', that great minds such as Darwin, Boyle or Hooke, or their lesser contemporary counterparts who beavered away in laboratories, formulated their problems in a way which 'merely' reflects the society around them. Some scientists, trapped by assumptions that all social science commentaries are tarred with the same simplistic post-modern brush, feel justified in resorting to the equally fatuous assumption that if sociologists make such superficial claims it is because they are 'unable to grasp the scientific arguments' (Dunbar 1995b: 157). The problem with the sociology and cultural history of science is not so much that it claims that scientists are creatures of their particular social and cultural circumstances, but that it does not go beyond this to examine the similar cross-cultural cognitive practices within which science might be embedded. It seems to me that the sociological 'strong theory' is a wholly illusory challenge to the credentials of science as a legitimate and powerful tool for understanding the world, and is now, anyway, so obviously true that it is no longer interesting. What is much more interesting is that despite its social determination, science is so obviously effective. With Anderson (2000), I take the view that even if we could demonstrate that science is one hundred percent socially constructed, generally speaking, it is still an accurate representation of the world. To say that something is socially constructed is not to say that it is inaccurate, only that people learn what they do (their 'social constructions') from each other. I shall return to this idea later, but in the following section provide the evidence for the apparently opposite view: that 'science-like thinking' is not merely a human universal, but perhaps even derives its universality from cognitive imperatives which are a propensity of all higher organisms.

Science-Like Cognition as a Human Universal

The growing recognition of, and respect for, traditional non-Western forms of knowledge of the environment led during the seventies and eighties of the last century to claims that it was a kind of science. This view gained support in the context of the many failures of non-participatory, apparently 'science-driven', top-down development projects [see Chapter 4 in the present volume], and the consequent increasing utilisation of discoveries originating in local knowledge systems. A revival in the recognition of the historical inputs of such systems into the growth of Western science, for example Indian innovations such as the decimal system, the concept of zero, and procedures in trigonometry and algebra, two millennia before Newton and Leibnitz, was also important in this respect. Partly due to the force of such claims, some scientists have themselves adopted the view that empirical science is a human capacity, traces of which can be found in all societies (Dunbar 1995b: 58). Indeed, although local ecological and social circumstances provide different constraints and opportunities, what is very clear is the remarkable extent to which cultures converge on the same answers and solutions. Among the most widely quoted anthropological evidence for this is the claim that classificatory knowledge of the kind which Brent Berlin calls *general purpose* reflects universal cognitive regularities. But there are also other kinds of evidence, such as the effective demonstration that farmers facing similar problems in widely separated parts of the world have developed basically the same dynamic understandings of the relationship between elements in an agroecological system, for example in relation to fodder crops and nitrogen fixation (Walker et al. 1999; cf. Iskandar and Ellen 2000). Other patterns of convergence in general perception of biological properties are observable in relation to medicinal plants: the widely recognised hot-cold frameworks, and patterns in the selection of taxonomically unrelated plants on the basis of chemical similarities, biases towards certain plant families displaying useful kinds of bioactivity, and a recognition that the properties of plants which make them toxic are the same as those which make them medically potent (T. Johns 1990; Moerman et al. 1999).

Such claims to the universality of particular practices and their outcomes are interpreted by some as evidence that all peoples share a basic way of apprehending the natural world grounded in a common evolutionary history. The notion of a shared infrastructure of perception and cognition with respect to biological knowledge has been termed by its proponents 'natural history intelligence' and is linked most prominently to modular theories of the mind. The diagnostic features of such intelligence, or such a module, generally include a shared concept of basic natural kind (a species-like concept) reflecting a view of the biological world as a series of discontinuous entities; an ability to recognise and respond to things as living matter (and more specifically an 'algorithm for animacy', or theory of 'aliveness', a set of core principles which guide identification and reasoning about animals arising from the recognition that they possess an internal source of movement); a capacity to intuit certain kinds of behaviour based on expectations arising in part from common experiences derived from phylogenetic similarities or observations of human behaviour, and strategies for classifying biological diversity (Atran 1990, 1998; Boster 1996; Carey 1996; Ellen 2003c; Gelman 1990; Keil 1994; Mithen 1996: 52–54).

Because none of this is accessible other than through its local cultural versions, distinguishing what are shared human universals from what are simply culturally widespread is problematic.[3] But whatever the degree and character of epigenetic embedding, strong evidence for the cognitive universality of science-like processes is found in the ability of people everywhere to generalise the principles of plant and animal biology on the basis of knowledge of individual organisms. In terms of understanding human cultural adaptation to different environments, knowledge of such general principles of biology may be more important than breadth of formal knowledge or depth of substantive knowledge of individual organisms, or indeed of any universality in the taxonomic ordering of biodiversity. What is central here is the ability to transfer general lessons learned with respect to one organism to another organism. To some extent this may encourage us to generalise a module for natural history intelligence, with its predisposition to recognise common aspects in the functioning of living things, but much substantive knowledge of individual types of animal derives from analogical reasoning with respect to human bodily functioning. Thus, knowledge of human anatomy mutually reinforces knowledge of animal anatomy. Knowledge of the human body is, therefore, partly based on knowledge of animal bodies acquired in hunting, food preparation and livestock keeping; while understanding of animal physiology, pathology, and even psychology derives from modified human experience.

But if science-like cognition is a pan-human universal, and if this universality is accompanied by evidence for common underlying cognitive operations under ontogenetic control, then the question must arise as to whether such cognition is uniquely human at all. Some would claim that it is not, and that the methods of low-level empirical science are practised by all advanced non-human animals, or in an even stronger formulation that 'Western science is a product of a highly formalised version of something very basic to life' (Dunbar 1995b: 58; see also 33, 57). Two processes underpin an organism's ability to learn about the world: classification and causal inference, on the basis of which are built up logical chains of cause-effect sequences which permit leaps of inference (ibid.: 58). Johnson-Laird (1982), for example, claims that storing knowledge as causal hypotheses (or models) is efficient because humans do not have sufficient memory to make the right responses by induction alone. The difficulty for anthropologists here has been in identifying cultural and cognitive traits of sufficient discreteness to be accepted as unitary memes in the first place, and the ways in which the human mind unhelpfully interferes with the conventional forces of selection by re-forming such units, linking them together in novel ways and attributing to them new (and sometimes contradictory) linkages and meanings (Aunger 2000).

Science as a Specialised Form of Folk Knowledge

We can see from both the preceding brief history of the category 'indigenous knowledge' and from the equally brief review of theories of science that where the dividing line between scientific biology and other kinds of biological knowledge lies is by no means obvious, and that both science and ethnoscience have common and interconnected origins. Indeed, 'the whole of science', as Einstein once famously remarked, 'is nothing more than a refinement of everyday thinking', an assertion which cognitive psychologists such as Deanna Kuhn (1996: 261–62, 275) have sought to substantiate, even citing hypothesis-testing in children's verbal exchanges and the way they learn word endings as evidence in support of this.

How ways of thinking (cognitive practices) develop and become available to individual humans can be instructively compared with how we develop ways of speaking. We are genetically provisioned with a range – if not an infinite variety then a very wide variety – of cognitive options, just as we are provided with a wide congenital range in terms of our ability to generate and recognise phonemes through the audio-vocal tract (Lieberman 1984). But these options become more limited and less flexible as we are habituated and socialised into local cultural practices – such as occupational or social role playing. Within this range of cognitive activity, the most obvious distinction is not necessarily between scientific thinking and the rest (Kuhn 1996: 276), but rather 'between thinking that is more versus less skilled, with skilled thinking defined in its essence as thinking that reflects on itself and is applied under the individual's conscious control'. For most of the time widely shared and deeply embedded cultural responses which do not involve too much skill and reflexivity serve us well. Only when habitual behaviour and rules of thumb fail do we resort to conscious and reflexive science-like activity. In order to understand any differences there might be between science as a specific kind of reified knowledge-making process and science as an underlying proclivity, it is useful to list the characteristics of both, which are often claimed to distinguish the first from the second.

1. The grounds for belief in science and folk science are the same. Both require *suspension of belief* and the free and vigorous expression of contrary views; not simply the mechanical application of existing knowledge. As Kuhn (1996: 275) has demonstrated, 'in both scientific and everyday reasoning, people must be able to distance themselves from their own beliefs to a sufficient degree to be able to evaluate them, as objects of cognition, in a framework of alternatives that compete with them and evidence that bears on them'. Thus, Richards (1993: 62) notes that the range of skills and strategies employed by farmers often extends beyond simple applied knowledge into a 'fluid body of improvisations' about inter-species ecological complementarity relevant to immediate needs, rather than the outcome of a prior fixed 'stock of knowledge'. An essential dimension of this kind

of thing is 'thought becoming aware of itself', which in developmental terms occurs very gradually rather than at some discrete point during maturation (Kuhn 1996: 277).
2. *Differentiated concepts of causality*. Causality is a universally understood notion, but as Lloyd (1990) suggests, it everywhere varies between different domains. In its widest understood form, it is based on mechanical or physical analogy.
3. Philosophers differ in their rational reconstruction of what constitutes a *theory* (Carey 1996: 190), and some cognitive anthropologists deny that ordinary cognition relies on theory-like representational structures, and assert that folk biology, for example, is a 'pretheoretical cognitive module', even among adults (Atran 1994; Sperber 1994). For Atran (1995: 132), 'the structures of ordinary conceptual domains may strongly constrain, and thereby render possible, the initial elaboration of corresponding scientific fields'. But for most cognitive psychologists, and, I suspect, ethnographers, theory is as much an instrument of ethno-scientific thinking about the natural world as it is of science. It may, however, make sense to distinguish framework theories (foundational theories) from specific theories. If Wellman (1990: 191) is correct when he argues that cognitive scientists who write about intuitive theories usually mean framework theories, then by this logic folk biology is a framework theory.
4. A common feature of ethnobiological knowledge is the way in which knowledge is structured in terms of *networks of understanding*, linking individual species together in living contexts and entire landscapes, in contrast to formal science in the West which historically early reified the species and species-centred approach to understanding. This kind of systemic knowledge differs from biological science in emphasising long-term processes, including cyclical environmental change. However, it re-emerges in modern science in ecology, climatology and the earth sciences.
5. Suspension of belief makes possible acceptance that the world is constructed differently from conclusions based on initial perceptions or pre-existing cultural authority. Some scientists have held such *counter-intuitivity* to be the main condition of thought practices we describe as 'scientific' (Wolpert 1992), though there is increasing evidence that this is not the case. Atran (1996: 234) notes, for example, that supernatural beliefs are just as counter-intuitive for those who think them true as those who think them false, an obvious biblical example of which is the miracle in which Jesus turns water into wine. The types of belief which we regard as intuitive depend in part on substantive domain, place and specialist training. For a physicist,

what is counter-intuitive is, in certain respects, not the same as for a non-physicist. For instance, the idea that ice freezes faster when hot water is added (the so-called Mpemba effect), is counter-intuitive for most of us (including most physicists), but for an ice cream maker or somebody who refills livestock troughs in freezing conditions it is not (Chaplin 2004).
6. *Experimentation.* All science and folk science requires that in some form or another its practitioners evaluate relevant data against a possible set of explanations, and embrace a methodology which requires an explanation which best fits the data. Evidence for the repeated and systematic evaluation of experimental situations has by now been well documented in the local agroecological knowledge literature, with respect to plant breeding and pest control (e.g. Cleveland and Soleri 2002; Richards 1985). Moreover, the experimental method in Europe preceded seventeenth-century prototypes by over 1,500 years, Aristotle in his *Metereologica* showing clear understanding of this knowledge generation technique (Lloyd 1991; Dunbar 1995b: 40).
7. It is not simply a matter of extending recognised characteristics of science to ethno-science, but also of the reverse. Thus, the emphasis given to mathematics and abstraction in modern science sometimes seems to deny the significance of *narrative*. As Oatley (1996: 123–24) has pointed out, scientists do not restrict themselves to mathematics, diagrams and experiments. They use narratives to spin stories but can switch from these to the 'paradigmatic mode', such as an equation, when necessary. Similarly, while Bruner (1996: 100) acknowledges that while there just might be 'branches of mathematics and of the physical and biological sciences that are so formally or propositionally entrenched as to permit deviations without the support of folk tales', this is rare, and recalls a claim by Niels Bohr that the inspiration for the Principle for Complementarity grew by an analogical story drawn from an autobiographical experience.

Nature, the *Etak* of Science

It is not just that the specific articular and underlying cognitive practices of science and ethno-science appear to be the same, but also the cultural 'doxa' in which they are embedded and through which their performance is measured. By doxa I mean here – following Bourdieu (1977) – that network or framework of shared assumptions, habitual practices and axioms which we take for granted, but which give meaning to individual acts and thoughts and which allow them to function as a system. Doxa, for Bourdieu (1990: 20), is 'the coincidence of the objective structures and the internalised structures which provides the illusion of immediate understanding, characteristic of practical experience'. I would include here also 'beliefs' in the sense of the kind of propositions described by Goodenough (1990), a propensity for which hominin brain evolution has permitted.

For science and folk science to work, there needs to be a framework of assumptions about how the world is constructed and how human actors relate to that world. Such a framework often corresponds to what we conventionally call 'nature', that is some kind of conscious broad-brush definition of the objects under scrutiny in relation to the human mind and actions in the world. Just as knowledge of individual organisms is embedded in ecological knowledge of the relations between them, and the relationship of assemblages of living things is understood in a wider landscape and in functional contexts, so there is a link between all culturally varied biological knowledges and local constructions of that aspect of the world we call 'nature'. Of course, this does not mean that this framework is everywhere constructed in the same way, nor does it mean that such a framework needs to be universally 'accurate', only sufficiently robust to serve as a shared point of investigative departure. We can draw a parallel here with other, more specific framework theories in science, such as those of Newtonian physics, which while inconsistent with prevailing conceptions of matter, and in other ways flawed, have nevertheless provided an essential practical basis for most engineering. Such frameworks are cognitively reminiscent of the Micronesian *etak* system (Akimichi 1996; Frake 1985; Gell 1985; Gladwin 1970; Oatley 1977), long a familiar ethnographic case study in undergraduate cognitive anthropology courses, included – one assumes – to demonstrate the impossibility of typologising modes of thought. The *etak* system, you will recall, combines detailed empirical observations of environmental data – tides, currents, animal movements, winds, star movements – with the imaginary existence of an island and other symbolic entities, to make calculations of distance and direction which achieve a remarkable degree of navigational accuracy in inter-island voyages. The Micronesian *etak*, like 'nature', is a moving target, if you will, a fiction, which nevertheless aids investigative focus, and only makes sense because it helps achieve the desired objectives.

But even if we acknowledge that nature is no more than a convenient fiction, it does appear that all conceptions of nature are themselves underpinned by pan-human conceptual universals: one being the notion of what is 'natural' (primordial, of the essence); second, a tendency to contrast ourselves as humans and individuals with those biological others which lie outside of and around us; and thirdly, a compulsion to recognise and classify natural kinds as things in ways which suggest that we are evolutionarily adapted to cognise the natural world in broadly the same way (Ellen 1996d). Thus, human biological knowledge, in whatever tradition or particular social world it has developed, always and simultaneously informs and reflects adaptive behaviour through flexible cultural learning constrained by a common human cognitive framework. The cognitive roots of 'nature' indicate clearly how important such constructions are to basic adaptive 'scientific' thought, in that without certain cultural interventions or stimuli the cognitive processes themselves are not activated.

What is notable about conceptions of nature, including and perhaps most obviously in the *etak* system, and what has long puzzled anthropologists, is the ambiguous relationship in all cultural repertoires between the empirically observable and the symbolically asserted. This is often portrayed as a tension between levels of understanding distinguished as *symbolic* and *technical* (mundane) knowledge (knowledge versus know-how, savoir versus savoir-faire, ontological knowledge versus practical knowledge), or slightly differently between knowledge of and knowledge for, a genus of distinctions which goes back beyond Durkheim and Mauss to earlier philosophical dualisms, particularly mind/body theories. Attempts to make such distinctions are not completely separate from attempts to distinguish knowledge from skills, and the difficulty with virtually all such qualitative contrasts is that they are never hard and fast. Those anthropologists (such as Brent Berlin) who have accepted the legitimacy of distinguishing the technical from the symbolic have, on the whole, been those who have undertaken specialised studies of kinds of indigenous knowledge, the ethnosciences in the sense used above. By contrast, those anthropologists who have avoided analysing technical knowledge, or who reject the distinction between technical and symbolic in the first place (such as Mary Douglas), have been more interested in symbolic and social knowledge *per se*. This convergence of cognitive and symbolic approaches (Colby, Fernandez and Kronenfeld 1980; Ohnuki-Tierney 1981) is consistent with the recognition that all human populations apprehend both the social in terms of the natural world and the natural in terms of the social world, making many claims of unidirectional metaphoric extension problematic. The two are intrinsically complementary. The classificatory language we use for plants and animals is derived from the way we talk about genealogical relations, and we understand the functional dynamics of both organisms and ecological systems in terms of our experience of participating in social systems, where technology provides numerous productive analogies: say, the heart as a pump, the blood vascular system as a thermostat or the brain as a computer. More generally people attribute meaning to parts of the natural world around them by investing them with human and spiritually anthropic qualities (animism). Indeed, there are striking similarities across cultures (Atran 1996: 234) between natural causality and the supernatural, in terms of symbolic content (e.g. animated substances and monstrous beings) organised through the same core set of cognitive mechanisms.

The symbolic merges, therefore, with the mundane, and both may be truly *local* knowledge. Local people themselves simultaneously embed their mundane knowledge in the symbolic, and their symbolic knowledge in the mundane, but are nevertheless often able to make inferences which imply the separation of one (or certain aspects of one) from the other when it matters. Recognition of this possibility is vital, since by emphasising the merging of local symbolic knowledge (e.g. worldviews) and technical knowledge, those who criticise the use of anything less than fully symbolically contextualised knowledge sometimes seem to deny the ability of people to discriminate different orders of inference or kinds of data at all, as well as the strong probability that people know that certain kinds of solutions to problems are easier to identify than others. Indeed, one of the major philosophical contradictions in science as we know it, is that while its effective conduct requires some foundational theory, a set of assumptions and metaphors which are beyond empirical testing (a kind of doxa), it is also part of a cultural tradition which ideologically *separates* the symbolic from the technical in terms of the latter involving the application of self-conscious rationality. It is a tacit acceptance (or avoidance) of this contradiction through a pragmatic division between spheres of rationality which permits NASA scientists to be simultaneously evangelical southern Baptists, and creationists molecular biologists. But if we accept this, then we must also accept that the same kinds of distinction might apply to Trobriand gardeners when evaluating the reasons for crop failure. We know that the art of good story-telling and science (see above) is for the authors to provide the conditions under which the reader can suspend disbelief, so we might reasonably expect there to be conditions in any belief system where the conditions are presented which allow for the suspension – or even the instantiation – of belief.

Science as an Instituted Model

If it is the case, as many argue, that insisting on seeing science as a special cognitive practice, or in denying the science in ethno-science or in the learning strategies of other species, is a result of confusing science as a general process of thinking with idealistic theories of particular individuals, then we still need to establish what it is which separates out what scientists really do in cognitive terms from what the rest of us do. As Kuhn (1996: 279) notes, it is difficult to deny that 'non trivial differences exist between everyday and scientific thinking', and to say that science is *no more than* common sense in a special institutional setting is to come dangerously close to saying nothing at all. But if science, in all its many cultural manifestations, is only possible through reliance on a doxic infrastructure which is rarely fully articulated or understood, I wish also to suggest that we treat science as it has developed since the sixteenth century in Europe and the neo-Europes as a more specific kind of cultural model. D'Andrade (1990: 809) defines a cultural model as 'a cognitive schema that is intersubjectively shared by a cultural group', but as Shore (1996: 45) has noted, this definition fails to distinguish between 'special purpose models' and 'foundational schemas'. There is no doubt also that historically Western biological science emerged as a special purpose knowledge in a very specific context of use, with a specific division of labour, and like other local knowledges has simply reflected the interests of a particular local culture – that of scientists – who work as a community within social organisations and according to shared social norms. Thus, science conforms closely to Shore's notion of an instituted model. For Shore (ibid.: 51–52), models become socially institutionalised when they are 'objectified as publicly available forms'. However, having originated through a process of 'intersubjective negotiation', modern science as an instituted model takes on a 'second life' as a series of mental representations or individual processes of 'meaning construction'. The practice of contemporary science provides some excellent examples of personal mental models derived from an instituted model, and where conflict arises between the two there also arise possibilities for innovation. This feedback effect is easier to understand if we start from the ethnographic assumption that cultural models are intersubjective representations created by individuals in a social environment, rather than from the base assumption of psychology, that mental models are subjective representations created by individuals. In looking at the growth of science, the interesting question becomes, therefore, how external, publicly available instituted models are reconstructed as cognitive models, and how the relations between relatively conventional and relatively personal mental models work for any individual (ibid.: 48–50).

Some of the main factors which make science so effective as a social and technical practice are the mechanisms for the establishment, shaping and maintenance of intersubjectivity, in other words for 'making meaning' (Bruner 1996: 94–95). In science, meaning is more secure than in other kinds of knowledge, and it is possible to more accurately establish that the receiver knows the message which the sender is transmitting. This is what Bruner has called 'memory externalisation' (ibid.: 102, following

Merlin Donald), through which process ideas and facts become independent of those individuals who innovated them, and remain as part of the 'exogram' because they are formally necessary for the descriptive and explanatory system to work (ibid.: 101). In terms of recent anthropological debates on the extent to which knowledge is shared, and of methodologies and modes of representation which conflate aggregate with individual knowledge, it may well be that in the exogram of certain scientific discourses we come the closest we ever can to that mythical figure, the 'ideal' or 'omniscient speaker-hearer' (see, e.g., Ellen 1993b: 43, 126–48).

For science to work there have to be mechanisms for securing intersubjectivity, for ensuring accurate memory externalisation, for distinguishing specialist knowledge from more generalised knowledge shared by a wider category of people, all of which in effect mean maintaining the boundary between scientists and non-scientists. In all of this, language use and literacy have historically been crucial: the determination of specialist terminologies and notations (e.g. anatomical Latin and Greek letters) and linguistic registers, use of metaphor and abbreviations (from memes to quarks), of international rules of practice (say of taxonomic nomenclature), methodological protocols, specialist journals and other forms of publication. But at the same time, what is de facto legitimated as technical necessity is simultaneously symbolic and social. Thus, these same devices, representations and instantiations may also evoke secrecy, mystery and therefore power, maintaining boundaries and conferring legitimacy, authority and status; or, within science, may equally serve to divide. Dunbar (1995b: 139, 142) compares, for example, the way immunologists have managed to develop a separate professional language, while physicists are forced to borrow the language of everyday (and social) experience to talk about abstract relations and entities which are not perceivable in any other way than through mathematics.

Beyond the oral and written forms of language, the instituted model of science is maintained by conferring authority through social markers outside of the scientific practices themselves. The most striking of these are special places of work and presentation of work to the public (e.g. laboratories and museums as temples of learning), and places of training (universities): 'real' science, note Chambers and Richards (1995: xiii), is generated in laboratories, research stations and universities. But science also has its rituals, rituals of election to the Royal Society or British Academy, the wearing of distinctive garments, and in art. For example, there is a striking difference between two portraits of Linnaeus: a contemporary likeness commissioned by Linnaeus himself as a Lapp, which we have already encountered (Figure 5.1), and a painting of Linnaeus in Thornton's *Temple of Flora*, published in 1807 (Figure 5.5). In the latter, Linnaeus

From Ethno-science to Science | 125

Figure 5.5. Illustration from R.J. Thornton, *Temple of Flora*, Volume II, 1807, showing Aesculapius, Flora, Ceres and Cupid paying homage to a bust of Linnaeus. Reproduced by permission of the Linnean Society, London.

has been deified, consistent with the enlightenment idea of science as the new religion. Thus, science maintains its separateness and status, and therefore effectiveness, by self-consciously appropriating the sacred and demonstrating again the inescapable intermingling of the symbolic and the technical. This role accorded to individually named scientists in establishing science as an instituted model might appear to be at variance with the concept of science as anonymised intersubjectivity discussed above. However, we need really to draw a distinction between the process by which scientific knowledge is created – in socially instituted instructional contexts and through biographised authors (a process which provides a necessary social legitimation and authority and which provides social rewards to individual scientists) – and its accumulated form as a body of shared knowledge.

The centrality of intersubjectivity and the maintenance of its stability through social means are therefore crucial also because they decentre the self in cognitive terms: science is a distributed process. Thus, while most researchers conceptualise thought as a process in the individual mind, it has been recognised since the work of Vygotsky (1978 [1930]) and Harré (1983) that it may first be social, and that only in later development can we think in certain ways as individuals. It has even been suggested that the social quality of science is reflected in an 'inner dialogue' of individual scientific minds. Thus, 'the social enters into thinking in the form of culturally elaborated methods of using inferences' (Oatley 1996: 135). But it is not simply the transferal of social thinking to the individual mind which is involved, but in addition reliance on social interaction itself to enhance cognitive processes which individual minds are by themselves ill-equipped to undertake. Thus, as Oatley (ibid.: 137) has pointed out, humans are not good at generating examples to disconfirm their own theories, and science would not work with individual knowers and doers. Empirical work in support of these generalisations can be found, for example, in the work of Kevin Dunbar (1995a), who found that most productive conceptual advances in molecular biology occurred in laboratories where there were weekly meetings of researchers from different specialist backgrounds, who were able to engage in analogical reasoning between different parts of the same 'region' of understanding. If something was difficult to understand, analogies drawn from another biochemical system, another subfield, or some other organism were found to be helpful; results could be interpreted from different viewpoints, while confirmation bias was counteracted by one person presenting results and others seeing different interpretations.

The Emergent Cognitive Features of Global Instituted Science

Global science, therefore, as we have come to understand it, is a social process, the product of self-reflective and meta-conceptual thought between consenting adults requiring sophisticated instruction (Carey 1996: 206), and we can only sensibly talk about its distinctive features having first defined it as an instituted process.

Since so much attention in science is paid to boundary maintenance, to effecting the conditions of intersubjectivity, to communication and to social institutionalisation, this in itself suggests that its modes of cognition are less different qualitatively from what pertains in the wider social world than they are by degree. This observation follows from the well-worn anthropological dictum that differences between categories will be emphasised much more where these are not reinforced by multiple perceptual discontinuities (as exemplified in Douglas 1973: 113–93). In turn, such accentuated features are those most likely to be used in promoting self-consciousness in the performance of certain kinds of cognitive operation which are a necessary part of sharing. None in themselves point to a crucial cognitive difference in the way science and ethnoscience work, but all, polythetically, contribute to the way in which we explicitly or implicitly maintain the boundary between science and ordinary thinking, communicating and doing. In the context of global science, I think we can point to six general processes which in the degree to which they are evident serve to distinguish those we call scientists from ethnoscientists.

The Lexicalisation of Implicit Knowledge

Science is a material practice, not just about thinking. Like other forms of knowledge, it is a combination of *conscious representational knowledge* (usually involving reflection: something we are aware of acquiring and using, and often do so purposely in order to solve various technical and social problems), and *bodily knowledge* (acquired and coded as part of doing and recognising in particular practical contexts which require sensory and motor skills that are readily transmitted trans-generationally). In traditional societies (see, for example, Ellen 1999b), much knowledge of the first kind (such as we find in plant and animal nomenclatures) is encoded in language, and is therefore *lexical*. Where this yields regularities in how people conceive relationships between different living kinds, it becomes classificatory knowledge. However, much knowledge, particularly of natural processes, is only partially lexically expressed. Where classificatory knowledge generates categories with no lexical markers, but where knowledge is manifestly evident though not necessarily systematically expressed in language, we might speak of *substantive knowledge*. Most folk knowledge of the biological world is substantive in this sense and classifications can be understood as codes to access and manipulate it. But modern science is also characterised by the degree to which practical procedures are lexicalised and formalised. Whereas in many folk contexts knowledge is not explicitly formulated into a set of rules, but rather acquired through mimicry, experience and informal apprenticeship, in science codification and formal instruction is much more central to learning *how to do things*. Thus, we have dissection manuals, field identification protocols, laboratory practice handbooks and so on. As we have seen, it is institutionalisation which makes this self-conscious instructional component effective, and to recognise its significance is not to deny the crucial role which the transfer of tacit knowledge may have had in actual scientific discoveries.

The Textualisation of Lexical Knowledge

The view associated with Goody (1968, 1977, 1986, 1987), and more recently with Olson (1996: 141), that literacy is the prime mover of qualitative changes in our mode of thinking about the world, and that science and certain kinds of logic were a historical by-product of literacy, must be substantially qualified in the light of other work. It is recognised that different traditions of literacy (say, Arabic versus English, versus Hanunóo) appear to have different implications (Foley 1997: 417–34), that orality and literacy are completely interdependent (Finnegan 1988), that analytic arguments have more to do with marketplace rhetoric than with private literacy (Lloyd 1979), that being literate in many local languages has little effect on cognitive performance, while being schooled in English or some other lingua franca associated with scientific culture can have dramatic effects (Scribner and Cole 1981). Nevertheless, there is equally little doubt that while ethno-science is possible without literacy, science as it has developed in the various scholarly traditions, was institutionalised in the West and has coalesced globally, has become dependent on the 'linear-sentential mode' (Bloch 1991) for its forms of organisation, range of possible sustained cognition manipulations, and on the written word for storing and transmitting knowledge.

The Formalisation of Textual Knowledge

Lexicalisation of data and the textualisation of utterance, as well as the diagrammatic and similar devices that we embed in and interpret through text, permit the routine use of formalised protocols by a community of scientists; that is, certain textual devices can be employed in a systematic way to better retrieve and manipulate information, and to ensure conduct of procedures in the same way everywhere. A formal description of this kind may include everything from the definitive writing-up of a new species according to acceptable taxonomic conventions, the use of anatomical

Latin in a medical diagnosis, a careful drawing of the reproductive organs of a plant, precision syllogism, a Euclidean proof, to the solving of a quadratic equation. Such formal conventions may exist independent of the rest of what we understand of science, but they can make all the difference between our superficial recognition of something as science rather than ethno-science. Thus, while illiterate farmers may year-on-year conduct experiments regarding the utility of different landrace seeds, proper recording on paper and analysis using abstract conventions permits a greater degree of experimental control and comparison. There has in the past been some resistance to the characterisation of science as merely careful perception and description, since it seems to deny the primacy of theory, and fudges the line of separation between, say, the artwork characteristic of the great scholarly traditions (say a Tibetan herbal: see Figure 10.1) and that of European science since the time of Vesalius or the microscopic images of Robert Hooke and Antony van Leeuwenhoek.

In some ways comparable to textual formalisation – and certainly involving the creation of texts such as labels and catalogues – are collections of specimens, whether in museums, laboratories, botanic gardens, herbaria or in living collections of animals. The accumulation of data – whether strictly textual or in some other form – typifies both scholarly and scientific ways of knowing.

Simplification and Abstraction

If textualisation permits more effective formalisation, then formalisation in turn allows for simplification and other forms of second-order manipulation. Data simplification is an essential part of handling large amounts of data, of comparison and therefore of inference. Simplification may be effected through visual depiction (consider, for example, a medical drawing compared with a photograph, or a microphotograph of a histological specimen stained to contrast its component parts), but in general the process is quintessentially associated with the application of mathematics, whether the grouping of like values in an equation, the ordering of statistical data through intervals or some similar procedure. Carey (1996: 206) describes, for example, how physicists translate from physical to mathematical description, look for regularities in the simpler mathematical version, and translate back to define what become physical laws.

The Application of Material Culture

Not only does the creation and dissemination of texts involve its own technology and material culture, but the doing of science from its earliest beginnings as such in the sixteenth century has involved the manufacture and use of instruments. Instrumentation may enhance empirical observation, in the way the microscopy of van Leeuwenhoek and Hooke revolutionised biological depiction, providing prostheses to extend the capacity of available human sensory organs; or they may aid the process of simplification, by – for example – permitting the recreation of organic, physical or behavioural processes in convenient laboratory spaces; or may simulate or model such processes by analogy. In this way, some cognitive practices may become concretised in material form. In addition, the technology of science has become a salient icon of the enterprise itself (the images conjured up by the retort and the test tube), while museums of science when they are not exhibiting the material data of science (plants, animals and minerals for example), comprise collections of tools used in its conduct.

The Routinisation of Intense Criticism and Argumentative Reasoning

Processes 1–5 by themselves might seem to suggest that what separates science from ethno-science is simply a number of mechanistic ways of eliciting, transforming and storing data, in which cognition is situated and distributed, and brain activity consequential and displaced rather than central. But, particularly idealistic, theories of science often put more emphasis on the quality of the reasoning involved. In sub-sections 2–5 I have provided arguments which would seem to cast doubt on this dimension, but it is nevertheless undeniable that we see in the development of modern science the foregrounding of 'a process of intensive criticism' (Dunbar 1995b: 31), the elevation of uncertainty to a matter of principle, a kind of 'argumentative reasoning' involving the systematic and self-reflective coordination of explicit theory and evidence (Carey 1996: 205; Kuhn 1996: 264, 275) in which investigators are able to reflect on their own theories as objects of cognition sufficiently to recognise that they might be wrong, and a methodologically explicit recognition that evidence might disconfirm a theory. Science, in other words, provides a set of tools – perhaps the best set we have – for choosing between rival theories. Modern science also involves cognitive operations – such as induction – which most modern people find intrinsically difficult because the default form of folk explanation involves deduction: testing a pre-existing model of the world or current hypothesis against new data (Oatley 1996: 136). For Carey (1996: 187), following Pierce, the dislodgement of this predisposition requires the ability to recognise and understand the abstract processes of inference: namely abduction, deduction and induction.

Processes 1–6 exist not as intrinsic characteristics of how individual scientists work, but rather are distributed within common institutional practices, in social entities, and in artefacts (such as books). Combined, they permit more effective sharing, codification and transmission of information. They also allow for increasingly stronger inference, logical rigour of description, of testing and of experimentation (Dunbar 1995b: 102); for coordination of theory and evidence (Kuhn 1996: 264) and for inductive reasoning skills, especially those involving causal inferences in a multivariable framework (ibid.: 275). But because science is detached from any one specific local context, these innovations have, most importantly, permitted the aggregation of knowledge from many localities and enabled trans-local generalisation and comparison through globalisation (Hunn 1993: 13–15). Thus, in a sense it was only when Linnaeus went beyond Lappland and applied his taxonomic criteria to 'coconuts and cardamoms' that he was arguably able to transcend what traditional scholarly knowledge systems had achieved (Koerner 1999). Lexicalisation, textualisation, formalisation and abstraction have, therefore, allowed scientific knowledge to escape its local roots, but trans-localism is not in itself unknown in local knowledge systems. Indeed, there is a uniquely human capacity for acquired biological knowledge to diffuse independently of what can be experienced in local habitats. Thus, people may have concepts for snakes, elephants, lions, even dragons, even though they have never seen one. Scientific biology is, in one sense, an extreme development of such an 'intuitive biology', augmented by the possibilities offered by effective cultural transmission, since the capacity to generalise and hypothesise is grounded in the way science aggregates knowledge of species and ecologies beyond what a scientist might have local first-hand experience of as a non-scientist. The corollary is that writing it down, the very thing which makes it more portable and permanent, also changes some of its fundamental properties, all of which reinforce dislocation. As several generations of development advisors have discovered, general comparative truths may often be at variance with the truth in a particular locality.

Conclusion

This chapter was originally published as part of a special issue of the *Journal of Cognition and Culture* devoted to the cognitive anthropology of science, yet I am claiming that science can never be wholly defined in cognitive terms. Science is not simply a way of thinking, but involves ways of doing (technical practices) and ways of representing (social practices), both to other scientists and to non-scientists. I also argue that although we need to distinguish between a general human aptitude for 'science' which is simultaneously pan-cultural and cognitive, and the socially constructed global science which has emerged since the seventeenth century, we must recognise the continuities between the two. Indeed, we will never understand modern global science, cognitively or otherwise, unless we look at it in the context of ordinary forms of reasoning and those specialist forms we call ethno-sciences. We need an integrated theory of science which incorporates them both, since continually redrawing the Rubicon will not work. Indeed, any approach which begins by reinventing a new version of the great cognitive divide, by opposing two meta-categories – science and traditional knowledge – is doomed to failure.

Because what counts as 'indigenous knowledge' is so protean and extensive, to claim that it is comparable or not comparable to science is misleading, a diversion from the real issue. It is not, in my view, particularly helpful to define indigenous knowledge as everything science is not, or in terms of tables of discrete opposing characteristics. While it may be useful as a beginning to characterise it as local, performative, organic, holistic, intuitive, socially constrained, practical, incremental and egalitarian, in contrast to modern global science which is rationalistic, reductionist, theoretical, generalisable, objectively verifiable, abstract, non-contextual, universal, based on cause-and-effect, and imperialistic, given the diversity of traditional knowledges, these sets of opposites do not take us very far, and exceptions and additions can always be found. The indigenous ethno-sciences can include propositional statements, experimental evidence, mathematical thinking and literacy. And while science may challenge the credibility of indigenous knowledge as science, the diversity of all that purports to be, or is by default treated as, indigenous knowledge, makes any kind of generalisation hazardous. Professional scientists and others have coped with this diversity and fluidity by essentialising, freezing, commodifying it, breaking it down into conveniently absorbable, observable and representational modules. But what we have to deal with as a result of such transformations and manipulations, even in some of the anthropological descriptions of indigenous knowledge, is something different, almost chimerical. I have – therefore – taken the view that the category of indigenous knowledge (which we may take to comprise the plethora of ethno-sciences) arises by default, as a counterpoint to what we call science, and is constructed largely on the basis of the kind of knowledge it is not. And as I have argued in Chapter 4, indigenous knowledge of a very important kind is ever present and constantly being reinvented to cope with new circumstances, existing as kind of buffer, an intuitive, informal knowledge which endures and inheres at every technical and social interface, and which enables technologies based on more formal abstract knowledge to work (cf. Fischer 2004).

But it is not just the antithesis – indigenous knowledge, the ethno-sciences – which defies placement in a single meta-category, but the thesis also. Science too exhibits disunity as a theorised set of practices, and the vested interest which scientists understandably have in maintaining a clear boundary between science and non-science is thus ever challenging. Unhelpfully, methods and criteria which might assist in precisely stating where the boundary lies tend to change from time to time, and from subject to subject (Barnes, Bloor and Henry 1996: 140), and as these boundaries change so certain theories become more marginalised, until they slip over the edge into non-acceptability. So, what is it that makes evolutionary psychology science, and cold fusion, scientology or psycho-analysis not? But despite the polythetic character of science, the fuzziness of its boundaries and the complexity of its historic interconnections with other knowledge systems, and despite the formidable difficulties of representing the totality of relations between kinds of knowledge, this does not mean that it is therefore impossible to describe or compare the cognitive, representational and social contours of different knowledge systems.

Within anthropology too, strong views exist as to what is scientific and what is not, as the ongoing factionalism between post-modernism and 'scientific' anthropology attests (Kuznar 1997). Indeed, in anthropology the debate may be even more intense because it is fratricidal, and because what separates one side from the other is sometimes philosophical sentiment as much as technical practice. Those who have tried to make sense of this grey area, and show how the boundaries between science and non-science uncomfortably correlate with convenient ideological and social currents, are sometimes accused of being engaged in some kind of pseudo-science themselves (Laudan 1981), or more straightforwardly of relativism. While some approaches to understanding how science works as theory and practice do make it sound like *no more than* pernicious ideology, text, 'rhetoric, persuasion and the pursuit of power' (Wolpert 1992: 117), we are always dealing with degrees of truth and plausibility. Since science is dependent on metaphors and cultural constructs to determine shared knowledge, and is conducted by sentient persons with values and social differences in intersubjective space, it will always be only *sufficiently precise,* but for all that a remarkably reliable model of the world.

Notes

First published in 2004 as 'From Ethno-science to Science, or "What the Indigenous Knowledge Debate Tells Us About How Scientists Define Their Project"' in the *Journal of Cognition and Culture* [4 (3-4), 409–450]. Reproduced courtesy of Brill.

1. See, e.g., the editorials (Anon 1999a, 1999b) and correspondence (Diamond 1986; Johannes 1987) in *Nature*. See also ICSU 2002.
2. Linnaeus exaggerated his dependency on Lapp knowledge and included various sleight-of-hand textual and illustrative devices in his *Flora Lapponica* to increase his scientific authority; he assembled a Saami costume for his grand tour of Europe and embroidered his travel tales. For Koerner (1999: 64), his 'Lappland invention' passed beyond 'self-aggrandisement' and 'became governed by a central fantasy: the coloniser masquerading as the colonised'. As for Linnaean lists generally, minerals were followed by plants, animals, and local technologies and ethnography. On a conceptual level, and within the master plot of import substitution that governed his natural history, Linnaeus had three Lapland strategies: to harvest natural resources; to support dairy and grain farming; and to introduce exotic cultivars (Koerner 1999: 77).
3. There is dispute as to whether folk biology is a non-theoretical innate core module, a congenitally innate module, an intuitive theory, or a framework theory constructed during the first decade of life (Carey 1996: 192; Keil 1992, 1994). For Carey (1996: 193), for example, the position espoused by Atran (and Sperber) that folk biology is a non-theoretical innate core module is problematic 'because features of folk biology which emerge in early childhood are not domain specific, and because those features which are domain specific are probably neither innate nor theory-neutral, because they fail to confront [the] full implications of perception, and because they face the "problem of theory-laden attribution"'. While Atran wants taxonomy and essentialism to be both biological and pretheoretical (ibid.: 196), for Carey they are 'plausibly innate but not specific to folk biological classification, and true only as properties of the adult system'. In support of this she cites child study data from the US and Nigeria (ibid.: 199) which suggest that only by age 10 does general reasoning become incorporated as intuitive biology, thus supporting Atran's claim that folk biological understanding is part of universal folk taxonomy but conflicting with his vision that this is part of an innate cognitive model. She concludes that there is no good evidence to see folk biology as an innate module like language, number, reasoning about objects, or reasoning about persons, but that it is rather a 'framework theory' (ibid.: 189).

CHAPTER 6

Local and Scientific Understandings of Forest Diversity

Introduction

Foresters, biogeographers and tropical forest ecologists have devised increasingly sophisticated classifications of forest types (e.g. Eyre 1980). Forest 'types' and their more localised and discrete components, which might variously be described as 'habitats', 'niches', 'biotopes' and 'ecotones', constitute what ecologists understand by 'secondary biodiversity': that is, diversity in terms of associations of species rather than the (primary) diversity measured in terms of the numbers of species (or other taxonomic categories). Although the classifications of foresters in particular have been largely determined by the practical considerations of the industry, during the latter part of the twentieth century they have been much influenced by the developing science of forest ecology, and the technologies of remote sensing (Howard 1991) and Global Information Systems (GIS) (C.A. Johnston 1998). The typologies of forest ecologists, while originally rooted in those of foresters, have become increasingly distanced from them in an attempt to model more accurately the dynamic character of forest diversity.

Although the pragmatic schemes used by national forest departments have often responded to local situations by incorporating categories that anthropologists would describe as 'folk', 'emic' or 'indigenous', on the whole the practice of modern forestry has markedly diverged from the representations of secondary biodiversity that these imply (see, e.g., Muraille 2000: 74–77). I shall show in this chapter how the categories and coordinates applied by Nuaulu in eastern Indonesia contrast with most official functional classifications of tropical forest type, in being dynamic, multidimensional, not tied to complex nomenclatures, and unashamedly *local*. I shall show how they anticipate recent modelling attempts in scientific ecology that emphasise the patchiness of tropical rainforest.[1] Studies of tropical forest peoples have revealed not only an extensive native knowledge of trees, but also local recognition of forest diversity and the existence of coherent vernacular classifications of forest types. The evidence suggests some variation in nomenclatural and classificatory patterns. Work in the Amazon region, for example, has reported folk classifications of considerable complexity (e.g. Shepard et al. 2001; Shepard, Yu and Nelson 2004; Fleck and Harder 2000: 1–3), which do not appear to be matched by comparable data from, for example, Southeast Asia and New Guinea [Chapter 7 in the present volume; also Sillitoe 1998]. However, my concern here is with the commonalities that such studies yield, using Nuaulu data as a point of departure; and with a comparison between ethnoecological classifications of tropical forest in general and those offered by scientists and officials. Thus, we are dealing with issues of *scale*, which as Sillitoe (2002a, 2002b) has shown, have increasingly become critical in judging the appropriateness of local and global knowledge respectively in the context of development practices.

There is one further important point which needs to be registered before embarking on this specific analysis, which is that technical forestry practice, especially including the typologies it has devised, was first formalised and institutionalised, and indeed continues, within an overt political context, which has shaped its underlying assumptions. Thus, in Indonesia, as in many other places, the definition and demarcation of land as 'forest' during the colonial period can be seen as a very concrete 'territorialisation strategy' in which first the colonial state (Boomgard 1994) and then an independent republic manifested its existence and legitimated its jurisdiction. Through the 'administrative ordering of nature', the remit of the state was made 'legible' (Scott 1998: 2, 4). Thus, forestry departments became one of the most important agencies in territorialising state power, and inevitably in doing so had the effect of simplifying the 'illegible' cacophony of local property regulations and communal tenure, which presented itself as an administrative nightmare (ibid.: 35, 37). But the process of simplification and of inscribing legibility had the consequence of excluding and including people within particular geographic boundaries and of controlling their access to natural resources; it provided the inevitable grounds for conflicts with local perceptions and values. In such a situation, 'tribal' peoples, already a 'problem' because of their administrative peripherality, became even more so through a forestry policy defined in such a way as to deny any merit in forms of extraction other than for timber, and which especially demonised swiddening or long fallow forms of agriculture (Dove 1983; Dove et al. 2007; Persoon et al. 2004: 26). And whereby the forested territory of the modern state could be understood in basically linear, abstract and homogenous terms as the monothetic management of wood, this is quite the opposite of how local people experience forest, or indeed any other kind of space (Vandergeest and Peluso 1995: 388–89; cf. Sivaramakrishnan 2000).

The main evidence that legitimated this new control, and therefore the problems which subsequently arose, were maps (cf. Dove et al. 2007). In other words, the territorialisation strategy only effectively became a reality as competent cartographic surveys were conducted, especially, but not exclusively, those which remapped forest on the basis of scientific criteria, such as soil type, slope, vegetation and timber utility, or what Vandergeest and Peluso (1995: 408) call 'functional territorialisation'. In the context of Indonesia, this emergence of an ideology of state forestry and of state and scientific classifications of land, as well as the very idea of the 'management' of natural resources (Ellen 2003b), happened first in colonial Java, with the establishment in 1808 of the Dienst van het [Ost-Indische] Boschwezen and the Administratie der Houtbosschen (Anon. 1917: 390; Boomgard 1994: 119; Departemen Kehutanan 1986; Peluso 1992: 6–8, 44–45). In the distant Moluccas, and on Seram in particular, such practices did not become a reality until the Topographische Dienst survey of 1917, which I shall return to in the final section of this chapter. But the conceptions of forest space that accompany this strategy are differentiated from pre-existing local conceptions again in terms of scale.

Methods for Studying Local Representations and Understandings of Forest Diversity

In order to understand how Nuaulu conceive and use their classification of types of forest, it is important to show in detail the composition and ecological character of the kinds of forest which they label. This entails the use of a plot methodology, in which all flora above a certain size and other features occurring in a specified area are logged, mapped and named with the help of local people. But one of the problems of comparing different compositional studies of tropical forest on a global scale has been inconsistency in the size of the plots, or quadrats, employed. The majority of ecological studies have relied upon plots of between 0.63 and 1.2 ha, most commonly 1 ha (e.g. Valencia, Balslev and Paz y Miño 1994; Richards 1996). While the problems of quadrat surveys generally have been widely discussed (e.g. Kershaw 1973; Kent and Coker 1992), in ethnobotany the problems are, if anything, greater, despite there being a smaller number of studies to which to refer (Martin 1995: 157–59). Rectangular plots, where one side is considerably longer than the other, have been used by Boom (1989), for example belt transects of 10 m by 1000 m in his work amongst the Chácobo of northern Brazil, and 40 m by 10 m plots have been used by Puri (2005) working among Penan Benalui in east Kalimantan. But most plots have conventionally been square, for example the use by Salick (1989: 191) of stratified random 5 m by 5 m plots to sample Amuesha swiddens. Bernstein, Ellen and Antaran (1997) used 0.23 ha (48 m by 48 m) plots divided into four quadrats in their work amongst the Brunei Dusun. Allan (2002: 137), in her Guyana work, used a plot size of 0.25 ha (50 m by 50 m) because the locally defined (largely Makushi) forest types often did not extend over areas large enough or symmetrical enough to allow a larger plot to be established within the forest type. Sillitoe (1998) has even used 10 m by 10 m quadrats to measure differences in tree flora.

Although the size of a plot must ultimately be determined by research objectives and practicalities, Greig-Smith (1964: 28–29) identifies two problems with smaller quadrats: that there is a greater chance of significant edge effects (due to an observer consistently including individuals which ought to be excluded); and that the frequency distribution for individuals is more likely to be Poisson than normal, with the magnitude of the variance related to the mean. This latter makes it difficult to apply some of the usual statistical procedures for comparing populations. The first effect can be corrected by including individual trees which fall on the edge of the plot only if 50 per cent or more of their canopy area is judged to fall within the plot; otherwise they are excluded. But although fieldworkers may make every effort to apply this rule consistently, it is inevitably a subjective assessment, and there will always be an unknown level of observer error. This must be acknowledged as a limitation of the data collected in plots of this size. The second problem identified by Greig-Smith can be tested for and potentially corrected using data transformation.

In 1996 the Nuaulu were a group of some two thousand individuals, engaged in swidden cultivation, sago extraction, hunting and forest extraction in lowland central Seram in the Indonesian province of Maluku, the Moluccas (Map 6.1). In that year I conducted eleven plot surveys in forest that Nuaulu exploited and which was acknowledged as belonging to them. The intention was to sample from as wide a range of mixed forest vegetation as possible with which Nuaulu were actively interacting. Deliberately excluded from the sample area were mangrove, littoral biotopes, groves and plantations, recently abandoned garden land, and swamp forest predominantly covered in sago (*Metroxylon sagu*). Also, because Nuaulu seldom extract from forest above 1,000 m asl (above sea level), mountain habitats above this altitude were excluded. As in some earlier studies (Allan 2002; Alcorn 1995; M. Johnston 1998; Sillitoe 1998), the object of the surveys was to obtain botanical composition data for locally recognised forest types, and for this reason plots were placed within areas identified by local informants as indicative of a particularly salient forest type, and within the range of that type, in locations which were relatively accessible. This inevitably resulted in a non-random, non-systematic distribution, which limited the quantitative analysis that could be performed on the data, and reduced their value as sources for a general ecological survey of the forest. It must, therefore, be borne in mind that the aim was an analysis of ethnoecological knowledge of different emically defined areas and not a study of forest ecology. The general characteristics of the plots surveyed, and their geographic location are indicated in Table 6.1 and Map 3.1 respectively.

Plots 1 to 6 were each 400 m² (20 x 20 m), and plots 7, 8, 9 and 11 were each 900 m² (30 x 30 m). Plot 10 was 430 m². The large 900 m² plots were surveyed because particular features of the plot were judged to be intrinsically interesting: plot 7 being sacred protected forest, plot 8 an area on the fringe of recent settlement, plot 9 a high-altitude site traditionally used for collecting *Agathis* resin, and plot 11 an old village site. All measurements were of surface areas, but surfaces that were often on steep slopes. Although angle of slope was measured, plot maps and density data were accordingly distorted: the steeper the slope, the greater the distortion.

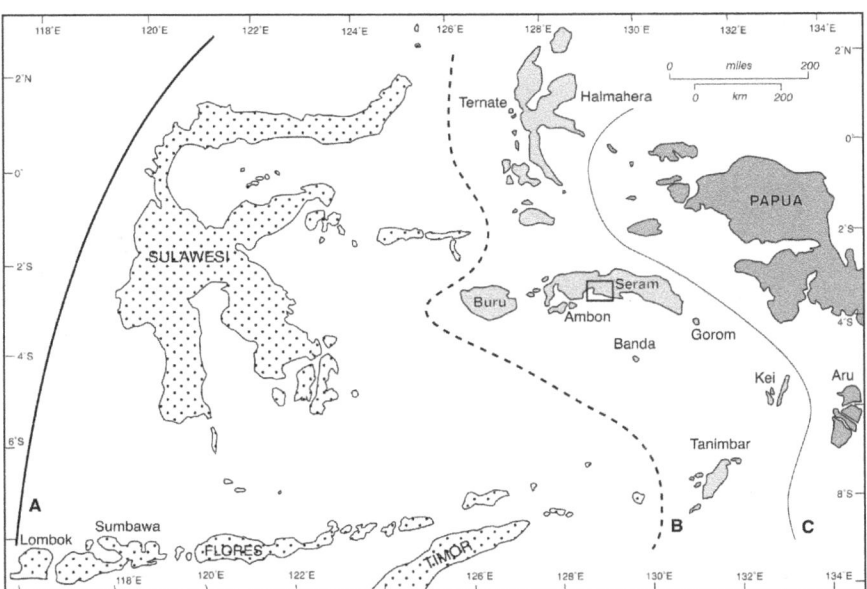

Map 6.1. Seram in the context of the eastern Indonesian archipelago, showing places mentioned in the text. Line A represents Wallace's Line of faunal balance, Line B is Weber's Line, and Line C is the western boundary of the Australo-Pacific region. The box indicates the area enlarged in Map 3.1. Map created by the author.

140 | Nature Wars

Table 6.1. Basic data on location and description of plots.

Plot number	Toponym	Location	Nuaulu description	Summary ecology	Altitude (m)	Distance from Rouhua (km)
1	Nahati Sanai	Near river Makoihiru	*nisi ahue*	Edge of cultivated area, depleted mixed forest	200	3.75
2	Mon	On river Mon, near Rouhua	*wesie*	Edge of cultivated area, depleted mixed forest	150	4.25
3	Nahane Hukune	Sama, north of Rouhua	*wesie*	Depleted forest, near logging road	200	2.00
4	Ratipanisa	Garden land on river Yoko, near Rouhua	*nisi ahue*	20 year old regrowth	100	0.75
5	Besi	Between Iana Ikine and Iana Onate	*nia monai*	Old settlement site	300	3.00
6	Iana Onate Matai	Garden site near river Upa	*nisi ahue*	30 year old regrowth	50	2.50
7	Mon Sanae	Head of river Mon, near Rouhua	*sin wesie*	Protected sacred forest (clan Peinisa)	300	4.50
8	Sokonana	Near transmigration site on river Ruatan	*wesie*	Debris of cut trees, far from gardens near new road	100	25.0
9	Rohnesi near Wae Sune Maraputi	West of trans-Seram highway	*wesie*	High altitude undisturbed forest	900	70.0
10	Wae Pia	East of trans-Seram highway near Tihasamane, Tanaa valley	*wesie*	Lowland forest	200	55.0
11	Amatene	Above headwaters of Iana river, trib. of Upa	*nia monai*	Old village site	400	5.00

Another problem associated with plot size was that small plots tended to underestimate species richness compared with larger plots in the same area. Figure 6.1 shows the relationship between the number of species and size of plot, from 0.05 to 0.5 ha, as used in a number of Moluccan studies. The inclination of the species-area curve is roughly consistent with species-area curves obtained in other studies of lowland rainforest in island Southeast Asia; though Edwards et al. (1990: 168, figure 15.2a) found that curves in the Manusela National Park generally flattened out at 0.25 ha, suggesting that enlarging plot size further would not have added more species. I shall return to a consideration of the implications of this pattern in the next section.

Each plot was surveyed with a minimum team of three adult males. They were not always the same persons, but there was a marked overlap in membership. All team members were trained in the use of measuring, marking and enumeration techniques before each survey. Plots identified by me were first measured and marked up using a 30-m fibreglass retractable tape and spray paint. Plants were included in the survey if they were 10 cm dbh (diameter at breast height) or above, effectively restricting the census to trees and large lianas. The 10 cm threshold has become standard practice, although it has been demonstrated (Valencia, Balslev and Paz y Miño 1994) that only counting trees over 10 cm dbh can underestimate the diversity of woody species present as saplings. The location of each tree above 10 cm dbh was marked on prepared graph paper and an inde-

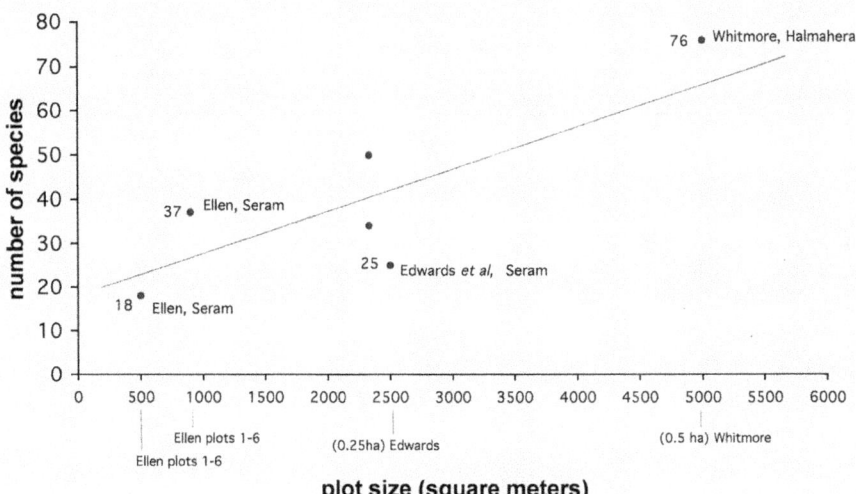

Figure 6.1. Species numbers in relation to plot size for various forest composition studies in the Moluccas. Figure created by the author.

pendent Nuaulu identification sought from each field assistant present. If there was any disagreement, discussion was allowed to see whether agreement might be reached or whether informants would agree to disagree. Where possible, voucher specimens were collected, including bark and wood, but seldom (especially for tall trees) fertile specimens. We would then move on to the next tree, and the same sequence would be repeated. Back in the village, voucher specimens would be further discussed, fully documented, preserved by drying or in alcohol-soaked newspaper. All specimens, collected in triplicate where possible, were checked and sorted at the Indonesian National Herbarium in Bogor. One set was retained in Bogor, a second was sent to Kew, and the third set deposited in the Ethnobiology Laboratory of the University of Kent. All systematic data were entered into the Nuaulu Ethnobotanical Database (NED). In the field, local names obtained during plot surveys were checked against earlier data entered into the NED, and revisions made as necessary, often involving further consultation with informants. Where voucher specimens were absent or insufficient, photographs, drawings and visual descriptions were used in combination with standard reference manuals. Where Nuaulu were also able to provide Ambonese Malay terms, these were matched where possible against standard lists of Moluccan tree species with vernacular glosses (e.g. Whitmore, Tantra and Sutisna 1989), but always back-translated several times in different contexts to minimise erroneous determinations. Table 6.2 lists the total number of standing trees recorded for each plot compared with: (a) numbers of trees for which Nuaulu informants

Table 6.2. Summary of selected 1996 plot data: levels of identification.

	Plot	1	2	3	4	5	6	7	8	9	10	11
1	N	34	30	37	26	28	54	124	116	80	35	68
2	N with Nuaulu name[a]	34[b]	28	37	26	28	54	124[b]	115	74	35	68[b]
3	Percentage N identified with agreed Nuaulu name	100	93	100	100	100	100	100	99	94	100	100
4	N identified to family level	30	25	35	25	16	50	108	98	54	25	68
5	N identified to generic level	20	21	32	24	16	49	103	90	37	25	58
6	N identified to species level	5	12	19	24	1	38	46	41	29	12	40

Key: N= number of standing trees 10 dbh or above; [a] = name agreed by minimum of three adult male field assistants; [b] = one doubtful.

could provide names, and (b) botanical identifications to different levels of taxonomic specificity obtained from the various authorities consulted. Although phylogenetic identifications have not been obtained for all vouchers (in some cases even to generic level), and there are some plot trees for which vouchers were not obtained, the general pattern of identification demonstrates a strong correlation between vernacular names provided and scientific species, suggesting that measures of species density, for example, might reasonably rely on vernacular names as proxies where determinations are unavailable.

The Ecology of Lowland Rainforest on Seram and the Classification of Vegetation Types

If we compare the forest composition of Seram with that of the large islands of Western Indonesia (Borneo and Sumatra) and New Guinea, it is clear that Seram lies in a zone of transition (Wallacea) between the predominantly Dipterocarp forests of Sunda (Asia) and the Australo-Pacific tree flora of Sahul (Oceania) (Figure 6.1). As we move eastwards, Dipterocarpaceae fade out and are replaced by other characteristic families, such as (in lowland areas) Myrtaceae (particularly the distinctive Eucalypts), Myristicaceae, Lauraceae and Guttiferae (Edwards et al. 1993: 66, table 2a; Glatzel 1992: 17–18). This same pattern is confirmed by my own data (Table 6.3), with the most numerous families represented in the Nuaulu plots being Myrtaceae, Myristicaceae and Guttiferae.

The Manusela National Park study, conducted in 1987 (Edwards et al. 1993), was primarily concerned with altitudinal variation. It was based on nine 0.25 ha (i.e. 50 m by 50 m) permanent sample plots at a range of altitudes from sea level to 2,500 asl south of Gunung Binaiya on the central mountain spine. There were two sequences, one over calcareous rocks and the other over non-calcareous rocks. Both show that soil pH decreases with altitude while organic carbon increases. In addition to a lowland zone (the primary focus of the present analysis), the Manusela study yielded data distinguishing alpine, sub-alpine (characterised by shrubby *Rhododendron*), montane (high-altitude tree fern grassland), and lower montane zones, the latter with an upper band dominated by Myrtaceae and Lauraceae, and a lower band by Fagaceae. The dominant species of lowland and lower montane forest (which occur at a lower altitude on smaller mountains, and are therefore of some interest to us here) are reported for four plots as, respectively: *Drypetes longifolia, Planchonella nitida* and *Astronia macrophylla; Lithocarpus* sp., *Litsea robusta* and *Shorea* sp.; *Lithocarpus* sp. and *Weinmannia*; and *Phyllocladus hypophyllus,* Myrtaceae

144 | *Nature Wars*

Table 6.3. Family frequencies for individual trees in 1996 plots.

Family	Plot 1	Plot 2	Plot 3	Plot 4	Plot 5	Plot 6	Plot 7	Plot 8	Plot 9	Plot 10	Plot 11	Total
MYRTACEAE	6	1	4	1	6	1	16	17	11	8	15	86
MYRISTACEAE		2	2		2	7	6	21		6		46
EUPHORBIACEAE	13	2		1	5	2	7		3	1	11	46
GUTTIFERAE	1		5				5	8	17	4		40
ARECACEAE		4				21	4		2	1	3	35
MORACEAE	1			17	1		8	1		2	3	33
FABACEAE	1	1	1	1		3	4	3	4		7	25
POLYPODIACEAE								23				23
LAURACEAE	1	2	1	1			7	2	4			18
BURSERACEAE			4	2		1	7	3			1	18
ANNONACEAE		2				1	11	3				17
EBENACEAE	2		1		1	1	8	1				14
LEEACEAE		3				3	5					12
RUBIACEAE	3	2					4		1		1	11
ROSACEAE			3			1	2	1	3			10
DIPTEROCARPACEAE			10									10
LOGANIACEAE						1					7	8
OLEACEAE			2					6				8
VERBENACEAE	2			1			2		2		1	8
STERCULIACEAE					3		1		1		2	7
MELIACEAE		3			1	1	2					7
LECYTHIDACEAE			1				5					6
APOCYNACEAE							2				3	5
PANDANACEAE					2						3	5
ARAUCARIACEAE									4			4
MELASTOMACEAE						1	2		1			4
POACEAE						1					3	4
ELAEOCARPACEAE			1								3	4
MALVACEAE											3	3
ANACARDIACEAE						1					2	3
FLACOURTACEAE						3						3
Eight families with two or fewer trees	3	1		1	3	1	3	1		13		
Unidentified		4	5	2	1	12	4	16	18	27	10	99

and *Trimenia*. By comparison, in the eleven Nuaulu plots (Tables 6.3 and 6.4), there are 39 families represented overall. There are no clear dominants in one, and in the others the dominants are Euphorbs and *Syzygium*; *Shorea selanica*; *Artocarpus integer*; Myrtaceae and *Mallotus*; *Areca catechu*; Myrtaceae and *Annona reticulata*, *Polymatodes nigrescens* and *Myristica*; *Calophyllum inophyllum*; *Syzygium* and *Myristica*; and finally Myrtaceae and *Macaranga involucrata*. In other words, despite a strong similarity between the Manusela data and my own at the family level, the only overlap of dominants at the generic level is with respect to *Shorea* (a genus which is numerically quite untypical of the Moluccas) and the important Myrtaceae genera, no doubt including *Syzygium* and *Eugenia*. The explanation for this difference may in part lie in the deliberate bias in the Nuaulu plots in favour of anthropogenic vegetation, but it also reflects the general diversity and patchiness of species composition of lowland rainforest on Seram below 1,000 m (mostly on low hill land), which had been evident from my work in 1970–71, at a time when there were no detailed studies of forest ecology for Seram (Ellen 1978: 67–68). Table 6.4 provides a summary of 1996 Nuaulu plot data for floristics and forest structure (see also Figures 6.2, 6.3 and 6.4).

Figure 6.2. Looking eastwards along the Nua valley towards Mount Binaiya from Notone Hatae on the trans-Seram highway; midway between the south coast and Sawai on the north coast, but on the southern watershed. Apart from the roadside strip, all forest here is described simply as *wesie*, and consists of long-term regenerated forest and forest which has not obviously been modified by humans. March 1996 (96-11-20). Photograph by the author.

Table 6.4. Summary of plot data: floristics and forest structure.

	Plot	Size (m²)	Alt.	N	S	N/m²	S/m²	H	E	1/D	Most Frequent Family/Genus (N reported for taxon)
1	Nahati	400	200	34	20	0.085	0.05	2.75	0.92	18.10	EUPHORBIACEAE (13), MYRTACEAE, *Syzygium* sp. (6)
2	Mon	400	150	30	21	0.075	0.053	3.01	0.99	48.33	ARECACEAE (4)
3	Nahane hukune	400	200	37	16	0.093	0.04	2.47	0.89	10.74	DIPTEROCARPACEAE *Shorea selanica* (10) GUTTIFERAE *Calophyllum inophyllum* (5)
4	Yoko	400	100	26	9	0.065	0.023	1.41	0.64	2.39	MORACEAE *Artocarpus integer* (17)
5	Benteng	400	300	28	9	0.07	0.023	1.77	0.80	4.97	MYRTACEAE (6) EUPHORBIACEAE *Mallotus* sp. (5)
6	Yana Onate	400	50	54	22	0.14	0.055	2.79	0.90	13.25	ARECACEAE (mainly *Areca catechu* (21) MYRISTACEAE (7)
7	Mon sanae	900	300	124	47	0.14	0.052	3.62	0.94	38.32	MYRTACEAE (16) ANNONACEAE *Annona reticulata* (11)
8	Sokonana	900	100	116	33	0.13	0.037	3.05	0.87	15.02	POLYPODIACEAE *Polymatodes nigrescens* (23) MYRTACEAE *Myristica* (17)
9	Rohnesi	900	900	80	28	0.089	0.031	2.92	0.88	14.77	GUTTIFERAE *Calophyllum inophyllum* (17)
10	Wae Pia	430	200	35	21	0.081	0.05	2.88	0.94	23.8	MYRTACEAE *Syzygium* sp. (8) MYRISTACEAE (Mainly *Myristica* sp.) (6)
11	Amatene	900	400	68	26	0.076	0.03	2.98	0.91	18.67	MYRTACEAE (15) EUPHORBIACEAE *Macaranga involucrata* (11)

Key: N = number of trees. S = number of species (see *Note*) = species richness. N/m² = tree density. S/m² = species density. H = Shannon diversity index: the value of H increases with both species richness and equitability (evenness with which individuals are distributed among the species). E = equitability H/lnS, 1 being where individuals are most evenly distributed amongst the species, and 0 being the least. D = Simpson's index of dominance: as D increases, diversity decreases. Simpson's index is therefore expressed as 1/D.

Note: S and formulae incorporating S are derived from Nuaulu vernacular terms for trees, and therefore an assumed equivalence between Nuaulu terms and taxonomic species.

Local and Scientific Understandings of Forest Diversity | 147

Figure 6.3. Plot 8. Riparian forest at Sokonana, north of the Ruatan river. February 1996 (96-08-25). Photograph by the author.

Both montane and lowland plots surveyed on Seram display low species diversity compared with many rainforests in the far east (Whitmore 1984), species declining with altitude above 600 m. If we take the mean of all plots (n = 4) within the altitude range 0–1,900 reported by Edwards et al. (1993) – that is, covering approximately the same altitudinal range as the Nuaulu plots, and including both lowland and sub-montane areas – the number of species per plot is 25. Species number for the Nuaulu plots was higher, even though plot size was smaller. Assuming an approximately proportionate increase in species number with plot size (Figure 6.1), Nuaulu species numbers for a 0.25 ha plot would likely be between 35 and 50, and projected to 0.5 ha then around 75. In terms of the index of species richness ($d = S/\sqrt{N}$), the Manusela data give a mean of 2.14 (range = 1.44 > 2.99, where N = 4) and the Nuaulu data a mean of 3.32 (range = 1.7 > 5.6, where N = 11). Whitmore, Sidiyasa and Whitmore (1987), in an enumeration study carried out on Halmahera at 630 m asl, recorded 76 species > 10 cm dbh, from 31 families within a 0.5 ha plot, giving a species richness index of 3.94, slightly higher than both the Manusela and Nuaulu data. Sidiyasa and Tantra (1984), working in the northern part of the Manusela National Park (Wae Mual), provide a very low species richness index of 0.97 for lowland rainforest, even for Seram. In contrast, a 1 ha plot in Brunei (Poulsen et al. 1996) had 550 trees, 231 species and an index of species richness of 9.85. The low species richness values reported for Seram, compared with Borneo (see also Proctor et al. 1983) or New Guinea (Paijmans 1970), appear to be related to the recent geological emergence of the island and the varying levels of isolation over a six million year period (Audley-Charles 1993).

There have been various attempts to distinguish distinct forest types for Seram, beginning with the colonial forestry department, and its successor in independent Indonesia (Departemen Kehutanan 1986). Map 6.2, for example, shows superimposed official forestry categories on a map of South Seram. More instructive, from an ecological standpoint, is the typology presented by Glatzel (1992: 17–18), based on work conducted in West Seram by the Agricultural Faculty of Pattimura University, in the same area in which the ethnobotanical work of Suharno (1997) was subsequently conducted (Table 6.5). What is significant about these official typologies, as we shall see, is their general lack of congruence with local folk classifications.

We now know that tropical rainforest is a less stable and more diverse vegetational regime than once thought, and that a great deal of forest, especially lowland forest, is relatively recent regrowth, much of it following human interventions. Little was known about the timescale of secondary successions at the time of Richards' classic benchmark study (1996 [1952]:

Local and Scientific Understandings of Forest Diversity | 149

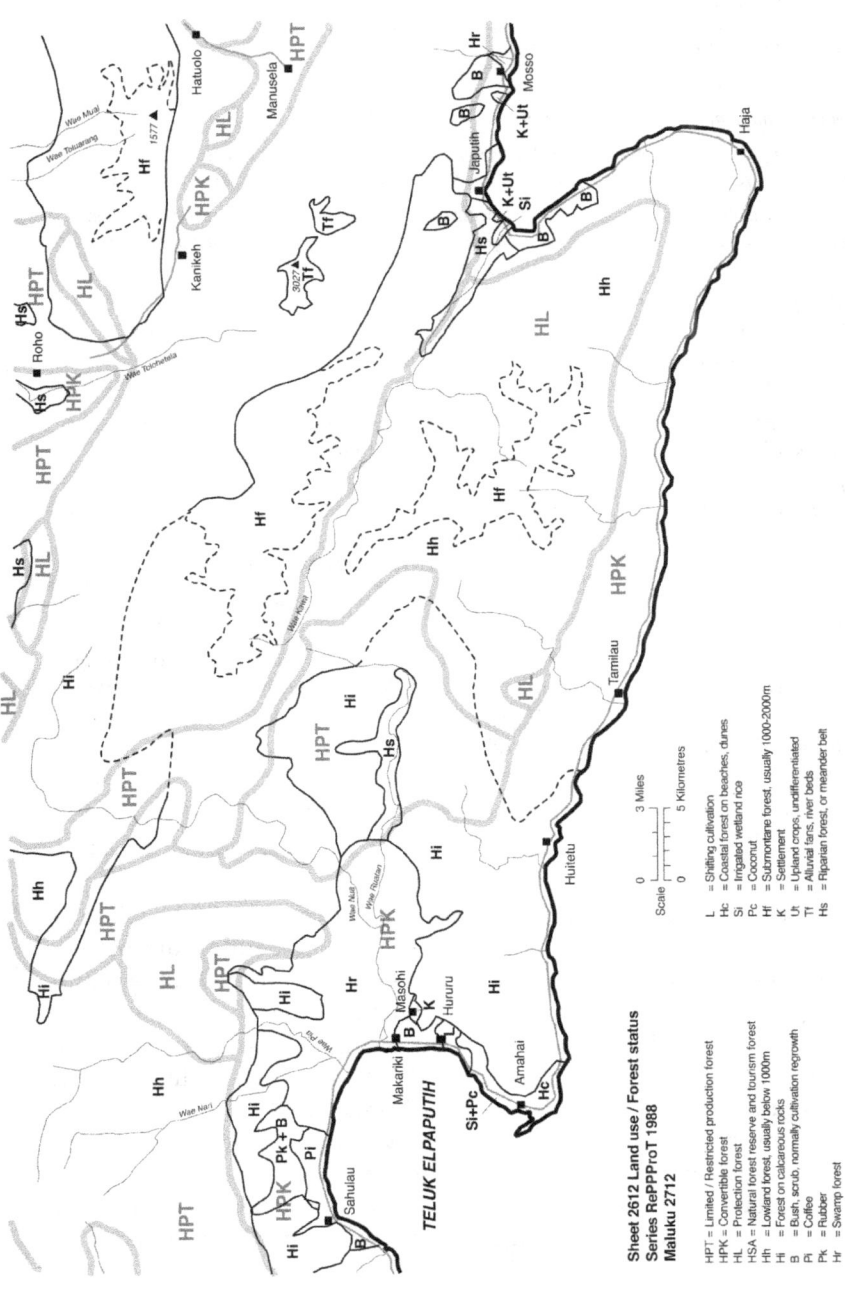

Map 6.2. South Seram, showing superimposed official forestry categories. Map created by the author, based on Original source Sheet 2612 Land use/Forest status Series RePPProT 1988 Maluku 2712.

Table 6.5. Forest types distinguished by Pattimura University Agricultural Faculty survey team and utilised by Glatzel (1992).

	Species association	Notes
1	*Imperata-Melaleuca* grassland	
2	*Melaleuca-Imperata* woodland	As 1, but *Pteridium* also characteristic
3	*Strombosia phillipensis* dense evergreen forest	*Anthocephalus macrophyllus, Vitex cofassus, Octomeles sumatrana, Macaranga* sp., *Pandanus* on disturbed sites
4	*Vitex-Pterocarpus* dense evergreen forest	No pronounced dominants. Most common species: *Vitex cofassus, Myristica insipia, Pterocarpus indicus, Eleaocarpus sphaericus*
5	*Anthocephalus-Intsia* dense evergreen forest	
6	*Intsia-Pterocarpus* dense evergreen forest	
7	*Canarium-Myristica* dense evergreen forest	Easy to walk in: dominants include *Canarium indicum, Myristica insipida* and *Pterocarpus indicus*
8	*Puteria-Metrosideros* dense evergreen forest	No real dominants, but common species include *Puteria obovata, Metrosideros vera, Calophyllum inophyllum, Litsea* sp., *Elaeocarpus sphaericus, Cananga odorata, Dysoxilum cautostachyum* and *Octomeles sumatrana*
9	*Metrosideros vera* dense evergreen forest	Almost exclusively monospecific
10	*Octomeles-Arenga* evergreen forest	Dominants are *Octomeles sumatrana, Ficus* sp., *Pinanga* sp., *Nauclea orientalis* and *Bambusa* sp. (*Arenga* very characteristic)
11	*Metroxylon-Bambusa* evergreen forest	*Metroxylon, Bambusa* and *Arenga*
12	*Sonneratia-Bruguira* evergreen forest	Coastal and estuarine mangrove

400), and it was generally accepted that primary forest could be taken as mature old forest which had reached a fairly stable equilibrium or ecological succession (Spencer 1966: 39). The certainties of these older equilibrium and functional models, and the static pristine rainforest concept are no longer accepted in their entirety, and a single forest ecosystem type concept based on notions of a stereotypical or 'essentialised' climax forest is inappropriate (Johns 1990: 144; see also Blumler 1996: 31). Instead, contemporary models of lowland forest ecology emphasise more the patchiness, historicity and diversity of composition. Moreover, measures of what is understood by diversity have become more sophisticated. For example, it is now usual to distinguish *alpha* diversity (the number of locally occurring species) from *beta* diversity (diversity at the level of species communities). Some argue that *alpha* and *beta* diversity are related, *alpha* diversity resulting from a mosaic of juxtaposed niches and microhabitats. Consequently, to attempt to measure empirically the number of different 'types' of vegetation in a tropical rainforest may seem so time-consuming and ultimately subjective as to be hardly worth the effort (Condit 1996). This makes establishing simple typologies difficult, though there may be good practical reasons (in connection with forest management) to devise and recommend them. Thus, the authoritative classification of Pires and Prance (1985: 112–13), which draws extensively on ethnically diverse local ethnoecologies, distinguishes about 22 separate vegetation types for the Brazilian Amazon. However, it appears to make increasing sense to interpret forest composition in terms of the distinguishable kinds of process that lead to variation (Sprugel 1991; Fairhead and Leach 1998: 186). Rainforest, it is now widely acknowledged, is a mosaic of patches of different sizes, whether looked at in terms of different silvigenic stages of development (Torquebiau 1987), or differences based on substrate, altitude and aspect, soil water content, or dynamics arising from species dispersion.

Human Use and Modification of Forest

Much tropical lowland rainforest – in Indonesia as elsewhere – is now seen as the product of many generations of selective human interaction and modification (deliberate and inadvertent), optimising its usefulness and enhancing local diversity. The outcome is a co-evolutionary process in which human activity is essential. Indeed, particular patterns of forest extraction and modification are often seen as integral to its sustainable future. For some authorities, the evidence for intentional rather than serendipitous human influence is so compelling as to invite the description of 'managed' forest (Clay 1988; Schmink, Redford and Padoch 1992: 7–8).

The empirical work supporting these claims comes mainly from the Amazon (e.g. Balée 1989, 1992, 1994; Anderson and Posey 1989), but more recently also from Africa (Fairhead and Leach 1996), and increasingly from large parts of Malaysia and the Western Indonesian archipelago (Aumeeruddy and Bakels 1994; Brookfield, Potter and Byron 1996; Colfer, Peluso and Chin 1997; Dove 1983; Maloney 1993; Padoch and Peters 1993; Padoch and Peluso 1996; Peluso 1996; Puri 2005; Rambo 1979). On Seram, the generally low tree diversity is much influenced by disturbance, and there is abundant evidence that human agency has had consequences for forest ecology. This has been largely through the long-term direct impact of small-scale long forest-fallow swiddening, the extraction of palm sago (*Metroxylon sagu*), and arboriculture over many hundreds of years featuring a small number of crucial nut and seed yielding trees, most notably *Canarium*, *Aleurites*, *Pandanus* and *Celtis* (Ellen 1988a, 2006a). For example, the mature mixed forests of central Seram contain a higher proportion of *Canarium* (Figure 6.5) than would be expected without human encouragement (Edwards 1994; Latinis 2000), and the high proportion of *Canarium* to other genera in the Nuaulu plot 7 (a protected area) is worth noting in this respect. The selective felling of large trees allows for small patches of characteristically secondary forest species (e.g. *Trevesia sundaica*, *Macaranga hispida*, *Artocarpus elasticus* and *Bombax* spp.), while species which are often regarded as being characteristically 'secondary' – *Prunea arborea*, *Platea excelsa* and *Chisocheton sandoricarpus* – have become typical of primary rainforest (Edwards et al. 1990: 171). In addition, the introduction through human agency of the pig (and almost certainly the cassowary), and in more recent centuries deer too, has had a marked impact on forest dynamics, both in terms of the feeding patterns of these megafauna, and also through systematic human predation. Extraction of a wide range of useful products, including timber for local use, selective logging and collection for exchange (resins, rattan, birds), has also been significant (Ellen 1985: 563; Ellen 1999a: 137). In addition to *Canarium*, among the endemic tree species whose distribution has been significantly affected by their

Figure 6.4. Upland forest with *Agathis dammara*, near plot 9 (Rohnesi), west of trans-Seram highway near Wae Sune Maraputi. March 1996 (96-11-21b). Photograph by the author.

Figure 6.5. *Canarium hirsutum* below the old village site of Amatene (plot 11). March 1996 (96-12-21). Photograph by the author.

importance in exchange are *Agathis dammara* (for its resin) at sub-montane altitude and *Melaleuca leucodendron* (for medicinal oil) in drier more open areas.

In earlier work (Ellen 1978: 67, map 8, p. 117), I have described the distribution of mature regrowth and 'primary' forest for 1970–71 in the vicinity of the Nuaulu settlement of Rouhua. The distribution showed a striking visual distinction between (a) the bulk of forest stretching from a very minimum of around 100 m from the coast northwards and mountainwards, and (b) isolated patches apart from the major block of forest and forming barriers between cultivated areas. This latter residual distribution tends to be along ridges and around steep knolls, unsuitable for cultivation under normal circumstances. As a result, these areas (together with the margins of the main forest block), within easy access of the village, are an important source of construction timbers and certain other products, leading to gradual thinning and denudation. Different kinds and degrees of extraction lead to different kinds of secondary regrowth, some directed (that is managed) and some arising by default (cf. Sillitoe 1996: 216–24). These include (1) young secondary growth: recently deserted clearings with rapidly growing herbs, shrubs and small trees of a relatively small number of genera – for example *Trema orientalis*, *Euphorbia hirta*, *Homalanthus populifolius* and many kinds of pteridophyte; (2) medium secondary regrowth: one to ten years, with small trees gradually becoming dominant, for example *Aleurites moluccana* and *Melastroma malabathricum*; (3) mature secondary forest, with a great variety of small and medium-sized trees, shrubs and vines in areas with over ten years of secondary growth; and finally (4) bamboo thicket, also found in combination with the three above associations.

The tendency to procure a wide variety of products, in particular rattans, timber and bamboo, from secondary and mature forest as near to the village as possible, and adjacent cultivated land, leads inevitably to the depletion of more stable associations of forest the nearer one is to the main loci of settlement. Consequently, when mature forest is cut for gardens it has almost always been considerably modified already and contains plant associations more typical of regenerated secondary forest, tends to lack rattan and is considerably thinned on account of the cutting of timber for construction purposes. Such depleted but ecologically distinctive areas, such as open secondary associations often subject to marginal cultivation as well as complete clearance (Ellen 1978: 76, 85, map 9; 1996c), were originally termed by Richards (1996 [1952]: 379, 400) *depleted* forest and by Fosberg *altered* forest (1962). Ecologically, these contain a combination of the properties of both mature and secondary forest growth. It is now widely acknowledged that the edges of garden land, swidden regrowth and disturbed and other secondary forest commonly represent the most important patches for hunting (e.g. Linares 1976), and sites of intensive plant extraction (Grenand 1992).

Nuaulu Terms and Categories Applied to Forest: Concepts and Plots

Nuaulu categorisation and general understanding of forest reflect (a) disturbance history, (b) topography and substrate, and (c) salient species associations; nuanced in terms of (d) land ownership and (e) toponyms. I argue in Chapter 7 of the present volume that this is a broad and flexible framework, which although employing a limited set of fixed and shared lexically-labelled concepts, accommodates knowledge of wide-ranging ecological differences in forest type, and indeed constitutes a pragmatic response to the recognition of its complexity. The Nuaulu term *wesie* broadly indicates all forest, but narrowly and prototypically is understood as mature forest, far away from human settlement, which has not been modified in recent times. Once cut, individual areas of cultivation are known as *nisi* (gardens), which in turn can be divided into three basic types: (1) *nisi honue*, recently cleared garden plots up until the end of the first year; (2) *nisi monai*, gardens after the first year; and (3) *nisi ahue*, secondary growth of various kinds. One special category based on disturbance history is indicated by the term *nia monai* (literally 'old village'), which refers to an old village that is still inhabited, but also to old village sites at different stages following abandonment.

In addition to disturbance history, Nuaulu describe forest locations in terms of four categories based on topography and altitude (Ellen 1978: 114, map 10): (1) *watane*: flat areas (the coastal margins, valley floors, alluvium); (2) *sanene*: valley sides; (3) *pupue*: ridge land, crests, the higher reaches of valley walls: (4) *tinete, pupue tinete*: mountains, peaks; or combinations of these terms, sometimes in conjunction with some reference to their underlying substrates. Shared labelled categories referring to areas dominated by a particular species are rare in Nuaulu, though any patch where a particularly salient species is dominant may be described with a term such as *wesi mukune* (tree-fern forest), *wesi iane* (*Canarium* forest), or *oni-oni* (*Cylindrica exaltata*, alang-alang grassland), but we should not mistake these for fixed terms, even though their use evokes widely-shared meanings and knowledge. Where there are special terms these tend to be for deliberate anthropogenic patches, groves or plantations. Thus, strictly ecological criteria elide with cultivation (*nisi*) and ownership (*wasi*) categories. A special case of tenure intruding into the lexicon to describe different kinds of forest is *sin wesie*, areas of sacred protected forest (e.g. plot 7). These are not necessarily historically undisturbed or unmanaged, but are generally ecologically mature, resource rich and with a composition which reflects their age and successional stage in the development of long fallow.

These cross-cutting ethnoecological and social categories are integrated and articulated through a detailed toponymic grid. No description of forest can make much sense for Nuaulu without such an annotation. The main components of this grid are named rivers, even small creeks, supplemented by names of peaks, hills, prominent rock outcrops, stones, waterfalls, lakes, swamps, caves and such like. In addition there are the transient features – large trees, paths, log bridges, burned patches, patches of grassland; plus the recorded evidence of human activity, gardens belonging to particular individuals, old gardens, abandoned gardens and – most importantly – old village sites, and sites of some other special significance, such as Kamnanai Ukune or Nusi Ukune, in these instances within the sago forest at Somau. The extensive character of participatory mapping exercises elsewhere has shown just how detailed this kind of knowledge can be. On the whole, as a reference system, these toponyms begin with the names of particular mountains on the one hand, and large rivers on the other. The mountains or hills are fixed points that also give their names to large areas surrounding them. Similarly, the large rivers indicate extensive riparian and valley areas rather than the rivers themselves. Linking a river name to a mountain, therefore, provides some general coordinates, which can then be refined further by referring to tributaries of the main rivers, and tributaries of tributaries. Only when this set of coordinates are insufficient to locate places will other indicators be introduced. This set of toponyms serves to identify particular patches of forest, which to some extent bypasses the need to identify forest in terms of floristic composition or habitat structure. The toponymic references clearly indicate the investment of history in the description of a particular landscape, no better revealed than through the narrative associations of old village sites. No stretch of vegetation is ever seen as an example of some generic ahistoric type, but rather as places whose character must be understood through their particular historical associations, and the overall cultural density (Brosius 1986: 175) of the landscape.

If we now look at the plot descriptions in terms of the words Nuaulu use to describe their overall character (Table 6.1), five are described as *wesie* (forest), three as *nisi ahue* (long-term fallow), two as *nia monai* (old village sites) and one as *sin wesie* (sacred forest). Only a small number of terms are consistently shared by Nuaulu to describe forest habitats, and there is a low degree of lexicalisation compared with what we find in official and scientific classifications, and indeed in the folk classifications of some Amazonian peoples [Chapter 7 in the present volume]. Systematic data on ecological knowledge and linguistic evidence indicate: (1) that the categories *wesie* (forest) and *nisi ahue* (long fallow) absorb a great deal of variation; (2) that disturbance history is the main and unifying basis for local understandings of variation, modified by occasional considerations of topography and substrate; (3) that forest is perceived as being in a constant state of flux, in large part due to interaction with humans; (4) that some stable categories are associated with specific species, but that named categories of this kind are rare; and (4) that ethnoecological understandings of forest are inseparable from categories dividing forest in terms of patterns of ownership and the cultural division of landscape reflected in the use of toponyms.

Discussion

Scientific and folk classifications have co-evolved in recent global history, and the relationship between folk knowledge and instituted scientific knowledge can be modelled as two interacting and mutually reinforcing streams: hybridising through mutual borrowings while maintaining permeable boundaries for social and professional reasons, and in the interests of cognitive efficiency [Chapters 4 and 5 of the present volume; Dove et al. 2007]. Because tropical forest ecology and forestry are field-based practices, they have absorbed more from local knowledge systems than the other way around, and also compared with some other sciences. Indeed, instituted professional forestry has adopted much from local artisanal forestry practices, nomenclatures and understandings. The precise form this has taken varies from one country to the next, but colonial forestry services certainly appropriated much from indigenous knowledge. Thus, the Brunei Forestry Service today utilises a typology developed by colonial foresters operating in Malaya, Sarawak and British North Borneo (Kathirithamby-Wells 2004) in which 'Peat Swamp Forest' is sub-divided using vernacular Malay terminology into, amongst other categories, 'atan bunga' and 'padang atan' (forms of forest dominated by *Shorea albida*), 'padang keruntum' (dominated by *Combretocarpus rotundatus*) and 'padang forest'; in addition to utilising the category 'kerangas' (tropical heath forest) (Brunei 1984). Whatever these terms once meant, they now reflect official categories.

A similar process of knowledge transfer can be identified in colonial map-making traditions. Thus, the maps produced by the Dutch Topographische Dienst in 1917 of Seram, and which surveyed in detail the entire island for the first time, show evidence of extensive reliance on Nuaulu (and other indigenous) topographic knowledge, through the use of recognisably Nuaulu toponyms over a large swathe of the central part of the island, approximately corresponding to that area which Nuaulu clans claim as their territory today. These descriptions were obviously generated by the map-makers surveying with Nuaulu guides in the first decade of the twentieth century. Conducting research on these issues from 1970 onwards, and particularly in 1996, both Nuaulu co-researchers and myself have been struck by the congruence between current Nuaulu knowledge, as indicated in culturally annotated sketch maps which Nuaulu produced for me (cf. Fernandez-Gimenez 1993), and the toponyms provided in the 1917 Dutch map. I have already indicated in the preceding section how crucial local toponymic knowledge is in providing a framework for understanding vegetational diversity more generally, and it is certainly not a coincidence that as *field*-based practices, colonial cartography and forestry converge in the way they made use of local knowledge.

But while colonial forestry and cartography depended heavily on the inputs of local people, at the same time there was increasing pressure to produce generic typologies of practical value to science and industry that applied over wider geographic areas. The possibilities permitted by new technologies of literary and graphic representation, in addition to the requirement to confirm qualitative intuitions with quantitative measurement, accelerated this tendency: routinising the use of plot surveys and yielding increasingly complex and contrastive typologies of forest habitats, but also raising issues of comparability between timber type maps using different categories in different places (Avery and Burkhart 1994: 262). Sometimes the process of generalisation encouraged dangerous distortions of local ecological realities which served to reinforce the 'territorialisation strategies' and official prejudice about local forestry practices and their consequences (e.g. Fairhead and Leach 1996). More recent technologies of GIS and remote sensing have had a similar effect, creating new opportunities for distancing official and local representations. The history of attempts by ecologists and foresters to impose overly rigid classifications is reminiscent of Campbell's (2002) instructive demonstration of how the predetermined conceptual assumptions and technical specifications of a GIS package prevented the absorption of relevant data on Namibian agropastoralist land tenure, which just like Nuaulu forest knowledge and tenure, is informal, flexible and overlapping.

Recent scientific modelling of rainforest in terms of a complex mosaic rather than as an aggregation of discrete types has been a response to the problems generated by the mechanical application of these methodologies and the assumptions associated with stereotypical, overgeneralised and essentialised representations. The diversity patterns we can now read into tropical rainforest make classifications of forest 'types' difficult. All lowland tropical rainforest is heavily influenced by patterns of human settlement and extraction over many thousands of years, and essentialist descriptions that ignore human disturbance are now widely acknowledged as misleading. And paradoxically, the problems of ground-truthing imagery based on remote sensing have led to the revision of just how such data should be interpreted, in some cases involving participatory mapping. We now appreciate much more how grouping secondary biodiversity at different levels of geographic aggregation may result in very different classificatory patterns and require different kinds of analysis and interpretation (Moran 1990), and how much professional forestry can learn from local people (Wiersum 2000). Indeed, what success recent strategies, such as Joint Forest Management (JFM), have had has been grounded in the partial resolution of the opposition between global scientific forestry knowledge and local knowledge (Sivaramakrishnan 2000: 61). Even in Indonesia, the rethinking of forest policies, in the light of the failure of top-down models, made possible by the 'Reformasi' following the end of the Suharto regime in 1998, has given more scope for social forestry, local voices, and for the recognition of local community rights and ecological knowledge.

We can observe, therefore, a convergence between how local tropical forest dwellers perceive and classify forest, in this case the Nuaulu, and how scientists have reacted to the inadequacies of an earlier generation of models. The spatial variation of secondary biodiversity (habitats, biotopes, ecosystems) must, on the whole, be understood very differently from variation at the species level. My data support the claim that a classificatory model composed of large numbers of forest types, analogous to folk taxonomic schemes reported for individual plant species and typified by morphological discontinuity, does not reflect accurately how Nuaulu perceive and encode forest differences. Rather, Nuaulu representation of forest is *non-taxonomic*, constructed on the basis of the intersection of a number of classificatory dimensions based on different criteria acknowledging its continuous variation, deployed in a flexible and non-mechanical way. Terminologies arising from classificatory stimuli are more likely to be ad hoc descriptions of difference rather than indicating the presence of widely shared and fixed categories. Nuaulu, therefore, seem to experience forest in the same way as those ecologists who have tried to use plots to measure compositional and structural diversity. To describe a 'patch' in terms of a permanent and simple ethnoecological category is to overgeneralise and reify in a way that is not always helpful to the representation and management of resources.

Notes

First published 2007 as 'Plots, Typologies and Ethnoecology: Local and Scientific Understandings of Forest Diversity on Seram', in *Global vs Local Knowledge*, edited by Paul Sillitoe (Oxford: Berghahn Books, pp. 41–74). Reproduced courtesy of Berghahn Books.

1. A patchy distribution pattern is one in which values, observations or individuals are more aggregated or clustered than in a random distribution, indicating that the presence of one individual or value increases the probability of another occurring nearby (Lincoln, Boxshall and Clark 1982). Alternatively, it might be defined as heterogeneity in the distribution of resources and of the patches themselves. In the context of forest ecology, patchiness reduces the possibility of accurate mapping using a neat classification of forest types.

CHAPTER 7

Why Aren't the Nuaulu Like the Matsigenka?

Introduction

Ethnobotanical studies of the knowledge of tropical forest peoples have demonstrated an extensive local knowledge of trees, local recognition of forest diversity, and the existence of coherent vernacular classifications of forest types. While folk classifications of habitats, biotopes and landscapes more generally have received much less attention than folk systematics (Sillitoe 1998: 104; Meilleur 1986: 54–90; Martin 1974; Torre-Cuadros and Ross 2003), the data that are available on indigenous forest classifications in particular suggest significant variation in the extent to which recognition of compositional diversity actually translates into complex, fixed and labelled categories for different types of forest. Although there are some early references to the importance of establishing ethnoecological categories in the Asian tropics (e.g. Bartlett 1936; Conklin 1954), the pioneer work on this subject was conducted in the Amazon, and has since extended elsewhere. Carneiro (1978) reports four forest types for the Kuikuru, as do Parker et al. (1983: 170–71) for the Brazilian Kayapó, with several subdivisions of gallery forest, as well as ten forest types for the Brazilian Yekuana around Lake Coari. Balée and Gély (1989: 131–32) report four Ka'apor forest categories (old swidden, fallow forest, mature forest, and swamp forest), plus a number of unspecified named ecotones. For New Guinea, Sillitoe (1998) lists nine basic Wola terms for vegetation types, with a further four sub-types; but this is not all forest, and covers an extensive altitudinal range, 1,600–2,000 m asl. Dependable data for island Southeast Asia are more difficult to obtain, but Puri (1997: 104), in his work on Penan forest knowledge, elicited just eight categories which map onto what we might generally accept as 'forest', despite systematic attempts to generate more detailed labelled categories. By contrast, a number of researchers working in the Amazon region have recently reported folk classifications of forest evidently more terminologically refined and extensive than these reports suggest. Thus, Andrello (cited in Shepard et al. 2001) has reported 53 natural habitat types. Fleck and Harder (2000: 1–3), working amongst the Peruvian Matses, list 47 labelled vegetation types overall, and claim that by combining vegetational and geomorphologic designations, Matses distinguish 178 habitats. Of these, 104 are described as types of primary rainforest, and 74 as types of successional forest. Shepard et al. (2001) suggest great similarities between Matses and Matsigenka, also in Peru, who operate with about 40 categories for lowland forest. That local peoples have a profound knowledge of forest diversity is now hardly doubted, but how can we account for such discrepancies in the lexicalisation of knowledge for people living in ecologically very similar environments?

In order to address this problem, we might consider a number of hypotheses:[1]

- that not all knowledge, everywhere, is equally lexicalised or that some research is less thorough;
- that ecological and subsistence differences influence the extent to which people categorise and lexicalise;
- that models based on the structure of folk taxonomies generated in studies of folk systematics bias our methodologies.

One approach to studying local knowledge of forest or more general habitat variation is to use a model based on the structure of folk taxonomies generated in studies of folk systematics. Unfortunately, such an approach treats forest types and habitats as kinds of folk species, and as functioning, organisational entities they are quite different: at the level of organism classification there are more terms and a greater fixity in the terms used. In other words, habitats are not 'things' in the sense, I think, implied in, say, Meilleur's multi-levelled lexically defined ranks of 'ethnoecosystem' and 'folk biotope', a system reminiscent of Berlin's (e.g. Berlin, Breedlove and Raven 1973) ranks for natural kind classification (Meilleur 1986: 54–90). By comparison with the morphological discontinuousness of individual species, where unidimensional characteristics, salient prototypes and contrasting segregates abound, the ecological variation of forest is multidimensional and continuous, and such variation does not encode well into simple taxonomic models. For example, many folk classifications of forest terminologically encode the phases of swidden cultivation and forest fallow regrowth, and the categories so established on the basis of these phases inevitably tend to merge with those on either side. Multidimensional models work better, especially as we now know that the tropical rainforest varies spatially much more in compositional terms than was at one time supposed. Even in the world of plant ecology, the basis for distinguishing habitats and vegetation types in rainforests is notoriously difficult [Chapter 6 in the present volume].

In the light of this, therefore, it is perhaps hardly surprising that Shepard et al. (2001: 7) provide Matsigenka data that they interpret as indicating no single hierarchy of habitat categories, but rather multiple systems of habitat description, intersecting to define forest types, and with habitat definitions overlapping. Nevertheless, they are sufficiently confident to report that these dimensions generate 76 biotically defined habitats, including 50 lowland primary forest types defined by indicator species. The categories of lexically recognised habitats are based on various kinds of criteria: abiotic, disturbance regimes, soil vocabulary, indicator species (palms, bamboos, ferns and herbs, as well as trees), characteristic secondary and weedy vegetation, typical montane vegetation types, those defined by overall vegetative aspect, and habitats defined by faunal association. Allan (2002) in her work on the Makushi of Guyana, provides further data which suggest similar intersecting frameworks, but without any evidence for extensive lexical complexity or, indeed, for the routine expression of such ecological differences in lexical terms. Shepard et al. (2001: 27) also suggest that there are a relatively small number of perceptual features underlying this otherwise elaborate scheme: flatland : montane, river mouth : headwaters, river edge : forest interior, weedy secondary growth : primary forest, terrestrial : arboreal, male : female, diurnal : nocturnal, natural : domesticated, and native : introduced. Allan (2002) too notes the small number of perceptual regularities underlying the forest classifications of her informants, and shows how Makushi forest classification can be understood through the intersection of four 'forest frameworks': disturbance history (high bush : low bush), land form (hill : swamp), soil category (sand : clay), and a small number of special associations with indicator species. These (mostly oppositional) criteria are seen to generate the 24 categories recorded for characterising forest: four based on landform, nine based on soil, two to three based on human disturbance history, two based on growth form, and six based on species association or dominance.

What is interesting about these two studies from tropical South America is that between them they indicate a number of organisational features of folk classifications of forest that I suspect are very widespread. Additionally, despite the extensive evidence of multidimensionality and flexibility, they also display continuing underlying assumptions of fixed hierarchical organisation, lexical fixity, and of shared knowledge, rather than it being suggested that the categories are the outcome of knowledge organised along a small number of dimensions to generate extensive, but essentially *ad hoc* terminologies and classifications. I wish here to show that the features highlighted are also evident in Nuaulu classifications of forest variation, but that unlike the Matsigenka, and more like the Makushi, Nuaulu are much more flexible in the way in which limited perceptual characters (such as toponyms) are used to generate organisational frameworks, variable in the classifications that become operative, and that the rather small fixed lexical repertoire of forest types systematically underestimates what people actually know. It does so because the amount of variation is so great that it cannot, and need not, be handled in a single static classification, which is anyway arguably less cognitively efficient.

Background

The study reported in this chapter compares local knowledge of tree vegetation and forest variation in a series of plots widely distributed spatially and in ecologically distinct areas [Chapter 6 in the present volume]. The plot surveys were conducted as part of long-term qualitative and quantitative ethnoecological fieldwork that I have been engaged in since 1970 among the Nuaulu, a people who in 1996 constituted of a group of intermarrying clans with a total population of about two thousand, located in south central Seram, Maluku, eastern Indonesia (Map 3.1). Nuaulu subsist largely through sago extraction, hunting, swidden cultivation and forest gathering, with some fishing. Historically and conceptually they perceive their subsistence and general cultural orientation as one of forest and mountain rather than of coast and sea. Until the late nineteenth century, most Nuaulu lived in dispersed inland settlements. Between about 1880 and the 1980s they concentrated in a small number of settlements surrounding the Muslim village of Sepa, though continuing to extract from a wide inland area. However, since the 1980s, the impact of transmigration, road-building and more recently civil disturbance has led once again to a more dispersed pattern of settlement, though one constrained by the new political realities.

The ecological differences between the Nuaulu plots selected reflect altitude, substrate, species composition and anthropic influence. One of the objectives in surveying them has been to measure the extent to which knowledge varies according to different kinds of forest, geographic area and between different adult male informants, and why. The analysis undertaken demonstrates a high ability to name trees consistently, irrespective of locality and ecology, and a high degree of shared knowledge between male informants. It also illustrates the extent to which Nuaulu understanding of forest diversity and patterning matches recent scientific ecological modelling of rainforest in terms of a complex mosaic rather than as an aggregation of discrete types, and how much of that variation is culturally informed. The data support the claim that simple folk classifications of large numbers of forest types based on the analogy of folk taxonomies of individual plants do not reflect accurately how Nuaulu perceive and encode forest differences. Rather, it is suggested that Nuaulu representation of forest is non-taxonomic, constructed on the basis of the intersection of a number of classificatory dimensions based on different criteria. While these multiple dimensions might be represented etically as interacting to generate a large number of discrete 'types', the evidence suggests that they are actually deployed in a more flexible and less mechanical way. Terminologies arising from classificatory stimuli are more likely to be *ad hoc* descriptions of difference rather than indicating the presence of widely shared and fixed categories. What encodes much of the difference is not recognition of ecological difference *per se*, but rather its cultural encoding. This relates back to the observation that what underlies many of the differences in lowland tropical forest are impacts made by humans that have short- and long-term ecological consequences.

Nuaulu Ethnoecological Classification of Forest

The data on the structural and compositional complexity of forest, as understood by Nuaulu, is evident from: (a) structured interview data and more discursive qualitative data obtained both from forest hikes and informal village group discussions; (b) patterns of differential use and extraction; and (c) linguistic evidence. The qualitative evidence is referred to in this chapter, but not presented in detail. The behavioural data on uses consist of both a cumulative data set for a period of some 30 years in which species are the units of record (the Nuaulu Ethnobotanical Database or NED), and household surveys (over a period of four months) of work inputs and consumption, based on work conducted in 1970–71.

Let us first consider the behavioural data. The entire forested area from which the Rouhua Nuaulu (180 persons) extracted during the period in which the 1970–71 fieldwork took place was some 900 square kilometres (Ellen 1978: 61, map 7). However, Nuaulu temporo-spatial interaction with this vast area of forest is very patchy. Work diary data indicate that more time was spent in two toponymically designated localities than in all other localities put together (some 62 per cent of the total number of man days) (ibid.: 79, table 12a). Together, these areas occupy about 62 square kilometres. Compared with the total area from which Nuaulu extract, say in one year, this is very small, and the productivity of such areas is accordingly high, though as these are quite large areas, other smaller terminologically designated localities have a higher productivity when area is divided by the number of days spent extracting (ibid.: table 12b). Since the 1970–71 survey, in-migration, population growth and movement, logging, market-driven patterns in forest product extraction, civil disturbance, the introduction of surfaced roads and therefore improved access, have all modified this picture somewhat, particularly through increased levels of extraction in more distant localities, where Nuaulu have either resettled or been allocated space and facilities within transmigration zones created by the provincial government during the 1980s. However, I have no reason to suspect that the general pattern revealed in the 1970–71 data – that extraction varies quite considerably from area to area according to vegetational cover, faunal composition, topography and relative accessibility – has altered over the intervening thirty years. This patchiness in human extraction patterns matches the patchiness in the ecology of the forest that has been described above, and underpins the way in which Nuaulu perceive forest.

The linguistic evidence includes both terminological data on individual forest plants, but also data suggesting the existence of categories grouping different plant species and other distinctive components of forest into broader categories based on ecological, social and cultural criteria. However, there is a marked contrast between the large number of folk species named and the small number of forest types indicated terminologically. Thus, there are in excess of 214 distinguishable Nuaulu terms for different non-domesticated tree species associated with the most inclusive forest category, *wesie*, compared with a total of 339 Nuaulu terms for trees as a whole coded in the NED. Approximately 156 tree species are listed for the 1996 plots, translating into about 153 distinguishable vernacular terms. Of course, compositional complexity is not only evident in woody tree species that might be considered as non-domesticated, but also in the presence of various domesticates and semi-domesticates that are either introduced or self-seeded, plus lianas, epiphytes and other species of the canopy, and ground cover. Overall, in excess of 234 distinguishable Nuaulu terminal plant categories are associated with *wesie*.

Wesie is the most general term applied to forest by Nuaulu.[2] At a symbolic level it connotes vastness, wildness and uncontrollability. It is opposed to *niane*, village, which is associated with the contrasting qualities of discreteness, tameness and controllability. Indeed, Nuaulu explicitly describe villages as 'islands' (*nusa*) within a sea of forest. The symbolic significance of this apparent contrast between the realms of nature and culture has been explored by me elsewhere (Ellen 1996b, 1999a). However, such an apparently rigid symbolic contrast belies a more fluid characterisation of forest which embodies cross-cutting distinctions and acknowledges the merging of categories. This too is reflected at a symbolic level, though from this point on, my primary concern will be only with the recognition of distinctions of material and practical significance.

Most of what Nuaulu describe as *wesie* covers both lowland rainforest, that stretches from sea level mountainwards, and montane rainforest. Although the Nuaulu recognise zonal variation within *wesie* areas, it is not systematically labelled. The only occasions on which montane zones are traversed are during journeys to north Seram, or on the longer hunting trips to the headwaters of the Nua, Ruatan, Kawa or Lata rivers (Map 3.1), or in collecting resin from the conifer *Agathis dammara*, a particularly prominent feature of the higher forest zones (plot 9). For the Nuaulu, the main features distinguishing *wesie* (largely unowned and uncultivated forest land) and *wasi* (land that is owned and has been cultivated) are the trees of which they are comprised, in particular their size. Thus, almost synonymous with the contrast set *wesie* : *wasi* is the set *ai ia onata* : *ai ia ana wasi*, 'great trees' : 'trees of the garden', or trees of mature and secondary forest associations respectively. *Wesie* has all the characteristics of *ai ia onata* and more: it is experienced as a source of useful plant materials and of game; it has a mystical dimension, particular visual, olfactory and acoustic qualities (Ellen 1978: 65; cf. Feld 1996), and its overall ecology is experienced synaesthetically.

Here I describe the much more limited Nuaulu lexicon and array of categories applied to forest in a broad etic sense, that for Nuaulu represents a fuzzy conceptual domain with *wesie* at its core, but necessarily including peripheral transitional vegetational types, that overlap cultivated land and patches of non-forest vegetation within areas overall designated *wesie*. In summary, Nuaulu categorisation and general cognition of forest reflect:

- disturbance history
- land form and substrate
- salient species associations

nuanced in terms of

- land ownership
- toponyms

I argue that the broadness and flexibility of such a framework, involving a limited set of fixed and shared lexically-labelled categories, do not reflect lack of knowledge of wide-ranging ecological differences in forest, but rather constitute a pragmatic response to the recognition of its complexity.

Terms and Categories Reflecting Disturbance History

Wesie broadly indicates all forest, but narrowly and prototypically is understood as mature forest, far away from human settlement, that has not been modified in recent times, what is sometimes called *wesie huie*, or 'empty forest' (Ellen 1978: 23–24). Once forest is cut by a known individual or household, it becomes *wasi* until such time as the rights which became so established have lapsed or have been forgotten. Clearly such distinctions are fundamental to an understanding of Nuaulu land tenure, and indeed conceptions of tenure have a bearing on Nuaulu ecological perceptions of forest, but for the time being we shall confine ourselves to those distinctions that indicate different kinds and degrees of disturbance. Once cut, individual areas of cultivation are known as *nisi*, 'gardens', and these in turn can be divided into three basic types:

(1) *nisi honue*, a recently cleared garden plot up until the end of the first year;
(2) *nisi monai*, a garden after the first year, including sago, clove and coconut groves, that may (as in the case of coconut) be up to 60 years old;
(3 *nisi ahue*, secondary growth of various kinds.

Of all new gardens created in a single year, on the basis of data for 1970–71, between 20 and 30 per cent are cut from mature forest growth, or rather from what Nuaulu describe as *wesie*. As such gardens tend to be larger than those cut from secondary growth (*nisi ahue*), the percentage area is somewhat greater: around 4–5 hectares or 30 to 36 per cent (Ellen 1978: 109, table 21). Neither *nisi honue* nor *nisi monai* are in any sense forest in terms of Nuaulu perceptions, though from an external perspective some *nisi monai* might be regarded as agroforest. However, for the Nuaulu themselves, the status of *ahue* is ambiguous, ranging from plots that have been cleared within the last three years to plots that are 25 years old or more. But not only is it a temporally wide category, it is also spatially extensive. Of all land within a 4-kilometre radius of Rouhua village in 1971, totalling some 2,430 hectares, 15 per cent was *ahue* and 58 per cent *wesie*. Of the 102 hectares designated *nisi* and cultivated by Rouhua Nuaulu in 1970–71, 23 per cent was classified as *nisi ahue* (ibid.: 185). While a stand of young sago (2–10 years) might be considered *nisi monai*, the same sago grove a few years later might be *ahue*. Despite the ecological distinctiveness and economic importance of depleted forest, and the reasonable assumption that its marginality and ambiguousness might create the kind of blur between the natural and cultural, *wesie* and *wasi*, that elsewhere might be considered symbolically salient, it is not terminologically distinct, or even categorically identifiable.

One special category based on disturbance history is indicated by the term *nia monai* (literally, 'old village'). This term may refer to an old settlement that is still inhabited, but also to old settlement sites at different stages following abandonment. Map 3.1 shows all existing Nuaulu settlements for 1996, and the plots surveyed in the same year. In 1996, *nia monai* was used to describe the site at Aihisuru six years following its abandonment as a village (marked as an open diamond in Map 3.1). The term was also applied to two areas surveyed: plot 5 at Pesi and plot 11 at Amatene (Figure 7.1) – both about 200 years old – as well as at least seven more old Nuaulu settlement sites (marked as empty squares in Map 3.1) dated variously within a period of 120 to 500 years since abandonment, and many

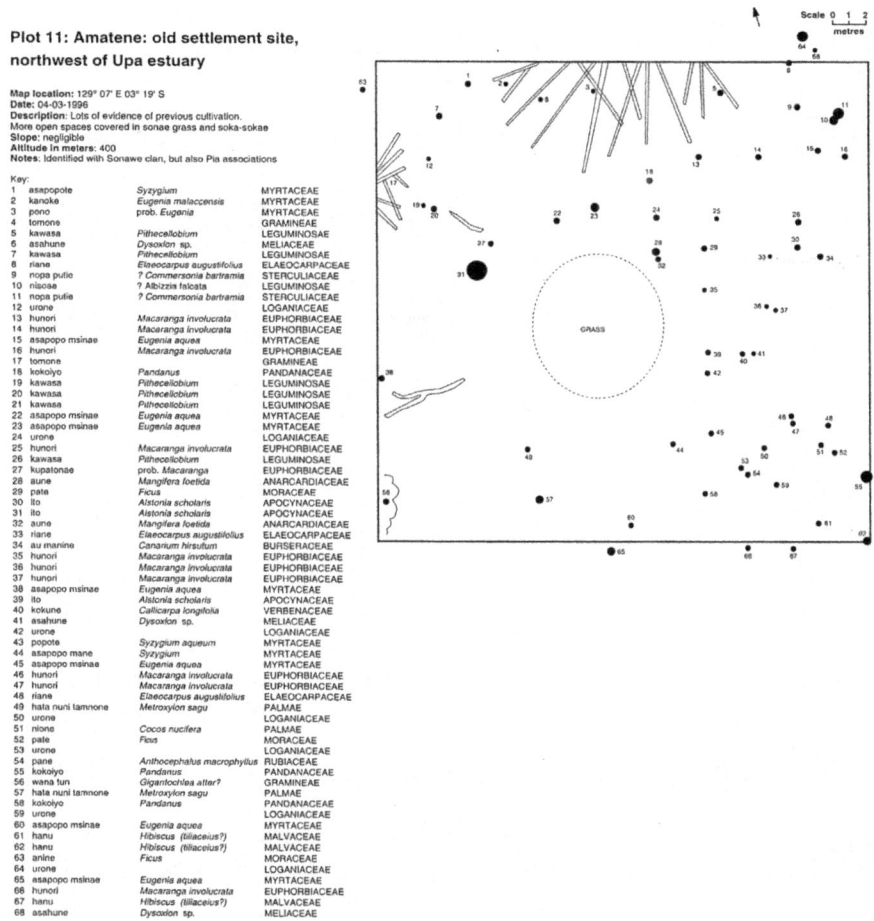

Figure 7.1. Plot 11. Amatene: old village site, northwest of Upa estuary. Much evidence of previous cultivation. Open patches covered in grass and *Selaginella*. Figure created by the author.

additional sites associated with other ethnic and political groupings. For example, Amahoru is an old Sepa clan site now mainly *Imperata* grassland, while the site of the old village of Ouh (which at least 500 years ago moved to the nearby island of Saparua) is now entirely covered in bamboo. Amatene (plot 11) was presumably vacated in the 1880s and has been periodically visited since; its active use today encourages perpetuation of the surrounding resources. The old Numanaeta clan site at Mamokoni, further inland than Amatene, is renowned for its density of sago. As we shall see, the category ***nia monai***, while clearly flagging an ecologically distinctive habitat characterised mainly by a high density of useful resources, also potently encodes history and a cultural reconstruction of the landscape.

Topography and Substrate

In addition to disturbance history, Nuaulu may also describe forest locations in terms of four categories based on topography and altitude (Ellen 1978: 114, map 10):

- *watane*: flat areas (the coastal margins, valley floors, alluvium);
- *sanene*: valley sides;
- *pupue*: ridge land, crests, the higher reaches of valley walls;
- *tinete, pupue tinete*: mountains, peaks.

Wesi pupue, therefore, may refer to ridge forest, and ***wesi tinete***, to montane forest.

The categorisation of forest in terms of its underlying substrate is even more basic. The soil underlying forest in the Nuaulu area, by and large favourable dark red and reddish brown latosols with little variation, is associated with an alluvial geology containing conglomerates and the characteristic outcrops of coralline limestone ('karang'), or with phyllite formations (Ellen 1978: 27, map 14). There are some elevated coral reefs and conglomerates in the area, but none of the plots were located on these. The neogenous soft white porous karang is called *nokase* by Nuaulu, the iron stained and weathered muscovite schists *ina inate*, the laminated schists *maia* (an allusion to the flat sago and 'kenari' nut food of the same name) and the iron stained quartzose sandstone ***tapune*** (ibid.: 216, table 41). Soils are either hard or soft, though they may be nuanced by using adjectival qualifiers referring to parent material (e.g. ***tapu msinae***, red ***tapune***). The plots were distributed as follows: coralline limestone (1, 4, 5, 7, 10), sandstone (2), alluvium (6, 8), schists (9), and limestone/phyllite (11). Soil in itself is not used to characterise forest, though the presence of ***nokase*** may be indicative. Otherwise, topographic terms are a significant encoder of substrate.

Categories Indicating Species-Specific Types

Shared labelled categories indicating species dominance are rare in Nuaulu, though the more salient species in particular areas are certainly recognised. Nevertheless, there is plenty of evidence to suggest that Nuaulu are well aware that the dominance of certain species or groups of plants in a particular area will indicate a particular micro-ecology and compositional pattern. For example, once while travelling to a plot, Nuaulu voluntarily remarked clearly and explicitly on how much *wesie* still existed on the north side of the Upa river, above Nepinama's extensive **nisi ahue**, that was noted as containing much **paune** (a kind of *Pandanus*) and, on another trek, on the density of **mukune** (*Cyathea* spp.) at the place they call Sama. Additionally, Nuaulu are well aware that all tree species have a particular autoecology that includes the presence of other indicative species (Ellen 1996a). This knowledge can be elicited easily enough employing queries based on the interrogative logic of 'if species x, then species y'. For example, in **onie** (*Shorea selanica*) dominated forest (e.g. plot 3), Nuaulu are aware that, unusually, relatively few other species are found, but that those other species often disproportionately represented include **niotune** (*Duabanga moluccana*) and **ai punara** (*Octomeles sumatrana*), and that **kinekane**, the polypod fern *Phymatodes nigrescens*, forms a characteristic understory ground cover. Species or groups of species that generate networks of ecological knowledge of this kind, and that would seem to justify distinct terminological recognition, include *Metroxylon sagu*, *Canarium*, the large bamboos, the grass *Imperata exaltata*, rattans, *Agathis dammara*, and *Cyathea*. Indeed, it is the case that any patch where a particularly salient species is dominant may be described with a term such as **wesi mukune** (tree-fern forest), **wesi iane** (*Canarium* forest), or **oni-oni** (*Cylindrica exaltata*), but we should not mistake these for fixed terms, even though their use evokes widely-shared meanings and bodies of knowledge. Interestingly, where there are special terms, these tend to be for deliberate anthropogenic patches, groves or plantations. Thus, strictly ecological criteria elide with cultivation and ownership categories.

For the most part, forest variation is fairly continuous and the size of discrete patches that could be described in this way is fairly small. However, on some well-trodden trails, the passage from one patch 'type' to another may be quite salient and encoded in shared memory as part of the landscape description used to evoke particular places and routes. Thus, in descending from plot 11, the old village site of Amatene, the traveller passes through fourteen zones that are distinguished by Nuaulu according to a diverse selection of indicators: mixed orchard arboriflora, highly indicative of an old habitation site (including clove: *Myrcianthes fragrans*, durian: *Durio zibethinus*, *Bambusa*, *Gigantochlea*, coconut: *Coco nucifera*, sago: *Metroxylon sagu*); open bamboo scrub; a belt of *iane* (*Canarium*, with some *meu munate* rattan); depleted *wesie*; *nisi ahue* with *oni* (*Imperata*, 'alang-alang'); a new Rouhua Nuaulu garden (*nisi honue*); *nisi ahue* with *kokoio* (*Pandanus* sp.); bamboo *ahue*; riparian vegetation along the banks of the small Wae Ia Ana Ikine river; a *tepine* (*Caryota rumphiana*) and rattan belt; an old Bunara Nuaulu garden (*nisi monai*); mixed secondary forest; old garden land; and coastal coconut grove. Some of this diversity is systematically labelled using ethnoecological categories, but most is not.

The Categories of Land Tenure

As we have seen, *wasi* is the local jural term for any patch of land that is owned by a particular clan, and it is subject to the ultimate authority of the Matoke clan, personified in the *ia onate Matoke*, the 'Lord of the Land'. Through its status as a senior and autochthonous clan to which all other clans owe their existence, Matoke is guardian of all land that the Nuaulu consider their original territory. This territory stretches as far as the upland divide between north and south of the island and around the drainage basins of the major Ruatan and Nua rivers (Ellen 1978: 86, maps 2 and 3). The *ia onate Matoke* is regarded as having ultimate jurisdiction over all Nuaulu cultivated land and tenurial arrangements, and all land–people and people–forest relationships. Swiddens cut from forest in the general sense are described as *nisi*. I shall not say anything further here about *nisi honue* (first year gardens) or *nisi monai* (gardens of approximately 2–15 years in age). Only *nisi ahue* (gardens acknowledged as being in fallow) are considered to be simultaneously gardens and forest, but even here land that might otherwise be described as forest will sometimes be identified using the name of the resource and the clan which owns it: thus *hata* Soumori ('Soumori sago'), or generically *hata ipan* or *ipane hatana* ('sago belonging to the clan'). Similarly, sago, or some other resource belonging to the village, becomes *hata niane* ('village sago'). Categories designating particular forest types with the name of the principle floristic component overlap with the terminology used for specialised gardens: thus we have *nisi* (or now sometimes *rusun*, from Ambonese Malay 'dusun') *hatane* ('sago garden'), *nisi kanai* ('betel palm garden') and so on.

A special case of tenure that intrudes into the lexicon to describe different kinds of forest is *sin wesie*. *Sin(e) wesie* are areas of sacred protected forest (e.g. plot 7) that are resource rich and whose composition may reflect age and successional stages of long fallow (cf. Balée and Gély 1989; Fernandez-Gimenez 1993). They are owned at the clan level, though at any one time not all clans in a village will have one. The *sin wesie* sampled in plot 7 (Figure 7.2) at the headwaters of the Mon river belongs to the Peinisa clan. Resources in such areas cannot be harvested without the express permission of a clan chief, and even sago that has reached fruition must be allowed to rot.

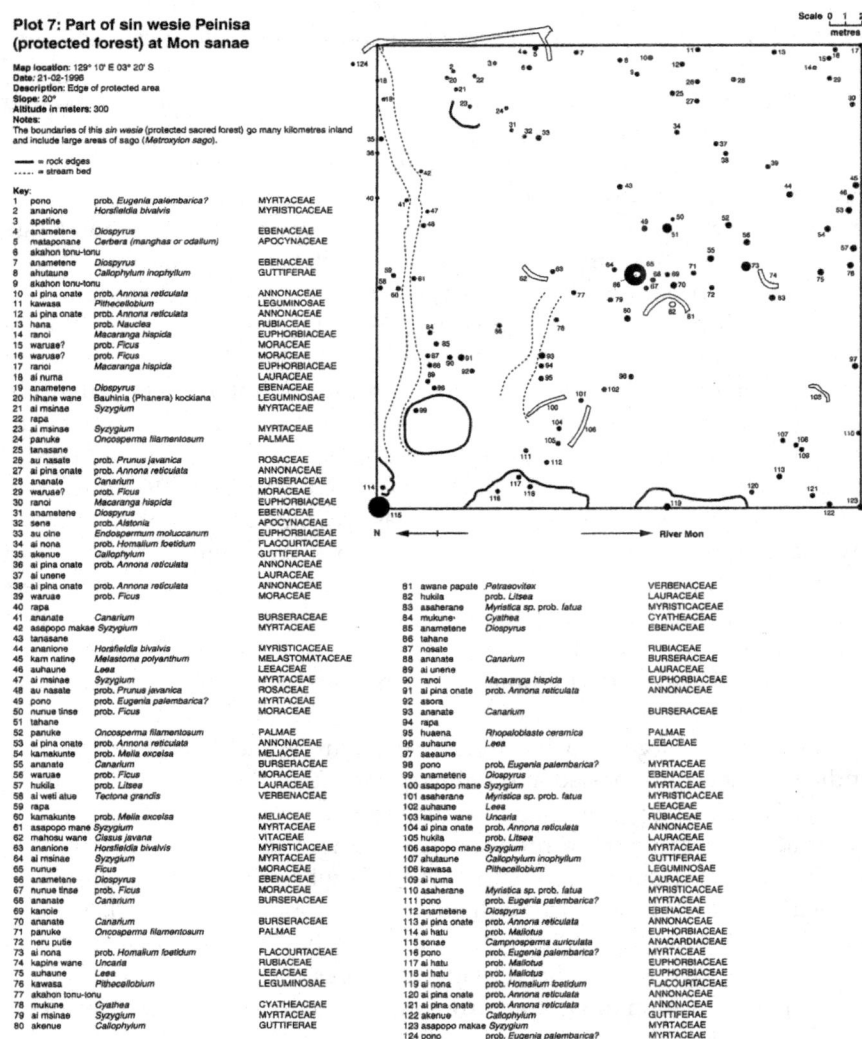

Figure 7.2. Plot 7. Part of *sin wesie* Peinisa (protected forest) at Mon Sanae. Figure created by the author.

Toponyms

Finally, Nuaulu perceive forest through a detailed toponymic grid. The main components of this grid are named rivers, even small creeks, supplemented by names of peaks, hills, prominent rock outcrops, stones, waterfalls, lakes, swamps, caves and the like. In addition, transient features such as large trees, paths, log bridges, burned patches, and patches of grassland are named, along with the recorded evidence of human activity such as gardens belonging to particular individuals, old gardens, abandoned gardens and – most importantly – old village sites, and sites of some locational specificity such as sites within the sago forest at Somau (Kamnanai Ukune or Nusi Ukune).

The extensive character of participatory mapping exercises elsewhere has shown just how detailed this knowledge can be. In the Nuaulu case, evidence of the geographic extensiveness of such toponymic knowledge comes not only from the mapping exercises that I have conducted with Nuaulu over a period of some thirty years, but from maps produced by the Dutch Topographische Dienst in 1917. A large swathe of central Seram, approximately corresponding to that area which Nuaulu clans claim as their territory, is annotated with river and mountain names that are clearly, and for the most part, Nuaulu. These names are presumably generated by the map-makers surveying with Nuaulu guides in the first decade of the twentieth century. Working with Nuaulu from 1970 onwards, and particularly in 1996, I was struck – as were the Nuaulu themselves – by the congruence between current Nuaulu knowledge as indicated in culturally annotated sketch maps that Nuaulu produced for me (cf. Fernandez-Gimenez 1993) and the toponyms provided in the 1917 Dutch map. On the whole, as a reference system, these toponyms begin with the names of particular mountains on the one hand and large rivers on the other. However, the mountains or hills are fixed points that also give their names to large areas surrounding them. Similarly, the large rivers indicate extensive riparian and valley areas rather than simply the rivers themselves. Linking a river name with a mountain name provides general coordinates, that are then refined by referring to tributaries of the main rivers and to tributaries of tributaries. Only when this set of coordinates is insufficient to locate places will other indicators be introduced. This set of toponyms serves to identify particular patches of forest, and which to some extent bypasses the need to identify forest in terms of its distinctive floristic composition or habitat structure. The toponymic references manifestly indicate the investment of history in the description of a particular landscape, and they are no better revealed than through the narrative associations of old village sites. No stretch of vegetation is ever seen as an example of some generic ahistorised type, but rather as places whose character must be understood only through particular historical associations and the overall 'cultural density' of the landscape (Brosius 1986: 175).

Plot Analysis in Relation to Local Knowledge and Use of Forest

Table 6.1 in the previous chapter summarises selected 1996 plot data reflecting Nuaulu botanical knowledge in relation to levels of identification. The first point to note is the completeness of Nuaulu terminological data. Of all the trees over 10 cm dbh in all the plots, there is a mean level of identification of 97.5 per cent, with seven of the eleven plots yielding 100 per cent agreed identifications. As might be expected, identifications in the more remote plots proved more difficult, including the most distant plot 9 in a sub-montane area, which yielded a 94 per cent identification rate. Some species were unfamiliar to Nuaulu assistants in this plot, but a more practical problem proved to be tall trees with little leaf visible below canopy level.

Table 7.1 summarises 1996 plot data relating to tree uses. The measure employed is a crude one that scored trees in each of the plots in terms of whether they had a volunteered use at all and then whether uses could be allocated to one or more of three aggregate categories: food, medicinals, and physical equipment. How some of the more marginal specific uses of trees were allocated between these three categories is explained in the key accompanying the table.

Table 7.1. Summary of selected 1996 plot data: selected and aggregated uses.

Plot	1	2	3	4	5	6	7	8	9	10	11
N trees above 10 dbh	34	30	37	26	28	54	124	116	80	35	68
N species	20	21	16	10	9	22	47	33	28	21	26
N species with indicated uses	14	17	12	9	4	18	28	17	15	10	19
N trees with indicated uses	22	23	31	25	5	45	78	56	39	20	55
N species used for food	1	3	4	5	0	10	6	5	1	2	9
N trees used for food	1	4	19	21	0	15	16	18	1	2	20
N species used medicinally	1	2	0	2	0	2	2	0	0	1	1
N trees used medicinally	1	2	0	2	0	4	2	0	0	1	1
N species used for equipment	11	12	11	6	3	14	21	15	11	9	14
N trees used for equipment	19	14	29	6	4	36	64	42	32	19	34

Note: Fuel is excluded as a use. Food includes additives such as spices. Medicinal uses include stimulants and cosmetics. Equipment includes manufactured items of all sizes, clothing and building timber.

However, when we look at the plot descriptions using the general words employed by Nuaulu to describe their overall character, five plots are described as *wesie*, three as *nisi ahue*, two as *nia monai* and one as *sin wesie* (Table 7.2). In describing the vegetation in these plots, no terms other than those applied to individual kinds of plants were elicited, despite demonstrably articulate descriptions provided by Nuaulu co-researchers for the relations between species found and the general ecological characteristics of the plots. Table 7.2 attempts to show the aggregate 'usefulness' of four Nuaulu categories applied to forest at the plot sites by measuring the number of trees listed with uses in the Nuaulu Ethnobotanical Database. The data are indicative rather than definitive, and more plots, over a wider spectrum of forest variation and of larger size, would provide a test of the plausibility of these patterns. For index of species richness (S), *sin wesie* (protected sacred forest: e.g. Figure 7.2) was found to have the highest value, followed by *nia monai* (old village sites), and then *wesie* (general mature forest) and *nisi ahue* (long-term fallow). These data provide evidence to support the hypothesis that long-term anthropic influences increase local tree diversity. If, however, we measure mean percentage of trees listed as 'useful' against the total number of trees in plots of that category, and against the index of species richness, we find that recent long fallow (*nisi ahue*) provides the greatest concentration of resources in areas most influenced by humans by whatever measure. While old village sites score well when total numbers of useful species are determined, and the old Sounaue village site of Amatene (plot 11) was still being regularly visited for its *Durio, Canarium* and *Artocarpus* in 1996, the percentage of actual trees indicated as useful is markedly the lowest of all the categories plotted. And in terms of species diversity and number of useful trees, protected sacred forest (*sin wesie*) is much like any *wesie*, which suggests that forest may not always be selected for special protection because it has a larger concentration of resources than any other area of forest, but rather because of its accessibility – physically and socially – to a particular clan. The usefulness numbers for *sin wesie* also suggest that forest is not

Table 7.2. General characteristics of Nuaulu forest patch categories based on 1996 plot data.

	Nuaulu description	Plots indicated	N plots	Mean S	Mean % N useful trees	Mean % S useful trees
1	*wesie*	2, 3, 8, 9, 10	5	25 (16, 22, 27, 28, 32)	57	61
2	*nisi ahue*	1, 4, 6	2	18 (10, 20, 23)	81	77
3	*nia monai*	5, 11	2	48 (28, 68)	26	66
4	*sin wesie*	7	1	50	63	60

necessarily likely to be protected because of its higher degree of anthropic influence. Finally, the data show wide variation within the category *wesie*, that is most unlikely to be maximally reflected in the plots selected in the 1996 survey.

Discussion: Why Aren't the Nuaulu Like the Matsigenka?

On the basis of the data provided in this chapter, we can conclude that Nuaulu forest classification conforms to a model in which there is evidence for subtle and extensive understanding of variation, and of the ecological properties of different vegetative associations. However, there are only a small number of shared and consistently organised categories, and a low degree of formal lexicalisation. Systematic data on ecological knowledge and linguistic evidence indicate that:

- The categories *wesie* (forest) and *nisi ahue* (long fallow) absorb a great deal of variation.
- Disturbance history is the main and unifying basis for local understandings of variation, modified by occasional considerations of topography and substrate. Nuaulu perceive all forest as in a state of flux, and recognise that this flux is in large part due to interaction with humans.
- Some stable categories are associated with specific species, but named categories of this kind are rare.
- Perception and classification of forest are inseparable from categories dividing forest in terms of patterns of ownership and the cultural reconstruction of landscape reflected in the use of toponyms.

Overall, what is remarkable about the classification of forest types is the small number of formal categories, the low degree of lexicalisation that could be elicited despite plot data indicating the objective ecological complexity and patchiness of forest, and the flexibility of content locally permitted with respect to the Nuaulu categories *wesie* (forest) and *nisi ahue* (long fallow) that describe them. While there are few widely shared terms systematically glossing types of forest composition and structure, there is good evidence from participant observation that this does not prevent Nuaulu being aware of, and fluently talking about, often quite subtle variation in floristics and in the ecological properties of different vegetative associations. Some of these conclusions now need to be explored in a bit more detail.

I do not think we should be surprised by the small number of labelled categories given the ecological and social conditions under which Nuaulu live, and given the body of existing contemporary evidence in cognitive anthropology that challenges some of the more simplistic versions of the Sapir-Whorf and Nida-Conklin hypotheses. In this context, I wish to argue that no useful purpose is served by a detailed classification of types, as opposed to recognition of some loose intersecting dimensions of variation. This finding is consistent with the observation that where peoples' folk knowledge is extensive and profound, and where there is a high degree of semantic contact between people and a nuanced and complex perceptual environment, experienced intricately and intimately on a daily basis, extensive, systematic and formal lexical codifications are often the least satisfactory way of organising that knowledge (Ellen 1999b). Indeed, they may be too inflexible and cumbersome to be a particularly productive way of retrieving and sharing information. In such situations, and especially where, as in this case, the subject of classification is highly variable, and patterns of extraction are very individualised rather than collectivised, and there is evidence of much intracultural variation, local categories need to be sufficiently flexible to incorporate personal experience, that may be more important than transmission of a formalised body of knowledge (e.g. Bulmer 1974a; Allan 2002: 179; Sillitoe 2002c).

The data presented here indicate the difficulty of separating categories based on ecology, resource use, social and cultural criteria, and thus challenge the idea of an 'ethnoecological classification' independent of other factors relating to land and vegetation that people see as being important. All forest is perceived as through a social grid. Moving through the forest constantly reinforces particular parts of its history as this has impinged on Nuaulu lives: the location of past villages, the territories of clans, or the patterns of extraction of particular individuals. In the same way that it is difficult to isolate a separate technical lexicon of forest types based solely on ecological criteria, so it is difficult to separate a classification of 'forest types' from general vegetation types and other land use categories. Forest, in the sense of *wesie*, is a fundamental cultural category with profound symbolic resonance, but in terms of peoples' ecological understanding it is continuous with other vegetative associations, including those created or modified by the Nuaulu themselves. However, none of this is to deny the rich understandings of forest ecology embedded and encoded in everyday experience and in superficially non-ecological language.

The analysis also demonstrates that ethnoecological categories are probably best not approached as analogues of folk classifications of individual organisms. There is little evidence of conventional taxonomic organisation; categories are only weakly contrastive, seldom easily identifiable as cognitive prototypes, and much better seen as *ad hoc* categories in which criteria clustering may better describe their mode of cognition.

There are particular dangers in deliberately looking for complex classifications of vegetation types that resemble the conventions of scientific ecology in their mode of organisation, at the very least because these latter conform to a narrow linguistic logic derived from the conventions of written language as these have been absorbed into Western science. To assume *a priori* that the underlying mode of organisation is such is to fall into the trap of the linear-sentential fallacy (Bloch 1991). How categories based on radically different kinds of criteria interact, and are presented in a field situation, will in the end be reflected by the way and context in which questions are asked that yield the data, which is basically the way the categories work and are shared amongst local decision-makers, a process I have elsewhere called *prehension* (Ellen 1993b: 229–34).

While we can agree that the frameworks of categories used to describe forest are based on essentially simple, sometimes binary distinctions, we must be wary of rejecting a conventional 'ethnotaxonomic' mode of representation only to replace it with a model of intersecting dimensions that is imagined as a matrix-like structure, capable of generating a larger number of categories simply by combining the dimensions of the matrix. Thus, when Allan (2002) derives 24 different categories for Makushi characterisations of forest, by linking terms for landform, soil, human disturbance history, growth form, and species association or dominance, we have to interpret such data with care. We should neither assume that we can generate additional 'local' categories by the simple logical manipulation of other categories that appear to cross-cut them, or to give undue, or even spurious, arithmetical or linguistic fixity to particular numbers of labelled categories discovered. While Nuaulu data reveal numerous simple contrasts of this type, I am sceptical as to the extent to which they can be formally constituted into a grid. There is not much cognitive evidence for this. Methodologically, we should operate with caution when it comes to cognitive models of dichotomous frameworks, treating them (until sufficient evidence to the contrary) as nothing other than a useful technique for yielding the range of criteria that might be involved in local classificatory behaviour. Such models are a useful preliminary analytic device to get some measure of the data rather than a definitive tool for yielding definitive knowledge of how people cognise their environment.

I want to suggest that the general model of understanding forest variation that I have elucidated here may apply more widely, and is – if you will – the default way in which tropical forest peoples comprehend and describe forest variation more generally. Because of the strong ecological and cultural similarities, a good starting point for any comparison is other material relating to the island of Seram. Conveniently, two studies exist of Alune (West Seram) vegetation classification conducted in two different areas, that by Suharno (1997: 153, 173) in the Eti-Lumoli area, and that by Florey and her associates in Lohiasapalewa and Lohiatala (Wolff and Florey 1998; Florey, personal communication). We find here the same mixture of criteria, the difficulty of distinguishing forest from other kinds of vegetation, and the primacy accorded disturbance regime, as we do with the Nuaulu. However, on the face of it we also find a greater terminological specification of different types of forest. This is in part due to more routine resource extraction from higher altitudes than is the case with the Nuaulu (an ecological difference), but it is also partly an artefact of the way in which the lexical data are presented. Thus, the Alune prefix 'lusun' can apparently be attached to any number of different cultivated trees grown in groves; as the number of tree species incorporated as adjectival qualifiers varies, so does the recorded number of vegetation types. It is also partly accounted for by including specific ecological descriptors for features which are not of themselves forest types, such as 'tape ial uwei' (rich soil found around *Canarium*), or 'lasa porole' (infertile ground around *Intsia bijuga*). It is impossible to say, for example, to what extent the categories 'mosole' (lower altitude montane forest) and 'lasa porole' are commensurable.

However, it is with respect to categories for forest regeneration – a dimension of disturbance history – where we can see some really interesting differences. Thus, the Alune term for the first year of regeneration is 'kwesie buini', forest of 4–8 years regeneration is called 'kwesie', and (in contrast) dense forest is called 'a ela uei' ('ela' = big, 'uei' = base of tree) (Suharno 1997: 153, 173). Thus, although the Alune term 'kwesie' is clearly cognate with Nuaulu *wesie*, its meaning is subtly different, and whereas Nuaulu *wesie* is all forest where specific garden histories are no longer traceable, 'kwesie' refers specifically to regrowth where specific histories are traceable. Indeed, Nuaulu forest that may not have been cultivated for 20 years, but whose history is still traceable, is still a kind of garden, ***nisi ahue***. The Alune term for garden, 'ndinu', only refers to the few years that a garden is being actively cultivated.

Other terminologies from other parts of island Southeast Asia are more consistent in having a single overarching word for forest, and in dividing this up into three to four stages of regrowth. We have already noted that, in his Penan Benalui work, Puri (1997: 104) elicited just eight categories for types of forest, despite systematic attempts to delineate more. However, he notes that further discriminations are possible by plotting these against a riverine ('la' bai') – inland ('la' daya') contrast. The geographically close Lundayeh in Sabah divide up the semantic domain forest ('fulung') into three categories of regrowth: 'amog darii' (less than 10 years), 'amog karar' (10–20 years) and 'amog balui' (20–50 years). Forest where histories of cultivation are no longer traceable are known as 'fulung karar' (Hoare 2002). Thus, some people have a generic term for cultivated land that includes productive and traceable regrowth (like the Nuaulu), while others have a separate term for regrowth that encompasses periods of different regrowth duration: 8 years in the case of the Alune and 50 years in the case of the Lundayeh. These differences may reflect the local importance attached to different kinds of extraction, pressure on resources, and general subsistence orientation. Thus, different peoples terminologically distinguish 'true' forest from 'ancient garden' in different ways, presumably because there are local differences in the correlation between usefulness and the age of the plot since being a swidden (Grenand 1992: 32).

Common Themes and Emerging Patterns

In looking more generally at the ethnoecological classifications used by tropical forest peoples to describe forest diversity, Shepard et al. (2001: 31–32) have noted that 'several common themes and patterns emerge . . . [and suggest] an overall pattern of extraordinary concordance between habitat classification by culturally distinct and geographically separate groups'. Their comparative data were largely Amazonian, but some of their core generalisations are upheld against the island Southeast Asian data examined here. They suggest that abiotic factors (topography, flooding and disturbance regimes, soils) are used to distinguish a small number of general categories. The distinction between river/coast and uplands is found in all indigenous systems. This is borne out in Allan's work and is reflected in the Nuaulu data presented here. Also, their suggestion that the distinction between primary forest and secondary forest, including various stages of swidden fallow regeneration, also appears as a salient category in all systems is confirmed, and indeed disturbance history turns out to be the single most important dimension in classifying forest for people engaged in swidden cultivation. Indeed, within the range of variation described, we detect a pan-cultural and geographically widespread conceptual model based on a limited number of dimensions of perceived experience.

Where my own data do not conform with the picture which emerges from these Amazonian studies, it is in terms of overall category differentiation, degree of lexicalisation and, most specifically, in relation to the claim of the extent to which biotic features – mostly indicator plant species – are used to define more specific habitat types. Even in tropical South America the pattern is far from uniform. For example, frameworks based on species association were only described by 4 per cent of Allan's Makushi participants (2002: 154). While I do not disagree that the concept of indicator species is widely understood by tropical forest peoples, and that substantive knowledge relating to recognised differences based on these is often extensive, I am not convinced that this is universally translated into systematic lists of labelled categories. My own data also show the difficulties of eliciting ethnoecological classifications that are independent of distinctions based on use strategies, land tenure and cultural significance. I am concerned about the dangers of treating complex multidimensional landscape categories in the same way that many have analysed folk classifications of species. I suggest that in many cases we should not expect the degree of shared systematic categorisation implied in the Matsigenka data, and indeed expect people to lexicalise their environment more flexibly and with more limited shared encoding.

Notes

First published in 2010 as 'Why Aren't the Nuaulu Like the Matsigenka? Knowledge and Categorization of Forest Diversity on Seram, Eastern Indonesia', in *Landscape Ethnoecology: Concepts of Biotic and Physical Space*, edited by Leslie Main Johnson and Eugene Hunn (Oxford: Berghahn Books, pp. 116–40). Reproduced courtesy of Berghahn Books.

1. Paul Sillitoe (2002c, and personal communication) has suggested that large numbers of formal categories might also imply the presence of some overarching authority to define them and arbitrate in disputes, whereas a flexibly constituted understanding is more consistent with a decentralised socio-political system. I can think of one clear example from a non-literate animist population for formal control over categories for certain kinds of primary biodiversity: the validation of the names for new landraces of rice by Kasepuhan ritual specialists in upland West Java (Soemarwoto 2007: 96–105). Something similar might well apply to categories of secondary biodiversity in populations where agricultural decision-making is linked to a complex divided landscape, such as for Balinese irrigation associations. However, I remain to be convinced that the distinction would be helpful in the context of the present discussion. If anything, Nuaulu political and ritual authority is more formal than that of the Matsigenka or the Wola. Nuaulu patrilineal clans are divided into complementary 'houses', each with ascribed leadership in a relation of formal diarchy with the other. In turn, clans are arranged in a mythically legitimised order of precedence, where the head of the most senior clan acts as a *primus inter pares*. Ritual and political authority does not necessarily or systematically translate into technical authority in matters relating to ethnoecological categories, except in literate societies.
2. *Apane* appears as a synonym for *wesie*. Thus, the leguminous vine *Derris trifoliata*, used locally as a fish poison, is described variously as *awane munu apane*, *(awane) munu wesie*, and *munu apane*.

CHAPTER 8

Roots, Shoots and Leaves
The Art of Weeding

> Today I think
> Only with scents –
> Scents dead leaves yield,
> And bracken, and wild carrot's seed,
> And the square mustard field;
> Odours that rise
> When the spade wounds the roots of tree,
> Rose, currant, raspberry, or goutweed,
> Rhubarb or celery;
> The smoke's smell, too,
> Flowing from where a bonfire burns
> The dead, the waste, the dangerous,
> And all to sweetness turns.
> It is enough
> To smell, to crumble the dark earth,
> While the robin sings over again
> Sad songs of Autumn mirth.
> —Edward Thomas, 'Digging', 1979

Introduction

Anthropological literature has nowadays a lot to say about the inter-generational transmission of knowledge and skills. The early empirical work – that stemming from cognitive anthropology and ethnobiology – tended to use lexical knowledge as a proxy for knowledge transmission in a particular domain of practice, for example how children acquire names for plants (Stross 1973; Zarger 2002), or it has looked at pre-defined second-order categories of skill to measure transmission, or knowledge loss, as a kind of linear process at an abstract level (Hewlett and Cavalli-Sforza 1986; Ohmagari and Berkes 1997). We now recognise that it is insufficient to know the names of things, or to transmit the names of things, for practical knowledge and practice to be acquired. 'Transmission' – the word itself is a bland and flowing abstraction – generally involves a much more interactive reproduction of cognitive, linguistic and bodily practice through imitation and (re-)discovery by doing (Ellen and Fischer 2013). This 'turn' in scholarship is reflected in the new ethnographies of craft activity, of 'making' (e.g. Marchand 2010; Ingold 2013; Hallam and Ingold 2014), that address the dynamic interface between the actions of the body (in particular the hands), memory, culture and social interaction. It also has much to say about skilled practice in relation to this. But while one can understand the fascination with fabrication because of its essential role in developing complex material cultures, human hands have evolved to undertake a much wider range of tasks than just making objects, or even serving as social organs. For example, hands present us with a sensory and motor apparatus that enables the manipulation of flora and fauna to achieve many different ends. One such practice is gardening, and within it techniques of weeding. The physical movements involved and the knowledge that motivates the use of the hand in this cultural domain, or which arises from such uses, are not necessarily the same as those employed in making things. Weeding – like gardening as a whole – and as evoked in the Edward Thomas poem 'Digging' – is a synaesthetic process in which the hand mediates a relationship between plant and body. It necessitates the mastery of various types of manual dexterity and tool manipulation, plus the coordination of different tactile skills, visual competence and the other senses in relation to acquired background knowledge.

This chapter begins by looking at weeding as a general ethnographic category, drawing upon the comparative literature, and then focuses on the physical actions involving hands, with a view to demonstrating how this is a complex and fully cultural phenomenon, while shedding some light on the process of how we 'learn to weed'. To this end it uses data drawn from an anthropological and ethnobotanical study of domestic gardening and allotment keeping in East Kent, a set of data on gardening practice in general accumulated during the Leverhulme British Homegardens Project, which had as a major theme the transmission of gardening knowledge and practice (Ellen and Platten 2011; Platten 2013). But I also draw on some home-grown domestic ethnography, indeed some experimental auto-ethnography, together with 287 photos of weeding downloaded from the internet, and a collection of pen and ink illustrations from gardening books, columns and strips in magazines and newspapers. Consider, for example, the graphical detail provided in the drawing of cutting and storing dahlia tubers in The Reader's Digest's *The Gardening Year* (1978: 256). What I find fascinating in this latter genre – as also found in the illustrations of home do-it-yourself manuals – is the attention given in the artwork to the precise positioning of the hands and fingers in relation to a particular physical activity, which of course we know is crucial for the proper execution of the task described.

Weeding as an Anthropological Category

At its core, weeding is a set of activities that comprise identifying growing plants that hinder the growth or appreciation of plants that are valued and harvested, followed by activity that physically removes them. We might suppose, therefore, that weeding cannot have existed as a practice until humans could recognise 'weeds', suggesting that there could be no weeding before the Neolithic, before cultivation and domestication, before gardens and fields. But even where humans extract plants in non-domesticated non-cultivated contexts, in what we still call the 'wild', there is plenty of evidence of humans protecting such plants by cutting back growth around them that might otherwise smother or out-compete them for nutritional resources and sunlight. The famous examples include yams in tropical forests (Headland 1987), but we might also admit the selective burning of vegetation as a strategy for removing unwanted undergrowth. Burning emerges also as a means of clearing unwanted vegetation prior to cultivation in swidden farming systems, and as a much more directed form of weed removal under intensive industrialised forms of agriculture.

Approached in this way, we might rather view weeding as a secondary cultural adaptation of a general foraging facility that draws upon the same cognitive and manipulative skills and must have evolved early in human (indeed in Hominin) evolutionary history. There is now no shortage of field evidence to show how chimpanzees and other great apes can selectively identify, manipulate and pick roots, shoots and leaves (e.g. Humle and Matsuzawa 2001, 2004), and we might therefore conclude that the selective pressures of a general foraging way of life and – one might also suppose – additional pressures encouraging the use of the hand as a social tool, 'pre-adapted' it for the precision picking of leaves and fruits, digging roots, breaking stems, making tools, stripping bark, and other activities that we associate with gardening and agriculture, including weeding.

Despite the protean and generic character of those cognitive and physical actions that constitute it, 'weeding' has been claimed by at least some anthropologists and others to be a useful analytic category of cross-cultural application, where it overlaps with similar practices such as cutting back, trimming and pollarding. Different forms of agriculture depend on weeding to differing extents. In swidden farming, weeding is, as a rule, less important than in intensive field horticulture or agriculture, but much depends on the crop and on the scale of farming. Weeding, for example, is much more important when cultivating grains than tubers, since grasses and sedges compete more effectively with domesticated grasses than they do with tubers, corms and root crops, such as yams or cassava. However, even in swidden populations, as Conklin (1957, 1961) has shown, weeding presents a complex domain of activity that can be instructively typologised, both emically and etically. And not only is weeding an activity which is functionally complex, it varies in the time it occupies across different production systems. While in some it occupies little time, in others it represents the most time-consuming activity in the gardening or agricultural calendar. Roy Rappaport (1971a: 120) famously measured the energy expenditure of various subsistence activities among the Tsembaga Maring of the New Guinea highlands and found that weeding absorbed 180,336 kilocalories per acre in a single year, 32 per cent of total expenditure on all inputs, from initial clearance to harvesting and cartage. Rappaport found weeding to be a fairly continuous activity between planting and harvesting, but in many farming regimes the types of weeds (and therefore the kind of weeding required) varies between different stages in the cultivation cycle, sometimes with dramatic consequences. In many agricultural calendars, especially those for rice, first and second weeding are fixed and vital calendrical phases, as among the Baduy of upland West Java (Iskandar 2007). Paul Richards (1986), working among the Mende of Sierra Leone, was able to show how weeds growing in a field prior to ploughing are different from those after ploughing. Traditional local methods of maintenance were able to take this into account and flexibly adapt weeding behaviour, but a UK science-driven attempt to advise Mende of the best way to deal with weeds failed miserably because it offered an unsubtle single generic solution. For example, the weed ranked by farmers as the most severe infestation before ploughing was 'Congo jute', *Urena lobata*, though this was far less significant after ploughing. On the other hand, sedges that were not significant before ploughing became very significant afterwards. Similar complexities in the ecology and consequences of weed distribution and applied practice are illustrated in Paul Sillitoe's (2010: 313) account of how Wola weeding activity varies depending on the target cultigen, for example whether taro or *Amaranthus*, and on the distance from a homestead. The typologising of weeding may also reflect the extent to which it is truly manual, the kinds of tools used and the extent to which the process as a whole is mechanised; or the amount of precision required, whether the fine-grained weeding we associate with the needs of the English domestic garden or the coarse-grained weeding of Nuaulu swiddens in eastern Indonesia (Ellen 1978: 177–78) where you either roughly cut back the undergrowth or selectively cut round individual plants and trees.

Weeding as a Cultural Domain

At the same time that the utility of the analytic category 'weeding' depends on the ecology, form and scale of cultivation practised, so its occurrence as a locally conceptualised type of activity varies. In this sense we can accept weeding as what Ingold (1993) calls a 'taskscape', meaning that it constitutes an 'array' of multiple overlapping activities over time in a landscape directed at solving the problems posed by weeds. Wherever such activities can be identified, the extent to which they are culturally recognised will be reflected in the degree to which as a domain it is labelled, and its constituent parts committed to specialist language; in other words the extent to which it comprises a 'taskonomy' (Dougherty and Keller 1982). This occurs where members of a speech community share subsistence problems and problem-solving, and agree to give those different components names. In the domain of weeding, detailed nomenclature and classification is rarely evident in the direct skilled practice of gardeners and farmers themselves – who take a much more intuitive approach based on experience. It is what I have elsewhere called substantive rather than lexical knowledge (e.g. Ellen and Fischer 2013: 17–18), but it may be reified in the manuals produced to aid gardeners in their work, or in the rhetoric of manufacturers of specialist weeding tools – about which more later. In other words, while we can begin to understand the complexity of weeding as an integrated cognitive, socio-cultural and physical activity by constructing a taskonomy, this is generally an etic rather than emic model. Weeding, for most people, is a less structured and more intuitive kind of knowledge.

The meanings attached to weeding vary between cultural populations depending on their history: on forms of agriculture, crops grown, ecology and plant geography. Indeed, languages vary in the extent to which they admit the category 'weed', and often a single word polysemously serves as a general-purpose category for a morphologically distinguishable kind of plant (grass) and a functional category (weed), as in the Nuaulu term *monote* (Ellen 1991a). The extent to which the special-purpose plant category is elaborated depends on the extent and ways in which local populations are transforming the environment, and it is hardly surprising that the ambiguity we find in the Nuaulu meanings is associated with a long-fallow swidden system, transitional between semi-managed agroforestry and proper field agriculture.

Weeding is not even always motivated by a desire to increase the size of a harvest, but can be essentially aesthetic and moral. In some cases, it is not even necessary to weed around plants to enhance growth, health or productivity, but people may do so because of preferred visual appearance. In many cases, weeding as an activity extends to practices quite unrelated to plant production. Nuaulu women seem to spend more time pulling out unwanted grass and other plants around houses than they do weeding swiddens, supported by periodic 'adat cuci negeri' (Ind., 'village washing') rituals through which all land in a village area – as if to define it as part of the domain of culture rather than unrestrained nature – is cleared of unwanted ground plant cover. It is a bit like removing unwanted bodily hair.

All categories formed from verbal substantives can be semantically simple or complex. The notion of 'pulling', for example, is semantically primitive and carries little cultural baggage. However, weeding as an emically recognised activity requires at the very least recognition of certain plants as 'weeds' and a set of values and notions about procedures that are undertaken in its name. Weeding is complex by virtue of referring to a pattern of activity that involves a range of different bodily actions (picking, pulling, digging, raking, hoeing, holding, lifting), other objects (tools and containers), and cognitive activity that combines with the purpose of removing those plants culturally classified as weeds. And not only does weeding involve the motor function of the hand and body in weeding, but also serves an important sensory function, without which the motor functions cannot operate. In order to weed, plants labelled as such must be identified. While this is initially generally a visual function, it is reinforced by tactile and – to a lesser extent – olfactory sensation. It is because of this that the visually impaired can generally adjust to weeding by shifting their reliance to different sensory perceptors.

Weeding therefore involves the whole sensorium, but we cannot effectively employ and connect those senses and translate them into motor activity without cognising the process. We have to know what we are doing, to identify weeds from non-weeds and to know why we are doing it. We have to recognise what has to come out and what has to stay: this is mainly visual, but may involve olfactory and tactile components, informed by cultural knowledge of what is and is not a weed, aided by plant names and the species-centric traits associated with them: size, shape, colour, characters of leaves, stems and flowers, the general habit of the plant, its feel (rough, smooth and other tactile properties) and its smell. Not only are weeds identified through their tactile properties, but how they are handled (including with or without tools, or with or without gloves) will depend on their woodiness, roughness, smoothness, whether stems or leaves are slimy or slippery, hairy, stinging, prickly, spiny or thorny. These are all properties that are primarily experienced through the hands. Just to take four examples from local Kentish domestic gardens. Hedge bindweed (*Calystegia sepium*) is intractable partly because of its slipperiness, nettles (*Urtica dioica, U. urens*) are problematic because of their stinging hairs, couch grass (*Elymus repens*) is tough and difficult to pull, and cleavers (*Galium aparine*), sometimes called 'velcro weed' in England, is rough but its stem is easily broken. Each species is by reputation and experience pernicious in its own way, and each poses a slightly different problem when it comes to removal, has to be handled in a slightly different way, because of its habit, rooting system, or the properties of its organs. Knowledge of weeds is essential for effective practice. As Richard Mabey (2010) notes, 'plants with strong taproots which could destroy the protective roof barrier layers and then the roof structure over time are to be identified as weeds and pulled up without mercy'. Weeds are aggressive 'Jack-of-all-places' and 'adaptive generalists' but vary in their resilience and intractability. Hoeing off weed leaves and stems as soon as they appear can eventually weaken and kill perennials, although this will require persistence in the case of plants such as bindweed. Nettle infestations can be tackled by cutting back at least three times a year, repeated over a three-year period, and bramble can be dealt with in a similar way.

Beginning with the Hands

Weeding as a cultural and technical phenomenon goes beyond the use of the hands, but it is with hands that we must begin, both logically and from the point of view of evolution. The person who first taught me about hands was John Russell Napier (1962), and it was perhaps no accident that his interest in the subject should connect with the fact that he was also a distinguished member of the Magic Circle. While our understanding of the mechanics of the hand and the taxonomy of grips is now much more sophisticated than Napier's, his distinction (1993 [1980]: 63; Figure 8.1) between power grip and precision grip (of the supposedly fifty-eight possible movements of the hand) is as good a place as any to start. He also identified a composite grip that is essentially a combination of the two, and a hook grip, associated mainly with carrying. Since Napier, classifications have become more complex (e.g. Cutkowsky and Howe 1990), but let us try and keep things simple here.

In weeding, we rely on both variations of the power and the precision grip: the power grip to remove tougher weeds out of the soil (pulling, dragging) and to hold tools, and the precision grip to manipulate (picking and plucking) smaller weeds, differentiate them from what surrounds

190 | *Nature Wars*

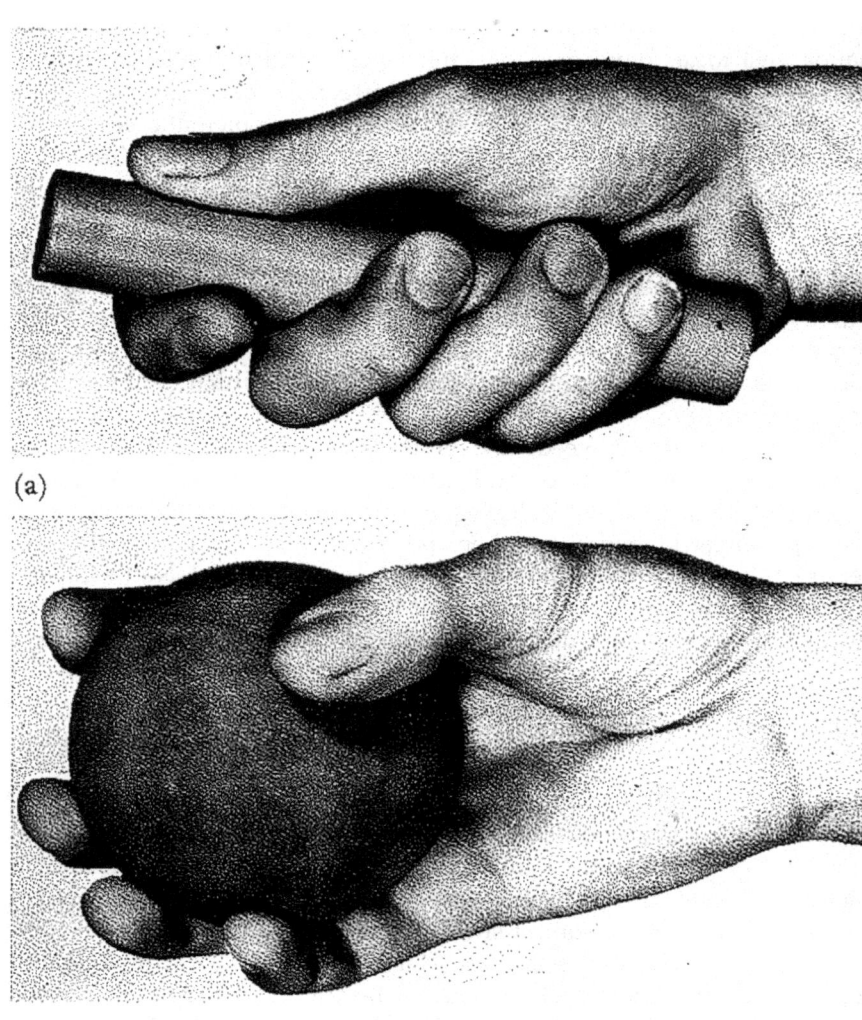

Figure 8.1. Power grip (a) and precision grip (b) (source: Napier 1993 [1980], figure 28).

them, and ensure that in working out a weed we do not break the stem or root and leave the offending organ in the earth. We can see here (Figure 8.2) examples of grasping actions involved in single-handed weeding, but weeding is seldom performed with one hand behind the back. The opposite hand is often called upon to assist where additional force, traction or support is required, or it may provide an adjunct role by holding

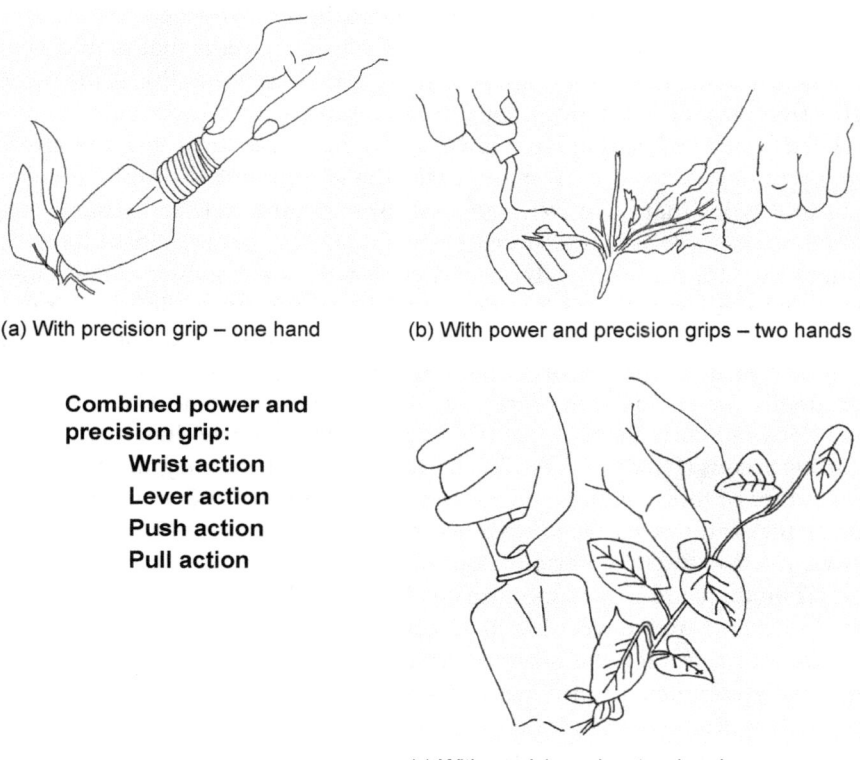

(a) With precision grip – one hand

(b) With power and precision grips – two hands

Combined power and precision grip:
    Wrist action
    Lever action
    Push action
    Pull action

(c) With precision grip – two hands

Figure 8.2. The default weeding action (in a Kentish country garden). Figure created by the author.

back vegetation, provide support for the body, or hold down the soil, or it may improve the efficiency of the weeding process by being used simultaneously and ambidextrously in performing the same task. But even the hands are not an independent physical system in this or in the context of any other activity. They can only be manipulated as part of the skeleto-muscular apparatus of the entire body through the elbow and shoulder, either to coordinate and balance activity or to provide additional force and leverage in heavy activity.

The Material Culture of Weeding

We usually associate weeding that employs only the hands with small domestic gardens, even though in large parts of the world weeds are removed entirely manually. Many gardeners still remove weeds by pulling them out of the ground, making sure to include the roots that would otherwise allow them to re-sprout. And there is no doubt that this is the most effective way of extracting many weeds; but as with most cultivation-related practices, people have always sought to use tools to more effectively undertake a task. In many cases the equipment is simple, involving tool types that have other general uses in gardening or farming. An obvious example is the all-purpose bushknife or 'parang' in Indonesia. But at least for the last two thousand years we have evidence of specialist weeding equipment. The Roman *Columella* advises us to 'let the careful gardener ... comb the ground with a two-pronged fork, and choking weeds cast from the furrows'. Similarly, Old English 'weed hoeks' were originally devised for removing weeds from standing wheat, while Samuel Pepys records using a 'spud' – with a narrow chisel-like blade – for cutting weeds (Huxley 1978: 178). By the nineteenth century, the specialist inventory of tools available to mediate between hand and weed included daisy forks and rakes, weeding pincers, root extractors, two-edged knives, lawn weed-extractors, various hoes and mattocks, small forks and trowels. Then there are gloves and arm coverings, tools of a kind which protect the body, and enable weeding in places where the hands might otherwise be damaged. In fact, the material equipment of weeding has become remarkably complex, improving and extending the kinds of manipulation possible with the hands alone.

Most weeding tools are operated in a squatting or bending posture, but others can be operated when standing or slightly bending, by adding a long handle to the kinds of devices already considered. This alters the biomechanics and ergonomics of weeding. The hoe, for example, works in a completely different way to a hand trowel, necessitating a whole-body movement in which the hands simply grip the handle and the arm and upper body does the work. How the hoe works to remove weeds varies with the design of the hoe. Weed control with a hoe can be by agitating the surface of the soil or by cutting foliage from the roots, and clearing soil of old roots and crop residues. While a normal hoe digs the top surface of the soil by dragging the soil towards the body, a Dutch or push hoe removes fewer recalcitrant weeds on the surface of the soil with a pushing motion. Then there are tools for precision weeding, which work through a combination of hand-eye coordination and the power grip holds the tool. In such a combination, the wrist may be used to work out the weed.

As Francois Sigaut (1993) has noted, there is an old strand of anthropological literature on material culture in which tools seem to stand apart from the hand and take on an autonomous analytic existence, yet how can we understand tools except as part of a system that includes the hand?

Even where the focus of a study is on skill and cognition, this dimension can sometimes be missing. Thus, Keller and Keller (1996) in their otherwise path-breaking book on blacksmithing have lots of pictures of tools, but none of these include hands. Tools are in essence prostheses or hand-extenders, the use of which can fundamentally change the way in which the hand is used. With a tool, the hand itself is no longer the 'business end' interfacing directly with the plant and soil, but may simply become that part of the entire apparatus that securely clamps the tool to the rest of the body, and where instead it is the arm and upper body that does much of the work. At the same time, the use of tools releases the hand to become the focus of other actions, for example wrist movement. When we use tools, the way we use our hands changes, depending on the tool.

Having noted the variety of tools available and the different biomechanical apparatus required in each case, most weeders prefer to use a single adaptable tool – such as the hand trowel. With a small trowel the typical instrument among Kentish weeders, it is not a power or a precision grip but rather a combination of the two (Figure 8.2), which facilitates a simultaneous or sequential use of a push action to get under the recalcitrant plant's root system, a wrist turning action to free it from surrounding soil, and a lever action to lift it. The free hand provides support for the entire operation, in particular allowing a pull action to remove the plant completely. The design of the trowel handle enables the grip. The design of the blade – its point and curvature – enables the user to precisely locate and free the plant. It can be used with a push action to get underneath a root, and then the back of the trowel used as a lever to force it out. The side of the blade can be used to cut. I observe that my partner Nikki Goward uses the trowel as a kind of scraper – so tools are often used for purposes for which they were not originally designed, but acquire a use through serendipity. Nikki only likes to use one tool, and the trowel is the best multi-purpose and flexible instrument at her disposal. She does not use a small fork because she does not wish to dig up the top layer of soil, which provides a protective barrier. Like most weeders, she synchronously uses both hands – tool in one hand, and the other hand picking up weeds and putting them into a container. In fact, this might be held as the basic and default tool–body arrangement in most weeding practice, of which there are numerous variations.

Thus, if we consider all permutations of physical actions involving the hands – singly, combined, in conjunction with the rest of the body, and those additional possibilities of adjunct physical action made possible by the hand or hands in conjunction with various tools, we have a highly differentiated set of actions that we can place in a taskscape of physical actions called 'weeding'. Techniques, however, will vary with micro-ecology of place and time. Compare, for example, the different techniques of weeding the grass edges of a bed in late spring where weeds are competing with new growth, with cutting back weeds to clean up beds after autumnal die-back. But while this may serve as an instructive and convenient analytic case, in terms of the ergonomics of material culture it places us firmly in the typological tradition of Leroi-Gourhan (1943, 1945). While in the normal way weeding is largely un-elaborated emically, is seldom experienced as a taskscape or organised as a taskonomy, none of this means that it is somehow 'outside' culture or sociality, as I shall now explain.

Weeding as a Social and Cultural Activity

Weeding is a relational practice: it occurs in situations made and pre-defined by its collective practitioners. Wherever the human hand operates, it does so in a cultural context, being an instrument the movements and capabilities of which influence and are influenced by the social mind within an immediate physical environment established through the actions of previous actors. Even if none of this were true, any physical action involving a fabricated tool must be cultural, since tool design, manufacture and mode of use are all the result of some transmitted cross-generational tradition. The difference between the way in which a rake and a hoe work is a cultural difference, and reflects the interaction of different individuals in some process of change and adaptation. Moreover, while we are accustomed to the image of the lone weeder in a domestic garden, weeding is often a highly sociable activity, whether in homegardens or big fields.

The pioneer theorist historically credited with grasping the socio-cultural significance of bodily movement in general – Marcel Mauss (1973 [1934]) – strangely has little to say about the hand. About fifteen years ago at a seminar at the University of Kent, my colleague Roger Just asserted that Mauss's *Les Techniques du Corps* was a very dull essay with nothing of interest to say to anthropologists. This observation was motivated by a discussion of the way in which Greek tobacconists cover the change they give you with the palm of the hand as they slide it across the kiosk counter in your direction. Mauss, it was suggested, would have nothing significant to say about what we might infer from this behaviour beyond the observation that it encodes and communicates moral values. I disagreed at the time, and still do. First of all, Mauss was part of the great Durkheimian project to uncover underlying elemental social forms, which in his essay he proceeds to do. In deprecating Mauss's achievement, we are simply confirming that we now take his insights for granted. Secondly, and most importantly, Mauss shows us that what is fundamental about human culture is the existence of multiple ways of enculturating the same physical process. Sometimes this variation is a statistical side-effect of transmission with no real social consequences, but at some point it becomes critical, as it is necessary to enculturate the body in a sufficiently similar way to make social behaviour possible, and to transmit it effectively. Consider, for example, Mauss's example of the problems encountered by closely ranked First World War troops when one or two march out of step, or the confusion that arises when different rules of right and left handedness confront each other, or his reference to the costs to military engineering when French troops were replaced with British troops unfamiliar with the French spades left behind for their use. Why should it be that, when the hand is at rest, women – as Mauss notes – close the fist with the thumb inside and men with the thumb outside? If this is true, it is simply because it conveniently routinises experience.

To ensure that the inconvenience of varied and unpredictable behaviours is minimised, we have social conventions to instil conformist behaviour: morally sanctioning 'wrong' somatic practices and mocking cultural practices that are unaccountably different from our own. From an evolutionary standpoint, such forms of cultural enforcement have more to do with the effective transmission of common technical practices than with the cultural supremacist claim that an English spade is better than a French spade. And it was Mauss who – long before the term was reified by students of Pierre Bourdieu – gave us the word 'habitus' to describe the physical demeanour of the body necessary to achieve a particular purpose, a demeanour that was necessarily cultural. Mauss, therefore, in his 'dull text' and relying heavily on autobiographical anecdotes, initiated the French tradition of material culture studies in which the dynamic interaction of cultural inputs through social transmission with the physical becomes a core methodological starting point, as in the work of Leroi-Gourhan (1943, 1945), Francois Sigaut (1993), Pierre Lemonnier (1992) or Robert Cresswell (1983).

In looking at weeding as a culturally embodied process, the differences in physical movement according to ethnicity, gender or age are the least important. What is important is how innovations allow the flexible adjustment of the body to different micro-ecologies, dependent on soil variation, crops grown and different weed regimes. Arbitrary cultural precedent too – which may indeed be linked to ethnicity, gender or age – influences how we use tools most comfortably and our ability to use the tools that are available. All of the actions I have described are cultural in that they are learned, through a combination of self-tuition and imitation, and these may vary between different cultural populations with degrees of what

Lemonnier (1992) would regard as arbitrariness. There is no single way of doing something, but many of roughly equal efficiency.

But weeding is not just a series of individual physical actions, but a process – a 'chaîne opératoire', a sequence of actions of the kind I have described in relation to the use of different kinds of tool in an English homegarden. The specific actions of weeding are interspersed with actions of carrying, lifting, loading and pushing. But the sequence is not of just connected technical actions, but comprises stretches of rhythmic action interspersed with moments of rest; it may be accompanied by singing or humming; if others are involved it will be interspersed with conversation. Over longer intervals, time will be taken out to pile up weeds, and remove them to a compost heap or bonfire. Thus, there is a complex sequence of different actions which repeat at lesser and greater intervals. While relying on and incorporating a variety of physical actions, what we see is a pattern of activity that cannot be understood by reducing it to biology. This is one of the reasons why the International Biological Programme (IBP) programme for the comparative study of human energy expenditure (e.g. Weiner and Lourie 1969) was so problematic: it could not control for the cultural component of human activity over a wide range of different ecologies and cultures. Human physical activity is 'biocultural' in the sense used by Ulijaszek (2007), at every possible turn.

Learning How to Weed – Some Provisional Conclusions

So, what does all this tell us about how we learn to weed? One of the main themes of the British Homegardens Project has been how gardening knowledge is transmitted inter-generationally in the modern world. At the highest level of abstraction, individual acts of transmission take place in a wide institutional context (Figure 8.3), a social world that frames and supports learning. Within this framework we can recognise that print and electronic media are an important element in the late twentieth-century growth of UK recreational gardening.

However, an underlying hypothesis in our work has been that because gardening is ultimately a practical bodily skill it must be acquired through direct physical activity and interaction between skilled and less-skilled gardeners. On the evidence presented here, the learning of weeding skills is not simply the transmission of rules and bodies of knowledge that exist prior to the physical actions involved, but depends on the actual undertaking of manual tasks. Books – even videos – are not the easiest medium through which to explain how to weed. It is much easier to physically show and do than to verbally tell, like learning to ride a bicycle or tie a

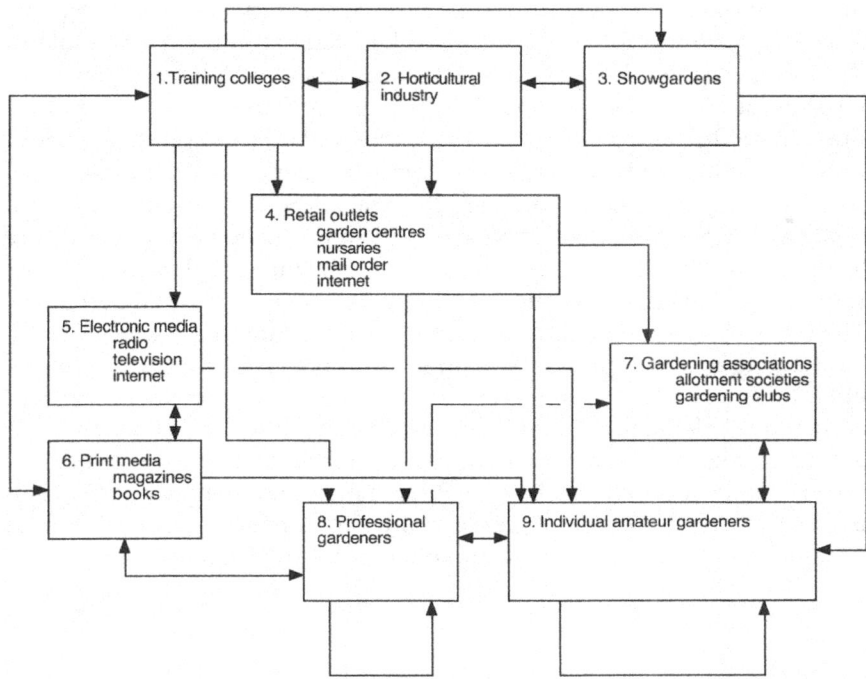

Figure 8.3. The institutional context of learning how to garden in the contemporary UK (source: Ellen and Platten 2011).

shoelace. To a considerable extent we have not developed the technical vocabulary (taskonomies again) to do this, though there is no reason in principle why we should not do so. Gardening books can provide pictures of weeds, to enable us to recognise what to pull out, but for a variety of reasons, well understood by field botanists and ethnobotanists, this can be a hazardous exercise. Micro-ecologies are diverse and instructional books have to write for the average situation in which gardeners find themselves. The ways in which tools, hands and plants physically interact are learned in complex cultural contexts. However far we drill down to find something that is untainted by culture, it strangely reappears, providing us with options for action and shaping our choices.

In some instances, the necessity to standardise the process of weeding, but at the same time maintain the reliability and specificity of the human mind–hand loop, has led to hybrid 'cyborg' forms of weeding mechanisation. One such example is the tractor-drawn platform on which several operatives lie face-down to manually weed along a furrow as the platform gradually moves forward. Such serial application of skilled labour has historically been the way in which factory systems have exploited the advantages of multiple bodies, by mechanically suppressing the role of the social. And while local knowledge and manual skills still prevail in most domestic gardening, both have diminished in commercial and industrial production. Where ecologies are simplified through standardised mono-cropping, generic solutions are possible. For example, in municipal park planting the selection of the appropriate designer varieties, chemical treatment of plants and soils and standardised management strategies are leading to a deskilling of weeding, in which the manual element and specialised knowledge requirement is diminished (Gieser 2014; Gilbert 2013). The hands have become progressively less important in weeding.

Weeding is a complex activity, in some ways no different from many other technical activities in its combination of physical, sensory, cognitive and cultural elements. I have looked at weeding here as a general ethnographic category, and drawn upon the comparative literature to explore how we learn to weed. At the same time, I have shown how by taking an ostensibly trivial subject we can explore fundamental issues of human behaviour, and show that substantively it is not so trivial after all.

CHAPTER 9

Tools, Agency and the Category of 'Living Things'

> Human cognition, it appears, is handily eclectic.
> —S. Atran, *Cognitive Foundations of Natural History*

Introduction: Thinking Like a Dog

I never cease to be amazed and intrigued by the way in which certain animals respond to humans using tools. Let me give two very specific examples from my own domestic life. When I am brushing away ashes in the fire hearth, our border collie will snap at the brush, but only when I am using it. As soon as the brush is put down, and my hand withdrawn, and the brush is completely inert, the snapping and barking ceases. Similarly, when I am outside, let us say, raking autumnal leaves, the collie will snap and bark at the rake, but as soon as the rake is put down it becomes completely disinterested and wanders off. The dog also reacts to wheelbarrows and tractor mowers in a similar way, and bites at the wheels, consistent with the widely reported canine 'grab-bite' predatory behaviour pattern (Coppinger and Schneider 1995: 27).

What is interesting about this observation is not simply the phenomenon itself (a characteristic of the breed), but a paradox that lies at the heart of our wonderment at the dog's perception and comprehension. It is a relatively uninteresting inference to say that when the tool is moving the dog responds to it as if the tool were animate. What is more interesting is to note that the tool becomes animate because it is attached to me. The dog knows me well enough and does not bark and snap when I am not raking or brushing, or whatever – only when the activity involves certain kinds of tool that interact with the ground. Thus, it does not happen when I am, say, using a hammer, or working at a bench. So, why, when the dog does not react aggressively to me normally, does it do so when I am using certain kinds of tool in a particular way? One possible explanation is that the dog responds to the rake or brush because it thinks it is an independent organism, and because of its close proximity must be threatening me. The collie has reverted to guard dog mode to protect me, responding to the rake or brush as if it were a recalcitrant sheep. So, although it can see that I am the agent moving the rake, it responds to the rake as though it was independent and itself had agency.

Can we therefore conclude that the dog is confused? Of course, not all animals respond in this way in such situations, certainly not all species and or most breeds of dog. Collies are trained as guard dogs to herd animals, and their behavioural features have been selected by humans and cultivated to encourage such behaviour. However, quite apart from the puzzle of canine perception and understanding that this raises, both the general observation that animals other than humans can attribute the qualities of living matter and agency to what we call tools or affordances, and the specific paradox concerning the simultaneous attribution of autonomy to the tool and the visual evidence that it is motivated by a human, are, I think, relevant. We can conclude that both humans and other animals attribute the qualities of living matter and agency to what we call tools and other cultural objects. And in both cases a paradox may arise when autonomy is attributed to the object at the same time that it is recognised that its life-like characteristics are motivated by human actions.[1]

My account of the interaction between dogs and human tools is relevant to anthropological debates about the differences between human cognition of living and non-living things (e.g. Atran 1990). Nuaulu people in eastern Indonesia describe many kinds of object as having the qualities we might otherwise reserve for biological organisms. They also distinguish entities that have many of the qualities of life but which ordinarily have no corporeal existence (spirits). While all cultural objects are potentially regarded in this way, in practice some objects are more alive and have more agency than others. I argue here that part of the problem with existing anthropological treatments of the category 'living things' is that they are either logical extrapolations through polythetic extension, or based on formal taxonomic deduction/induction. Using examples of meat skewers, outboard motors, coconut graters and sago-processing devices, together with certain forms of 'peripheral' biological life such as slime fungi and algae, I shall try to demonstrate how Nuaulu ideas of what is animate and agentive are always fuzzy and contingent, and that by combining data from different kinds of ethnographic context, using different elicitation procedures, a more complex picture emerges.

Tools, Machines and Engines

Nuaulu people of eastern Indonesia provide us with plenty of examples of tools that might be said to have agency, but not all tools are the same. They attribute to many kinds of object the qualities that we might otherwise reserve for biological organisms, and although I have continued unashamedly to describe Nuaulu as 'animists' despite the nuanced theorising of the ontological turn in anthropology, I do not have in mind here simply practices that we might formally understand as animism. Nuaulu do not animate every inanimate thing in their environment, all of the time. Neither by describing Nuaulu as animist do I mean that they exclusively resort to what Descola (2005b) would understand by an animist ontology. Totemic, analogical, naturalist and animist 'ontologies' are all available to Nuaulu, who like many people resort to each and all as and when the context makes them appropriate. I think we need to resist turning these important cognitive and representational distinctions into a mechanical typology. However, in examining the case of tools, it is impossible to avoid notions of 'animation' wherever we find the property of physical motion.

Tools have been classified in many ways, but here it helps to distinguish between: (A) tools that once made do not move (e.g. a fence or a stake in a pit trap), and (B) tools that move when activated by the human body and are often characterised ergonomically or in terms of physiological mechanics as an extension of a body part. These would include a hammer, sago pounder, or the fire hearth brush that featured in my opening example of dog–human interaction. Type (C) tools are those having simple moving parts that relay energy released by initial human motion, such as the Nuaulu sago flour extraction device, a treadle-operated coconut grater, or a hand-held string-making apparatus. These are effectively 'machines', or 'tended facilities' (Oswalt 1976) using mechanical power, having several parts for performing a particular task. Finally, there are (C) tools that are also machines in the sense outlined but that run on stored energy, and do not require continuous human inputs, only initially to prime them or to add fuel. In the Nuaulu material universe these might include clocks, trucks, chainsaws or outboard motors. We would usually describe these as 'engines', in that they each convert energy into useful mechanical motion. Let us now examine Nuaulu examples of each of these.

A common type (A) tool would be, as I have indicated, a fence or a pit trap stake. Although Nuaulu might in theory attribute some independent agency to either of these under certain circumstances, I have no examples of this ever being the case. A more interesting example would be a meat skewer or *asunaete*. These are made of wood or bamboo and used in the preparation and transport of meat, but they are also a material instrument facilitating communication between the living and ancestral spirits. Thus, after a wild pig has been killed, it will first be singed to remove most body hair near to the place where it was caught and before returning to the village. A fire is lit and a wooden stake cut to serve as a skewer to manipulate the carcase. A chip (*kakomate*) from the skewer – representing its soul or spirit – is placed inside the belly of the pig, removed after singeing and reunited with the *asunaete*. The pig is butchered by first stripping out the lower jaw bone (*penesite*), throat and lungs. After the pig has been butchered, the skewer will be stuck in the ground and the throat and lungs (the organs of breath) attached to the top as an offering to ancestral spirits, before being taken back to the village. A similar skewer (*asunaete marane*) is used for marsupial cuscus of the genera *Phalanger* and *Spilocuscus* that are the most frequent animal species hunted by Nuaulu (Ellen 1996b). In this case, however, the skewers are not used to remove the fur through singeing and do not have the lungs and trachea tied to them. Instead, having served their purpose in cooking and for transport they are stuck into the ground, and the chip, initially removed to make the spike, is reattached to the skewer. The soul is thus reunited with the body, and it is believed that the spirit of the cuscus will return in another body, which will be eaten again. Thus, the *asunaete* has a simultaneous purpose of skewering the meat, roasting it or carrying it, but by virtue of this role also ensures that the spirit of the animal returns to the cosmos to sustain the population of cuscus for further hunting (Figure 9.1). *Asunaete* for the four different kinds of cuscus are differentiated by the presence or absence of notches, or the number of notches on the skewer. The skewer for *mara kokowe* (male *Phalanger orientalis*) has no notches, while that for *mara osu* (female *Phalanger orientalis*) has one or two notches. Thus, the *asunaete* works in a similar way to the Huarani blowpipe, 'being a regulatory instrument inserted in webs of systemic relations through which the reproduction of society' (Rival 2013: 97) is effected through the reproduction of the cuscus population.

Type (B) tools conform to our prototypical notion of what a tool should be, and readily fit the idea of tool as prosthesis, as an extension of the living human anatomy, moving with the body and sometimes even resembling human body parts: for example a sago pounder. But while tools become animated by virtue of being extensions of the human body, this – unlike the case of dog–brush interaction in my opening example – is in itself insufficient to make them 'animate' in the sense understood by animism. Most Nuaulu tools, most of the time, are not attributed with animacy. However, some are more likely to be, and we need to identify what the conditions might be to satisfy this condition. In the first place, these

Figure 9.1. Series of *asunaete*: cuscus (*Phalanger*) skewers planted as an offering to ancestral spirits; June 1970 (Ellen 70-06-25). Photograph by the author.

conditions relate to the kind of subsistence activity with which they are connected. Thus, hunting (and in a previous era warfare) are high-risk activities in which supernatural support can make a difference. Secondly, some technologies are less under the continuous control of an operator. A bamboo pounder never leaves the hand that holds it during the actions entailed in pounding sago pith. However, arrows, once they leave the projectile release mechanism we call a bow, are subject to a variety of hazards over which the archer has no direct control: wind, movement of the prey, or of objects intervening between the hunter and his prey. In this situation, to attribute an arrow with agency and to make a preliminary offering to its embodied spirit to ensure its effectiveness in flight makes sense.

However, in addition to such technological contexts, there is a category of tool that is always regarded as fully animate because of the simultaneous status of such tools as ritual objects. In the first place, any tool or other artefact that has been used in ritual becomes sacred and cannot be disposed of, being stored until it disintegrates in the smoky lofts of clan houses. But there are other ritual objects, such as shields nowadays used only in ceremonial contexts (Ellen 1990, 2018b). Most of these are not subject to special ritual attention, but others are produced and stored with anthropomorphic regard under controlled ritual circumstances. They well illustrate Gell's (1998: 230–31) notion of 'objectified personhood' through deferred or abducted human agency, existing both 'objectively', and subjectively as persons. But not only are there sacred shields but also sacred spears and baskets (Ellen 2012) and other objects, all of which are exemplary instances of each kind of tool. To have all baskets, spears and shields accorded special respect would be inconvenient, but to have just some objects in a given category with sacred agency is sufficient to make the point. The logic here is similar to the totemic logic prohibiting one species within a category of potential food animals or plants, the rest of which can be eaten (Ellen 1998b: 254–55).

The third category of tool (type C) contains those with moving parts, and those that I will discuss here are the sago flour extraction apparatus and the treadle-operated coconut grater. Although like type B tools they are, in a sense, like any tool, an extension of the body, part of the extended phenotype, they are so in a less obvious way and rather than simply being a specialised extension to a limb, such as a sago pounder, the relationship between tool and person is more complex, the body and apparatus entwining in each other holistically. This appears to be the case for many tools that we describe as machines, and we need to examine whether it makes a difference when attributing agency or animacy. The first of these two cases (Figure 9.2), what Nuaulu call the *aha*, is a device of great antiquity and of wide distribution in the Moluccas and New Guinea, used for separating starch granules from pith residue. The apparatus consists, basically, of two troughs made from sago leafstalk resting on a frame, in which one – the input trough or *sihane* – overlaps with and is slightly higher than the lower (*solo-solo*) output trough. Attached to the overlapping end of the *sihane* is a filter mesh (*nunte*), usually of stitched coconut fibre matting, which acts as a semi-permeable membrane. The upper part of the membrane is attached by string to a flexible sapling that acts as a spring-loaded assembly (*hehune hatai*). As water flows into the upper trough, the resulting mulch is pressed against the filter with one hand and the string pulled down with the other. Because of the flexibility of the sap-

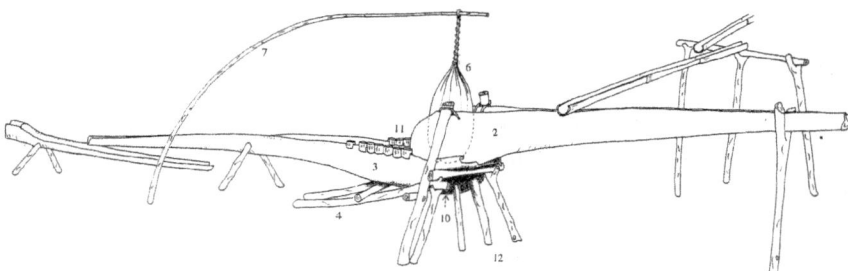

Figure 9.2. *Aha*, Nuaulu sago-processing apparatus. Figure created by the author.

ling, the membrane automatically retracts, enabling further compression of the mulch, and is ready for the operator to press once more. Thus, the latent energy produced by the bent sapling assists the process of efficient filtering. There is a process of complex bodily engagement between the individual and the apparatus. Here the tool is not simply motivated by the arm, but in a process initiated by the operator, actually collaborates in the process of filtering in a multifunctional kind of way (Ellen 2004b). This is such a common and culturally embedded technique that Nuaulu seldom reflect on its mode of function. As far as I know, it is never described in terms that would lead to an understanding that it is anthropomorphised, though the success of the processing activity is routinely ensured by making a small offering to the ancestral spirits who own the sago, consisting of tobacco, *Areca* betel pepper fruits wrapped in a leaf, and tucked into a convenient joint in the apparatus.

By contrast, the rotary action treadle-operated coconut grater (Figure 9.3) is a relatively recent introduction, and is perhaps no older than the late nineteenth century, part of a new technological repertoire associated with an increase in the planting of coconut palms for commercial copra production, and an increase in oil production for local consumption. The operator (usually male) presses the treadle with one foot, which pulls a string that rotates a cutting head, first in one direction and then in the other, using successive actions on the treadle. The head is made of wood in which metal cutting blades are embedded, and this assembly attached to a spindle at waist height. As can be seen from Figure 9.3, the action – like the sago flour processing apparatus, requires engagement with the whole body. To my knowledge, there are no associated ritual practices, though in several technical respects the treadle-operated coconut grater is comparable to the much older sago-washing device.

Finally, there are type (D) tools, machines driven by a non-human source of power, which in the historical experience of the Nuaulu consist of devices reliant on steam power, diesel or petrol. These have been familiar parts of the Nuaulu world for over a century, with steam and diesel-driven boats, and power-driven band saws used in timber yards. The internal combustion engine found in trucks and generators mainly became familiar along with aircraft during the Second World War, and through increased travel to Ambon and other islands. With independence, the road system deteriorated and most devices with engines were out of the reach of most people in rural areas of Seram. As the economy grew under the New Order, so Nuaulu became more familiar with road vehicles, tools such as chainsaws, and especially the outboard motor, the ubiquitous and eponymous 'motor jonson'. Outboard motors became common with local fisherman and small-scale traders during the 1980s, though being es-

Figure 9.3. Treadle-operated coconut grater, Rouhua village, Seram; December 1970 (Ellen 70-15-07). Photograph by the author.

sentially forest-oriented, Nuaulu have acquired them only recently. What is relevant to our discussion here is that Nuaulu treat outboard motors as essentially animate and motivated by a spirit even though some have a good knowledge of the practicalities of how they work. Nevertheless, when they go wrong, as they often do, Nuaulu will, after physical inspection and adjustment, make offerings and invocations to get them moving. These offerings are basically no different from those that they might offer before hunting, or tuck into the joints of a sago-processing apparatus. I was first introduced to this practice by a chance observation of Rosemary Bolton of Nuaulu 'feeding an outboard motor' in 1996. Up until that time, no Nuaulu of my acquaintance had owned an outboard motor and I was determined to follow through on the observation. To some extent this fits in with existing ritual practices relating to outrigger canoes and other sailing craft found in central Moluccan waters, that are anthropomorphised and subjected to life-cycle rituals and rituals at various stages in their manufacture (Ellen 2003a: 161–62). However, the outboard motor confers new properties to the vessel, namely a source of propulsion independent of human bodily action. While this has obvious technical advantages, it has the disadvantage that the operation of the vessel is less under the control of the crew. In a sailing boat, the crew can appeal to the spirits of the wind and may encourage them to blow by supplication in the form of banging gongs or similar metal objects. This is not possible with a 'jonson', and it is hardly surprising that the crew seek to maximise the forces working in their favour when the risk is increased.

In making ontological sense of these machines and the practices that accompany them, it is also relevant that outboard motors and sago-grating machines move, whirr, hum and get hot when they are used. Moreover, tools that have a quasi-independent existence in not needing to rely on continuous human manual power also resemble biological life in their capacity to 'die'. Paul Taylor (1990: 49) in his componential analysis of biotic forms claims that Tobelo define life as anything that has the capacity to die, and there is something paradoxically potent in this definition. Nuaulu speaking of an outboard motor that has just spluttered to a standstill having run out of fuel will say **mataenya** – 'it is dead', just as we would use the same word to describe a malfunctioning vehicle or power tool. Interestingly, Bloch (1998: 48) notes that Zafimaniry speak of life in relation to entities as diverse as clouds, quartz and motor engines, and use 'maty' (an Austronesian cognate of Nuaulu **matae**) for almost anything that breaks down. So, the attribution of the qualities of life to engines is hardly unique to the Nuaulu, and in Western societies too these same properties encourage modes of behaviour, emotion and linguistic expression that are wholly comparable.

The point I want to make is that these various attitudes concerning the degree to which tools have animacy, agency or intentionality reveal an underlying pan-human tendency. We all anthropomorphise tools (especially Western males) to the extent that some, such as cars, might be said to be fetishised (Miller 1987: 85–108). We develop an intimate relationship with them that can involve by turns love and anger when they do not perform as expected. Who has not shouted at a printer for breaking down when racing to meet a deadline – an example that Alfred Gell (1998) has felicitously explored – notwithstanding a clear distinction between intentional persons and inanimate things in dominant Euro-American ontology. Many of you will know the famous scene in 'Gourmet Night', an episode of the British comedy show *Fawlty Towers*, in which Basil (John Cleese) attacks his mini car that has mechanically failed while delivering food from a local restaurant to the hotel. Here is the dialogue to remind you:

> 'Come on! Start! Start, you vicious bastard! Come on! Oh, my God! I'm warning you! If you don't start I'll count to three. . . . One two three right! That's it! I've had enough! You stalled just once too often! Right! Well, don't say I haven't warned you! I've laid it on the line to you time and time again! Right! Well, this is it! I'm gonna give you a damn good thrashing!'

We laugh at this because we see in Basil's behaviour an exaggeration and mocking of our own attempts to interact with tools, where there is a clear dissonance between our rational techno-scientific selves and the more intuitive compulsion to treat an object as if it were biological and wilful.

Life as a Taxonomic Category

I think I can fairly claim that Nuaulu ideas about animacy are – like our own – generally fuzzy and contingent. However, if we look at scientific definitions, there have been repeated attempts to define the boundaries of living matter and what this might imply. These approaches come from philosophy, developmental/cognitive psychology, twentieth-century anthropology and particularly ethnobiology or ethnoscience. Let us start with the ethnoscience model. Brent Berlin (1992) describes the concept of 'living things' as a 'unique beginner' in a general taxonomy of biological organisms. For example, Taylor (1990) in his work on Tobelo ethnobiological classification uses a strict componential form of semantic analysis. Quite reasonably, he begins by indicating that Tobelo distinguish living from non-living, defining the former (as we have seen) as entities with the characteristic of being able to die. But rather than talk of living things, he uses the term 'biotic forms', which he then says are divided up by Tobelo into 'sexual biotic forms' that contrast with four other groups at the same taxonomic level: coral, sponges, fungi, and (a single category) 'moss, mould, bryozoans, small algae'. 'Sexual biotic forms' are in turn divided into 'breathers' and 'non-breathers', the latter exemplified by seaweed and black coral, and the former by fauna and flora (Figure 9.4).

Edmund Leach (1964) approached the issue in a different way, but with much the same result. Leach makes no reference to ethnoscience literature, and would probably be scathing in his dismissal of it if he had. Instead, he adopts a kind of logical formalism derived from Lévi-Strauss and Mary Douglas. The main problem with Leach, however, is not his underpinning theory, but his methods, or lack of them. The diagram in Figure 9.5 is drawn from Leach's imagination, augmented by his knowledge of the role of certain oppositions and notions from English popular culture and sacred texts. Leach uses the category 'nature' in a way that he has presumably derived from Lévi-Strauss, though he is sceptical of naive dualism and ambiguous on the universal proclivity of the nature–culture opposition (e.g. Leach 1972, 2000 [1977]). Nature is, therefore, not the same as 'life' or 'living organisms', or even less Taylor's 'biotic forms'. He divides 'nature' into animate and inanimate, though we are left to speculate whether this means that the category 'inanimate' includes some

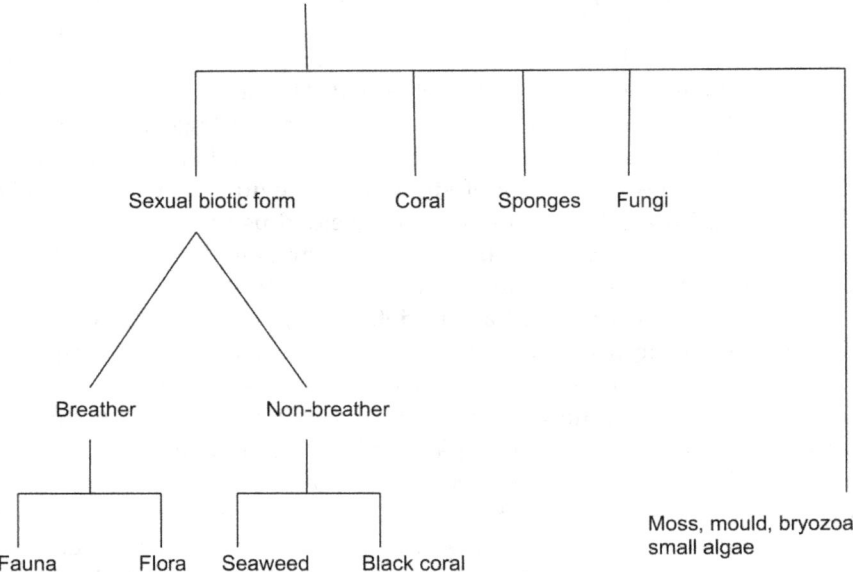

Figure 9.4. Tobelo taxonomy of 'biotic forms' based on semantic componential analysis (Taylor 1990: 48). Figure created by the author.

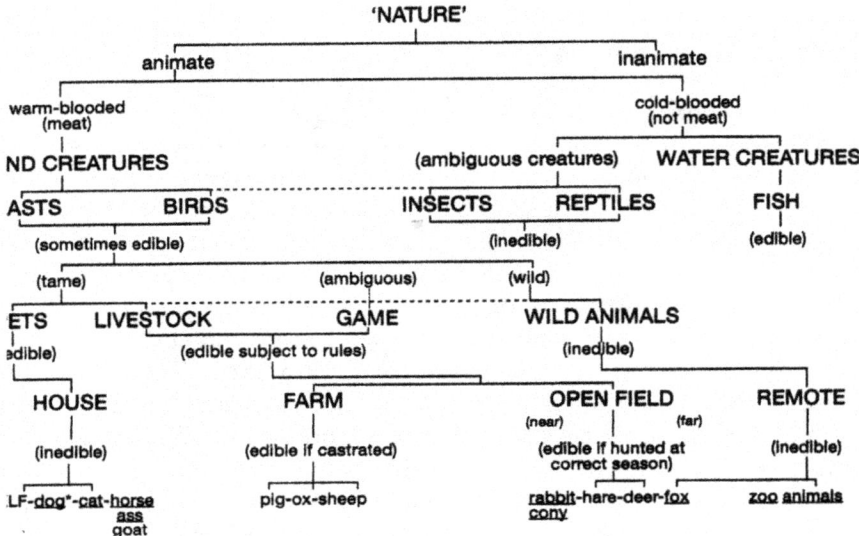

Figure 9.5. Edmund Leach's (1964) version of the English classification of nature. Reprinted courtesy of The MIT Press.

living organisms, most obviously plants. His category 'animate' (lexicologically) applies only to animals, given that it is then sub-divided into warm-blooded and cold-blooded. However, although I have often used Leach's folk-English scheme as a useful teaching example, it has always struck me as highly problematic. Not only does it suspiciously provide a convenient taxonomy of all living things that fits the logical conventions of a taxonomic approach, but it conflates discourses that we know to be separate, and flies in the face of ethnographic evidence. Unfortunately, 'living things' is a category that is easily yielded using formal elicitation techniques, but it is less obvious once you aggregate data from different ethnographic contexts using different research procedures.

Possibly because of the pitfalls in defining it, or in order to avoid the problems of using it as a unique beginner in a taxonomic description, many accounts of ethnobiological classification avoid considering what is meant by a 'living thing', and simply get on with the business of describing categories within the separate plant and animal domains. This approach is adopted by Hunn (2008) in his recent Zapotec natural history, and not even Berlin (1992), while adopting the over-riding rubric of 'ethnobiological classification' and dwelling on the formal criteria for establishing 'folk-kingdoms' of (often nomenclaturally covert) plants and animals, is interested in considering the unique beginner that might define the domain of 'living things' overall. Such approaches, however, logically (that is inferentially or syllogistically) assume that 'living things' must exist as a categorical phenomenon. Thus, if plants are living things and animals are living things, then there must be a superordinate or more encompassing category that both belong to. But this definition assumes that we are only dealing with what might be conventionally understood as 'biological taxa'.

For an example of an early ethnoscience analysis of the category 'living thing' which, unlike the example imagined by Leach, is based on real ethnographic data, we can do no better than look at a paper published by Mary Black in 1969 on the Ojibwa category '/bema.diziwa.d/'. This Black describes as the 'head-term of the taxonomic universe' and it indicates just how complex the concept can be in a particular local manifestation. Black uses a classic lexicographic distinctive feature approach. In her table 1 (1969: 186), 'living things' are divided into 'indians', 'white people', 'negroes' and 'asiatics'; and in another context into 'large animals', 'insects' and 'other'. In her table 2, 'living things' are divided into 'human', 'large animals', 'small animals', 'birds', 'fish' and 'spirits'. And we might recall here that Hallowell (1960) sees Ojibwa spirits as ontologically 'nonhuman persons'. Moreover, '/bema.diziwa.d/', depending on informants, sometimes also includes 'trees', 'stones', 'leaves', 'berries', 'shells', 'sun' and the 'moon' (Black 1969: 178). Well aware of the problems of confusing category with label, Black explains that choice of label here depends on 'context and type of contrast or relation'. They are taxonomically homonymous – sometimes just people, sometimes all living things. So, in Black's understanding of Ojibwa ontology, 'living things' may be biological taxa, human racial groups, spirits or astronomical entities.

Comparing Biological and Non-biological Classifications

Although we might now dismiss some of the formal approaches discussed above as methodologically naive, they do seem to point at some interesting similarities in the way in which the cultured mind makes sense of domains as diverse as biodiversity, human groups, the spirit realm, and other 'natural kinds' such as minerals. Sixteenth- and seventeenth-century European natural history routinely incorporated minerals as 'natural kinds'. Early attempts to systematically describe the 'mineral kingdom' and related entities 'dug out of the earth' often followed closely the organisation of local floras (Cooper 2007: 87–88). This approach was hardly novel even then. Rumphius in his *Ambonese Curiosity Cabinet* (1999 [1705]) follows Pliny, who discussed minerals in his *Natural History*. Rumphius juxtaposes descriptions of species of crustacea, echinoderms, coelenterates, seaworms, molluscs, cephalopods, stones, metals, minerals, gemstones, concretions, and objects that come from animals and plants often used medicinally. Thus, a kind of crystal found in Ambon is named *Crystallus ambonica*, while *Amianthus ambonicus* is a variety of asbestos (ibid.: 538). Also included are curiosities such as *Mestica sontong* (cuttlefish stones, ibid.: 531) and *Dendrites metallica* (small pieces of iron found in trees), or *Ambra grysea* (ambergris, the intestinal secretion of the sperm whale, ibid.: 499). Many of these objects are described using a version of the Latin binomial system. Then there are fossils such as *Cancri lapidescentes* (said to live under water but which petrify when removed), and prehistoric tools and weapons. In such schemes, fossils provided both a link with living biota and a problem. The idea that stones might reproduce, as Theophrastus had suggested in his *On Stones*, had still not been entirely repudiated. Following Rumphius, Linnaeus too attempted a 'taxonomy' of mineral 'species', and in the tenth edition (1758–59) of the *Systema Naturae* proposed four 'classes': Petræ, Mineræ, Fossilia and Vitamentra. Such classifications and attempts to integrate minerals in a more general taxonomic approach to natural history were eventually abandoned, superseded in global science by different arrangements based on chemical composition. But as both the history of science and the comparative ethnographic record attest, there have been repeated attempts since to integrate various domains of natural history knowledge (Atran 1990: 78), but generally resulting in the confrontation between irreconcilably different organising principles.

The same thinking has been extended to the humanly made world of artefacts. Drawing his inspiration from Berlin's work on the universal features of folk ethnobotanical classifications, Brown (Brown et al. 1976) claimed to find the same formal features of taxonomy in the organisation of other domains, including both human artefacts and spirits, referencing also the work of Frake (1961: on disease categories) and Spradley (1970: on social categories). Brown et al. conclude that 'principles originally attributed solely to biological classification' (ibid.: 73) extend beyond biological and perhaps even beyond taxonomic classification (ibid.: 84). He has in mind hierarchical depth, class contrast and inclusion, partonymy, and how nomenclature relates to category level. We can see some of these features in his rendering of American English tool taxonomy (Figure 9.6).[2]

In addition to treating certain tools in a 'life-like' way, Nuaulu distinguish entities that have many of the qualities of life, but which in the ordinary way have no corporeal existence. Thus, Nuaulu – like many peoples – think of spirits as a kind of pseudo-organism and represent them as species-like entities that can be ordered in terms of family resemblances (Ellen 1993b: 176–90), even if, as Boyer (1994: 97) argues, their conception as such violates the intuitive principles that some psychologists (e.g. Keil

Hierarchic level	Taxonomic rank	Term	Nomenclatural status
L0	UB	tool	PL
L1	lf	hammer	PL
L2	gn	hammer	PL
L2	gn	ballpeen hammer	PPL
L2	gn	sledge hammer	PPL
L2	gn	mallet	PL
L1	lf	vice	PL
L2	gn	clamp	PL
...			
L1	gn	saw	PL
L2	sp	sabre saw	SL
L3		crosscut saw	
L2	sp	regular screwdriver	
And so on ...			

Key: UB = unique beginner, lf = life-form, gn = generic, sp = specific; PL = unanalyzable productive lexeme, PP = productive primary lexeme, SL = secondary lexeme, UPL = unproductive primary lexeme.

Figure 9.6. American English tool taxonomy (after Brown et al. 1976: 78). Figure created by the author.

1979) have demonstrated for the domain-specificity of living kinds. Because spirits have these qualities, they are sometimes also attributed with corporeal manifestations: they become birds, or lizards, or indeed certain animals may always be regarded as the physical manifestations of spirits, such as scarab and long-horned beetles, or the death adder (*Acanthophis antarcticus*). In a way this is not surprising, since we can only imagine the spirit world through our experience of the physical and social world.

It was difficulties of this kind – both ontological and epistemological – that preoccupied Scott Atran in much of his *Cognitive Foundations of Natural History* (1990). For Atran, there is only a superficial similarity between biological and non-biological domains, 'living things [. . . being . . .] everywhere ranked into transitively structured taxonomies, with no other natural-object domain so structured' (ibid.: 47). In concluding thus, he draws on the support of field experiments in child psychology (ibid.: 50) and the work of Keil (1979). Keil has argued that children possess an ontological category of living things that includes animals and plants, allowing Atran (1990: 73–74) to claim that young children 'categorically distinguish artefacts from living things' and come to presume that only the latter constitute 'natural kinds' with underlying essences, while limiting certain concepts (such as growth) to living things. For Atran (ibid.: 5), there is a significant contrast both in regard to the 'ordinary categorization of artefacts and the extraordinary scientific classification of living kinds'. Thus, science is based on a kind of universal ethnoscience in which 'our universally held conception of the living world is both historically prior to, and psychologically necessary for, any scientific – or symbolic – elaboration of that world' (ibid.: 13).

As well as using experimental data, Atran (1990: 55–56) argues his case on formal logical grounds, assuming this to be a universal grammar. Thus, 'furniture' cannot be part of the definition of 'chair', although 'animal' is part of the definition of 'cat'. Transitive hierarchy, he therefore reasons, works for living kinds but not for artefacts, because the domain of artefacts fails to meet the inductive and deductive requirements of ranked taxonomies. Biota, like artefacts, are often placed in different categories (whether we call these taxa or not), and although he recognises that people often 'confound' artefacts with living kinds and 'confuse' plants with things made from plants, the underlying field structures are quite different. But one reason that artefacts are not conveniently organised taxonomically is because Atran has defined taxonomy in such a way that it can only be used for biota (ibid.: 57). If we are to argue on the basis of logical formalism, then we might forgive ordinary people for deviating from it in the practices of their ordinary lives. No wonder Atran (ibid.: 71) dismisses that work in developmental psychology (e.g. Carey 1985; see also Gelman 2003) which shows that children will spontaneously attribute a common invented property, a kind of underlying nature, to dogs, flowers and inanimate objects. Such theories and data tend to support the idea of the integration of domains of knowledge, and of fundamental ambiguity in the concept of natural kind.

The Body, Social Cognition and the Limits of Modularity

While we may still wish to argue that there are special features in ethnobiological classifications that distinguish them from the organisation of other domains, I would suggest that this has less to do with the cognitive apparatus brought to bear on them than the pattern of empirical discontinuities found in a particular ecological context. Similarly, the mind cognises tools in the same way as living organisms, partly because of a shared cognitive architecture but also fundamentally because our models of apprehending and thinking about the world derive from our own bodily experience, and from the social worlds of which we are part.

It has long been recognised that at the core of human cognition is a necessary duality and tension whereby humans understand the natural world through their experience of society, and the social world through their experience of nature (e.g. Lévi-Strauss 1962). This is why, despite repeated attempts to counter naive dualism and challenge the culture–nature divide, the divide keeps on re-emerging (Leach 2000 [1977]: 340; Astuti 2001). Thus, there is a general tendency in human relations with the inanimate world to attribute and represent that world in organic terms, and to attribute inanimate objects with the properties of living things (Ellen 1988b). It happens because we are bound to model our world directly on our experience of our own body (Mauss 1973 [1934]) and we employ this self-same model as a source of labels and concepts to interpret the world outside the body. The lexicon of animal parts is, after all, for the most part that of human anatomy. Botanical nomenclature is less so, and that of inanimate objects less still, but body terms – or at least terms that appear concurrently in anatomical lexicons – are still crucial (Ellen 1977a). More than this, if we 'thingify' or 'entify' parts of a living system, and then observe that the things move, so to speak, it logically follows that the things may well be regarded, or spoken of, as if they were sentient beings; they will appear as though they were indeed animated. Thus, phenomena that have life are turned into objects, only to be re-animated in turn (Ellen 1988b: 223). The organic models we use vary along a continuum from general organic analogies (organomorphs) to plant analogies (phytomorphs), animal analogies (zoomorphs), general human analogies (anthropomorphs), and the attribution of particular personalities (personification) (ibid.: 224). It is as if the mind progressively 'enlivens' non-living entities, and humanises other entities in which it recognises life. I have elsewhere illustrated this point in relation to the personification of sacred shields that Nuaulu attribute with soul (*wanui*). The shields and other sacred valuables (such as sacred spears or barkcloth beaters) are treated with reverence, anthropomorphically, granted personhood and have complex biographical histories, as reported for other parts of Indonesia (Ellen 1990; Hoskins 1998). When Viveiros de Castro (2004b: 465) tells us that Amazonian beliefs attributing perceptual perspectives of the world to different species are connected with their belief that animals are ex-humans, this is not only an example of mythic legitimation but of how objects are treated as subjects and species as persons. We can see the same process at work when Carrithers, Bracken and Emery (2011) refer to 'the person-like character of a species' in conservation and taxonomic discourse and show how the 'axiom of amity' finds an afterlife in the same. At this point too even Atran (1990: 74) seems to concede the point that 'because humans and animals are adjacent overlapping domains, then one might expect children to borrow from knowledge of humans to organize animals and plants, and vice versa'.

Because the role of the social world in the way we organise and understand nature is so entrenched in ordinary thought and discourse, this has been taken as good evidence that the faculties of social cognition have evolved in humans to eclipse other modules of knowledge (Mithen 1996). At some point in our evolutionary history the barriers between hitherto specialised intelligences distributed as quasi-separate neural networks in the brain – natural history cognition, intuitive physics and others – break down and merge with the hegemonic module of social cognition. Thus, if we are to understand those cultural behaviours we describe as 'animistic', we must take into account a fundamental fact of human cognition: that we use social intelligence to make sense of the natural world. What we call animism is in a way the reification of multiple instances of such thinking, of repeated observations, reinforced by cultural elaboration into something approaching a coherent set of connected beliefs.

Organomorphism, Motion, Agency, Intention

Thus, through the working out of the recent evolutionary history of the embodied brain, and polythetic linkage between different cognitive and semantic domains in any particular cultural population, we will find a group of things that are regarded as like life, or life-like. But in attributing the notion of 'life', and more narrowly 'animacy', what features does the mind latch on to? The evidence of the previous section would suggest that we start with physical resemblance, especially since given our dominant sense of vision it is visually salient attributes that first register and that are most easily encoded in memory. In other species it might be other senses that occupy this position, but even in humans these other senses can be critical in determining whether something is likely to be living. Imagine a world in which life is mainly apprehended and registered through the senses of sound or tactility (which we can perhaps imagine, especially if we are blind) or through smell (which we can only imagine with difficulty). In reality, of course, our cognition of life is multi-sensorial and synaesthetic, but we must start with physical form.

Some of the classic boundary problems of the category 'living matter' are raised through an engagement with forms of life that do not fit easily into the cognitively universal (but not lexically universal) prototypical categories of 'plant' or 'animal', that are peripheral to biological life as most ordinary people experience it. Our different senses register different qualities on the life/non-life continuum, but combined offer a sufficiently discriminating instrument. In my work on Nuaulu ethnobiological classification, fungi and algae are classic liminal forms (Ellen 2008). In the classifying and naming strategies that Nuaulu employ, there is a tension between placing fungi with plants and according them their own separate 'kingdom', while seaweed is nomenclaturally aligned with fungi. The term *unate* refers to all visible fungi, with the exception of lichen-forming Ascomycetes; and is also applied to sponges (*unate nau moti*, literally, 'mushrooms of the reef'), and to all algal seaweed (*una nuae*), despite the first being phylogenetically Animalia and the latter either Plantae or Protista. All *unate* are marked lexically by the contracted prefix *una-* followed by an adjectival or other qualifier: for example, *una msinae* ('red mushroom') for *Pycnoporus sanguineus*, or *una pate* ('fig-tree mushroom') for *Trametes corrugata*. The broadly inclusive character of *unate* is in itself interesting, given that mushrooms as a phylogenetic grouping are extremely varied in shape, structure, colour, habit and reproduction. Since there can be considerable morphological difference, say between rigid shelf mushrooms or bracket fungi, fragile fleshy mushrooms and the highly salient coral mushrooms, we must assume that placing them together in a single clearly labelled category (whether 'mushrooms' or *unate*) must reflect some combination of cognitive prototype and common distinctive features. Not subsumed under *unate* are forms such as *Usnea*, a fruticose lichen which Nuaulu call *ahane*, and moulds and mildew (which they call *rekunai*). Slime moulds, which are not fungi, are given their own category as well: *sona*, literally 'sago jelly' which they are said to resemble. Freshwater and terrestrial algae are described as *mapunua* by Nuaulu and seen as related forms, for example *lumu-lumu* (*Chaetomorpha javanica*) found commonly on trees. For Nuaulu, all these forms are undeniably living, even though some seem to lack movement, others much evidence of growth, and others still a capacity for reproduction. Movement in the narrow sense is easily observable, growth less so, but reproduction in many cases has to be inferred. In most folk biologies, while sexual biotic forms clearly reproduce, entities such as sponges merely endure.

So, by deliberately selecting liminal forms we can test the extent to which the notion of 'life' applies, and if that test is passed whether such entities conform best to animal or to plant prototypes. But we also need to recognise that both these prototypes are in semantic tension, simultaneously sharing features and contrasting them. All living matter could be said to have both a vegetal and animalistic aspect, there being a 'vegetal quality' especially found in plants, and an 'animal quality' especially found in animals. This is why where certain peripheral organisms are placed in classificatory space varies between cultures, compared with the greater regularities reported for core plants and animals. But it is also reflected in the evolutionary convergence of forms that we might otherwise have no problem is assigning to one or other of the taxonomic kingdoms. Thus, for Nuaulu, certain plants have attributes of animals, such as the insectivorous pitcher plants (**koitipi**: *Nepenthes* spp.) found in the Manusela National Park, and certain animals the attributes of plants, as in various phasmid stick and leaf insects (**kau ai otoe**, e.g. *Platycrana viridana*). But in addition, we are constantly also primed to look out for what is potentially human in other parts of the living world, as we have seen from the previous section. We try to make things anthropomorphic, but while the basic attributes of morphology make this more promising in the case of, say, the Nuaulu marsupial cuscus, with its simian anatomy and multiple symbolic resonances (Ellen 1972), conservationists struggle to convince us of the humanity in the hapless pearl mussel (Carrithers, Bracken and Emery 2011).

In the attribution of life, and even more so of animacy in the sense of 'animality' (Reed 1988), morphological resemblance is not enough. Equally indispensable is motion, in all or any of its manifestations. Everywhere that liminal biological forms are attributed with animacy it is because in some way or another they display a characteristic that is semantically rooted in movement or its metaphorical extension, such as 'locomotion', 'growth', 'reproduction', 'fission', 'fusion', 'fragmentation'. Even 'eruption' and 'erosion' are recognisably for all humans 'kinds of motion'. When we talk about the 'living' landscape, we have in mind the idea that it is dynamic, whether vegetally, animalistically or geomorphologically. Time, change and cause are all described in various contexts as if they were like motion. But to qualify for the condition of life, the source of motion has to be independent of any interlocutor. So, as we move between the different types of Nuaulu tool in the order that we considered them above, the cognitive stimuli amenable to the attribution of life seem to increase. In the transition from skewer to sago pounder, and from sago pounder to the sago flour extraction apparatus, from the treadle-operated coconut grater to the power-assisted sago grater and the outboard motor, there is a gradual shift in the source of the motion – and therefore seemingly of agency: from the using subject to the tool itself.

We now come to agency in the strict sense. As Gell (1998: 72) puts it, 'agency implies the possession of a mind which intends actions prior to performing them', and 'what matters is where an animated object stands in a network of social relations' (ibid.: 123). For Gell (ibid.: 132), there is only a slight dividing line between the intentionality of humans and of anthropomorphic objects. The problem with this is that, conceptually, it mixes up not only agency with intention, but with animacy and sociality as well. The term agency has been much stretched in recent anthropological discussions of animism and technology, but in this context I think we need to shrink it back to its core meaning: an intervention to produce a particular result, or something with 'the faculty of an agent' (SOED 1973: 37). Thus, a sago-processing device has agency in the sense that it can produce unique outcomes in the context of human–object interaction. This neither makes it animate nor gives it intentionality. So, looking at our selected Nuaulu tools, on material grounds neither the meat skewer nor the sago pounder can be said to have agency, though more complex machines with many parts which form a system with emergent properties not entirely under the control of the operator might indeed be said to possess agency. Thus, this would be the case for the sago-processing device, the coconut grater and the outboard motor.

A quality that Nuaulu commonly associate with the essentials of animal and human life is breath (*nahai*), and breath too is a kind of motion. At the birth of a child, the moment at which a child breathes independently, when the chest begins to move and the lungs ventilate, is the beginning of autonomous human life, while death is the expiration of breath and the end of movement, and therefore is (paradoxically) also a characteristic of life. Breath as a concept is recurrent in ritual and attributed to physical entities that are anthropomorphised, such as sacred houses or ritual shields. Ritual shields, like the meat skewer, retain their organs of breath in the first chip of wood to be cut, and which is thereafter kept in the loft of a sacred house. Most salient of all, however, is the literal extraction of the organs of breathing (the lungs and trachea) of large game animals and their offering as a sacrifice to the clan ancestors in the form of a gift to the clan head. In the *asunaete* ritual these same organs are attached to a wooden skewer as a form of repayment for a life taken and to ensure that life will thereby be replenished. In humans and large animals, the physicality of breath is clear enough, but in other biological organisms and non-biological entities it is not, and here we find that sound (more specifically vocalisation) may sometimes serve as a proxy, for sound is only possible where there is breath or motion to produce it. So, when cicadas sing it is evidence of breath, or even when the wind blows through certain rocks to produce eerie sounds it may be taken as evidence of life, recalling somewhat the remarks of Herodotus on the Colossi of Memnon at Thebes.

Finally, we come to intentionality. In the Nuaulu world, humans, some animals, spirits, the godhead, animals and some plants that have become coterminous with spirits might be said to act intentionally. Their actions in the world do not simply have consequences independent of the humans that interact with them, but they have minds that permit them to make plans and act in the world in ways that are deliberate responses to human and other behaviour, and which are often contrary.

Life as a Matter of Degree, While Animacy Is Not Animism

I am hardly the first to argue that the attribution of life is necessarily gradual, contextual and, from a biological perspective, sometimes inconveniently deviant. Bloch (1998: 53) calls this the 'more-or-less' character of life. Ingold (2006) argues that we can make anything seem alive, but we do not always choose to do so. Moreover, there is much ethnographic evidence that people do not agree about what life is and no universal distinctions as to what is alive and what is not. Ingold (2011: 29) further speaks of 'bringing things to life', of 'things in life, rather than life in things', suggesting that life is less a property of individual entities than a phenomenon of which those entities are part. In this model, the animacy of the 'lifeworld' is 'ontologically prior to their differentiation' (Ingold 2006: 10). What I have tried to do here is to unpack those conditions for the recognition of life and to show how they might constitute a series of progressive cognitive steps that when aggregated are more likely to prompt the attribution of life. These are: recognition of morphological resemblance, recognition of motion, and recognition of independent motion.[3] As we have seen, these are each reflected in a pattern of conceptual attribution that follows a broadly phylogenetic progression: we apprehend physical entities as being plant-like, animal-like, human-like and – ultimately – like individual human persons (Ellen 1988b).

Part of the problem in the literature is that the discourses on biocognition, life and animism begin from different starting points and have different intellectual histories. While analytically we need to separate these and certainly not confuse and conflate the concepts and terms employed, in particular ethnographic cases it is unlikely that we will ever discover a convenient congruence. It may be that we need to separate vital from symbolic forces – that we need both 'vital and symbolic ontologies' – just as Mauss suggested we separate technical from symbolic classifications, and Berlin general-purpose 'natural' schemes from special-purpose schemes. Unfortunately, real-life examples do not give us much hope that this is possible. In some cases we may find evidence of two life forces (spiritual and biological), as Rival (2012) suggests for Makushi cassava, but my informed bet is that because 'vital and technical processes [are] already situated in a complex relational complex when we experience them', in practical everyday life organisms and things are treated as though they are motivated by a single underlying force, unless otherwise prompted to reconsider. This would be my reading of the Nuaulu data.

While all cultural objects are potentially regarded in this way, in practice some objects are more alive, are more likely to evoke the characteristics of agency or indeed intentionality than others. Part of the problem with existing anthropological treatments of the category 'living things' is that they are either logical extrapolations through polythetic extension, based on formal ethnotaxonomic deduction/induction, rooted in observations of how children under artificial conditions perform in field experiments of a very abstract kind, or (completely differently) assume that life is recognised phenomenologically prior to its differentiation. Nuaulu ideas of what is animate and agentive are always fuzzy, and always contingent. By combining data from different contexts, by using different elicitation procedures, a more complex picture has emerged.

The same applies to animism, with which the attribution of life is too readily conflated. If, following Descola (2005b: 183–84), animism is 'the granting by humans to non-humans of an interiority identical to theirs, an attribution that humanizes animals (and plants)' (Rival 2012: 70), I would say that it is virtually impossible to separate ethno-theories of life processes from what is sometimes described as animism. However, not every object in nature is animated, and animism is not totalising. Recent work (including my own) suggests much selectivity with which it is evoked ontologically, and limits to the extension of personhood as a human-like category. Praet (2014) even argues that the outstanding feature of animism is its peculiar restrictiveness.

Regardless of the arguments surrounding how we might best understand 'animism' as a specific worldview, whether we are considering humans or other species (including dogs), we can observe a tendency for the mind to use an understanding of living bodies to interpret experience of artefacts, including tools. When they exhibit evidence of motion, and especially independent motion, objects prompt responses and interactions that suggest recognition of animacy, agency and intentionality to different degrees. If you do not know whether something is alive, then, as Ingold suggests, it is better to assume that it is. We have evolved a tendency to attribute the characteristics of life to parts of the world and to the world as a whole, since our experience of existence is how we must represent, model, understand and act in the world. Life in its most generalised phenomenological sense must emerge, in terms of our experience, from the aggregation of lives in particular. When Nuaulu refer to *mahai* (life), they are first and foremost thinking of human life, but this does not mean that they do not also readily extend the notion to other biota and non-biota as necessary.

A final word on motion as a condition of life. Motion is often necessary, but is seldom sufficient. Motion is often accompanied by multi-sensorial – often synaesthetic – characteristics that are shared with biological life, for example the expenditure of heat and the emission of sound. But while none of the clanking, whirring and buzzing of the treadle-operated coconut grater, or even the sloshing and slapping of a sago-processing device are sufficient for Nuaulu to conceive of them as living entities, the same features in an outboard motor or power-assisted sago grater are intrinsic to recognition of its animate status. For while the treadle-operated coconut grater and sago-processing device have the technical characteristics of a machine, they do not have the autonomy of an engine. Once primed and fuelled, the engine will run by itself until the fuel runs out or it malfunctions. These technical processes are fully understood and Nuaulu have wondrous ways of fixing malfunctioning engines, but the combined features that give them quasi-autonomy also give them the vitality that is more than just the combination of the parts and crosses a boundary that places them with other vital biological and quasi-biological entities such as spirits. This is so despite their not sharing other characteristics that are often focal to our definitions of life, such as growth and reproduction. Humanly operated machines may have agency, but engines can also appear to act intentionally. When Basil Fawlty is thrashing the car, he is exacting revenge through punishment from an entity that has 'stalled just once too often'. It has wilfully disobeyed its owner and driver. We laugh because we recognise that all of us, while fully accepting the technical reasons for mechanical failure, insist on treating the vehicle as if it were a sentient person who is deliberately contrary.

Notes

First published in 2017 in *Classification from Antiquity to Modern Times: Sources, Methods, and Theories from an Interdisciplinary Perspective*, edited by Tanja Pommerening and Walter Bisang (Berlin: De Gruyter, pp. 239–62). Reproduced courtesy of De Gruyter.

1. It may be that dogs behaving in this way are responding to a 'key stimulus', an old ethological concept that refers to specific stimuli that have the potential to release a specific behaviour (modal action pattern). The rapidly moving stimuli of the kind described here release the predatory behaviour, more effectively in collies and in particular dogs. In some cases, this behaviour can become stereotypical (obsessive-compulsive) and therefore abnormal. In such

cases, what we see has little to do with seeing/perceiving directly, but rather reflects the brain's sensitivity to certain stimulus configurations.
2. In considering the ranks in non-biological domains, Brown is content to employ the term 'life form' for level 1, though without flagging up any sense of irony. Of course, the 'generic' level, like many concepts employed in Western scientific and other folk classifications of living things, frequently reflects social categories (genus, family, tribe . . .), echoing another broadly understood principle, that is how – of necessity – we use social categories to make sense of the natural world and non-social categories to make sense of nature (Lévi-Strauss 1966). The relationship between tool and organism displays the same conceptual mutuality, one domain being used to explain the other. Consider, for example, Aristotle's use of 'organon' in his natural history, and the long post-Aristotelian tradition of explaining animal function using mechanical analogies (e.g. Smith 2011).
3. Compare this with a similar progression noted by Rival (2012: 71) in the contributions from Ingold and others in the animism debate regarding the logical implicatory relationships between communication, intentionality, consciousness, life and movement. The problem, as Rival observes, is in a 'hazardous slippage' between concepts.

CHAPTER 10

Is There a Role for Ontologies in Understanding Plant Knowledge Systems?

Introduction

For the meeting of the International Society for Ethnobiology in 2005, I put together a panel on the theme 'Ethnobiology and the Science of Humankind' (Ellen 2006b), with the intention of engaging with Richard Ford's (1978) now famous assertion that ethnobotany is a common discourse lacking a unifying theory. My intention was to explore what might have changed in the meantime and to monitor the growth of the subject. My conviction then – and remains – is that ethnobiology (of which, of course, ethnobotany is still the major part) was too important to be left in the gaps between the main disciplines and was, from my perspective as an anthropologist, central and integral to addressing some of the main questions about what makes us human. It is appropriate to return to this theme, almost a decade later, as the issues under discussion have become more prominent, and arguably more urgent too (Miller et al. 2016).

It is important not to reify disciplines themselves, which are inevitably situated practices, often convenient coalitions of researchers sustained by institutional structures and cultural working patterns, training regimes and core methodologies. Some of the tensions we might identify are not between disciplines in the most conventional sense at all, but between those defending older – normal – paradigms against proponents of new peripheral paradigms. Disciplinary and subject boundaries are nowadays extremely fluid, and different kinds of cross-disciplinarity have become standard, though disciplines still provide essential coherence to bodies of thought and findings, and offer practical advantages in organising practice. Evolutionary biology, for example, unites many older subjects traditionally separated by their physical subject matter in terms of life-forms. There is no particular reason to expect that ethnobotany should be any different, or for its value to be measured simply through possession of a shared and distinct body of theory and practice. But academic subjects characterised as interdisciplinary will continue to lack theoretical coherence as long as the different disciplines involved are seen to be pulling apart, and this we sometimes find in ethnobotany. So I begin here by acknowledging these tensions, and suggest that we might find some of their causes in those frictions that others have called ontological. I do so by looking at a number of intellectual entanglements that lie at the heart of any attempt to make the subject more homogenous and discipline-like.

On Ontologies

Let us first talk ontologies. Over the last few years, I have relaxed my resistance to the apparently irresistible tide of 'the ontological turn', as those around me all seem to think that an argument has to ontologise just about everything. While I acknowledge that there is an important debate going on, what I think many are trying to say is often what scholars and scientists have been grappling with for a long time, only using a different conceptual baggage. The word ontology has been embraced with a quasi-religious passion in some quarters, and used where it need not be, setting up wild goose chases. For example, if we remove the word in a phrase (as in 'ontological division', or 'ontologically separate'), frequently nothing changes in an argument.

It is no coincidence that in the human sciences – and especially in anthropology – the rise of the concept of ontology has been especially connected with ways of apprehending the natural world, emerging from debates about nature–culture dualism, the idea of the social construction of nature and recognition that not all peoples everywhere or in different contexts of engagement define nature in the same way, if at all. In other words, its definition is relational. And then, ontology, after all, is often described as focusing on the 'nature' (in this sense, essence) of being, and on the nature of different beings. More recently it has been associated in particular with scholars challenging those non-reflexive interpretations of the world we call anthropocentric, with actor network theory (ANT), the 'new materialities' turn and the critique of 'human exceptionalism' (e.g. Bennett 2010; Haraway 2008; Latour 2005).

So, one definition of ontology is 'the investigation and theorisation of diverse experiences and understandings of the nature of being' (Scott 2013: 859). But another is 'a set of propositions urging a particular viewpoint on reality' (Carrithers, in Carrithers et al. 2010: 160). Rather differently, in computer and information science, an ontology is what formally represents knowledge as a set of concepts within a domain, using a shared vocabulary to denote the types, properties and interrelationships of those concepts. In yet other texts, a large part of its intention is covered by the phrase 'a framework for thinking'. But if this is so, then it comes close to Clifford Geertz's (e.g. 1973) 'webs of significance', which was of course his pithy definition of culture.

If we understand ontology in terms of the logical relations and cosmological assumptions underpinning a particular discourse or set of practices, there is also problematic slippage in the way specific philosophical themes are nested within broader cultural traditions. So, how does something called 'Western' ontology relate, say, to Cartesian or Kantian ontology? There are plainly major differences in terms of epistemology and basic working assumptions between scientific disciplines and between theoretical strands within the same discipline, which in other respects might be said to share aspects of a single overarching ontology. Moreover, in terms of the convenient binaries we like to invent, we might ask whether 'Western ontology' is constructed in the same way as other ontologies we distinguish on quasi geo-cultural grounds when we reify cultures and speak of – say – 'Nuaulu ontology' or 'Maori ontology'. In my view, the term ontology has to be used sparingly, and only where there is no other way of expressing the scale or quality of underlying conceptual difference. Otherwise we risk undermining its productivity altogether.

For the time being, I prefer to remain agnostic as to which definition, if any, is the most persuasive. However, in terms of any and several, ethnobotany is undeniably at a frontier of some kind, probably in a variety of ways (epistemological, methodological, theoretical). Comprehending how people conceptualise the relationship between plants and people might be claimed by some as work of 'ontological translation'. Indeed, I have tried to manage a challenge of such proportions every year when teaching students on the Kent MSc in Ethnobotany, some of whom come from biological science backgrounds and others from the social sciences and humanities. How can we grasp the meanings and uses of plants in terms of the paradigms and language of global science and scholarship, and at the same time acknowledge that plants exist for many people as parts of a system of significance and practice that is quite different? Why do we feel compelled to give priority and even authority to one representation at all? I would like to argue that ethnobotanists are well positioned to mediate the contexts in which various worldviews about plants intersect. Plants exist in many and varied contexts, and how they are represented and employed, and the consequences of their interactions with people, depend on what those contexts are. The socially embedded process of cognition through which both people's representations and our research findings are generated and framed is what I have previously described as 'prehension' (Ellen 1986a). So here I look briefly at some entanglements encountered in ethnobotanical research where prehension varies. These are: post-Linnaean taxonomic orthodoxy versus local plant classification, pre-Linnaean natural history versus science, phytopharmaceutical orthodoxy versus medical anthropology, museum practice versus lived practice, ecological versus phylogenetic explanation, plant and knowledge movement and stability, and shifts in understanding contingent on membership of different intra-cultural domains. There is no particular underlying logic to this selection, though examples of each can be found in the ethnobotanical literature of the last fifty years, and in my experience repeatedly in the professional lives of working ethnobotanists.

Post-Linnaean Scientific Taxonomic Orthodoxy versus Local Folk Classification

A major preoccupation of ethnobotany from its beginnings as a self-conscious subject has been with basic identification and translation.[1] Indeed, this might be said to engage with that frontier between frameworks for thinking most widely encountered in the ethnobotanical literature, mainly because its entanglements must be traversed in order to establish our basic units of analysis – scientific taxa or local categories. It finds a theoretical manifestation in the body of work initiated by Brent Berlin on the way in which we might map the particularities of folk categorisation onto the language of taxonomic science. Berlin does this by proposing an underlying naturalist framework that helps us explain and compare all folk schemes. Without going into the difficulties he encountered in achieving this, and without denying the importance of the Berlinian project, I think it is fair to say that the approach tends to play down some key differences between those schemes shared and promoted in science and any one local folk scheme. This is because although in many cases language data can be seen to yield some of the uniformities claimed (e.g. psychological salience, transitivity, ranking and so on), the way people interact and experience plants in traditional non-literate societies is rather different from the way a taxonomist in the Kew Herbarium interacts with them. Although there is a range of variation between clusters of individuals in any situated practice, and simplistic dualities are always to be avoided, in the first people interact with plants holistically, as part of a wide-ranging network of material and symbolic resources, while in the second taxonomists (in their role as taxonomists) are working within a much tighter set of professional guidelines, narrower objectives, and with written texts and collections of dried specimens. Tsing (2005: 155–70) captures some of the complexities of this transformation in her evocative account of collaborating with Meratus Dayak on a biodiversity assessment.

Let us take the example of Nuaulu palms. Nuaulu, a people of the island of Seram in eastern Indonesia, amongst whom I have worked intermittently since 1970, recognise and name 14 scientific genera and 15 species of palm. Nuaulu organise their knowledge of these species by using 13 uninomials and 28 binomials, 11 of which describe folk-varieties of the sago palm, *Metroxylon sagu* Rottb. Nuaulu are well aware of the similarities between what we call standing palms, in terms of their overarching architecture and reproductive pattern, and together these might be said to form a weak covert category – a grouping that can be inferred to exist in local thought and practice but which is not named. Rattans by contrast are explicitly named as a group (***meute***), and include the genera *Calamus*, *Daemonorops* and possibly *Korthalsia*, and are distinguished from other palms. This is a classification based on growth form, which contemporary scientific taxonomists and palm biologists recognise as a folk category, useful when engaging with the wider public, but not significant for formal scientific classification, and with low phylogenetic meaning (see, e.g., Dransfield and Manokaran 1994; and also the Ngaju Dayak case discussed in Schreer 2016). *Nypa*, which has a more or less prostrate stem, and some rattan-like characteristics, is grouped separately by Nuaulu in the covert category PALM. Nuaulu do not label palms as trees (*ai*), which are woody and branching, but palms are disproportionately important symbolically given their high utilitarian value (Ellen 1998a: 64).

Some palm species are grouped together by Nuaulu on account of their edible starch: *M. sagu* and *Nypa fruticans* Wurmb., but also the mature – but only the mature – *Caryota rumphiana* Mart., which is labelled using a quite different word (***panuke***) from the immature form (***katue***). However, *M. sagu* is a keystone, multi-purpose mega-species that is so significant for Nuaulu that their identity as a cultural group is strongly connected with its continued use and management (Ellen 2004b, 2006a).

Another group of palms (Ellen 1991b) are identified by Nuaulu because they provide fruits that can be chewed with other ingredients to produce or simulate mild psychoactive effects, the sharing of which is important in many ritual and other social contexts: *Areca catechu* L., *Areca macrocalyx* Zipp. Ex Blume [syn. *A. glandiformis* Lam.], *Calyptrocalyx spicatus* (Lam.) Blume, *Drymophloeus oliviformis* (Giseke) Miq., *Gronophyllum microcarpum* Scheffer, *Pinanga punicea* (Blume) Merr.

As some of these functional groups overlap, we have further evidence for the existence of the larger covert grouping of PALMS, following the principle of analytic induction (Ellen 1998a). Moreover, Nuaulu terms for palm morphology vary slightly, but in significant ways that point to a subgrouping within the larger covert category. For example, there are three terms for inflorescence: (a) that used for coconut palm and betel palms, (b) that used for sugar and 'nibung' palms, and (c) that used for the sago palm. Separate in other ways from the starch and betel nut-producing palms is coconut (*Cocos nucifera* L.), which is consumed with virtually every meal, and which is also of major commercial importance.

Formally speaking, it would be possible to compare how Nuaulu classification of palms conforms to the Linnaean categories (in terms of over- and under-differentiation), how it relates to Berlin's universalist scheme of ranks or to any other scheme that might be proposed. However, what we need to remember is that the picture of Nuaulu vernacular classification that I have provided constitutes a set of features and relations that the Nuaulu linguistic and ethnographic data permit us to yield; they do not conform to any pseudo-Linnaean local ontology. Indeed, if we are to understand Nuaulu palms we need to see these in the context of their local ecology, uses and in the cultural narratives people construct around them. Particular folk (emic) classifications presented in ethnobotanical reports are not in themselves ontologies, but simplified representations drawing on selected features of plants put together in a particular scientific (etic) framework, an example of the process which I have described as prehension, and which is reflected in the experience of Tsing's (2005: 155–70) Meratus research collaborations.

Thus, in understanding folk classification there is a constant imperative to compare the categories and relations of a folk system with those of the phylogenetic system as this has emerged in the global scientific tradition, what I have previously and admittedly loosely called the 'Linnaean grid' (Ellen 2006b: 4). The problem is that this might seem to immediately set up an opposition between two reified purported ontologies, that of science and that of the folk system subject to analysis. Whereas we can be fairly clear as to the philosophical underpinning of the scientific system, because it has developed historically as a set of self-conscious principles that are published and agreed upon by scientists committed to a kind of logical coherence, the status of the folk system is never quite clear. Sometimes the folk system is represented as a kind of weak reflection of the scientific system, and this is the case with that large body of work that claims that there is a universal bio-taxonomic model that underpins both biology and folk biology (Atran 1990; Berlin 1992). Insofar as this says anything about deep cognition, it is not an ontology in the usual sense of the word at all, though may be an important element in various ontologies.

If we look at folk understandings of plants and how they should be organised as part of a system of knowledge in a particular place or cultural tradition, there is seldom evidence of the kind of coherent and self-conscious ontology that we associate with science. In many cases the descriptions ethnobotanists provide are partial, and simply reflect the questions they ask of their data, and again often mimic the scientific ontology that they operate within. Unless there is a reflexive tradition of science among the subjects being researched, the very idea of 'plant classification' as a separate department of knowledge might seem very strange. But as Theresa Miller (2016) shows, local people may come to endorse new ways of (scientifically) representing their plant knowledge as these valorise it in terms of legitimate official representations and because they are recognised as a practical means of storing and transmitting knowledge.

Pre-Linnaean Natural History versus Science

Something that Scott Atran (1990) has drawn to our attention is how we might look at historic European proto-science in the same way that we look at modern folk classification embedded in different languages and knowledge systems. In this context the first 'cultural other' is constructed through what Lévi-Strauss might have described as diachronic separation, and the second through synchronic separation. Depending on the magnitude of distance, it is possible to devise a break between the productions of pre-Linnaean European natural history and the phylogenetic orthodoxy of the 'modern synthesis' underpinning twenty-first-century botanical science. Older, more innocent histories of early European botany tend to adopt a presentist stance, in seeing early modern (say seventeenth-century) science as a malformed or weak version of modern science, selecting from it those elements that make for a progressive cumulative narrative. So, in the hagiographical accounts, Georg Everard Rumpf (Rumphius), the celebrated German naturalist, who for most of his life worked for the Dutch East India Company and resided in Ambon in the spice islands of Indonesia, is presented as a 'Pre-Linnaean'. Understandably, his own way of looking at the plant world could not in any meaningful sense be said to have anticipated Linnaeus, and rather had as its point of reference the scholarly concerns of late seventeenth-century Europe and the mercantilist concerns of his employer, set in the context of the everyday life of a gentleman living in a tropical colony (Beekman 2011). For example, Rumphius writes in his most famous work, the *Herbarium Amboinense*, of a matter-of-fact observation that the leaves of overhanging mangrove trees when they touch the water turn into perches, and indicates throughout his work a belief in the spontaneous generation of living matter. In seventeenth-century Holland, these things were taken for granted, just as Newton was not unusual in his time in subscribing to alchemy, astrology, mysticism and the occult (Cowling 1977; Figala 2004). Such things only became a legacy embarrassment for younger acolytes, admirers and biographers. So too with Rumphius. We can see from the images accompanying his texts (Figure 5.4) acceptance of the idea that nymphs of certain crustacea emerged as minute homunculi, but this was no more credulous than the comparable belief of the great contemporaneous European microscopists, such as Van Leeuwenhoek. Many of Rumphius's assumptions about the natural world were shared with his Ambonese informants, just as Linnaeus a generation later shared many assumptions with his Lapp informants, whom he regarded as highly credible sources of data [Chapter 5 in the present volume]. So, while Rumphius could be critical of some of the claims of his informants, his brilliant work reflected a set of essentially seventeenth-century European world-framing assumptions that in terms of perception of the natural world overlapped with the cosmologies of the cultural others with whom he lived (and even married), and from whom he obtained his specimens and contextual data. Indeed, a focus on the work of many early modern naturalists shows us that ontologies are not fixed and tightly bounded as some commentary sometimes suggests, but were in a state of flux, in Rumphius's case reflecting an engagement between his everyday folk experience and the emerging practices of enlightenment science. This becomes even clearer if we look at the life of Linnaeus, whose early contributions to natural history were very much in the Rumphian mode, but who by the time of his death was hailed a demi-god in the pantheon of the new scientific age (Koerner 1999).

There is another feature of what some might call the early modern naturalist ontology that comes through in the work of Rumphius, and this has less to do with underlying beliefs and assumptions than with technical possibilities of representation. Rumphius, ostensibly to please his patrons, produced three major works of natural history, *The Herbal*, *The Ambonese Curiosity Cabinet* and the *Amboinsch Dierboek* (the 'Animal Book') that was lost, but which appeared in a heavily plagiarised form through the work of François Valentijn (2002–2003 [1726]). *The Herbal* (which is now available in a wonderful English translation by the late E.M. Beekman) follows the patterns of other early compendia of exotic plants, listing them species by species, grouped into books using practical, what Berlin would call special-purpose criteria. For example, Book 1, 'Containing all sorts of trees, that bear edible fruits, and are husbanded by people', reflects a structure that historically arrives with the technologies of the written word that reduce oral knowledge to lists (see also Tsing 2005: 155–70), but which can then reorganise the content of those lists in novel ways (e.g.

Goody 1977), opening up new forms of intellectual scrutiny. However, this same conversion radically separates the names of individual plants and their uses from their context as part of a local physical landscape, ecology and cultural world, in a set of representations that are not fixed or tightly bounded, but fluid and complex. Thus, Rumphius's description (2011 [1743]: vol. 3, 86–87) of *Albizia falcataria* (L.) Fosberg is beautiful, but the simple reference to its use in making shields does little justice to, say, the Nuaulu perception of 'the shield tree', which is intricately bound up in the way this species is sought out for making sacred shields (*aniaue monne*) that are then invested with symbolic qualities and used in ritual contexts (Ellen 1990, 2018b). Thus, different kinds of representation significantly change the cultural construction of Nuaulu plant knowledge. As Latour (1993) might put it, whereas modern botanical ontologies separate things, nature and society through the activity of science, other ontologies bring them together. The development of European botanical knowledge depended on local field collaborations that were subsequently erased, while the multi-dimensional complexities of human–plant interaction were simplified in the pursuit of global knowledge (Ellen and Harris 2000). As Tsing (2005: 94) puts it, 'the system takes precedence over the plant'.

Scientific Phytomedicine versus Medical Anthropology

We now move to a conjuncture of a different order: the way science, purportedly constructed as an ontological whole, confronts other radically different cultural constructions, and examine how the same problems can be seen within epistemologically different traditions of Western scholarship. In her introduction to *Plants, Health and Healing*, which she co-edited with Stephen Harris, Elisabeth Hsu (2010a) addresses an observation I made in my 2005 overview regarding the disconnect at the interface between medical ethnobotany and medical anthropology. While we may suspect that in practice these two approaches show great internal diversity and some overlap, medical anthropology as represented by some of its major exponents is primarily about relations between healers and their patients and how sickness is socio-culturally constructed (see Waldstein and Adams 2006). My question had been partly an observation that most people who describe themselves as medical anthropologists are just not interested in how the healing practices of most of the world involve plants, and are more interested in illness and healing as a socio-cultural phenomenon; and that where they do take an interest in everyday therapies they often avoid robust methodologies that look at treatment episodes and the way in which plant preparations are sourced, introduced, explained, and have material bodily consequences that are themselves interpreted culturally. Of course, there were major exceptions to this picture even in 2005 – the work, for example, of Nina Etkin (1986, 1993), Elois and Brent Berlin (1996) and Francis Zimmerman (1989) – but despite dramatic growth in scholarly work on medicinal plants, this remains an under-researched area within medical anthropology as a whole.

As Hsu points out, medical anthropology seems to prioritise local epistemologies (how knowledge is generated) and ontologies (questions as to what constitutes being), while much ethnobotany (e.g. Berlin and Berlin 1996) is concerned in the first instance with mapping local classifications on to botanical taxa in the ways already discussed; concerned more with examining objective empirical knowledge derived in a subject–object relation in which the investigator is detached from the complexities of cultural context and local experience by the conventions of a particular scientific tradition for reporting nature. Although simplified and reconfigured to conform with a particular – no less cultural – view of the world, science provides us with a convenient baseline for comparative work, hypothesis-testing and deep generalisation, sustained by the practical experience of scientists themselves. While ethnobotanical approaches provide us with evidence against the strong programme of social constructionism and cultural relativism, in showing how there is an aggregate tendency for people to select plants that really do have beneficial therapeutic effects, there is no perceivable empirical fact that is not also metaphoric or symbolic (Hsu 2010a: 20), and therefore relational. Hsu argues that the interface is not much explored because of differences in dominant epistemologies. While medical ethnobotany tends to treat knowledge of plants as empirical knowledge, medical anthropology is engaged with problems of knowledge production itself. However, this is not the whole problem: medical anthropology has not engaged well with the problems that the materiality of medical cultures pose (Hsu 2010a: 36). For example, herbal medicines are not natural herbs but cultural artefacts (ibid.: 38); at every stage in selection, harvesting, treatment and healing, local and cultural factors are at play. Hsu illustrates the issue by looking at the Chinese lexical item 'qing hao', which designates both a living kind and the drugs related to modern botanical species. The category references – though not exclusively – *Artemisia annua* L. (or sweet wormwood) from which is nowadays extracted artemisinin used to treat malaria. In one of the first longitudinal studies of a particular drug in the Chinese material medica, she shows how the history of cultural practices in preparing the plant is accompanied by changes in its attributed efficacy. The case of 'qing hao' beautifully illustrates how the medicinal use of plants poses explanatory problems for medical anthropologists, how knowledge arises in negotiation with the materiality of the plants and human bodies, and how plants become part of social life. The example shows us that while we must begin by accepting the materiality of plants, it is necessary to address this in a variety of ways, from their chemistry to phenomenological appearance, through different dimensions of the sensorium, and as both common sense and enskilled practice. Indeed, the same taxonomic plant can yield different materialities in different contexts of use. Thus, the materiality of 'qing hao' identified as *Artemisia annua* when used for extracting artemisinin to treat malaria is not the same as that used to treat female haemorrhoids.

Museum Practice versus Lived Practice

Another institutional context in which ethnobotanists work, and in which the materiality of the plant is central, is the museum. The museum (of which we must regard the herbarium as a special case) is a way of arranging knowledge physically. As embedded in the Western intellectual tradition, the museum objectifies, sub-divides and rearranges the world according to specialised cultural logics (Durrans 2012). It therefore reflects the kinds of change in representation that accompanied the technologies of literacy that I have discussed above in connection with early descriptive botanical texts, such as those of Rumphius. Depending on the kinds of object and the overarching purpose of the museum, the organising principles will vary, for example according to whether the emphasis is on, say, natural history, geography, science, particular cultural groups, historical periods, and so on. But because the museum arranges objects in physical space, the materiality of the objects themselves (size, vulnerability, the substances from which they are made) is an additional consideration when storing and displaying. Moreover, objects in museums are – literally – tied to that particular icon of literacy we call 'the label'. In museum parlance, objects only become 'specimens' once they have a label (Sturtevant 1969: 29), which to varying degrees interprets the object through its collection history, physical analysis and cultural and ecological background. Sometimes labels are textually minimal and information-light, but others may be extensive and connect with other kinds of texts: published books and papers, herbaria, databases, photographs and so on.

Ethnobotanical objects that find themselves part of a museum collection may be represented very differently depending on the kind of museum. Emily Brennan (2017) has been researching barkcloth, mainly at Kew, but also in the field, and using my own data on contemporary Nuaulu ethnography. Her particular concern is the way in which barkcloth presents itself in different cultural contexts. In an ethnographic museum, the context will be the material culture of the particular population that produced it, either organised geographically (as in the British Museum), or in terms of functionality or assumed evolutionary relationship (as in the case with the Pitt Rivers Museum, Oxford). In all this, the plant qualities of the object – the species, extracts and plant parts employed – are subsumed within the larger cultural context of the object.

In an economic botany museum, such as we find at Kew, the emphasis is on the taxonomic identity of materials transformed into cultural objects. Whereas ethnographic labels define the object culturally, once placed within the overarching scheme of the museum catalogue, the logic of economic botany is taxonomic identification, use and the properties of the comprising taxa. Emily Brennan (2013: 4–5) puts it this way (but see also Brennan 2017):

> At Kew, approaches to material culture and techniques serve to homogenise barkcloth. Science shapes the way that barkcloth is perceived, i.e. as transformed chemical and physical matter, and serves to frame its coming into being and properties, by finding patterns through comparative systems; whilst quietly taking effect throughout barkcloth reference. This conceptual landscape is materialised at the collection through the organisation and categorisation of the material. Rather than the objects in the collection representing people and places, they create and imagine them within their own frames of reference, as indexes . . . barkcloth is indexical of natures, and of technologies that are situated amongst those natures.

By contrast, among Nuaulu, for Brennan (2003: 15): 'barkcloth is wrapped around the male groin in abrasive fibrous and tough strips, produced by beating in flowing water, harvested from the forest, is both restricted and restrictive, and is active and efficacious in ritual'. I would add that, at the present time at least, barkcloth is wholly a sacred and gendered fabric (at least when made from those tree species used for male puberty ceremonies). It connects living trees with living human bodies, and through its continuing materiality in exchange and patrilineal descent embodied in its storage in clan houses, acts out what is a local interiority in contrast to those exchanges involving trade valuables (porcelain and textiles) that reflect exteriority and lateral links between clans. This is a very (social) anthropological reading, of course, emphasising 'the sociality embedded in things'. In ethnobotany, as we have seen already, and as exemplified in the preponderance of papers published in periodicals such as *Economic Botany* and the *Journal of Ethnobiology*, it often seems that cultural aspects are determined and universalised through natural science paradigms; with biodiversity and objective evidence predominating over diversity of human perception. Having said this, it could also be argued that any scholarly attempt to understand local cultural perceptions of plants using terms that are outside that culture (including and perhaps especially its language) are going to use some paradigm that is alien to that culture.

A related feature of the economic botany collection is the foregrounding of the word 'use' and its role as an organising concept (see also Lewis-Jones 2016). We can see some of the consequences of its reification in *Economic Botany Data Collection Standard* published by Kew in 1995 (Cook 1995). This is a manual that assists the measurement of usefulness and provides a set of terms that can be agreed internationally to dis-ambiguate the descriptions of plant resource properties. Whilst convenient and necessary for botanists with no anthropological training, it inevitably distorts the way living botanical knowledge systems work, by first reifying the use and then splitting up what might be regarded as separate uses for local users and then putting uses together again in a scheme that particularly emphasises biomedical descriptors and marginalises and warps the contextual, experiential and social role of plants; separating what should be together and bringing together what may be experienced separately. For example, there are two pages of 'social uses' compared with 37 for biomedical uses and 19 for the rest; thus reflecting the perceptions of plants in applied laboratory science, from which the 'lived ontologies' of those peoples for whom a particular use is reported – be it Nuaulu barkcloth makers at the time a collection was made or those who later use the barkcloth in some previously unanticipated way – are quite excluded. It is important to recognise that all plants that have a use become cultural artefacts in some form or another and must, by definition, be socially embedded. Exploring just what that means with respect to the myriad species involved – in, say, phytotherapy – is the proper work of ethnobotany.

Taxonomic Versus Ecological Paradigms

The phylogenetic episteme of modern biology developed through the gradual displacement of ways of thinking about natural history that were essentially local and culturally embedded (Cooper 2007). Of course, what we call 'scientific' biology is no less cultural than any other way of understanding the world, only organised in a way that allows for shared and privileged insights that cut across other social differences that we also call cultural. The process by which modern biology emerged was in part driven by European expansion into the rest of the world and the discovery of new species that challenged existing representations, and required new ways of explaining biological difference and relatedness. As early modern scholars grappled with what they encountered, they generated a complex array of phylogenies, names and classifications, which Linnaeus and others were to make sense of through radical transformation. What replaced local knowledge, therefore, was an increasingly reductionist model of the world that grew to accommodate the growth in diversity encountered, but which in so doing had to simplify the number and type of organising principles. Such scientific schemes consequently became remote from the experience of ordinary people living in local environments where all was materially connected and situated in a symbolically meaningful cosmology, but provided the essential framework that Darwinism could later work with.

Paradoxically, while Darwinism had by the late nineteenth century become the instrumental force driving an economy of explanation in relation to biodiversity, Darwin himself provided us with the tools for another paradigm organised around the metaphors of the 'tangled bank' and the 'web of life'. Through the work of Ernst Haeckel and others, this was to underpin the modern science of ecology, and to some extent had more affinity with the complex local ecologies of interconnection than with the Linnaean grid and evolutionary descent with modification models, which had replaced these folk models. Modern ecology was, therefore, to restore to some degree the contextual logics of folk natural histories, and to rediscover local knowledge. It was also to pragmatically resolve the logical tension between the evolutionarily linear-temporal and the present-systemic through the flexible tool-kit of modern plant science and evolutionary biology, although that tension is still refracted in modern ethnobotany. We can see it in the relationship between approaches drawn from plant systematics on the one hand, and from ecology on the other: the one universalist, inductive and reductionist, the second local and system-oriented.

The logic of fieldwork requires that we investigate the local and use epistemologies and techniques that are locality-grounded. For example, we undertake plot surveys and measure transects [Chapter 6 in the present volume]. But plot surveys can either be used to sample a locality, and to provide a collecting regime, all in support of a universalist paradigm of phylogenetic biodiversity and systematic plant taxonomy; or they may be the basis for understanding local environmental dynamics and plant interactions. The kind of ethnobotany that relies on insights obtained using the phylogenetic paradigm works by comparing local knowledge and practice within an evolutionary context. Thus, to take another example from *Plants, Health and Healing* – this time the paper by Caroline Weckerle and her associates (2010) – every plant species that produces caffeine has become a culturally known plant in disparate regions and in completely different societies. This is remarkable because caffeine is only produced by six genera from entirely unrelated families. Different ways in which caffeine-containing plants are used affects and is affected by different forms of sociality. A more extended and influential illustration of this approach is found in the important work of Tim Johns (1990) on the evolutionary origins of human vegetal diet and medication, particularly in relation to the handling of toxicity. So, in this perspective we can see local knowledge as something that changes, adapts and converges over the longer term as people interact with plants with similar properties.

A comparable tension exists in the way local people organise their plant knowledge. Undeniably, at one level, people operate with a weak version of systematic botany, in that they often organise information around whatever concept of natural kind approaches most closely what we would regard as an individual species or genus, and with which they interact on a regular multi-dimensional basis. Each taxon is – if you like – encapsulated in a body of associated knowledge that varies depending on frequency of interaction and socio-cultural importance. However, at the same time people are clearly able to generalise and to adjust their knowledge of how one species of plant works, in order to understand another, at the same time as understanding their local environments as systems, and as systems within systems, with emergent properties above the species level. There are, we might say, folk-biological homologies of autoecology and synecology (Ellen 2003c). There is a point, also, where these largely oral – but intermittently written – bodies of plant knowledge take on the appearance of global science in their manifest contradictions, for example in the great Asian scholarly healing traditions. Thus, as the Tibetan system (see, e.g., Ghimire, McKey and Aumeeruddy-Thomas 2005) spread beyond its heartland down through the Himalayas and northwards and eastwards into central Asia, Mongolia and China, it had to rely on different plants and engaged in exchange relations to ensure the supply of others. Forms of representation for teaching and spiritual purposes – such as the pictorial herbals (e.g. Figure 10.1) – presented a problem, as these were created in the context of local ecologies and monastic disciplines that were decreasingly shared in the environmentally diverse areas to which the system had spread.

Plant Movement and Knowledge Disjunction

If the historical transition from local to universal knowledge schemes is accompanied by a paradigm shift as local plant knowledges are necessarily aggregated and simplified, then the physical synchrony of movement from one place to another can result in equal surprises, as plants cross

Is There a Role for Ontologies in Understanding Plant Knowledge Systems? | 239

Figure 10.1. One of a set of 77 medical paintings copied in the time of the Thirteenth Dalai Lama in the 1920s for the training of physicians in Buryiatia. The original paintings were made in the late seventeenth century, to accompany a medical text compiled by the then Regent of Tibet, Desi Sangye Gyatso (sde srid sangs rgyas rgya mtsho). See Parfionovitch and Meyer (1992). The present image (Item 40928) is from a private collection and reproduced courtesy of *Himalayan Art* and the Shelley and Donald Rubin Foundation.

cultural and ecological boundaries. Local human populations are very selective about the properties of plants that interest them. Plants travel around the world, but the knowledge does not necessarily travel with them, or at least not all of the knowledge all of the time. Thus, as Elizabeth

Hsu (2010b) explains, the earliest Chinese records for the use of *Artemisia annua* concern the treatment of female haemorrhoids, although nowadays it is best known as an anti-malarial. Another example of cultural shift engendered by the global movement of plants is the story Michael Dove (2000) tells of the introduction of *Hevea brasiliensis* (A. Juss.) Muell.-Arg. into Malaysia and Indonesia from South America. This, of course, is a well-known tale of imperial derring-do that illustrates the economic role of the great botanic gardens such as Kew (Brockway 1979). In Dove's telling, however, the focus is on indigenous knowledge, and what we might mean by it. Those who acquired the germplasm in Brazil, nurtured it at Kew and introduced it to Malaya had certainly taken steps to note the optimal growing conditions of trees from which the latex was tapped in Brazil, and so were disappointed when initial attempts to establish Malayan plantations were unsuccessful. It was only when trees were cultivated experimentally by local Malay smallholders that success was achieved. The reason for this is that while local farmers shared little knowledge of how to grow *Hevea* with their Brazilian tapping counterparts, they (unlike the plantation owners) had a considerable and subtle knowledge of their own environment, which was what mattered in this case.

A similar case can be found in the movement of *Manihot esculenta* Crantz or cassava from its homeland in northwest Amazonia out into the diaspora. Laura Rival (e.g. Rival and McKey 2008) has conducted work on cassava diversity, domestication, and how this interacts with local knowledge in a tropical American context. However, as a result of the great Columbian Exchange, cassava has since the sixteenth century become a crop of increasing global importance. The history of how it spread is complex, but we can be sure that much of the local management knowledge accrued by Amerindian farmers was lost in the process, and effectively had to be rediscovered in the diaspora in the context of different cultures and ecologies. Whenever cassava first arrived in Indonesia, it did not become widespread until the end of the nineteenth century, and then spread quickly, particularly in deforested areas of relative aridity and social poverty where the toxic hydrogen cyanide conferred an advantage. For example, in a recent project with Indonesian colleagues (Ellen, Soselisa and Wulandari. 2012), I have shown how in less than 100 years farmers in the Kei islands learned to adapt and diversify particularly toxic forms of cassava ('enbal') from a low knowledge base, having formerly relied on yams, millet and sago as their starch staples. They did this through innovation, local experimentation, the sharing of knowledge and the exchange of germplasm with other farmers. But exactly what has been going on can be illuminated through DNA analysis in a phylogenetic framework, of the clonal folk-varieties of cassava in two very different populations. Nuaulu swidden cultivators on Seram who are not incentivised to diversify by encroaching aridity, who have other starch alternatives, and who have few named folk-varieties, also have folk-variety DNA profiles that are all relatively speaking genetically remote from each other. By comparison, Kei farmers have 16 or so named and disproportionately bitter varieties that are all quite closely related in terms of their DNA, indicating high and recent selection activity and management.

Understanding Contingent Membership of Different Functional Domains

Plants pass through different regimes of understanding as they move physically through different ecologies and cultural contexts. But not only do they acquire new meanings and uses as they are adopted in new settings, but their position in relation to natures of being and existence can change too. My final example demonstrates that plants do not have to move physically or between cultures to reflect a changed position. This may occur simply through altered situations of use and significance (Magnani 2016). In the context of any one knowledge system, we might see that a plant can exist as part of many overlapping cultural domains that emphasise different and often partial properties. So, a plant may be part of a body of knowledge concerned with healing, or it might be part of a domain concerned with food, or with manufacturing objects, or it may be part of a geographically defined grouping, an element in a particular kind of ecosystem or landscape. Amongst the Semelai 'dammar' collectors of the Malay peninsula, the many types of resin harvested have very different meanings at the production end, in the forest and in local cosmologies, than they do for the Chinese traders who buy them (Gianno 1990). As commodities they have properties that come into being not through experience of the forest and of extraction, but through the market and the consumption-driven needs of users of specific resins. We can see something similar in relation to Nuaulu knowledge of rattan that is delivered to the market, and the plants used by Nuaulu to make baskets (Ellen 2009). Plants used for making ritual baskets are embedded in a somewhat different (but overlapping) set of meanings than those for plants used for cooking, or for healing. In each case the relations established between the plants and other elements in the domain vary. These domains have often been described as special purpose, in contrast to those general-purpose classifications based on biological resemblance rather than utility, but conceptual difference may also emerge between domains based on different kinds of use: regimes of function compared, say, with regimes of making.

Markets can also be places of semantic and knowledge disjunction, as in the way in which medicinal plant traders in urban Bolivia (e.g. Wilkin 2014) serve as brokers, mediating worlds of plant knowledge based on varied altitudinal zonation, other floras and different cultural traditions, and the worlds of healers of different kinds who lack knowledge of the ecology of the living plants but who possess privileged knowledge by virtue of their experience of particular systems of healing.

Conclusion

If, like Dick Ford, we still imagine ethnobotany to be a common discourse without a unifying theory, then we can now see why this might be so. It has disjunctions and 'frictions' at its heart: cultural, epistemological, methodological. Whether we want to add 'ontological' as an adjective is hardly the point. If, as Henare, Holbraad and Wastell (2007: 27) suggest, 'there are as many ontologies as there are things to think through', then the concept might be considered entirely superfluous. I have examined here a few cases of radical disjuncture reflected in different kinds of ethnobotanical text. In discussing each, I have tried to avoid use of the term ontology, but have expressed radical conceptual disjuncture in other ways. I have referred to contrasting paradigms, practices, perspectives, frameworks for thinking, worldviews, cosmologies and epistemologies. Now, of course I accept that these notions are not necessarily semantically identical, and in some instances express important and subtle distinctions that we need to respect. But according to the definitions and usages of many, they are virtually interchangeable, while the meaning of 'ontology' itself has become woolly and inconsistent in its application (Woolgar and Lezaun 2013). Better, perhaps, to eschew the implication of discrete ontological distinctions altogether and – as Joseph Powell (2016) suggests – focus on actor-networks of people and things where knowledge is just one of several properties inhering within relations within a landscape.

In anthropology the ontological turn is generally associated with the work of Philippe Descola (e.g. 2005b), who famously distinguishes animist, totemic, analogical and naturalist ontologies. Descola was responding to the special difficulties he faced in accounting for Amazonian perceptions of the world that seemed inherently positional, relational and unstable. But in order to solve this problem, he develops a kind of typological approach, distinguishing societies that have animist ontologies from those that have totemic ontologies, and so on. In this vision it becomes what Des Fitzgerald (2013) has called 'a grand project in the old style'; one that flirts with a dangerous sociological holism, if not explicitly with mechanistic determinism. So, when we look at actual cases it is clear that all four ontologies can in principle – as amongst the Nuaulu – co-exist within the same society, different underlying assumptions emerging in different contexts.

One way to apprehend the intellectual space of ethnobotany is to envisage it as a set of overlapping circles circumscribing an infinite number of contexts in which a plant species might be placed. Each of these circles might be theoretically constituted as a cultural domain, but whether they additionally involve distinct epistemologies or ontologies must be a matter for further investigation. I find it helpful to make a threefold meta-conceptual distinction between *cultural domain* (distinguishing knowledge and practice on the grounds of content), *episteme* (loosely following Foucault, distinguishing knowledge in terms of the methods and approaches used to acquire it), and finally *ontologies* (defined in terms of underlying logical relations and cosmological assumptions). Most likely the claim of ontological difference will only be appropriate when aggregating several otherwise distinct cultural domains for a particular plant. This is because whatever else distinguishes ontologies, in practice history and the fuzziness of their boundaries must be taken into account. Ontologies are always products of change through time and space. At the beginning of the twenty-first century, ethnobotany – with its interstitial character and centrifugal forces – stands at an important junction between biology, culture and sociality. This is why it is such a challenge. In studies of systems of environmental knowledge, technical practice and cultural cognition, ethnobotany has provided – and will continue to provide – a convenient intellectual space in which to explore and test key concepts and methodologies about the capacity of the human mind to store, evaluate and utilise knowledge of the natural world.

Notes

First published in 2016 as 'Is There a Role for Ontologies in Understanding Plant Knowledge Systems?' in a special issue of the *Journal of Ethnobiology* (36 [1], 10–28) entitled 'Botanical Ontologies'. Reproduced courtesy of the Society of Ethnobiology.

1. See, for example, Chamberlain (1909), but Conklin's (1972) bibliography contains a larger number of illustrative references.

References

Agrawal, A. 1995. 'Indigenous and Scientific Knowledge: Some Critical Comments', *Indigenous Knowledge and Development Monitor* 3(3): 5. Elaborated as: (1995) 'Dismantling the Divide between Indigenous and Scientific Knowledge', *Development and Change* 26: 413–39.

———. 2005. 'Environmentality: Community, Intimate Government, and Environmental Subjects in Kumaon, India', *Current Anthropology* 46(2): 161–90.

Akimichi, T. 1996. 'Image and Reality at Sea: Fish and Cognitive Mapping in Carolinean Navigational Knowledge', in R. Ellen and K. Fukui (eds), *Redefining Nature: Ecology, Culture and Domestication*. Oxford: Berg, pp. 493–514.

Alcorn, J. 1995. 'Ethnobotanical Knowledge Systems: A Resource for Meeting Rural Development Goals', in D. Michael Warren, L. Jan Slikkerveer and David Brokensha (eds), *The Cultural Dimension of Development: Indigenous Knowledge Systems*. London: Intermediate Technology Publications, pp. 1–12.

Allan, C.L. 2002. 'Amerindian Ethnoecology, Resource Use and Forest Management in Southwest Guyana', Unpublished Ph.D. thesis. University of Surrey (Roehampton).

Anderson, A.B., and D.A. Posey. 1989. 'Management of a Tropical Scrub Savanna by the Gorotire Kayapó of Brazil', in D.A. Posey and W. Balée (eds), 'Resource Management in Amazonia: Indigenous and Folk Strategies', special issue of *Advances in Economic Botany* 7: 159–73.

Anderson, E.N. Jr. 1969. 'The Life and Culture of Ecotopia', in D. Hymes (ed.), *Reinventing Anthropology*. New York: Random House, pp. 264–83.

Anderson, E.N. 2000. 'Maya Knowledge and "Science Wars"', *Journal of Ethnobiology* 20(2): 129–58.

Anderson, J.N. 1973. 'Ecological Anthropology and Anthropological Ecology', in J.J. Honigmann (ed.), *Handbook of Social and Cultural Anthropology*. Chicago: Rand-McNally, pp. 179–239.

Anon. 1917. 'Boschwezen', in *Encyclopaedie an Nederlansch-Indië*, 2nd ed., Part 1, A–G. Leiden: Brill/The Hague: Nijhoff, pp. 385–92.

———. 1999a. 'Caution: Traditional Knowledge: Principles of Merit Need to Be Spelt Out in Distinguishing Valuable Knowledge from Myth', *Nature* 401: 623 (14 October, issue 6754).

———. 1999b. 'ICSU Seeks to Classify "Traditional Knowledge"', *Nature* 401: 631 (14 October, issue 6754).

Astuti, R. 2001. 'Are We All Natural Dualists? Cognitive Developmental Approach', *Journal of the Royal Anthropological Institute (N.S.)* 7: 429–47.
Atran, S. 1990. *Cognitive Foundations of Natural History: Towards an Anthropology of Science*. Cambridge: Cambridge University Press.
———. 1994. 'Core Domains Versus Scientific Theories: Evidence from Systematics and Itza-Maya Folkbiology', in L. Hirschfeld and S. Gelman (eds), *Mapping the Mind: Domain Specificity in Cognition and Culture*. New York: Cambridge University Press, pp. 316–40.
———. 1995. 'Classifying Nature Across Cultures', in E.E. Smith and D.N. Osherson (eds), *Thinking: An Invitation to Cognitive Science*. Cambridge, MA: MIT Press, pp. 131–174.
———. 1996. 'Modes of Thinking about Living Kinds: Science, Symbolism, and Common Sense', in D.R. Olson and N. Torrance (eds), *Modes of Thought: Explorations in Culture and Cognition*. Cambridge: Cambridge University Press, pp. 216–60.
———. 1998. 'Folk Biology and the Anthropology of Science: Cognitive Universals and Cultural Particulars', *Behavioural and Brain Sciences* 21: 547–609.
Audley-Charles, M.G. 1993. 'Geological Evidence Bearing upon the Pliocene Emergence of Seram, an Island Colonizable by Land Plants and Animals', in I.D. Edwards, A.A. MacDonald and J. Proctor (eds), *Natural History of Seram, Maluku, Indonesia*. Andover: Intercept, pp. 13–18.
Aumeeruddy, Y., and J. Bakels. 1994. 'Management of a Sacred Forest in the Kerinci Valley, Central Sumatra: An Example of Conservation of Biological Diversity and Its Cultural Basis', *Journal d'Agriculture Tropicale et de Botanique Appliquée* 36(2): 39–65.
Aunger, R. (ed.). 2000. *Darwinizing Culture: The Status of Memetics as a Science*. Oxford: Oxford University Press.
Avery, T.E., and H.E. Burkhart. 1994. *Forest Measurements*. New York: McGraw-Hill.
Balée, W. 1989. 'The Culture of Amazonian Forests', in D.A. Posey and W. Balée (eds), 'Resource Management in Amazonia: Indigenous and Folk Strategies', special issue of *Advances in Economic Botany* 7: 1–21.
———. 1992. 'People of the Fallow: A Historical Ecology of Foraging in Lowland South America', in K.H. Redford and C. Padoch (eds), *Conservation of Neotropical Forests: Working from Traditional Resource Use*. New York: Columbia University Press, pp. 35–57.
———. 1994. *Footprints of the Forest: Ka'apor Ethnobotany: The Historical Ecology of Plant Utilization by an Amazonian People*. New York: Columbia University Press.
Balée, W., and A. Gély. 1989. 'Managed Forest Succession in Amazonia: The Ka'apor Case', in D.A. Posey and W. Balée (eds), 'Resource Management in Amazonia: Indigenous and Folk Strategies', special issue of *Advances in Economic Botany* 7: 129–58.
Bamford, S. (ed.). 1998a. 'Identity, Nature and Culture: Sociality and Environment in Melanesia', special issue of *Social Analysis* 42(3).
———. 1998b. 'Introduction: The Grounds of Melanesian Sociality', *Social Analysis* 42(3): 4–11 (special issue on 'Identity, Nature and Culture: Sociality and Environment in Melanesia', ed. S. Bamford).

———. 1998c. 'Humanized Landscapes, Embodied Worlds: Land and the Construction of Intergenerational Continuity among the Kamea of Papua New Guinea', *Social Analysis* 42(3): 28–54 (special issue on 'Identity, Nature and Culture: Sociality and Environment in Melanesia', ed. S. Bamford).

Barnes, B., B. Bloor and J. Henry. 1996. *Scientific Knowledge: A Sociological Analysis*. London: Athlone.

Barnes, J.A. 1962. 'African Models in the New Guinea Highlands', *Man* 62: 5–9.

Barnes, R.H. 1995. 'Introduction', in R.H. Barnes, A. Gray and B. Kingsbury (eds), *Indigenous Peoples of Asia*. Ann Arbor: Association for Asian Studies (Monograph no. 48), 1–12.

Bartlett, H.H. 1936. 'A Point of View and a Method for Rapid Fieldwork in Tropical Phytogeography', in *Botany of the Maya Area*. Miscellaneous Papers, I-13. Washington, DC: Carnegie Institution, pp. 1–13.

Bates, D. 1995. *Knowledge and Scholarly Medical Traditions*. Cambridge: Cambridge University Press.

Baviskar, A. 2000. 'Claims to Knowledge, Claims to Control: Environmental Conflict in the Great Himalayan National Park, India', in R. Ellen, P. Parkes and A. Bicker (eds), *Indigenous Environmental Knowledge and Its Transformations: Critical Anthropological Perspectives* (Studies in Environmental Anthropology 5). Amsterdam: Harwood, pp. 101–20.

Beekman, E.M. (ed. and trans.). 1981. *The Poison Tree: Selected Writings of Rumphius on the Natural History of the Indies*. Amherst: University of Massachusetts Press.

———. 2011. 'Introduction', in G.E. Rumphius, *The Ambonese Herbal*, vol. 1 (trans. E.M. Beekman). New Haven/London: Yale University Press/National Tropical Botanical Garden, pp. 1–169.

Bellwood, P. 1978. *Man's Conquest of the Pacific: The Prehistory of Southeast Asia and Oceania*. London: Collins.

Bennett, J. 2010. *Vibrant Matter: A Political Ecology of Things*. Durham, NC: Duke University Press.

Berkes, F. 1992. *Traditional Ecological Knowledge in Perspective*. Winnipeg: Natural Resources Institute.

Berlin, B. 1992. *Ethnobiological Classification: Principles of Categorization of Plants and Animals in Traditional Societies*. Princeton, NJ: Princeton University Press.

Berlin, B., D.E. Breedlove and P.H. Raven. 1973. 'General Principles of Classification and Nomenclature in Folk Biology', *American Anthropologist* 75: 214–42.

Berlin, E.A., and B. Berlin. 1996. *Medical Ethnobiology of the Highland Maya of Chiapas, Mexico*. Princeton, NJ: Princeton University Press.

Bernstein, J., R.F. Ellen and B. Antaran. 1997. 'The Use of Plot Surveys for the Study of Ethnobotanical Knowledge: A Brunei Dusun Example', *Journal of Ethnobiology* 17(1): 69–96.

Bessire, L., and D. Bond. 2014. 'Ontological Anthropology and the Deferral of Critique', *American Ethnologist* 41(3): 440–56.

Black, M.B. 1969. 'Eliciting Folk Taxonomy in Ojibwa', in S.A. Tyler (ed.), *Cognitive Anthropology*. New York: Holt, Rinehart and Winston, pp. 165–89.

Blaser, M. 2009. 'The Threat of the Yrmo: The Political Ontology of a Sustainable Hunting Program', *American Anthropologist* 111(1): 10–20.

———. 2013. 'Notes Toward a Political Ontology of "Environmental" Conflicts', in L.J.F. Green (ed.), *Contested Ecologies: Dialogues in the South on Nature and Knowledge*. Cape Town, South Africa: HSRC Press, pp. 13–27.

Bloch, M. 1974. 'Symbols, Song, Dance and Features of Articulation: Is Religion an Extreme Form of Traditional Authority?', *European Journal of Sociology* 15(1): 55–81.

———. 1991. 'Language, Anthropology and Cognitive Science', *Man* 26(2): 183–98.

———. 1998. 'Why Trees, Too, Are Good to Think With: Towards an Anthropology of the Meaning of Life', in L. Rival (ed.), *The Social Life of Trees: Anthropological Perspectives on Tree Symbolism*. Oxford: Berg, pp. 39–56.

Blumler, M.A. 1996. 'Ecology, Evolutionary Theory and Agricultural Origins', in D.R. Harris (ed.), *The Origins and Spread of Agriculture in Eurasia*. London: UCL Press, pp. 25–50.

Blust, R. 1976. 'Austronesian Culture History: Some Linguistic Inferences and Their Relations to the Archaeological Record', *World Archaeology* 8(1): 19–43.

Bonnemere, P. 1998. 'Trees and People: Some Vital Links: Tree Products and Other Agents in the Life Cycle of the Ankav-Anga of Papua New Guinea', in L. Rival (ed.), *The Social Life of Trees: Anthropological Perspectives on Tree Symbolism*. Oxford: Berg, pp. 113–31.

Boom, B.M. 1989. 'Use of Plant Resources by the Chácobo', in D.A. Posey and W. Balée (eds), 'Resource Management in Amazonia: Indigenous and Folk Strategies', special issue of *Advances in Economic Botany* 7: 78–96.

Boomgard, P. 1994. 'Colonial Forest Policy in Java in Transition, 1865–1916', in R. Cribb (ed.), *The Late Colonial State in Indonesia: Political and Economic Foundations of the Netherlands Indies, 1880–1942* (Verhandelingen an het Koninklijk Instituut voor Taal-, Land- en Volkenkunde 163). Leiden: KITLV Press, pp. 117–37.

Boster, J. 1996. 'Human Cognition as a Product and Agent of Evolution', in R.F. Ellen and K. Fukui (eds), *Redefining Nature: Culture, Ecology and Domestication*. Oxford: Berg, pp. 269–89.

Bourdieu, P. 1977. *Outline of a Theory of Practice* (Cambridge Studies in Social Anthropology 16, trans. R. Nice). Cambridge: Cambridge University Press.

———. 1990. *The Logic of Practice*. Cambridge: Polity.

Boyer, P. 1993. *Cognitive Aspects of Religious Symbolism*. Cambridge: Cambridge University Press.

———. 1994. *The Naturalness of Religious Ideas: A Cognitive Theory of Religion*. London: University of California Press.

Brennan, E. 2013. 'Heterogenous Cloth: An Ethnography of the Coming Into Being of Barkcloth Artefacts at the Royal Botanic Gardens, Kew, and amongst the Nuaulu of Seram, Indonesia', Unpublished Ph.D. proposal. University College London.

———. 2017. 'Heterogenous Cloth: An Ethnography of the Coming Into Being of Barkcloth Artefacts at the Royal Botanic Gardens, Kew, and amongst the Nuaulu of Nua Nea Village, Maluku, Eastern Indonesia', Unpublished PhD thesis. University College London.

Brockway, L. 1979. 'Science and Colonial Expansion: The Role of the British Royal Botanic Gardens', *American Ethnologist* 6: 449–65.

Brookfield, H.C., L. Potter and Y. Byron. 1996. *In Place of the Forest: Environmental and Socio-economic Transformation in Borneo and the Eastern Malay Peninsula.* Tokyo: United Nations University Press.

Brosius, J.P. 1986. 'River, Forest and Mountain: The Penan Gang Landscape', *Sarawak Museum Journal* 36(57) (New Series): 173–84.

———. 2000. 'Endangered Forest, Endangered People: Environmentalist Representations of Indigenous Knowledge', in R. Ellen, P. Parkes and A. Bicker (eds), *Indigenous Environmental Knowledge and Its Transformations: Critical Anthropological Perspectives* (Studies in Environmental Anthropology 5). Amsterdam: Harwood, pp. 293–318.

Brown, C.H., J. Kolar, B.J. Torrey, T. Trung-Quang and P. Volkman. 1976. 'Some General Principles of Biological and Non-biological Folk Classification', *American Ethnologist* 3: 73–85.

Brunei. 1984. *Brunei Forest Resources and Strategic Planning Study, Forest-type Map.* Sheet 4. Singapore: Anderson and Marsden.

Bruner, J. 1996. 'Frames for Thinking: Ways of Making Meaning', in D.R. Olson and N. Torrance (eds), *Modes of Thought: Explorations in Culture and Cognition.* Cambridge: Cambridge University Press, pp. 93–105.

Brutti, L. 1997. 'Waiting for God: Ecocosmological Transformations among the Oksapmin (Sandaun Province - PNG)', in P.J. Stewart and A. Strathern (eds), *Millennial Markers.* Townsville: Centre for Pacific Studies, University of North Queensland, pp. 87–131.

Budiansky, S. 1995. *Nature's Keepers: The New Science of Nature Management.* London: Weidenfeld and Nicolson.

Bulmer, A. 1991. 'Ralph Bulmer – A Bibliography', in A. Pawley (ed.), *Man and a Half: Essays in Pacific Anthropology and Ethnobiology in Honour of Ralph Bulmer.* Auckland: The Polynesian Society, pp. 45–54.

Bulmer, R.N.H. 1970. 'Which Came First, The Chicken or the Egg-Head?', in J. Pouillon and P. Maranda (eds), *Echanges et Communications; Mélanges Offerts a Claude Lévi-Strauss.* The Hague: Mouton, pp. 1069–91.

———. 1974a. 'Folk Biology in the New Guinea Highlands', *Social Science Information* 13(4/5): 9–28.

———. 1974b. 'Memoires of a Small Game Hunter: On the Track of Unknown Animal Categories in New Guinea', *Journal d'Agriculture tropicale et de Botanique appliquee* 2(1): 79–99.

Burkill, I.H. 1935. *A Dictionary of Economic Products of the Malay Peninsula*, 2 vols. London: Crown Agents for the Colonies.

Cadena, M. de la. 2015. *Earth Beings: Ecologies of Practice across Andean Worlds.* Durham, NC: Duke University Press.

Cadena, M. de la, and M. Blaser. 2018. *A World of Many Worlds*, Durham, NC: Duke University Press.

Callenbach, E. 1978. *Ecotopia.* London: Pluto Press.

Campbell, J.R. 2002. 'Interdisciplinary Research and GIS: Why Local and Indigenous Knowledge Are Discounted', in P. Sillitoe, A. Bicker and J. Pottier (eds), *Participating in Development: Approaches to Indigenous Knowledge.* London: Routledge (ASA Monograph Series no. 39), pp. 189–205.

Capra, F., and C. Spretnak. 1984. *Green Politics: The Global Promise*. London: Hutchinson.
Carey, S. 1985. *Conceptual Change in Childhood*. Cambridge, MA: MIT Press.
———. 1996. 'Cognitive Domains as Modes of Thought', in D.R. Olson and N. Torrance (eds), *Modes of Thought: Explorations in Culture and Cognition*. Cambridge: Cambridge University Press, pp. 187–215.
Carneiro, R. 1978. 'The Knowledge and Use of Rainforest Trees by the Kuikuru Indians of Central Brazil', in R.I. Ford (ed.), *The Nature and Status of Ethnobotany* (Anthropological Papers, no. 67). Ann Arbor: Museum of Anthropology, University of Michigan, pp. 201–16.
Carrithers, M. 1990. 'Why Humans Have Cultures', *Man (N.S.)* 25: 189–206.
Carrithers, M., L.J. Bracken and S. Emery. 2011. 'Can a Species Be a Person? A Trope and Its Entanglements in the Anthropocene', *Current Anthropology* 52: 661–85.
Carrithers, M., M. Candea, K. Sykes and M. Holbraad. 2010. 'Ontology Is Just Another Word for Culture: Motion Tabled at the 2008 Meeting of the Group for Debates in Anthropological Theory', *Critique of Anthropology* 30: 152–200.
Carroll, L. 1960 [1871]. *Alice's Adventures in Wonderland* and *Through the Looking-Glass*. London: Collins.
Cepek, M.L. 2011. 'Foucault in the Forest: Questioning Environmentality in Amazonia', *American Ethnologist* 38(3): 501–15.
Chamberlain, R.V. 1909. 'Some Plant Names of the Ute Indians', *American Anthropologist* 11(1): 27–40.
Chambers, R. 1983. *Rural Development: Putting the Last First*. Harlow: Longman.
Chambers, R., and P. Richards. 1995. 'Preface', in D.M. Warren, L.J. Slikkerveer and D. Brokensha (eds), *The Cultural Dimension of Development: Indigenous Knowledge Systems*. London: Intermediate Technology Publications, pp. xiii–xiv.
Chaplin, M. 2004. *Water Structure and Behaviour*. http://www.lsbu.ac.uk/water/.
Chua, L. 2015. 'Troubled Landscapes, Troubling Anthropology: Co-presence, Necessity, and the Making of Ethnographic Knowledge', *Journal of the Royal Anthropological Institute* 21: 641–59.
Clay, J.W. 1988. *Indigenous Peoples and Tropical Forests: Models of Land Use and Management*. New York: Cultural Survival Inc.
Cleese, J., C. Booth and Waterfall Productions. 1988. *The Complete Fawlty Towers*. Cambridge, MA: Da Capo Press.
Cleveland, D.A. and D. Soleri (eds). 2002. *Farmers, Scientists and Plant Breeding: Integrating Knowledge and Practice*. Wallingford: CABI Publishing.
Clifford, J. 1986. 'Introduction: Partial Truths', in J. Clifford and G.E. Marcus (eds), *Writing Culture: The Poetics and Politics of Ethnography*. Berkeley: University of California Press, pp. 1–26.
Coiffier, C. 1994. 'L'ecorce et la Moelle du Rotin: Tshimbe Kuvu, Kwiya Kuvu, Conception Iatmul de l'Universe', vol. 2, Unpublished Ph.D. thesis. École des Hautes Études en Sciences Sociales.
Colby, B., J. Fernandez and D. Kronenfeld. 1980. 'Toward a Convergence of Cognitive and Symbolic Anthropology', *American Ethnologist* 8: 422–50.

Colchester, M. 1993. 'Forest Peoples and Sustainability', in M. Colchester and L. Lohmann (eds), *The Struggle for Land and the Fate of the Forests*. Penang, Malaysia: World Rainforest Movement, The Ecologist, Zed Books, 61–95.

Colfer, C.J.P., N. Peluso and S.C. Chin. 1997. *Beyond Slash and Burn: Building on Indigenous Management of Borneo's Tropical Rainforests*. New York: The New York Botanical Garden.

Condit, R. 1996. 'Defining and Mapping Vegetation Types in Mega-Diverse Tropical Forests', *Trends in Ecology and Evolution* 11: 4–5.

Condominas, G. 1954. *Nous Avons Mangé la Forêt de la Pierre-Génie Gôo (Hii saa Brii Mau-Yaang Gôo)*. Paris: Mercure de France.

Condominas, G. 1977. *We Have Eaten the Forest: The Story of a Montagnard Village in the Central Highlands of Vietnam*. London: Allen Lane.

Conklin, B., and L. Graham. 1995. 'The Shifting Middle Ground: Amazonian Indians and Eco-politics', *American Anthropologist* 97(4): 695–710.

Conklin, H.C. 1954. 'An Ethnoecological Approach to Shifting Agriculture', *Transactions of the New York Academy of Sciences* 17: 133–42.

———. 1957. *Hanunóo Agriculture: A Report on an Integral System of Shifting Cultivation in the Philippines* (Forestry Development Paper no. 12). Rome: Food and Agriculture Organization of the United Nations.

———. 1961. 'The Study of Shifting Cultivation', *Current Anthropology* 2: 27–61.

———. 1972. *Folk Classification: A Topically Arranged Bibliography of Contemporary and Background References through 1971*. New Haven, CT: Yale University, Department of Anthropology.

Cook, F.E.M. 1995. *Economic Botany Data Collection Standard*. Kew, UK: Royal Botanic Gardens.

Cooper, A. 2007. *Inventing the Indigenous: Local Knowledge and Natural History in Nearly Modern Europe*. Cambridge: Cambridge University Press.

Coppinger, R., and R. Schneider. 1995. 'Evolution of Working Dogs', in J. Serpell (ed.), *The Domestic Dog: Its Evolution, Behaviour and Interactions with People*. Cambridge: Cambridge University Press, pp. 21–47.

Cotgrove, S. 1982. *Catastrophe or Cornucopia: The Environment, Politics and the Future*. Chichester: Wiley.

Cotton, C.M. 1996. *Ethnobotany: Principles and Applications*. Chichester: Wiley.

Coursey, D.G. 1978. 'Some Ideological Considerations Relating to Tropical Root Crop Production', in E.K. Fisk (ed.), *The Adaptation of Traditional Agriculture: Socio-economic Problems of Urbanisation* (Development Studies Centre Monogr. 11). Canberra: Australian National University, pp. 131–41.

Cowling, T.G. 1977. *Isaac Newton and Astrology*. Leeds: Leeds University Press.

Cresswell, R. 1983. 'Transferts de Techniques et Chaînes Opératoires', *Techniques et Cultures* (n.s.) 2: 143–63.

Croll, E. 1993. 'The Negotiation of Knowledge and Ignorance in China's Development Strategy', in M. Hobart (ed.), *An Anthropological Critique of Development*. London: Routledge, pp. 161–78.

Croll, E., and D. Parkin. 1992. 'Cultural Understandings of the Environment', in E. Croll and D. Parkin (eds), *Bush Base: Forest Farm: Culture, Environment and Development*. London: Routledge, pp. 11–36.

Crumley, C.L. (ed.). 1994. *Historical Ecology: Cultural Knowledge and Changing Landscapes*. Santa Fe: School of American Research Press.
Cutkowsky, M.R., and R.D. Howe. 1990. 'Human Grasp Choice and Robotic Grasp Analysis', in S.T. Venkataraman and T. Iberall (eds), *Dextrous Robot Hands*. New York: Springer-Verlag, pp. 5–31.
Damon, F.H. 1998. 'Selective Anthropomorphization: Trees in the Northeast Kula Ring', *Social Analysis* 42(3): 67–99 (special issue on 'Identity, Nature and Culture: Sociality and Environment in Melanesia', ed. S. Bamford).
D'Andrade, R.G. 1980. 'Cultural Cognition', in M.I. Posner (ed.), *Foundations of Cognitive Science*. Cambridge, MA: MIT Press, pp. 795–830.
Deacon, T. 1997. *Symbolic Species: The Co-evolution of Language and the Brain*. New York: W.W. Norton.
Departemen Kehutanan. 1986. *Sejarah Kehutanan Indonesia*, 2 vols. Jakarta: Menteri Kehutanan.
Descola, P. 1992. 'Societies of Nature and the Nature of Society', in A. Kuper (ed.), *Conceptualizing Society*. London: Routledge, pp. 107–26.
———. 1996. 'Constructing Natures: Symbolic Ecology and Social Practice', in P. Descola and G. Pálsson (eds), *Nature and Society: Anthropological Perspectives*. London: Routledge, pp. 82–102.
———. 2005a. *Par-delá Nature et Culture*. Paris: Gallimard.
———. 2005b. 'Beyond Nature and Culture: Radcliffe-Brown Lecture in Social Anthropology', *Proceedings of the British Academy* 139, 2005 Lectures. doi:10.5871/bacad/9780197263945.003.0006.
Descola, P., and G. Pálsson (eds). 1996. *Nature and Society: Anthropological Perspectives*. London: Routledge.
Desmond, A., and J. Moore. 1991. *Darwin*. London: Michael Joseph.
Diamond, J.M. 1966. 'Zoological Classification System of a Primitive People', *Science* 151: 1102–4.
———. 1986. 'The Environmentalist Myth', *Nature* 324: 19–20.
Dobbs, B.J.T. 1975. *The Foundations of Newton's Alchemy, or 'The Hunting of the Greene Lyon'*. Cambridge: Cambridge University Press.
Dougherty, J.W.D., and C.M. Keller. 1982. 'Taskonomy: A Practical Approach to Knowledge Structures', *American Ethnologist* 9: 763–74.
Douglas, M. (ed.). 1973. *Rules and Meanings: The Anthropology of Everyday Knowledge*. Harmondsworth: Penguin.
Dove, M.R. 1983. 'Theories of Swidden Agriculture and the Political Economy of Ignorance', *Agroforestry Systems* 1(3): 85–99.
———. 2000. 'The Life-Cycle of Indigenous Knowledge, and the Case of Natural Rubber Production', in R. Ellen, P. Parkes and A. Bicker (eds), *Indigenous Environmental Knowledge and Its Transformations: Critical Anthropological Perspectives* (Studies in Environmental Anthropology 5). Amsterdam: Harwood, pp. 213–51.
Dove, M.R., D.S. Smith, M.T. Campos, A.S. Mathews, A. Rademacher, S. Rhee and L.M. Yoder. 2007. 'Globalisation and the Construction of Western and Non-Western Knowledge', in P. Sillitoe (ed.), *Global vs Local Knowledge*. Oxford: Berghahn Books, pp. 129–54.

Dransfield, J., and N. Manokaran (eds). 1994. *Plant Resources of South-East Asia. No 6. Rattans*. Bogor: PROSEA.
Dunbar, K. 1995a. 'How Scientists Really Reason: Scientific Reasoning in Real-World Laboratories', in R.J. Steinberg and J. Davidson (eds), *Mechanisms of Insight*. Cambridge, MA: MIT Press, pp. 365–95.
Dunbar R.I.M. 1995b. *The Trouble with Science*. London: Faber and Faber.
Durrans, B. 2012. 'Anthropology and Museums', in R. Fardon, O. Harris, T.H.J. Marchand, M. Nuttall, C. Shore, V. Strang and R.A. Wilson (eds), *The SAGE Handbook of Social Anthropology*. Los Angeles: Sage, pp. 197–211.
Durrenberger, E., and G. Pálsson. 1986. 'Finding Fish: The Tactics of Icelandic Skippers', *American Ethnologist* 13(2): 213–29.
Dwyer, P.D. 1976. 'An Analysis of Rofaifo Mammal Taxonomy', *American Ethnologist* 3: 425–45.
———. 1996. 'The Invention of Nature', in R.F. Ellen and K. Fukui (eds), *Redefining Nature: Ecology, Culture and Domestication*. Oxford: Berg, pp. 157–86.
Edwards, I.D. 1993. 'Introduction', in I.D. Edwards, A.A. Macdonald and J. Proctor (eds), *Natural History of Seram, Maluku, Indonesia*. Andover: Intercept, pp. 1–12.
———. 1994. 'Rainforest People', in *Between the Leaves: The DPI Forest Service Journal*. Brisbane: Queensland Forest Service, Summer.
Edwards, I.D., R.W. Payton, J. Proctor and S. Riswan. 1990. 'Altitudinal Zonation of the Rain Forests in the Manusela National Park, Seram, Maluku, Indonesia', in P. Baas, K. Kalkman and R. Geesink (eds), *The Plant Diversity of Malesia*. Amsterdam: Kluwer, pp. 161–75.
———. 1993. 'Rainforest Types in the Manusela National Park', in I.D. Edwards, A.A. MacDonald and J. Proctor (eds), *Natural History of Seram, Maluku, Indonesia*. Andover: Intercept, pp. 63–74.
Ellen, R. 1972. 'The Marsupial in Nuaulu Ritual Behaviour', *Man* 7: 223–38.
———. 1975. 'Non-domesticated Resources in Nuaulu Ecological Relations', *Social Science Information* 14(5): 51–61.
———. 1977a. 'Anatomical Classification and the Semiotics of the Body', in J. Blacking (ed.), *The Anthropology of the Body*. London: Academic Press, pp. 343–73.
———. 1977b. 'Resource and Commodity: Problems in the Analysis of the Social Relations of Nuaulu Land Use', *Journal of Anthropological Research* 33: 343–73; 50–72.
———. 1978. *Nuaulu Settlement and Ecology: The Environmental Relations of an Eastern Indonesian Community* (Verhandelingen van het Koninklijk Instituut voor Taal-, Land- en Volkenkunde no. 83). The Hague: Martinus Nijhoff.
———. 1979. 'Introductory Essay', in R.F. Ellen and D.A. Reason (eds), *Classifications in Their Social Context*. London: Academic Press, pp. 1–32.
———. 1982. *Environment, Subsistence and System: The Ecology of Small-Scale Social Formations*. Cambridge: Cambridge University Press.
———. 1985. 'Patterns of Indigenous Timber Extraction from Moluccan Rain Forest Fringes', *Journal of Biogeography* 12: 559–87.
———. 1986a. 'Ethnobiology, Cognition and the Structure of Prehension: Some General Theoretical Notes', *Journal of Ethnobiology* 6: 83–98.

———. 1986b. 'What Black Elk Left Unsaid: On the Illusory Images of Green Primitivism', *Anthropology Today* 2 (6 December): 8–12.

———. 1986c. 'Microcosm, Macrocosm and the Nuaulu House: Concerning the Reductionist Fallacy as Applied to Metaphorical Levels', *Bijdragen tot de Taal-, Land- en Volkenkunde* 142(1): 1–30.

———. 1987. 'Environmental Perturbation, Inter-island Trade and the Re-location of Production along the Banda Arc; or, Why Central Places Remain Central', in T. Suzuki and R. Ohtsuka (eds), *Human Ecology of Health and Survival in Asia and the South Pacific*. Tokyo: University of Tokyo Press, pp. 35–61.

———. 1988a. 'Foraging, Starch Extraction and the Sedentary Lifestyle in the Lowland Rainforest of Central Seram', in T. Ingold, D. Riches and J. Woodburn (eds), *Hunters and Gatherers: History, Evolution and Social Change*. London: Berg, pp. 117–34.

———. 1988b. 'Fetishism', *Man* 23: 213–35.

———. 1988c. 'Ritual, Identity and the Management of Interethnic Relations on Seram', in D.S. Moyer and H.M. Claessen (eds), *Time Past, Time Present, Time Future: Essays in Honour of P.E. de Josselin de Jong (*Verhandelingen van het Koninklijk Instituut voor Taal-, Land- en Volkenkunde 131). Dordrecht: Foris, pp. 117–35.

———. 1990. 'Nuaulu Sacred Shields: The Reproduction of Things or the Reproduction of Images?', *Etnofoor* 3: 5–25.

———. 1991a. 'Grass, Grerb or Weed? A Bulmerian Meditation on the Category "Monote" in Nuaulu Plant Classification', in A. Pawley (ed.), *Man and a Half: Essays in Honour of Ralph Bulmer*. Auckland: Uniprint, pp. 95–101.

———. 1991b. 'Nuaulu Betel Chewing: Ethnobotany, Technique and Cultural Significance', *Cakalele: Maluku Research Journal* 2: 97–122.

———. 1993a. 'Rhetoric, Practice and Incentive in the Face of the Changing Times: A Case Study in Nuaulu Attitudes to Conservation and Deforestation', in K. Milton (ed.), *Environmentalism: The View from Anthropology*. London: Routledge, pp. 126–43.

———. 1993b. *The Cultural Relations of Classification: An Analysis of Nuaulu Animal Categories from Central Seram* (Cambridge Studies in Social and Cultural Anthropology 91). Cambridge: Cambridge University Press.

———. 1993c. 'Human Impact on the Environment of Seram', in I.D. Edwards, A.A. Macdonald and J. Proctor (eds), *Natural History of Seram, Maluku, Indonesia*. Andover: Intercept, pp. 191–205.

———. 1996a. 'Introduction', in R.F. Ellen and K. Fukui (eds), *Redefining Nature: Culture, Ecology and Domestication*. Oxford: Berg, pp. 1–36.

———. 1996b. 'Individual Strategy and Cultural Regulation in Nuaulu Hunting', in R. Ellen and K. Fukui (eds), *Redefining Nature: Ecology, Culture and Domestication*. Oxford: Berg, pp. 597–635.

———. 1996c. 'Putting Plants in Their Place: Anthropological Approaches to Understanding the Ethnobotanical Knowledge of Rainforest Populations', in D.S. Edwards, W.E. Booth and S.C. Choy (eds), *Tropical Rainforest Research – Current Issues*. Dordrecht: Kluwer, pp. 457–65.

———. 1996d. 'The Cognitive Geometry of Nature: A Contextual Approach', in P. Descola and G. Pálsson (eds), *Nature and Society: Anthropological Perspectives*. London: Routledge, pp. 103–23.

———. 1996e. 'Cuscus and Cockerels: Killing Rituals and Ritual Killings among the Nuaulu of Seram', in S. Howell (ed.), *For the Sake of Our Future: Sacrificing in Eastern Indonesia*. Leiden: Research School, CNWS, pp. 263–82.

———. 1998a. 'Palms and the Prototypicality of Trees: Some Questions Concerning Assumptions in the Comparative Study of Categories and Labels', in L. Rival (ed.), *The Social Life of Trees*. Oxford: Berg, pp. 57–79.

———. 1998b. 'The Inedible and the Uneatable: Totemic and Other Restrictions on the Use of Biological Species among the Nuaulu', in S. Pannell and F. von Benda-Beckman (eds), *Old World Places, New World Problems: Exploring Issues of Resource Management in Eastern Indonesia*. Canberra: Australian National University, pp. 243–66.

———. 1998c. 'Comparative Natures in Melanesia: An External Perspective', *Social Analysis* 42(3): 143–58 (special issue on 'Identity, Nature and Culture: Sociality and Environment in Melanesia', ed. S. Bamford).

———. 1999a. 'Forest Knowledge, Forest Transformation: Political Contingency, Historical Ecology and the Renegotiation of Nature in Central Seram', in T. Li (ed.), *Transforming the Indonesian Uplands: Marginality, Power and Production*. Amsterdam: Harwood, pp. 131–57.

———. 1999b. 'Modes of Subsistence and Ethnobiological Knowledge: Between Extraction and Cultivation in Southeast Asia', in D.L. Medin and S. Atran (eds), *Folkbiology*. Cambridge, MA: MIT Press, pp. 91–117.

———. 2003a. *On the Edge of the Banda Zone: Past and Present in the Social Organization of a Moluccan Trading Network*. Honolulu: University of Hawaii Press.

———. 2003b. 'A Synoptic View of the Co-management of Natural Resources', in G.A. Persoon, D.M.E. van Est and P. Sajise (eds), *Co-management of Natural Resources in Asia: A Comparative Perspective*. Copenhagen: NIAS Press, pp. 281–92.

———. 2003c. 'Variation and Uniformity in the Construction of Biological Knowledge across Cultures', in H. Selin (ed.), *Nature across Cultures: Views of Nature and the Environment in Non-western Cultures*. Amsterdam: Kluwer, pp. 47–74.

———. 2004a. 'From Ethno-science to Science, or "What the Indigenous Knowledge Debate Tells Us about How Scientists Define Their Project"', *Journal of Cognition and Culture* 4(3–4): 409–50.

———. 2004b. 'Processing Metroxylon sagu (ARECACEAE) as a Technological Complex: A Case Study from South Central Seram, Indonesia', *Economic Botany* 58: 601–25.

———. 2006a. 'Local Knowledge and Management of Sago Palm (*Metroxylon sagu* Rottboell) Diversity in South Central Seram, Maluku, Eastern Indonesia', *Journal of Ethnobiology* 26: 83–123.

———. 2006b. 'Introduction', in R. Ellen (ed.), *Ethnobiology and the Science of Humankind* (vol. 12, special issue of the *Journal of the Royal Anthropological Institute*). Oxford: Blackwell, pp. 1–22.

———. 2007. 'Plots, Typologies and Ethnoecology: Local and Scientific Understandings of Forest Diversity on Seram', in P. Sillitoe (ed.), *Global vs Local Knowledge*. Oxford: Berghahn Books, pp. 41–74.

———. 2008. 'Ethnomycology among the Nuaulu of the Moluccas: Putting Berlin's "General Principles" to the Test', *Economic Botany* 62: 483–96.

———. 2009. 'A Modular Approach to Understanding the Transmission of Technical Knowledge: Nuaulu Basket-Making from Seram, Eastern Indonesia', *Journal of Material Culture* 14: 243–77.

———. 2010a. 'Why Aren't the Nuaulu Like the Matsigenka? Knowledge and Categorization of Forest Diversity on Seram, Eastern Indonesia', in L.M. Johnson and E.S. Hunn (eds), *Landscape Ethnoecology: Concepts of Biotic and Physical Space* (Studies in Environmental Anthropology and Ethnobiology, vol. 9). Oxford: Berghahn Books, pp. 116–40.

———. 2010b. 'Theories in Anthropology and "Anthropological Theory"', *Journal of the Royal Anthropological Institute* 16: 387–404.

———. 2012. *Nuaulu Religious Practices: The Frequency and Reproduction of Rituals in a Moluccan Society*. Leiden: KITLV Press.

———. 2016. 'Is There a Role for Ontologies in Understanding Plant Knowledge Systems?', in T. Miller (ed.), 'Botanical Ontologies', special issue of *Journal of Ethnobiology* 36(1): 10–28.

———. 2017. 'Tools, Agency and the Category of Living Things', in T. Pommerening and W. Bisang (eds), *Classification from Antiquity to Modern Times: Sources, Methods, and Theories from an Interdisciplinary Perspective*. Berlin: De Gruyter, pp. 239–62.

———. 2018a. *Kinship, Population and Social Reproduction in the 'New Indonesia': A Study of Nuaulu Cultural Resilience*. London: Routledge.

———. 2018b. 'Understanding Geometrical Features of Nuaulu Shield Design', *Journal of Material Culture*. Published online 10 October 2018, https://doi.org/10.1177/1359183518803393.

Ellen, R.F., and J.H. Bernstein. 1994. 'Urbs in Rure: Cultural Transformations of the Rain Forest in Modern Brunei', *Anthropology Today* 10(4): 16–19.

Ellen, R., and M.D. Fischer. 2013. 'Introduction: On the Concept of Cultural Transmission', in R. Ellen, S.J. Lycett and S.E. Johns (eds), *Understanding Cultural Transmission in Anthropology: A Critical Synthesis*. Oxford: Berghahn Books, pp. 1–54.

Ellen, R., and K. Fukui (eds). 1996. *Redefining Nature: Ecology, Culture and Domestication*. Oxford: Berg.

Ellen, R.F., and N.J. Goward. 1984. 'Papeda Dingin, Papeda Dingin . . . Notes on the Culinary Uses of Palm Sago in the Central Moluccas', *Petits Propos Culinaires* 16: 28–34.

Ellen, R., and H. Harris. 2000. 'Introduction', in R.F. Ellen, P. Parkes and A. Bicker (eds), *Indigenous Environmental Knowledge and Its Transformations: Critical Anthropological Perspectives*. Amsterdam: Harwood (Routledge), pp. 1–33.

Ellen, R., P. Parkes and A. Bicker (eds). 2000. *Indigenous Environmental Knowledge and Its Transformations: Critical Anthropological Perspectives* (Studies in Environmental Anthropology 5). Amsterdam: Harwood.

Ellen, R., and S.J. Platten. 2011. 'The Social Life of Seeds: The Role of Networks of Relationships in the Dispersal and Cultural Selection of Plant Germplasm', *Journal of the Royal Anthropological Institute (N.S.)* 17: 563–84.

Ellen, R., S.J. Platten and R. Kaleta. N.d. 'The Transmission of Gardening Knowledge in UK Allotments and Domestic Plots: "Traditional' Knowledge" in a Complex Society'. Unpublished.

Ellen, R., H.L. Soselisa and A.P. Wulandari. 2012. 'The Biocultural History of *Manihot esculenta* in the Moluccan Islands of Eastern Indonesia: Assessing the Evidence for the Movement and Selection of Cassava Germplasm', *Journal of Ethnobiology* 32: 157–84.

Escobar, A. 2017. 'Sustaining the Pluriverse: The Political Ontology of Territorial Struggles in Latin America', in M. Brightman and J. Lewis (eds), *The Anthropology of Sustainability: Beyond Development and Progress*. New York: Palgrave Macmillan, pp. 237–56.

Etkin, N.L. 1986. *Plants in Indigenous Medicine and Diet: Biobehavioural Approaches*. New York: Gordon and Breach.

———. 1993. 'Anthropological Methods in Ethnopharmacology', *Journal of Ethnopharmacology* 38: 93–104.

Eyre, F.H. (ed.). 1980. *Forest Cover Types of the United States and Canada*. Washington, DC: Society of American Foresters.

Fairhead, J., and M. Leach. 1994. 'Declarations of Difference', in I. Scoones and J. Thompson (eds), *Beyond Farmer First*. London: Intermediate Technology Publications, pp. 75–79.

———. 1996. *Misreading the African Landscape: Society and Ecology in a Forest-Savanna Mosaic*. Cambridge: Cambridge University Press.

———. 1998. *Reframing Deforestation: Global Analysis and Local Realities – Studies in West Africa*. London: Routledge.

Fajans, J. 1998. 'Transforming Nature, Making Culture: Why the Baining Are Not Environmentalists', *Social Analysis* 42(3): 12–27 (special issue on 'Identity, Nature and Culture: Sociality and Environment in Melanesia', ed. S. Bamford).

Farquhar, J. 1995. 'Rewriting Traditional Medicine in Post-Maoist China', in D. Bates (ed.), *Knowledge and the Scholarly Medical Traditions*. Cambridge: Cambridge University Press, pp. 251–76.

Feld, S. 1996. 'A Poetics of Place: Ecological and Aesthetic Co-evolution in a Papua New Guinea Rainforest Community', in R. Ellen and K. Fukui (eds), *Redefining Nature: Ecology, Culture and Domestication*. London: Berg, pp. 61–87.

Fernandez-Gimenez, M. 1993. 'The Role of Ecological Perception in Indigenous Resource Management: A Case Study from the Mongolian Forest-Steppe', *Nomadic Peoples* 33: 31–46.

Figala, K. 2004. 'Newton's Alchemy', in I.B. Cohen and G.E. Smith (eds), *The Cambridge Companion to Newton*. Cambridge: Cambridge University Press, pp. 370–86.

Finnegan, R. 1988. *Literacy and Orality*. Oxford: Blackwell.

Fischer, M.D. 2004. 'Powerful Knowledge: Applications in a Cultural Context', in A. Bicker, P. Sillitoe and J. Pottier (eds), *Development and Local Knowledge: New*

Approaches to Issues in Natural Resource Management, Conservation and Agriculture. London: Routledge Harwood, pp. 19–30.

Fitzgerald, D. 2013. 'Philippe Descola's "Beyond Nature and Culture"', *Somatosphere: Science, Medicine, and Anthropology* 11 (October), http://somatosphere.net/2013/10/philippe-descolas-beyond-nature-and-culture.html.

Flach, M. 1976. 'Yield Potential of the Sagopalm and Its Realisation', in K. Tan (ed.), *Sago-76: First International Sago Symposium: The Equatorial Swamp as a Natural Resource.* Kuala Lumpur: Kemajuan Kanji, pp. 157–77.

Fleck, D.W., and J.D. Harder. 2000. 'Matses Indian Rainforest Habitat Classification and Mammalian Diversity in Amazonian Peru', *Journal of Ethnobiology* 20(1): 1–36.

Foley, W.A. 1997. *Anthropological Linguistics: An Introduction.* Oxford: Blackwell.

Ford, R.I. 1978. 'Ethnobotany: Historical Diversity and Synthesis', in R.I. Ford (ed.), *The Nature and Status of Ethnobotany* (Anthropological Papers 67). Ann Arbor, MI: Museum of Anthropology, University of Michigan, pp. 33–50.

Fosberg, F.R. 1962. 'Nature and Detection of Plant Communities Resulting from Activities of Early Man', in *Symposium on the Impact of Man on Humid Tropics Vegetation, Goroka, Territory of Papua and New Guinea, 1960.* Djakarta: UNESCO Science Cooperation Office for Southeast Asia, pp. 251–52.

Foucault, M. 1970. *The Order of Things: An Archaeology of the Human Sciences.* London: Tavistock.

Fox, J.J. 1971. 'Sister's Child as Plant: Metaphors in an Idiom of Consanguinity', in R. Needham (ed.), *Rethinking Kinship and Marriage* (ASA Monograph in Social Anthropology 11). London: Tavistock Publications, pp. 219–52.

———. 1980. 'Models and Metaphors: Comparative Research in Eastern Indonesia', in J.J. Fox (ed.), *The Flow of life: Essays on Eastern Indonesia.* Cambridge, MA: Harvard University Press, pp. 327–33.

Frake, C.O. 1961. 'The Diagnosis of Disease among the Subanun of Mindanao', *American Anthropologist* 63: 113–32.

———. 1983. 'Did Literacy Cause the Great Cognitive Divide?', *American Ethnologist* 10: 368–71.

———. 1985. 'Cognitive Maps of Time and Tide among Medieval Seafarers', *Man* 20(2): 254–70.

Franklin, S. 2003. 'Re-thinking Nature-Culture: Anthropology and the New Genetics', *Anthropological Theory* 3(1): 65–85.

Geertz, C. 1973. *The Interpretation of Cultures: Selected Essays.* New York: Basic Books.

Gell, A. 1985. 'How to Read a Map: Remarks on the Practical Logic of Navigation', *Man* 20(2): 271–86.

———. 1995. 'The Language of the Forest: Landscape and Phonological Iconism in Umeda', in E. Hirsch and M. O'Hanlon (eds), *The Anthropology of Landscape: Perspectives on Space and Place.* Oxford: Clarendon Press, pp. 232–54.

———. 1998. *Art and Agency: An Anthropological Theory.* Oxford: Clarendon Press.

———. 1999. 'Strathernograms, or, the Semiotics of Mixed Metaphors', in A. Gell (ed. E Hirsch), *The Art of Anthropology.* London: Athlone Press, pp. 29–75.

Gelman, R. 1990. 'First Principles Organize Attention to and Learning about Relevant Data: Number and the Animate-Inanimate Distinction as Examples', *Cognitive Science* 14: 79–106.

Gelman, S. 2003. *The Essential Child: Origins of Essentialism in Everyday Thought*. Oxford: Oxford University Press.

Ghimire, S., D. McKey and Y. Aumeeruddy-Thomas. 2005. 'Heterogeneity in Ethnoecological Knowledge and Management of Medicinal Plants in the Himalayas of Nepal: Implications for Conservation', *Ecology and Society* 9(6), http://www.ecologyandsociety.org/vol9/iss3/art6/.

Gianno, R. 1990. *Semelai Culture and Resin Technology*. New Haven, CT: Connecticut Academy of Arts and Sciences Memoir 22.

Gieser, T. 2014. 'Enskillment Inhibited: "Industrial Gardening" in Britain', *Journal of the Royal Anthropological Institute (N.S.)* 20(1): 131–49.

Gilbert, P.R. 2013. 'Deskilling, Agrodiversity and the Seed Trade: A View from Contemporary British Allotments', *Agriculture and Human Values* 30(1): 101–14.

Gillison, G. 1980. 'Images of Nature in Gimi Thought', in C. MacCormack and M. Strathern (eds), *Nature, Culture and Gender*. Cambridge: Cambridge University Press, pp. 143–73.

Gladwin, T. 1970. *East Is a Big Bird: Navigation and Logic on Pulawat Atoll*. Cambridge, MA: Harvard University Press.

Glatzel, G. 1992. *Report of a Fact Finding Mission on the Proposal for a Centre for Sustainable Land Use on Forested Islands of the Moluccas*. Vienna: Bundeskanzleramtes der Republik Österreich.

Glick, L. 1964. 'Categories and Relations in Gimi Natural Science', *American Anthropologist* 66: 273–80.

Goodenough, W.H. 1990. 'Evolution of the Human Capacity for Beliefs', *American Anthropologist* 92: 597–612.

Goody, J.R. 1968. 'Introduction', in J. Goody (ed.), *Literacy in Traditional Societies*. Cambridge: Cambridge University Press, pp. 1–26.

———. 1977. *The Domestication of the Savage Mind*. Cambridge: Cambridge University Press.

———. 1986. *The Logic of Writing and the Organisation of Society* (Studies in Literacy, Family, Culture and the State). Cambridge: Cambridge University Press.

———. 1987. *The Interface between the Written and the Oral*. Cambridge: Cambridge University Press.

Gray, A. 1995. 'The Indigenous Movement in Asia', in R.H. Barnes, A. Gray and B. Kingsbury (eds), *Indigenous Peoples of Asia* (Monograph no. 48). Ann Arbor: Association for Asian Studies, pp. 35–58.

Greigg-Smith, P. 1964. *Quantitative Plant Ecology*. London: Butterworths.

Grenand, P. 1992. 'The Use and Cultural Significance of the Secondary Forest among the Wayãpi Indians', in M. Plotkin and L. Famolare (eds), *Sustainable Harvest and Marketing of Rain Forest Products*. Washington, DC: Island Press, pp. 27–40.

Grimes, B. 1993. 'The Pursuit of Prosperity and Blessing: Social Life and Symbolic Action on Buru Island, Eastern Indonesia', Ph.D. dissertation. Canberra: The Australian National University.

Grove, R. 1995. *Green Imperialism: Colonial Expansion, Tropical Island Edens and the Origins of Environmentalism, 1600–1860*. Cambridge: Cambridge University Press.
———. 1996. 'Indigenous Knowledge and the Significance of South-West India for Portuguese and Dutch Constructions of Tropical Nature', *Modern Asian Studies* 3011: 121–43.
Grzimek, B.R. 1991. 'Social Change on Seram: A Study of Ideologies of Development in Eastern Indonesia', Thesis submitted for the Degree of Doctor of Philosophy. London: School of Economics and Political Science, University of London.
Guddemi, P. 1992. 'When Horticulturalists Are Like Hunter-Gatherers: The Sawiyano of Papua New Guinea', *Ethnology* 1(4): 303–14.
Gudeman, S. 1988. 'Frontiers as Marginal Economies', in J.W. Bennett and J.R. Bowen (eds), *Production and Autonomy: Anthropological Studies and Critiques of Development* (Monographs in Economic Anthropology 5). Lanham, MD: University Press of America, pp. 213–16.
Hacking, I. 1999. *The Social Construction of What?* Cambridge, MA: Harvard University Press.
Hallam, E., and T. Ingold (eds). 2014. *Making and Growing: Anthropological Studies of Organisms and Artefacts*. Farnham: Ashgate.
Hallowell, A.I. 1960. 'Ojibwa Ontology, Behavior and World View', in S. Diamond (ed.), *Culture in History: Essays in Honor of Paul Radin*. New York: Columbia University Press, pp. 19–52.
Hämäläinen, P. 2008. *The Comanche Empire*. New Haven, CT: Yale University Press.
Haraway, D. 2008. *When Species Meet*. Minneapolis: University of Minnesota Press.
Hardjono, J. 1991. 'The Dimensions of Indonesia's Environmental Problems', in J. Hardjono (ed.), *Indonesia: Resources, Ecology and Environment*. Oxford: Oxford University Press, pp. 1–16.
Harré, R. 1983. *Personal Being: A Theory for Individual Psychology*. Oxford: Blackwell.
Harris, H. 1996. 'A Critical Analysis of the Concept "Indigenous Knowledge" within Current Development Discourse', Dissertation presented for MA degree. University of Kent at Canterbury.
Hart, G. 1989. 'Agrarian Change in the Context of State Patronage', in G. Hart, A. Turton and B. White (eds), *Agrarian Transformations: Local Processes and the State in Southeast Asia*. Berkeley: University of California Press, pp. 31–49.
Hastrup, K. 2011. 'Nature: Anthropology on the Edge', in K. Hastrup (ed.), *Anthropology and Nature*. New York: Routledge, pp. 1–26.
Haudricourt, A. 1962. 'Domestication des Animaux, Culture des Plantes et Traitement d'Autrai', *L'Homme* 2(1): 40–50.
———. 1964. 'Nature et Culture dans la Civilisations de l'Igname: l'Origine des Clones et des Clans', *l'Homme* 4(1): 93–104.
Hays, T. 1983. 'Ndumba Folk Biology and General Principles of Ethnobiological Classification and Nomenclature', *American Anthropologist* 85: 592–611.
Headland, T.N. 1987. 'The Wild Yam Question: How Well Could Independent Hunter-Gatherers Live in a Tropical Rainforest Ecosystem?', *Human Ecology* 15(4): 463–91.
Healey, C. 1978–79. 'Taxonomic Rigidity in Folk Biological Classification: Some Examples from the Maring of New Guinea', *Ethnomedizin* (3–4): 361–84.

———. 1993. 'The Significance and Application of TEK', in N. Williams and G. Baines (eds), *Traditional Ecological Knowledge: Wisdom for Sustainable Development*. Canberra: Centre for Resource and Environmental Studies, Australian National University, pp. 21–26.

Henare, A.J.M., M. Holbraad and S. Wastell. 2007. *Thinking through Things: Theorising Artefacts Ethnographically*. London: Routledge.

Henrich, J., S. Heine and A. Norenzayan. 2010. 'The Weirdest People in the World?', *Behavioral and Brain Sciences* 33(2–3): 61–83.

Herzfeld, M. 1997. *Cultural Intimacy: Social Poetics in the Nation-State*. New York: Routledge.

Hewlett, B.S., and L.L. Cavalli-Sforza. 1986. 'Cultural Transmission among Aka Pygmies', *American Anthropologist* 88: 922–34.

Hirsch, E. 1995. 'Introduction. Landscape: Between Place and Space', in E. Hirsch and M. O'Hanlon (eds), *The Anthropology of Landscape: Perspectives on Space and Place*. Oxford: Clarendon Press, pp. 1–30.

Hoare, A.L. 2002. 'Cooking the Wild: The Role of the Lundayeh of the Ulu Padas (Sabah, Malaysia) in Managing Forest Foods and Shaping the Landscape', Unpublished Ph.D. dissertation. University of Kent at Canterbury.

Hobart, M. (ed.). 1993. 'Introduction: The Growth of Ignorance?', in M. Hobart (ed.), *An Anthropological Critique of Development*. London: Routledge, pp. 1–30.

Hobsbawm, E., and T. Ranger (eds). 1983. *The Invention of Tradition*. Cambridge: Cambridge University Press.

Holbraad, M. 2008. 'Definitive Evidence from Cuban Gods', *Journal of the Royal Anthropological Institute (N.S)* 14(s1): s93–s109.

Hollis, M., and S. Lukes (eds). 1982. *Rationality and Relativism*. Oxford: Basil Blackwell.

Hooke, R. 1961 [1665]. *Micrographia, or Some Physiological Descriptions of Minute Bodies Made by Magnifying Glasses with Observations and Enquiries Thereupon*. New York: Dover.

Horton, R., and R. Finnegan (eds). 1973. *Modes of Thought*. London: Faber and Faber.

Hoskins, J. 1998. *Biographical Objects: How Things Tell the Stories of People's Lives*. New York: Routledge.

Howard, J.A. 1991. *Remote Sensing of Forest Resources: Theory and Application*. London: Chapman and Hall.

Howell, N. 1976. 'The Population of the Dobe area !Kung', in R.B. Lee and I. DeVore (eds), *Kalahari Hunter-Gatherers: Studies of the !Kung San and Their Neighbours*. Cambridge, MA: Harvard University Press, pp. 137–51.

Howell, S. 1992. 'Time Past, Time Present, Time Future: Contrasting Temporal Values in Two Southeast Asian Societies', in S. Wallman (ed.), *Contemporary Futures: Perspectives from Social Anthropology*. London: Routledge, pp. 124–37.

———. 2011. 'Divide and Rule: Nature and Society in a Global Forest Programme', in K. Hastrup (ed.), *Anthropology and Nature*. New York: Routledge, pp. 147–65.

Hsu, E. 2010a. 'Introduction: Plants in Medical Practice and Common Sense', in E. Hsu and S. Harris (eds), *Plants, Health and Healing: On the Interface of Ethnobotany and Medical Anthropology*. Oxford: Berghahn Books, pp. 1–48.

Hsu, E. (in consultation with F. Obringer). 2010b. 'Qing Hao (Herba Artemisiae Annuae) in the Chinese Material Medica', in E. Hsu and S. Harris (eds), *Plants, Health and Healing: On the Interface of Ethnobotany and Medical Anthropology.* Oxford: Berghahn Books, pp. 83–130.

Humle, T., and T. Matsuzawa. 2001. 'Behavioural Diversity among the Wild Chimpanzee Populations of Bossou and Neighbouring Areas, Guinea and Cote d'Ivoire, West Africa', *Folia Primatologica* 72: 57–68.

———. 2004. 'Oil Palm Use by Adjacent Communities of Chimpanzees at Bossou and Nimba Mountains, West Africa', *International Journal of Primatology* 25: 551–81.

Hunn, E. 1993. 'What Is Traditional Ecological Knowledge?', in N. Williams and G. Baines (eds), *Traditional Ecological Knowledge: Wisdom for Sustainable Development.* Canberra: Centre for Resource and Environmental Studies, ANU, pp. 13–15.

———. 2008. *A Zapotec Natural History: Trees, Herbs and Flowers, Birds, Beasts and Bugs in the Life of San Juan Gbëë.* Tucson, AZ: University of Arizona Press.

Hurst, P. 1990. *Rainforest Politics: Ecological Destruction in Southeast Asia.* London: Zed Books.

Huxley, A. 1978. *An Illustrated History of Gardening.* New York: Paddington Press.

Hyndman, D. 1982. 'Biotope Gradient in a Diversified New Guinea Subsistence System', *Human Ecology* 10(2): 219–59.

ICSU (International Council for Science). 2002. *Science, Traditional Knowledge and Sustainable Development,* ed. D. Nakashima and D. Elias (ICSU Series on Science for Sustainable Development no. 4). ICSU and UNESCO.

Ingold, T. 1992. 'Culture and the Perception of the Environment', in E. Croll and D. Parkin (eds), *Bush Base, Forest Farm: Culture, Environment and Development.* London: Routledge, pp. 39–56.

———. 1993. 'The Temporality of the Landscape', *World Archaeology* 25(2): 152–74.

———. 1996. 'Hunting and Gathering as Ways of Perceiving the Environment', in R. Ellen and K. Fukui (eds), *Redefining Nature: Ecology, Culture and Domestication.* Oxford: Berg, pp. 117–55.

———. 1997. 'Environmental Perception and Cognitive Categories', unpublished paper delivered in a seminar series entitled 'Cognition and the Representation of Living Kinds', Department of Anthropology, University of Kent at Canterbury.

———. 2000a. 'On Weaving a Basket', in T. Ingold, *The Perception of the Environment: Essays in Livelihood, Dwelling and Skill.* London: Routledge, pp. 339–48.

———. 2000b [1995]. 'A Circumpolar Night's Dream', in T. Ingold, *The Perception of the Environment: Essays on Livelihood, Dwelling and Skill.* London: Routledge, pp. 89–110.

———. 2006. 'Rethinking the Animate, Re-animating Thought', *Ethnos* 71: 9–20.

———. 2011. *Being Alive: Essays on Movement, Knowledge and Description.* London: Routledge.

———. 2013. *Making: Anthropology, Archaeology, Art and Architecture.* London: Routledge.

Iskandar, J. 2007. 'Responses to Environmental Stress in the Baduy Swidden System, South Banten, Java', in R. Ellen (ed.), *Modern Crises and Traditional Strategies: Local Ecological Knowledge in Island Southeast Asia* (Studies in Environmental Anthropology and Ethnobiology 6). Oxford: Berghahn Books, pp. 112–32.

Iskandar, J., and R. Ellen. 2000. 'The Contribution of *Paraserianthes (Albizia) falcataria* to Sustainable Swidden Management Practices among the Baduy of West Java', *Human Ecology* 28(1): 1–17.

Johannes, R.E. 1987. 'Primitive Myth', *Nature* 325: 478.

———. 1989. *Traditional Ecological Knowledge*. Cambridge: IUCN, The World Conservation Union.

Johns, R.J. 1990. 'The Illusory Concept of the Climax', in P. Baas, K. Kalkman and R. Geesink (eds), *The Plant Diversity of Malesia*. Dordrecht: Kluwer, pp. 133–46.

Johns, T. 1990. *With Bitter Herbs They Shall Eat* (also published under the title *The Origins of Human Diet and Medicine*). Tucson, AZ: Arizona University Press.

Johnson, M. 1992. *Lore: Capturing Traditional Environmental Knowledge*. Ottawa: IDRC.

Johnson-Laird, P. 1982. *Mental Models*. Cambridge: Cambridge University Press.

Johnston, C.A. 1998. *Geographic Information Systems in Ecology*. Oxford: Blackwell Science.

Johnston, M. 1998. 'Tree Population Studies in Low-Diversity Forests, Guyana. II. Assessments on the Distribution and Abundance of Non-timber Forest Products', *Biodiversity and Conservation* 7: 73–86.

Jorgensen, D. 1998. 'Whose Nature? Invading Bush Spirits, Travelling Ancestors and Mining in Telefomin', *Social Analysis* 42(3): 100–16 (special issue on 'Identity, Nature and Culture: Sociality and Environment in Melanesia', ed. S. Bamford).

Karim, W.A. 1981. 'Mah Betisek Concepts of Humans, Plants and Animals', *Bijdragen tot de Taal-, Land-en Volkenkunde* 137: 135–60.

Kathirithamby-Wells, J. 2004. *Nature and Nation: Forests and Development in Peninsular Malaysia*. Honolulu: University of Hawaii.

Keil, F.C. 1979. *Semantic and Conceptual Development: An Ontological Perspective*. Cambridge, MA: Harvard University Press.

———. 1992. 'The Origins of an Autonomous Biology', in M.R. Gunnar and M. Maratsos (eds), *Modularity and Constraints in Language and Cognition* (The Minnesota Symposium on Child Psychology 25). New York and London: Psychology Press, pp, 103–37.

———. 1994. 'The Birth and Nurturance of Concepts by Domains: The Origins of Concepts of Living Things', in L. Hirschfeld and S. Gelman (eds), *Mapping the Mind: Domain Specificity in Cognition and Culture*. New York: Cambridge University Press, pp. 234–54.

Keller, C.M., and J.D. Keller. 1996. *Cognition and Tool Use: The Blacksmith at Work*. Cambridge: Cambridge University Press.

Kent, M., and P. Coker. 1992. *Vegetation Description and Analysis*. London: Bellhaven Press.

Kershaw, K.A. 1973. *Quantitative and Dynamic Plant Ecology*. London: Arnold.

Kingsbury, B. 1995. 'Indigenous Peoples as an International Legal Concept', in R.H. Barnes, A. Gray and B. Kingsbury (eds), *Indigenous Peoples of Asia*. Ann Arbor: Association for Asian Studies (Monograph no. 48), pp. 414–57.

Kirsch, S. 2001. 'Changing Views of Place and Time along the Ok Tedi', in A. Rumsey and J. Weiner (eds), *Mining and Indigenous Lifeworlds in Australia and Papua New Guinea*. Adelaide: Crawford House, pp. 243–72. Second printing 2004, Oxford: Sean Kingston Publishing, pp. 182–207.

Kluckhohn, E.R., and F.L. Strodtbeck. 1961. *Variations in Value Orientations*. Evanston, IL: Row Peterson.

Knight, D. 1981. *Ordering the World: A History of Classifying Man*. London: Andre Deutsch.

Knight, J. 2000. '"Indigenous" Regionalism in Japan', in R. Ellen, P. Parkes and A. Bicker (eds), *Indigenous Environmental Knowledge and Its Transformations: Critical Anthropological Perspectives* (Studies in Environmental Anthropology 5). Amsterdam: Harwood, pp. 151–76.

Kocher-Schmid, C. 1991. *Of People and Plants: A Botanical Ethnography of Nokopo Village, Madang and Morobe Provinces, Papua New Guinea* (Basler Beitrage zur Ethnologie 33). Basel: Ethnologisches Seminar der Universitat und Museum für Volkerkunde.

———. 1997. 'Les Oiseaux Volés', *Le Courrier de l'Environnement de l'INRA* 31: 79–83.

Koentjaraningrat. 1993. 'Pendahuluan', in Koentjaraningrat (ed.), *Masyarakat Terasing di Indonesia* (Seri Etnografi Indonesia 4). Jakarta: Gramedia Pustaka Utama, pp. 1–18.

Koerner, L. 1999. *Linnaeus: Nature and Nation*. Cambridge, MA: Harvard University Press.

Kohn, E. 2007. 'How Dogs Dream: Amazonian Natures and the Politics of Trans-species Engagement', *American Ethnologist* 34(1): 3–24.

———. 2015. 'Anthropology of Ontologies', *Annual Review of Anthropology* 44: 311–27.

Kopnina, H. 2016. 'Nobody Likes Dichotomies (But Sometimes You Need Them), Special Forum: Environmental and Social Justice?' *Anthropological Forum* 26(4): 415–29.

Kuhn, D. 1996. 'Is Good Thinking Scientific Thinking?', in D.R. Olson and N. Torrance (eds), *Modes of Thought: Explorations in Culture and Cognition*. Cambridge: Cambridge University Press, pp. 261–81.

Kuper, A. 1992. 'Introduction', in A. Kuper (ed.), *Conceptualizing Society*. London: Routledge, pp. 1–14.

Kuznar, L.A. 1997. *Reclaiming a Scientific Anthropology*. Lanham, MD: Altamira Press.

Laidlaw, J. 2012. 'Ontologically Challenged', *Anthropology of This Century* 4 (May), http://aotcpress.com/srticles/ontologically-challenged/.

Latinis, D.K. 2000. 'The Development of Subsistence System Models for Island Southeast Asia and Near Oceania: The Nature and Role of Arboriculture and Arboreal-Based Economies', *World Archaeology* 32(1): 41–67.

Latour, B. 1993. *We Have Never Been Modern*, trans. Catherine Porter. Cambridge, MA: Harvard University Press.
———. 2005. *Reassembling the Social: An Introduction to Actor-Network Theory*. Oxford: Oxford University Press.
———. 2008. *What Is the Style of Matters of Concern? Two Lectures in Empirical Philosophy*. Amsterdam: Van Gorcum.
———. 2009. 'Perspectivism: "Type" or "Bomb"', *Anthropology Today* 25(2): 1–2.
Laudan, L. 1981. 'The Pseudo-science of Science?', *Philosophy of the Social Sciences* 11: 173–98.
Leach, E. 1964. 'Anthropological Aspects of Language: Animal Categories and Verbal Abuse', in E. Lenneberg (ed.), *New Directions in the Study of Language*. Cambridge, MA: MIT Press, pp. 23–63.
———. 1965. 'Claude Lévi-Strauss – Anthropologist and Philosopher', *New Left Review* 34: 12–27.
———. 1970. *Lévi-Strauss*. London: Fontana/Collins.
———. 1972. *Humanity and Animality* (Fifth Conway Memorial Lecture). London: South Place Ethical Society.
———. 2000 [1977]. 'Anthropos', in S. Hugh-Jones and J. Laidlaw (eds), *The Essential Edmund Leach*. New Haven, CT: Yale University Press, pp. 324–80.
Lecuyer, J., and R. Pujol. 1975. 'L'oie Plumassiere du Poitou, Utilisation des Peaux et des Plumes', in R. Pujol (ed.), *L'homme et l'animal: Premier Colloque d'ethnozoologie*. Paris: Institut International d'Ethnosciences, pp. 205–16.
Lemonnier, P. 1992. *Elements for an Anthropology of Technology* (Anthropological Papers of the Museum of Anthropology 88). Ann Arbor, MI: University of Michigan.
———. 1993. 'The Eel and the Ankave-Anga of Papua New Guinea: Material and Symbolic Aspects of Trapping', in C.M. Hladik, A. Hladik, O.F. Linares, H. Pagezy, A. Semple and M. Hadley (eds), *Tropical Forests, People and Food: Biocultural Interactions and Applications to Development*. Paris: UNESCO, pp. 673–82.
Leroi-Gourhan, A. 1943. *L'homme et la Matiere: Evolution et Techniques*. Paris: Albin Michel.
———. 1945. *Milieu et Techniques: Evolutions et Techniques*. Paris: Albin Michel.
Lévi-Strauss, C. 1962. *Le Totémisme Aujourd'hui*. Paris: Presses Universitaires de France.
———. 1966. *The Savage Mind*. London: Weidenfeld and Nicholson.
Lewis-Jones, K.E. 2016. '"Useful to Us in Unknown Ways": Seed Conservation and the Quest for Novel Human-Plant Relationships for the 21st Century', *Journal of Ethnobiology* 36(1): 66–84.
Li, T.M. 2000. 'Locating Indigenous Environmental Knowledge in Indonesia', in R. Ellen, P. Parkes and A. Bicker (eds), *Indigenous Environmental Knowledge and Its Transformations: Critical Anthropological Perspectives* (Studies in Environmental Anthropology 5). Amsterdam: Harwood, pp. 121–50.
Lieberman, P. 1984. *The Biology and Evolution of Language*. Cambridge, MA: Harvard University Press.
Linares, O.F. 1976. '"Garden Hunting" in the American Tropics', *Human Ecology* 4(4): 331–49.

Lincoln, R.J., G.A. Boxshall and P.F. Clark. 1982. *A Dictionary of Ecology, Evolution and Systematics*. Cambridge: Cambridge University Press.
Linnaeus, C. 1758–59. *Systema Naturae*, 10th ed. Holmiae: Impensis Direct. Laurentii Salvi.
Lloyd, G.E.R. 1979. *Magic, Reason and Experience*. Cambridge: Cambridge University Press.
———. 1990. *Demystifying Mentalities*. Cambridge: Cambridge University Press.
———. 1991. *Methods and Problems in Greek Science*. Cambridge: Cambridge University Press.
Lyotard, J. 1979. *The Postmodern Condition: A Report on Knowledge*. Minneapolis: University of Minnesota Press.
Mabey, R. 2010. *Weeds: The Story of Outlaw Plants*. London: Profile.
MacAndrews, C. 1986. *Land Policy in Modern Indonesia*. Boston: Lincoln Institute of Land Policy.
MacCormack, C. 1980. 'Nature, Culture and Gender: A Critique', in C. MacCormack and M. Strathern (eds), *Nature, Culture and Gender*. Cambridge: Cambridge University Press, pp. 1–24.
MacCormack, C., and M. Strathern (eds). 1980. *Nature, Culture and Gender*. Cambridge: Cambridge University Press.
Magnani, N. 2016. 'Reconstructing Food Ways: Role of Skolt Sami Cultural Revitalization Programs in Local Plant Use', *Journal of Ethnobiology* 36(1): 85–104.
Maloney, B.K. 1993. 'Climate, Man, and Thirty Thousand Years of Vegetation Change in North Sumatra', *Indonesian Environmental History Newsletter* 2: 3–4.
Marchand, T.H.J. (ed.). 2010. 'Making Knowledge', special issue of *Journal of the Royal Anthropological Institute*.
Martin, G.J. 1995. *Ethnobotany: A Methods Manual*. London: Chapman and Hall.
Martin, M. 1974. 'Essai d'Ethnophytogeographie Khmere', *Journal D'Agriculture Tropicale et de Botanique Appliquée* 22(7–9): 219–38.
Masipiqueña, A., G.A. Persoon and D.J. Snelder. 2000. 'The Use of Fire in Northeastern Luzon (Philippines): Conflicting Views of Local People, Scientists and Government Officials', in R. Ellen, P. Parkes and A. Bicker (eds), *Indigenous Environmental Knowledge and Its Transformations: Critical Anthropological Perspectives* (Studies in Environmental Anthropology 5). Amsterdam: Harwood, pp. 177–212.
Mauss, M. 1973 [1934]. 'Techniques of the Body', trans. B. Brewster. *Economy and Society* 2: 70–88.
McKibben, W. 1989. *The End of Nature*. London: Anchor.
Meilleur, B.A. 1986. 'Alluetain Ethnoecology and Traditional Ecology: The Procurement and Production of Plant Resources in the Northern French Alps', Dissertation submitted in partial fulfillment of the requirements for the degree of Doctor of Philosophy. Seattle: University of Washington.
Miller, D. 1987. *Material Culture and Mass Consumption*. Oxford: Blackwell.
Miller, T.L. 2016. 'Living Lists: How the Indigenous Canela Come to Know Plants through Ethnobotanical Classification', *Journal of Ethnobiology* 36(1): 105–24.
Miller, T.L., N. Eoin, L. Daly and K. French (eds). 2016. 'Botanical Ontologies', special issue of *Journal of Ethnobiology* 36(1).

Milton, K. 1996. *Environmentalism and Anthropology: Exploring the Role of Anthropology in Environmental Discourse*. London: Routledge.

Mithen, S. 1996. *The Prehistory of the Mind: A Search for the Origins of Art, Religion and Science*. London: Thames and Hudson.

Moerman, D.E., R.W. Pemberton, D. Kiefer and B. Berlin. 1999. 'A Comparative Analysis of Five Medicinal Floras', *Journal of Ethnobiology* 19(1): 49–67.

Moniaga, S. 1991. 'Toward Community-Based Forestry and Recognition of Adat Property Rights in the Outer Islands of Indonesia', in J. Fox, O. Lynch, M. Zimsky and E. Moore (eds), *Voices from the Field: Fourth Annual Social Forestry Writing Workshop*. Honolulu: East-West Center, pp. 113–33.

Moran, E.F. 1990. 'Levels of Analysis and Analytical Level Shifting: Examples from Amazonian Ecosystem Research', in E.F. Moran (ed.), *The Ecosystem Approach in Anthropology: From Concept to Practice*, 2nd ed. Ann Arbor: University of Michigan Press, pp. 279–308.

Morgan, C. 1997. 'The State at the End of the Universe: Madness and the Millennium in Huli', in P.J. Stewart and A. Strathern (eds), *Millennial Markers*. Townsville: Centre for Pacific Studies, University of North Queensland, pp. 59–86.

Morris, B. 1997. 'In Defence of Realism and Truth: Critical Reflections on the Anthropological Followers of Heidegger', *Critique of Anthropology* 17(3): 313–40.

Muraille, B. 2000. 'Associating People and Industrial Forestry: Joint Forest Management in Lao PDR', in A. Lawrence (ed.), *Forestry, Forest Users and Research: New Ways of Learning*. Wageningen, The Netherlands: European Tropical Forest Research Network, pp. 71–84.

Nader, L. (ed.). 1996. *Naked Science: Anthropological Enquiry into Boundaries, Power and Knowledge*. New York: Routledge.

Napier, J.R. 1962. 'The Evolution of the Hand', *Scientific American* 12: 49–115.

———. 1993 [1980]. *Hands*. New York: Pantheon Books.

Neihardt, J.O. 1972 [1932]. *Black Elk Speaks: Being the Life Story of a Holy Man of Oglala Sioux*. London: Barrie and Jenkins.

Oatley, K.G. 1977. 'Inference, Navigation and Cognitive Maps', in P.N. Johnson-Laird and P.C. Wason (eds), *Thinking: Readings in Cognitive Science*. Cambridge: Cambridge University Press, pp. 537–47.

———. 1996. 'Inference in Narrative and Science', in D.R. Olson and N. Torrance (eds), *Modes of Thought: Explorations in Culture and Cognition*. Cambridge: Cambridge University Press, pp. 123–40.

Ohmagari, K., and F. Berkes. 1997. 'Transmission of Indigenous Knowledge and Bush Skills among the Western James Bay Cree Women of Subarctic Canada', *Human Ecology* 25(2): 197–222.

Ohnuki-Tierney, E. 1981. 'Phases in Human Perception/Cognition/Symbolization Processes: Cognitive Anthropology and Symbolic Classification', *American Ethnologist* 8(2): 451–67.

Olson, D.R. 1994. *The World on Paper: The Conceptual and Cognitive Implications of Writing and Reading*. Cambridge: Cambridge University Press.

———. 1996. 'Literacy, Consciousness of Language, and Modes of Thought', in D.R. Olson and N. Torrance (eds), *Modes of Thought: Explorations in Culture and Cognition*. Cambridge: Cambridge University Press, pp. 141–51.

Osseweijer, M. 2000. '"We Wander in Our Ancestors' Yard": Sea Cucumber Gathering in Aru, Eastern Indonesia', in R. Ellen, P. Parkes and A. Bicker (eds), *Indigenous Environmental Knowledge and Its Transformations: Critical Anthropological Perspectives* (Studies in Environmental Anthropology 5). Amsterdam: Harwood, pp. 55–78.

Oswalt, W.H. 1976. *An Anthropological Analysis of Food-Getting Technology*. New York: Wiley.

Overing, J. (ed.). 1985. *Reason and Morality* (ASA Monographs 24). London: Tavistock.

Padoch, C., and N. Peluso (eds). 1996. *Borneo in Transition: People, Forests, Conservation and Development*. Kuala Lumpur: Oxford University Press.

Padoch, C., and C. Peters. 1993. 'Managed Forest Gardens in West Kalimantan, Indonesia', in C. Potter, J. Cohen and D. Janczewski (eds), *Perspectives on Biodiversity: Case Studies of Genetic Resource Conservation and Development*. Washington, DC: AAAS, pp. 167–76.

Paijmans, K. 1970. 'An Analysis of Four Tropical Rainforest Sites in New Guinea', *Journal of Ecology* 58: 77–101.

Pálsson, G. 1994. 'Enskilment at Sea', *Man* 29(4): 901–27.

———. 2018. 'Nature, Concepts of', in H. Callan (ed.), *The International Encyclopedia of Anthropology*, vol. VIII. Hoboken, NJ: Wiley-Blasckwell, pp. 4250–60.

Pálsson, G., and P. Durrenberger. 1982. 'To Dream of Fish: The Causes of Icelandic Skippers' Fishing Success', *Journal of Anthropological Research* 38: 227–42.

Parfionovitch, D., and R. Meyer (eds). 1992. *Tibetan Medical Paintings: Illustrations to the Blue Beryl Treatise of Sangye Gyamtso (1653–1705)*. London: Serindia Publications.

Parker, E., D. Posey, J. Frechione and L. Francelano da Silva. 1983. 'Resource Exploitation in Amazonia: Ethnoecological Examples from Four Populations', *Annals of the Carnegie Museum of Natural History* 52(8): 163–203.

Parkes, P. 2000. 'Enclaved Knowledge: Indigent and Indignant Representations of Environmental Management and Development among the Kalasha of Pakistan', in R. Ellen, P. Parkes and A. Bicker (eds), *Indigenous Environmental Knowledge and Its Transformations: Critical Anthropological Perspectives* (Studies in Environmental Anthropology 5). Amsterdam: Harwood, pp. 253–92.

Pedersen, M.A. 2007. 'Talismans of Thought: Shamanist Ontologies and Extended Cognition in Northern Mongolia', in A. Henare, M. Holbraad and S. Wastell (eds), *Thinking through Things: Theorising Artefacts Ethnographically*. Abingdon: Routledge, pp. 141–66.

Peeters, A. 1979. 'Nomenclature and Classification in Rumphius's Herbarium Amboinense', in R.F. Ellen and D. Reason (eds), *Classifications in Their Social Context*. London: Academic Press, pp. 145–66.

Peluso, N.L. 1992. *Rich Forests, Poor People: Resource Control and Resistance in Java*. Berkeley: University of California Press.

———. 1996. 'Fruit Trees and Family Trees in an Anthropogenic Forest: Ethics of Access, Property Zones, and Environmental Change in Indonesia', *Comparative Studies in Society and History* 38: 510–48.

Peluso, N., and C. Padoch. 1996. 'Changing Resource Rights in Managed Forests of West Kalimantan', in C. Padoch and N. Peluso (eds), *Borneo in Transition: People, Forests, Conservation and Development*. Kuala Lumpur: Oxford University Press, pp. 121–36.

Persoon, G.A. 1994. *Vluchten of Veranderen: Processen van Verandering en Ontwikkeling bij Tribale Groepen in Indonesie*. Leiden: Rijksuniversiteit te Leiden, Faculteit der Sociale Wetenschappen.

Persoon, G., T. Minter, B. Slee and C. van der Hammer. 2004. *The Position of Indigenous Peoples in the Management of Tropical Forests* (Tropenbos Series 23). Wageningen, The Netherlands: Tropenbos International.

Pfaffenberger, B. 1992. 'Social Anthropology of Technology', *Annual Review of Anthropology* 21: 491–516.

Pina-Cabral, J. de. 2014. 'World: An Anthropological Examination (Part 1)', *Hau: Journal of Ethnographic Theory* 4(1): 49–73.

Pires, J.M., and G.T. Prance. 1985. 'The Vegetation Types of the Brazilian Amazon', in G.T. Prance and T.E. Lovejoy (eds), *Key Environments: Amazonia*. Oxford: Pergamon Press – IUCN, pp. 109–45.

Platten, S. 2013. 'On the Transmission of Gardening Knowledge: Innovation and Consensus in the Planting of Allotment Vegetables', in R. Ellen, S.J. Lycett and S.E. Johns (eds), *Understanding Cultural Transmission in Anthropology: A Critical Synthesis*. Oxford: Berghahn Books, pp. 300–19.

Posey, D.A. 1988. 'Kayapo Indian Natural-Resource Management', in J.S. Denslow and C. Padoch (eds), *People of the Tropical Rainforest*. Berkeley: University of California Press, pp. 89–90.

———. 1996. *Protocols and Mechanisms of the Convention of Biological Diversity for Access to Traditional Technologies and Benefit Sharing for Indigenous and Local Communities Embodying Traditional Lifestyles* (Research Paper 6). Oxford: Oxford Centre for Environment, Ethics and Society.

———. 2000. 'Ethnobiology and Ethnoecology in the Context of National Laws and International Agreements Affecting Indigenous and Local Knowledge, Traditional Resources and Intellectual Property Rights', in R. Ellen, P. Parkes and A. Bicker (eds), *Indigenous Environmental Knowledge and Its Transformations: Critical Anthropological Perspectives* (Studies in Environmental Anthropology 5). Amsterdam: Harwood, pp. 35–54.

Poulsen, A.D., I.C. Nielsen, S. Tan and H. Balslev. 1996. 'A Quantitative Inventory of Trees in One Hectare of Mixed Dipterocarp Forest in Temburong, Brunei Darussalam', in D.S. Edwards, W.E. Boloth and S.C. Choy (eds), *Tropical Rainforest Research – Current Issues*. Dordrecht: Kluwer, pp. 139–50.

Powell, J.B. 2016. 'White Maize to Pigarro: An Actor-Network Analysis of an Improved Crop Variety in Northwest Portugal', *Journal of Ethnobiology* 36(1): 45–65.

Praet, I. 2014. *Animism and the Question of Life*. London: Routledge.

Prance, G.T., W. Balée, B.M. Boom and R.L. Carneiro. 1987. 'Quantitative Ethnobotany and the Case for Conservation in Amazonia', *Conservation Biology* 1: 296–310.
Proctor, J., J. M. Anderson, P. Chai and H.W. Vallack. 1983. 'Ecological Studies in Four Contrasting Rainforests in Gunung Mulu National Park, Sarawak. 1. Forest Environment, Structure and Floristics', *Journal of Ecology* 71: 237–60.
Pujol, R. 1975. 'Définition d'un Ethnoécosystème avec Deux Exemples: Etude Ethnozoobotanique des Cardères *(Dipsacus)* et Interrelations Homme-animaltruffe', in R. Pujol (ed.), *L'homme et L'animal: Premier Colloque d'Ethnozoologie.* Paris: Institut International d'Ethnosciences, pp. 91–114.
Puri, R.K. 1997. 'Hunting Knowledge of the Penan Benalui of East Kalimantan Indonesia', Unpublished Ph.D. dissertation. Honolulu: University of Hawai'i.
———. 2005. 'Post-abandonment Ecology of Penan Fruit Camps: Anthropological and Ethnobiological Approaches to the History of a Rain-forested Valley in East Kalimantan', in M.R. Dove, P.E. Sajise and A. Doolittle (eds), *Conserving Nature in Culture: Case Studies from Southeast Asia* (Yale Southeast Asia Studies Monograph Series). New Haven, CT: Yale University Council on Southeast Asia Studies, pp. 25–82.
Rambo, A.T. 1979. 'Primitive Man's Impact on Genetic Resources of the Malaysian Tropical Rainforest', *Malaysian Applied Biology* 8(1): 59–65.
Rapoport, A. 1969. 'The "Pueblo" and the "Hogan"', in P. Oliver (ed.), *Shelter and Society*. London: The Crescent Press, pp. 66–79.
Rappaport, R.A. 1971a. 'The Flow of Energy in an Agricultural Society', *Scientific American* 224: 116–33.
———. 1971b. 'The Sacred in Human Evolution', *Animal Review of Ecology and Systematics* 2: 23–44.
———. 1984 [1968]. *Pigs for the Ancestors: Ritual in the Ecology of a New Guinea People*. New Haven, CT: Yale University Press.
Rayner, S., and C. Heyward. 2014. 'The Inevitability of Nature as a Rhetorical Resource', in K. Hastrup (ed.), *Anthropology and Nature*. New York: Routledge, pp. 125–46.
Reader's Digest. 1978. *The Gardening Year*. Pleasantville, NY: Reader's Digest Association.
Reed, E.S. 1988. 'The Affordances of the Animate Environment: Social Science from the Ecological Point of View', in T. Ingold (ed.), *What Is an Animal?* London: Unwin Hyman, pp. 110–26.
Rhoades, R., and A. Bebbington. 1995. 'Farmers Who Experiment: An Untapped Resource for Agricultural Research and Development', in D.M. Warren, L.J. Slikkerveer and D. Brokensha (eds), *The Cultural Dimension of Development: Indigenous Knowledge Systems*. London: Intermediate Technology Publications, pp. 296–307.
Richards, P. 1985. *Indigenous Agricultural Revolution: Ecology and Food-Crop Farming in West Africa*. London: Hutchinson.
———. 1986. *Coping with Hunger: Hazard and Experiment in an African Rice-Farming System*. London: Allen and Unwin.

———. 1993. 'Cultivation: Knowledge or Performance?', in M. Hobart (ed.), *An Anthropological Critique of Development*. London: Routledge, pp. 61–78.
Richards, P.W. 1996 [1952]. *The Tropical Rain Forest*. Cambridge: Cambridge University Press.
Rival, L.M. (ed.). 1998. *The Social Life of Trees: Anthropological Perspectives on Tree Symbolism*. Oxford: Berg.
Rival, L. 2012. 'Animism and the Meaning of Life: Towards an Understanding of Manioc Domestication ', in O. Ulturgasheva, M. Brightman and V.E. Grotti (eds), *Animism in Rainforest and Tundra: Personhood, Animals, Plants and Things in Contemporary Amazonia and Siberia*. Oxford: Berghahn Books, pp. 69–81.
———. 2013. 'The Materiality of Life: Revisiting the Anthropology of Nature in Amazonia', in G. Harvey (ed.), *The Handbook of Contemporary Animism*. Durham, NC: Acumen, pp. 92–100.
Rival, L., and D. McKey. 2008. 'Domestication and Diversity in Manioc (Manihot esculenta Crantz ssp. Esculenta, Euphorbiaceae)', *Current Anthropology* 49: 1119–28.
Robertson, R. 1996. 'Glocalization: Time-Space and Homogeneity-Heterogeneity', in M. Featherstone, S. Lash and R. Robertson (eds), *Global Modernities*. London: Sage, pp. 25–44.
Rodman, M.C. 1998. 'Creating Historic Sites in Vanuatu', *Social Analysis* 42(3): 117–34 (special issue on 'Identity, Nature and Culture: Sociality and Environment in Melanesia', ed. S. Bamford).
Roepstorff, A., N. Bubant and K. Kull (eds). 2003. *Imagining Nature: Practices of Cosmology and Identity*. Aarhus: Aarhus University Press.
Roszak, T. 1972. *Where the Wasteland Ends: Politics Post Industrial Society*. London: Faber.
———. 1978. *Person Planet: The Creative Disintegration of Industrial Society*. Garden City, NY: Anchor, Doubleday.
Rumphius, G.E. 1999 [1705]. *The Ambonese Curiosity Cabinet*, trans. E.M. Beekman. New Haven, CT: Yale University Press.
———. 2011 [1743]. *The Ambonese Herbal*, vol. 3, trans. E.M. Beekman. New Haven, CT/London: Yale University Press/National Tropical Botanical Garden.
Sahlins, M. 1968. 'La Première Société d'Abondance', *Les Temps Modernes* 268: 641–80. Reissued and extended in English translation in 1972 as 'The Original Affluent Society', Chapter 1 of *Stone Age Economics*. Chicago: Aldine-Atherton, pp. 1–40.
———. 2013. 'Foreword', in P. Descola, *Beyond Nature and Culture*. Chicago: University of Chicago Press, pp. xi–xiv.
Salick, J. 1989. 'Ecological Basis of Amuesha Agriculture, Peruvian Upper Amazon', in D.A. Posey and W. Balée (eds), 'Resource Management in Amazonia: Indigenous and Folk Strategies', special issue of *Advances in Economic Botany* 7: 189–212.
Schmid, J., and C. Kocher-Schmid. *1992. Sohne des Krokodils: Mannerhausrituale und Initiation in Yensan, Zentral-Iatmul, East Sepik Province, Papua New Guinea* (Basler Beitrage 36). Basel: Ethnologischen Seminar der Universität und Museum für Volkerkunde.

Schmink, M., K.H. Redford and C. Padoch. 1992. 'Traditional Peoples and the Biosphere: Framing the Issues and Defining the Terms', in K.H. Redford and C. Padoch (eds), *Conservation of Neotropical Forests: Working from Traditional Resource Use*. New York: Columbia University Press, pp. 3–13.

Schreer, V. 2016. 'Learning Knowledge about Rattan (CALAMOIDAE ARECACEAE) and Its Uses amongst Ngaju Dayak in Indonesian Borneo', *Journal of Ethnobiology* 36(1): 125–46.

Scoones, I., and J. Thompson (eds). 1994. *Beyond Farmer First*. London: Intermediate Technology Publications.

Scott, M.W. 2013. 'The Anthropology of Ontology (Religious Science?)', *Journal of the Royal Anthropological Institute* 19: 859–72.

Scott, J.C. 1998 *Seeing Like a State: How Certain Schemes to Improve the Human Condition Have Failed*. New Haven, CT: Yale University Press.

Scribner, S., and M. Cole. 1981. *The Psychology of Literacy*. Cambridge, MA: Harvard University Press.

Secord, J. 1981. 'Nature's Fancy: Charles Darwin and the Breeding of Pigeons', *Isis* 72: 163–86.

———. 1985. 'Darwin and the Breeders: A Social History', in D. Kohn (ed.), *The Darwinian Heritage*. Princeton, NJ: Princeton University Press, pp. 519–42.

Shepard, G.H., D.W. Yu, M. Lizarralde and M. Italiano. 2001. 'Rainforest Habitat Classification among the Matsigenka of the Peruvian Amazon', *Journal of Ethnobiology* 21(1): 1–38.

Shepard, G.H., D.W. Yu and B.W. Nelson. 2004. 'Ethnobotanical Ground-Truthing and Forest Diversity in the Western Amazon', in L. Maffi, T. Carlson and E. Lopez-Zent (eds), *Ethnobotany and Conservation of Biocultural Diversity* (Advances in Economic Botany vol. 15). New York: New York Botanical Gardens, pp. 133–71.

Shiva, V., and R. Holla-Bhar. 1993. 'Intellectual Piracy and the Neem Tree', *The Ecologist* 23(6): 223–27.

Shore, B. 1996. *Culture in Mind: Cognition, Culture and the Problem of Meaning*. Oxford: Oxford University Press.

Sidiyasa, K., and I.G.M. Tantra. 1984. 'Tree Flora Analysis of the Way Mual Lowland Forest, Manusela National Park, Seram-Maluku', *Bulletin Penelitian Hutan* 462: 19–34.

Sigaut, F. 1993. 'How Can We Analyse and Describe Technical Actions?', in A. Berthelet and J. Chavaillon (eds), *The Use of Tools by Human and Non-Human Primates*. Oxford: Clarendon Press, pp. 381–97.

Sillitoe, P. 1979. *Give and Take: Exchange in Wola Society*. New York: St. Martins.

———. 1996. *A Place against Time: Land and Environment in the Papua New Guinea Highlands* (Studies in Environmental Anthropology 1). Amsterdam: Harwood.

———. 1998. 'An Ethnobotanical Account of the Vegetation Communities of the Wola Region, Southern Highlands Province, Papua New Guinea', *Journal of Ethnobiology* 18(1): 103–28.

———. 2002a. 'Participant Observation to Participatory Development: Making Anthropology Work', in P. Sillitoe, A. Bicker and J. Pottier (eds), *Participating in Development: Approaches to Indigenous Knowledge* (ASA Monograph Series 39). London: Routledge, pp. 1–23.

———. 2002b. 'Globalizing Indigenous Knowledge', in P. Sillitoe, A. Bicker and J. Pottier (eds), *Participating in Development: Approaches to Indigenous Knowledge* (ASA Monograph Series 39). London: Routledge, pp. 108–38.

———. 2002c. 'Contested Knowledge, Contingent Classification: Animals in the Highlands of Papua New Guinea', *American Anthropologist* 104(4): 1162–71.

———. 2010. *From Land to Mouth: The Agricultural 'Economy' of the Wola of the New Guinea Highlands.* New Haven, CT: Yale University Press.

Singer, C. 1959. *A History of Biology to About the Year 1900: A General Introduction to the Study of Living Things.* London: Abelard-Schuman.

Sivaramakrishnan, K. 2000. 'State Sciences and Development Histories: Encoding Local Forestry Knowledge in Bengal', *Development and Change* 31(1): 61–90.

SKEPHI. 1992. 'Logging and the Sinking Island', *Inside Indonesia* 33: 23–25.

SKEPHI and R. Kiddell-Monroe. 1993. 'Indonesia: Land Rights and Development', in M. Colchester and L. Lohmann (eds), *The Struggle for Land and the Fate of the Forests.* Penang, Malaysia: World Rainforest Movement, pp. 228–63.

Smith, J. 2011. *Divine Machines: Leibnitz and the Sciences of Life.* Princeton, NJ: Princeton University Press.

SOED. 1973. *The Shorter Oxford English Dictionary.* Oxford: Clarendon Press.

Soedjito, H., A. Suyanto and E. Sulaeman. 1986. *Sumber Daya Alam di Pulau Seram Barat, Propinsi Maluku.* Jakarta: Lembaga Biologi Nasional.

Soemarwoto, R. 2007. 'Kasepuhan Rice Landrace Diversity, Risk Management and Agricultural Modernization', in R. Ellen (ed.), *Modern Crises and Traditional Strategies: Local Ecological Knowledge in Island Southeast Asia.* Oxford: Berghahn Books, pp. 84–111.

Spencer, J.E. 1966. *Shifting Cultivation in Southeastern Asia.* Berkeley: University of California Press.

Sperber, D. 1994. 'The Modularity of Thought and the Epidemiology of Representations', in L. Hirschfeld and S. Gelman (eds), *Mapping the Mind: Domain Specificity in Cognition and Culture.* New York: Cambridge University Press, pp. 39–67.

Spradley, J.P. 1970. *You Owe Yourself a Drunk.* Boston: Little, Brown.

Sprugel, D.G. 1991. 'Disturbance, Equilibrium and Evironmental Variability: What is "Natural" Vegetation in a Changing Environment?', *Biological Conservation* 58: 1–18.

Staal, F. 1993. *Concepts of Science in Europe and Asia.* Leiden: International Institute for Asian Studies.

Stark, K., and K. Latinis. 1992. 'Research Report: The Archaeology of Sago Economies in Central Maluku', *Cakalele: Maluku Research Journal* 3: 69–86.

Strathern, A., and P.J. Stewart. 1997. 'Introduction: Millennial Markers in the Pacific', in P.J. Stewart and A. Strathern (eds), *Millennial Markers.* Townsville: Centre for Pacific Studies, University of North Queensland, pp. 1–17.

Strathern, M. 1980. 'No Nature, No Culture; The Hagen Case', in C. MacCormack and M. Strathern (eds), *Nature, Culture and Gender.* Cambridge: Cambridge University Press, pp. 174–222.

———. 1992a. *After Nature: English Kinship in the Late Twentieth Century.* Cambridge: Cambridge University Press.
———. 1992b. 'Parts and Wholes: Refiguring Relationships in a Post-plural World', in A. Kuper (ed.), *Conceptualizing Society.* London: Routledge, pp. 75–104.
———. (ed.). 1995. *Shifting Contexts.* London: Routledge.
Street, B. 1975. *The Savage in Literature: Representations of 'Primitive' Society in English Fiction, 1858–1920.* London: Routledge.
Stross, B. 1973. 'Acquisition of Botanical Terminology by Tzeltal Children', in M.S. Edmonson (ed.), *Meaning in Mayan Languages.* The Hague, Mouton, pp. 107–41.
Sturtevant, W.C. 1969. *Guide to Field Collecting of Ethnographic Specimens.* Washington, DC: Smithsonian Institution.
Suharno, D.M. 1997. 'Representation de l'Environment Vegetal et Pratiques Agricoles chez les Alune de Lumoli, Seram de l'Ouest (Moluques Centrales, Indonesie de l'Est)', These de Doctorat de l'Université Paris VI.
Sundar, N. 2000. 'The Construction and Destruction of "Indigenous" Knowledge in India's Joint Forest Management Programme', in R. Ellen, P. Parkes and A. Bicker (eds), *Indigenous Environmental Knowledge and Its Transformations: Critical Anthropological Perspectives* (Studies in Environmental Anthropology 5). Amsterdam: Harwood, pp. 79–100.
Swift, J. 1977. 'Sahelian Pastoralists: Underdevelopment, Desertification and Famine', *Annual Review of Anthropology* 6: 457–78.
Sylvan, R. 1985. 'A Critique of Deep Ecology', *Radical Philosophy* 40: 2–12.
Tallis, R. 2003. *The Hand: A Philosophical Enquiry into Human Being.* Edinburgh: Edinburgh University Press.
Taylor, P.M. 1990. *The Folk Biology of the Tobelo People: A Study in Folk Classification.* Washington, DC: Smithsonian Institution.
Thomas, G. (ed.). 1979. *Edward Thomas: Collected Poems.* London: Faber and Faber.
Thomas, K. *1983. Man and the Natural World: Changing Attitudes in England, 1500–1800.* London: Allen Lane.
Torquebiau, E.F. 1987. 'Forest Mosaic Pattern Analysis', in H.P. Nooteboom (ed.), *Report of the 1982–1983 Bukit Raya Expedition.* Leiden: The Rijksherbarium, pp. 25–42.
Torre-Cuadros, M., and N. Ross. 2003. 'Secondary Biodiversity: Local Perceptions of Forest Habitats, the Case of Soferino, Quintana Roo, Mexico', *Journal of Ethnobiology* 23(2): 287–308.
Traube, E.G. *1986. Cosmology and Social Life: Ritual Exchange among the Mambai of East Timor.* Chicago: University of Chicago Press.
Truswell, A.S., and J.D.L. Hansen. 1976. 'Medical Research among the !Kung', in R.B. Lee and I. DeVore (eds), *Kalahari Hunter-Gatherers: Studies of the !Kung San and Their Neighbours.* Cambridge, MA: Harvard University Press, pp. 166–94.
Tsing, A. 2005. *Friction: An Ethnography of Global Connection.* Princeton, NJ: Princeton University Press.
———. 2011. 'More-than Human Sociality: A Call for Critical Description', in K. Hastrup (ed.), *Anthropology and Nature.* New York: Routledge, pp. 27–42.
Turnbull, C. 1961. *The Forest People.* London: Cape.

Turnbull, D. 2000. *Masons, Tricksters and Cartographers: Comparative Studies in the Sociology of Scientific and Indigenous Knowledge*. Amsterdam: Harwood Academic.

Ulijaszek, S. 2007. 'Bioculturalism', in D. Parkin and S. Ulijaszek (eds), *Holistic Anthropology: Emergence and Convergence*. New York: Berghahn Books, pp. 21–51.

Valencia, R., H. Balslev and G. Paz Y Miño. 1994. 'High Tree Alpha-Diversity in Amazonian Ecuador', *Biodiversity and Conservation* 3: 21–28.

Valentijn, F. 2002–2003 [1726]. *Oud en Nieuw Oost-Indiën*, facsimile ed. Franeker: Van Wijnen.

Valeri, V. 1989. 'Reciprocal Centers: The Siwa-Lima System in the Central Moluccas', in D. Maybury-Lewis and U. Almagor *(eds)*, *The Attraction of Opposites*. Ann Arbor: University of Michigan Press, pp. 117–41.

———. 1990. 'Both Nature and Culture: Reflections on Menstrual and Parturitional Taboos in Huaulu (Seram)', in J.M. Atkinson and S. Errington (eds), *Power and Difference: Gender in Island Southeast Asia*. Stanford, CA: Stanford University Press, pp. 235–72.

Vandergeest, P., and N.L. Peluso. 1995. 'Territorialization and State Power in Thailand', *Theory and Society* 24: 385–426.

Vayda, A.P., and R.A. Rappaport. 1968. 'Ecology, Cultural and Non-cultural', in J.A. Clifton (ed.), *Introduction to Cultural Anthropology: Essays in the Scope and Methods of the Science of Man*. Boston: Houghton-Mifflin, pp. 476–97.

Vigh, H.E., and D.B. Sausdal. 2014. 'From Essence Back to Existence: Anthropology beyond the Ontological Turn', *Anthropological Theory* 14: 49–73.

Vilaça, A. 2002. 'Making Kin Out of Others in Amazonia', *Journal of the Royal Anthropological Institute* 8(2): 347–65.

Vitebsky, P. 1995. 'From Cosmology to Environmentalism: Shamanism as Local Knowledge in a Global Setting', in R. Fardon (ed.), *Counterworks: Managing the Diversity of Knowledge*. London: Routledge, pp. 182–203.

Viveiros de Castro, E. 2004a. 'Perspectival Anthropology and the Method of Controlled Equivocation', *Tipití: Journal of the Society for the Anthropology of Lowland South America* 2(1): 3–22.

———. 2004b. 'Exchanging Perspectives: The Transformation of Objects into Subjects', *Common Knowledge* 10: 463–84.

Vygotsky, L.S. 1978 [1930]. 'Tool and Symbol in Child Development', in M. Cole, V. John-Steiner, S. Scribner and E. Souberman (eds), *Mind in Society: The Development of Higher Mental Processes*. Cambridge, MA: Harvard University Press, pp. 19–30.

Wagner, R. 1998. 'Environment and the Reproduction of Human Focality', *Social Analysis* 42(3): 55–66 (special issue on 'Identity, Nature and Culture: Sociality and Environment in Melanesia', ed. S. Bamford).

Waldstein, A., and C. Adams. 2006. 'The Interface between Medical Anthropology and Medical Ethnobiology', in R. Ellen (ed.), 'Ethnobiology and the Science of Humankind', special Issue of *Journal of the Royal Anthropological Institute* 12: 95–117.

Walker, D.H., P.J. Thorne, F.L. Sinclair, B. Thapa, C.D. Wolod and D.B. Subba. 1999. 'A Systems Approach to Comparing Indigenous and Scientific Knowledge:

Consistency and Discriminatory Power of Indigenous and Laboratory Assessment of the Nutritive Value of Tree Fodder', *Agricultural Systems* 62: 87–103.
Warren, D.M., L.J. Slikkerveer and D. Brokensha (eds). 1995. *The Cultural Dimension of Development: Indigenous Knowledge Systems*. London: Intermediate Technology Publications.
Watt, G. 1889–96. *Dictionary of the Economic Products of India, 6 vols*. Calcutta: Superintendent of Government Printing.
Wear, A. 1995. 'Epistemology and Learned Medicine in Early Modern England', in D. Bates (ed.), *Knowledge and the Scholarly Medical Traditions*. Cambridge: Cambridge University Press, pp. 151–73.
Weckerle, C., V. Timbul and P. Blumenshine. 2010. 'Medicinal, Stimulant and Ritual Plant Use: An Ethnobotany of Caffeine-Containing Plants', in E. Hsu and S. Harris (eds), *Plants, Health and Healing: On the Interface of Ethnobotany and Medical Anthropology*. Oxford: Berghahn Books, pp. 262–301.
Weiner, J. 1998. 'Revealing the Grounds of Life in Papua New Guinea', *Social Analysis* 42(3): 135–42 (special issue on 'Identity, Nature and Culture: Sociality and Environment in Melanesia', ed. S. Bamford).
Weiner, J.S., and J.A. Lourie. 1969. *Human Biology: A Guide to Field Methods* (International Biological Programme Handbook 9). Oxford: Blackwell.
Wellman, H.M. 1990. *The Child's Theory of Mind*. Cambridge, MA: MIT Press.
White, L., Jr. 1969. 'The Historical Roots of Our Ecological Crisis', in P. Shephard and D. McKinley (eds), *The Subversive Science*. Boston: Houghton Mifflin, pp. 341–51. First published [1967] in *Science* 155: 1203–7.
Whitmore, T.C. 1984. *Tropical Rain Forests of the Far East*. Oxford: Clarendon Press.
Whitmore, T.C., K. Sidiyasa and T.J. Whitmore. 1987. 'Tree Species Enumeration of 0.5 Hectare on Halmahera', *Garden Bulletin Singapore* 40: 31–34.
Whitmore, T.C., I.G.M. Tantra and U. Sutisna (eds). 1989. *Tree Flora of Indonesia: Check List for Maluku*. Bogor: Ministry of Forestry, Agency for Forestry Research and Development (Forest Research and Development Centre).
Wiersum, K.F. 2000. 'Incorporating Indigenous Knowledge in Formal Forest Management: Adaptation or Paradigm Change in Tropical Forestry', in A. Lawrence (ed.), *Forestry, Forest Users and Research: New Ways of Learning*. Wageningen, The Netherlands: European Tropical Forest Research Network, pp. 19–32.
Wilkin, P.J. 2014. 'Transmission and Commoditisation of Medicinal Plant Knowledge in the Marketplaces of Oruro, Bolivia', Ph.D. dissertation. University of Kent.
Wilson, B.R. (ed.). 1970. *Rationality*. New York: Harper and Row.
de Wit, H.C.D. (ed.). 1959. *Rumphius Memorial Volume*. Baarn: Hollandia N.V.
Wolff, X.Y., and M. Florey. 1998. 'Foraging, Agricultural and Culinary Practices among the Alune of West Seram, with Implications for the Changing Significance of Cultivated Plants as Foodstuffs', in S. Pannell and F. von Benda-Beckman (eds), *Old World Places, New World Problems: Exploring Issues of Resource Management in Eastern Indonesia*. Canberra: Australian National University, pp. 267–320.

Wolpert, L. 1992. *The Unnatural Nature of Science*. London: Faber and Faber.
Woolgar, S., and J. Lezaun. 2013. 'The Wrong Bin Bag: A Turn to Ontology in Science and Technology Studies?', *Social Studies of Science* 43: 321–40.
Yearly, S. 1996. *Sociology, Environmentalism, Globalization: Reinventing the Globe*. London: Sage.
Zarger, R.K. 2002. 'Acquisition and Transmission of Subsistence Knowledge by Q'eqchi Maya in Belize', in J.R. Stepp, F.S. Wyndham and R.K. Zarger (eds.), *Ethnobiology and Biocultural Diversity: Proceedings of the Seventh International Congress of Ethnobiology*. Athens, GA: International Society of Ethnobiology, pp. 593–603.
Zeitlyn, D., and R. Just. 2014. *Excursions in Realist Anthropology: A Merological Approach*. Newcastle-upon-Tyne: Cambridge Scholars Publishing.
Zerner, C. 1990. *Community Rights, Customary Law and the Law of Timber Concessions in Indonesia's Forests: Legal Options and Alternatives in Designing the Commons*. Jakarta: FAO Forestry Studies TFIINS/065.
———. 1994. 'Through a Green Lens: The Construction of Customary Environmental Law and Community in Indonesia's Maluku Islands', *Law and Society Review* 28(5): 1079–122.
Zimmerman, F. 1989. *Le Discours des Remèdes au Pays des Épices*. Paris: Payot.
———. 1995. 'The Scholar, the Wise Man, and Universals: Three Aspects of Ayurvedic Medicine', in D. Bates (ed.), *Knowledge and the Scholarly Medical Traditions*. Cambridge: Cambridge University Press, pp. 297–319.

Index

abandoned villages, 153, 155–56, 169–70, 174, 176
Actor Network Theory (ANT), 225, 242
adaptation
　concept, 4, 30, 34–35, 194
　cultural, 116, 185
adat, 56
'administrative ordering of nature', 136
affordances, 200
age differentiation, 106
agency, 25, 93, 199–201, 204, 208, 216, 218–19, 221–22
Agrawal, A., 22, 90–91, 100
agricultural intensification, 70
agroforestry, 93, 168, 187
Akimichi, T., 120
Alaska, 30
alchemy, 231
Alcorn, J., 92–93, 138
algae, 200, 209, 217
Allan, C.L., 139, 163, 178–79, 181
allotments, 184
alterity, 16–17
　radical, 7
Alune, 179–81
Amazonia, 7, 11–12, 14–15, 24, 44, 59, 136, 151, 157, 161, 181, 215, 240, 242
Ambon, Amboina and Ambonese, 54, 58, 84–85, 205, 212, 230–31
Ambonese Herbal. See *Herbarium Amboinense*
Ambonese Malay, 142, 172
Amuesha, 138
analogy and analogism, 12, 126, 130, 201, 242

Anderson, E.N., 31, 35, 103, 114
Anderson, J.N., 29
Anderson, A.B., 151
Andes, 99
animacy, 202, 208–10, 216, 218–21
animality, 218
animation, 200–202
animism, 7, 12–15, 25, 66, 122, 182, 201, 216, 219–21, 223n3, 242
Ankave-Anga, 102n8
Antaran, B., 138
anthropocene, 20, 26
anthropologies of the environment, 2
anthropomorphism, 41, 49, 205, 207–8, 215, 219–20
anti-science, 103
anti-taxonomy, 11
Apollonian cultures, 32
Arabs, 83–84, 128
arbitrariness in design, 196
arboriculture, 151
archaeology, 54, 64
Aristotle, 119, 223n2
artefacts, 212, 214. See also tools
Aru Islands, 97
astrology, 110, 231
Astuti, R., 9, 215
Atran, S., 9, 12, 20, 46, 80, 82, 107, 115, 118, 122, 134n3, 200, 212–14, 216, 229–30
Attenborough, D., 71
audio-visual aids, 196
Audley-Charles, M.G., 148
Aumeeruddy(-Thomas), Y., 59, 151, 238
Aunger, R., 116
autoecology, folk, 238

Avery, T.E., 158
Ayurvedic medicine, 77, 84, 94, 106
Austronesian, 64, 66, 207
axiom of amity, 216

Bacon, F., 34
Baduy, 186
Baining, 41, 47
Bakels, J., 59, 151
Balée, W., 4, 59, 64, 151, 161, 172
Bali, 182n1
Bamford, S., 40–42, 47, 49, 51
Barbarian culture, 29
barkcloth, 234–36
Barnes, B., 133
Barnes, J., 44
Barnes, R.H., 78
Bartlett, H.H., 161
Basic Agrarian Law, Indonesia, 56
Basic Forestry Law, Indonesia, 56
Bates, D., 95, 106
Baviskar, A., 97
Bebbington, A., 99
Beekman, E.M., 84, 230–31
Bellwood, P., 64
Benedict, R., 32
Bennett, J., 225
Berkes, F., 102n2, 183
Berlin, B., 12, 46, 80, 115, 121, 162, 208, 210, 212, 220, 227, 229, 233
Berlin, E.A., 233
Bernstein, J.H., 44, 138
Bessire, L., 26
Bicker, A., 96
Bidayuh, 17–18
Biersack, A., 44
binary distinctions. *See* dualism
bio-cognition, 220
biocultural concept, 196
biodiversity, 9, 211, 228, 235, 237
  loss, 2
  secondary, 135, 159
biology, 104
  intuitive, 131
biomechanics, 189, 192–93
bio-prospecting, 91

biotaxonomic model, universal, 229
biotic form concept, 209
Black Elk, 28–29, 34, 38
Black, M.B., 11, 211
Blaser, M., 10, 20, 22, 27n
Bloch, M., 61, 128, 179, 207, 220
Bloor, B., 133
Blume, C.J. von, 85
Blumler, M.A., 150
Blust, R., 64
body, 214–16
  engagement, 204
  movement, 194
  practical skills of, 196
Bogor, 142, 212
Bohr, N., 119
Bolivia, 242
Bolton, R., 67–68, 74, 207
Bond, D., 26
Bondt, J., 83
Bonnemere, P., 48
books, 81, 106, 196
  gardening, 197
Boom, B.M., 137
Boomgard, P., 136–37
Borneo, 17, 143, 148
Boster, J., 82, 107, 115
botanic gardens, 84
botany, history of, 230
Botswana, 36
Bourdieu, P., 119–20, 195
Boyer, P., 61, 212
Boyle, R., 113
brain, embodied, 216
Brazil, 97, 138, 151, 161, 240
breath
  as motion, 219
  vocalisation as evidence for, 219
Breedlove, D.E., 46, 162
Brennan, E., 234–35
British Homegardens Project, 24, 196
Brockway, L., 240
Brokensha, D., 88, 90, 92, 99, 102n2
Brookfield, H.C., 151
Brosius, J.P., 98, 156, 175
Brown, C.H., 212–13, 223n2

Brunei, 138, 148, 157
Bruner, J., 113, 119, 123
Brutti, L., 52n2
Bubant, N., 9
Buchanan-Hamilton, F., 85
Budiansky, S., 87
Buddhism, 31, 34
Bulmer, A., 47
Bulmer, R.N.H., 47, 178
Burkhart, H.E., 158
Burkill, I.H., 85
Burman, J., 85
Buryiatia, 239
Butonese, 54, 57–58

Cadena, M. de la, 20, 27n
caffeine, 237–38
Callenbach, E., 29
Campbell, J.R., 158
Capra, F., 28
Carey, S., 9, 115, 118, 127, 129–30, 134n3, 214
Carneiro, R., 161
Carrithers, M., 6, 48, 216, 218, 225
Carroll, L., 1
cartography, 137, 158, 174. *See also* map-making
cash-cropping, 55–57, 65–66
cassava, 62, 65, 186, 220, 240
  DNA analysis of landraces, 240–41
Castaneda, C., 29
causality, differential concepts of, 118
Cavalli-Sforza, L.L., 183
Cepek, M.L., 22
Chácobo, 138
'chaîne operatoire', 196
Chamberlain, R.V., 243n1
Chambers, R., 79, 86, 102n2, 124
Chaplin, M., 119
chimpanzees, 185
China, 54, 238
Chinese, 54, 97, 241
  medicine, 94–95, 106, 233, 240
Chua, L., 17–18, 20, 26
classifications
  ad hoc, 163, 165, 178

  biological and non-biological compared, 211–14
  cross-cutting, 166, 179
  ethnobiological, 208, 210, 214, 217
  ethnoecological, 136, 156, 161, 172, 178, 181–82
  European folk, 82
  flexibility in, 163, 165, 177, 182
  folk, 115, 229
  folk classification of natural kinds, 162
  general-purpose versus special-purpose, 115–220, 241
  local (*see* folk classifications)
  non-taxonomic features of, 159
  official, 230
  social authority influences shared, 182n1
  of vegetation types, 162 (*see also* Nuaulu *and* secondary biodiversity)
  See also forest types
Clay, J.W., 59, 151
Cleese, J., 208
Cleveland, D., 119
Clifford, J., 107
climate change, 5
Clusius (C. d'Ecluse), 83
coconut grater, 218, 222
codification of folk knowledge, 81–82, 85, 89–91, 93, 95, 98, 105–106, 110, 131
co-evolution, 4, 52, 59
cognition
  cultural, 243
  of natural history knowledge, 82–83, 115, 216
  social, 214–16
cognitive anthropology, 9, 12, 23, 104, 118, 120, 131, 178, 183
cognitive prototypes, 178, 217
Coiffier, C., 48, 52n3
Coker, P., 137
Colby, B., 121
Colchester, M., 56
Cole, M., 128

Colfer, C.J.P., 151
colonialism, Dutch, 53–54, 64–66, 83, 95, 136–37, 157
commodification
    of nature, 43, 50, 70
    of indigenous knowledge, 96
common-sense, 20, 78, 100, 103, 123
comparison, 11–13, 16–18, 44–45, 48, 51–52
componential analysis, 207–208
Condit, R., 150
Condominas, G., 48
confirmation bias, 126
Conklin, B., 87
Conklin, H.C., 161, 186, 243n1
conservation, 77, 218
consubstantiality, 51
Cook, F.E.M., 236
Cooper, A., 211, 236
Coppinger, R., 199
cosmology, 231, 237
Cotgrove, S., 31
Cotton, C.M., 81
Coursey, D.G., 62
covert categories, 228–29
Cowling, T.G., 231
Creswell, R., 195
critical realism, 19, 26
criteria clustering, 178
Croll, E., 61, 93
Crumley, C.L., 4
Cuba, 16–17
cultural model, 123
Cultural Survival, 78
cuscus, 202, 218
Cutkowsky, M.R., 189

Dahad Monogolians, 14
Damon, F.H., 41–42, 45, 48
D'Andrade, R.G., 123
Daribi, 42, 44, 48, 51–52n2
Darwin, C. and Darwinism, 4, 29, 34, 79, 82, 113, 237
Deacon, T., 15, 18
deforestation, 22, 31, 33, 68, 70, 74

Deleuze, G., 7
demography, 36–37
Descartes, R., 13, 51–52, 226
Descola, P., 3, 6–7, 9–14, 51, 201, 221, 242–43
Desmond, A., 82
development, 58, 76–77, 86, 88, 90–97, 99, 105, 136
    discourse, 89, 97
    participatory, 93
Diamond, J.M., 47, 87, 134n1
diachronic separation, 230
Dionysian cultures, 32
Dioscorides, 81
disciplinarity, 224–25
distinctive feature analysis, 211
disturbance history, 155, 157, 163, 167–70, 177, 179–81
Dobbs, B.J.T., 110
dogs, 15–17
    thinking like, 199–200, 202, 221–22, 222n12
domain
    cultural, 243
    mutualism, 9 (see also mutualism)
    specificity, 9, 213
Donald, M., 124
Dougherty, J.W.D., 187
Douglas, M., 121, 127, 209
Dove, M.R., 59, 86, 97, 136–37, 151, 157, 240
doxa, 119–20, 122–23
Dransfield, J., 228
dualism, 3–4, 8, 10, 18–19, 23, 30, 51, 66, 79, 104, 121, 179, 209, 215, 225, 227
Duna, 52n2
Dunbar, K., 126
Dunbar, R.I.M., 106, 113–16, 119, 124, 130–31
Durkheim, E., 121, 195
Durrans, B., 234
Durrenberger, E., 82
Dusun, 138
Dwyer, P.D., 47, 50

East India Company, Dutch (VOC), 54, 64, 83–84, 107, 230
Ecotopia, 28–29
Edwards, I.D., 56, 60, 141, 143, 148, 152
ecological
　anthropology, 4, 8
　change (*see* environmental change)
　Eden, concept of, 76
ecology
　historical, 4, 59, 62
　as science, 28, 118, 179, 237
　as systems theory, 237
Einstein, A., 117
emic. *See* folk knowledge
enclavement, 98
engineering, 120
engines, 201–208, 222
entification. *See* thingification
environmental
　change, 41, 43, 52–54, 56, 63–64, 67–68, 71–72, 118
　conflict, 27, 68
　consciousness, 53, 71
　degradation, 2, 44, 53, 67
　harmony (balance), 31–32, 34–36, 38, 87
environmentalism, 29, 89
　spiritual environmentalism, 31
environmentalist
　movements, 21, 32, 76, 96
　'myth', 87
　rhetoric, 22, 53, 67, 87
environmentality, 22
epidemiology of ideas, 84, 107
episteme
　concept, 243
　of modern biology, 236
epistemic divide, 107, 110
epistemology, 14, 18, 226
ergonomics, 192, 194, 201
Escobar, A., 8, 22, 27n
essentialism, 134n3, 159
etak, 20, 119–21
Etkin, N.L., 233

ethnobiology, 9, 23, 46, 105, 134n3, 183, 208, 217, 224
ethnobotany, 25, 83, 91, 96, 137, 148, 161, 184, 197, 226–27, 230, 234–37, 243
　definition, 224
　medical, 232–33, 236
　theory, 224, 242
ethnoecological categories, 24, 159
ethnoecology, 46, 77, 151, 157, 164
ethnography, 118
　of making and craft activity, 184
ethnoscience, 9, 25, 103–34, 104, 118–19, 121–22, 127–30, 132–33, 208–209, 211, 214
　hybridity with science, 157
Euclid, 129
evolutionary biology, 224, 237
exogram, 124
experimentation, 79, 119, 129, 131, 214, 221, 240
Eyre, F.H., 135
Ezhavas, 84

'factish', 10
Fairhead, J., 88, 93, 151, 158
Fajans, J., 41, 47
fallow, 162, 172, 187
falsification, 112
Farquhar, J., 95
Feld, S., 43, 50, 167
Fernandez-Gimenez, M., 158, 172, 174
fetishization, 208
Feyerabend, P., 113
fieldwork, logic of, 237
Figala, K., 231
Finnegan, R.H., 100
fire in resource management, 97, 185
Fischer, M.D, 133, 184, 187
Fitzgerald, D., 11, 242
Flach, M., 62
Fleck, D.W., 136, 162
Florey, M., 180
Foi, 42
Foley, W.A., 128

folk biology. *See* ethnobiology
Ford, R.I., 224, 242
forest, 54, 97
  anthropic, 59
  climax, 150
  conceptions of, 50, 53, 63, 66, 155, 178
  degradation and depletion, 56, 154, 168
  ecology, 135, 145, 178
  ethnoecology methods, 137–43
  extraction from, 53, 55
  as fuzzy concept, 167
  historicity of, 150
  human use of, 151–55
  knowledge of, 23–24, 161–62
  managed, 59, 151
  modification of, 151–55
  Nuaulu categories of, 61–62, 155–57
  Nuaulu concept of, 166
  official classifications of, 135, 148–50
  politics, 136
  primary (mature), 154, 162–63, 181
  riparian, 147
  sacred and protected, 156, 172–73, 176–77
  secondary growth, 154–55, 172, 181
  variation, knowledge of, 164, 179
  See also forest diversity, forest types *and* rainforest
forest diversity, 135–60, 162, 164, 181
  local and scientific understanding compared, 135–60, 161–62
forest types, folk classification of, 135–37, 161–63. *See also* Nuaulu
  influence of land tenure, 172–73, 177, 182
  influence of social factors, 178
  'lexical repertoire' of, 164
  species-specific categories, 171–72, 177
  influence of topography and substrate, 170, 177 (*see also* toponymy *and* disturbance)
  history

forestry, 157–58
  administration, 137
  politics of, 136
formalisation of textual knowledge, 128–29, 131
Fosberg, F.R., 154
Foucault, M., 7, 22, 107, 243
Fox, J.J., 48
Frake, C.O., 104, 212
Franklin, S., 10
Frazer, J., 17
Fukui, K., 9
fungi, 200, 209, 217

Gaia, 28
Galen, 94, 106
gardening, 24–25, 64–65, 184–85, 187, 192, 196–97
  learning as physical practice, 196
Geertz, C., 6, 226
Gell, A., 21, 43, 51, 120, 203, 208, 218–19
Gély, A., 161, 172
Gelman, R., 115
Gelman, S., 214
gender, 2, 40, 42, 63, 80, 106
geographical isolation, 30, 37
Ghimire, S., 238
Gianno, R., 241
Gieser, T., 198
Gilbert, P.R., 198
Gillison, T., 42
Gladwin, T., 120
Glatzel, G., 143, 148, 150
Glick, L., 47
Global Information Systems (GIS), 135, 158
globalization, 72–73, 83–84, 131
  and electronic media, 71, 76, 95, 196
  of knowledge, 101
glocalisation, 101
Goodenough, W.H., 120
Goody, J.R., 128, 232
governmentality, 22
Goward, N.J., 63, 193
Graham, L., 87
Gray, A., 78

great cognitive divide, 100, 104, 132
great Columbian exchange, 240
great and little traditions, 106
Greenland, 30
Greenpeace, 30
green politics, 21, 28, 32–34, 38–39
Grenand, P., 155, 181
Griegg-Smith, P., 138
Grimes, B., 48
Grove, R., 84–85, 102n6, 107
Grzimek, B.R., 58
Guattari, F., 7
Guddemi, P., 50
Gudeman, S., 70
Guinea, 89
Guyana, 138, 163

habitats are not 'things', 162
Hacking, I., 113
Haeckel, E., 237
Haggard, H. R., 28
Haida, 32–33
Hallam, E., 184
Hallowell, A.I., 10–11, 17, 211
Hämäläinen, P., 39n2
hands, 185, 188, 191–94
   evolution of human, 184
   grasping, 190
   power and precision grips, 189–91, 193
   role in weeding, 189–91
   taxonomy of grips, 189
   wrist, lever and push actions, 193
Hansen, J.D.L., 36
Hanunóo, 128
Haraway, D., 225
Harder, J.D., 136, 162
Hardjono, J., 56
Harré, R., 126
Harris, H., 22, 86, 89, 232
Harris, S., 232
Hart, G., 70
Hastrup, K., 3
Haudricourt, A., 62
Hausa, 91
Hays, T., 47

head-hunting, 58
Headland, T.N., 185
Healey, C., 47, 96
Heidegger, M., 7
Hempel, C., 113
Henare, A.J.M., 26, 242
Henrich, J., 17
Henry, J., 133
Henschel, A.W.E.T, 85
herbalism, 106, 129
herbals, pictorial, 238–39
herbaria, 234
Herbarium Amboinense, 84–85, 230–31
Herodotus, 219
Herzfeld, M., 19
Hewlett, B.S., 183
Hinduism, 34
Hippocrates, 83
Hirsch, E., 47, 51
Hoare, A.L.,181
Hobart, M., 80, 88–89, 93
Hobsbawm, E., 79
Holbraad, M., 7, 13, 16–17, 26, 242
holism, 227
Holla-Bhar, R., 86
Holland, 85, 230
Hollis, M., 100
homeostasis, 30, 37
homunculus, concept of, 110–11, 231
Hooke, R., 113, 129–30
Hooker, J.D., 85
Horton, R., 100
Hoskins, J., 215
Howard, J.A., 135
Howe, R.D., 189
Howell, N., 2, 36
Howell, S., 48
Hsu, E., 232–33, 239–40
Huarani, 202
Huaulu, 51
Huli, 52n2
human exceptionalism, 7, 225
Humle, T., 185
Hunn, E., 79, 85, 89, 131, 210
hunting, 50, 93, 97, 137–38, 155, 164, 202–203

Hurst, P., 56
Huxley, A., 192
Hyndman, D., 46

Iatmul, 48
Icelandic fishing, 82
International Council for Science (ICSU), 134n1
Ifugao, 31
India, 54, 83–85, 97
indigeneity, concept of, 77
indigenous activism, 76, 94
indigenous ecological wisdom, 30, 32, 34, 58, 76, 87–88, 96
indigenous environmental knowledge (IEK), 76–102. *See also* indigenous knowledge
  changes in, 76–102
indigenous knowledge
  concept, 20, 23, 27, 76, 105, 132, 240
  and cultural identity, 96
  decontextualisation of, 93, 98
  definition, 77–80, 98, 103, 106
  embeddedness, 89, 102
  end of, 98
  history of, 103–105, 116
  and history of science, 77
  legal status, 86
  as local knowledge, 79
  marginalization, 85–87, 105, 110, 1123
  recording, 90–94
  rediscovery, 105
  reinvention, 87–89, 95
  and science, 103–104
  as science, 114
  in the West, 81
  versus Western knowledge, 92
indigenousness as applied to knowledge, 77–78
indigenous rights, 78, 94, 96
Indonesia, 6, 36–37, 40–41, 44, 54–55, 59–60, 66, 68, 72–75, 78, 83, 85, 93, 97, 135–39, 143, 151, 159, 164, 186, 192, 200–201, 215, 230, 240
Indonesian National Herbarium, 142

induction, 130–31
inference, 130–31
Ingold, T., 2, 7, 10–11, 15, 18–19, 62, 100, 184, 187, 220, 223n3
instituted process, 127
intellectual property rights, 96
intentionality, 208, 216, 219–21, 223n3
International Biological Programme (IBP), 196
International Society of Ethnobiology (ISE), 224
intersubjectivity, 123–24, 126, 133
intracultural variation, 178
intuitive physics, 46, 216
irrigation, 182n1
Iskandar, J., 115, 186
International Working Group for Indigenous Affairs (IWGIA), 78

Japan, 97
Java and Javanese, 37, 50, 54, 84, 137, 182n1, 186
Johannes, R.E., 86–87, 134n1
Johns, R.J., 150
Johns, T., 115, 238
Johnson, M., 102n2
Johnson-Laird, P., 116
Johnston, C.A., 135
Johnston, M., 138
Joint Forest Management, 159
Jorgensen, D., 43, 47
Judaeo-Christianity, 28, 34
Just, R., 19, 194

Ka'apor, 161
Kalasha, 98
Kalimantan, 138. *See also* Borneo
Kaluli, 43, 50
Kamea, 41–42, 45, 48–49, 51
Kant, I., 13, 226
Karim, W.A., 63
Karimojong, 33
Kasepuhan, 182n1
Kathirithamby-Wells, J., 157
Kayapó, 98, 161
Kei Islands, 240–41

Keil, F.C., 9, 115, 134n3, 212, 214, C.M., 187, 193
Keller, J.D., 187, 193
Keller, C.D, 187, 193
kenari, 60, 63, 152–53, 155, 171, 180
Kent, M., 137
Kent (English county), 191–94
Kershaw, K.A., 137
Kew, 142, 234–36, 240
  herbarium, 227
Kiddell-Monroe, R., 56
Kingsbury, B., 78
Kirsch, S., 42–43, 50, 52n1
Kluckhohn, E.R., 31
Knight, D., 82
Knight, J., 97
knowledge
  agroecological knowledge, 119
  bodily,127, 184, 191
  disjunction in market places, 242
  distributed, 80
  European folk, 81–83, 106–107
  flexibility, 80
  folk, 81, 106, 112, 135 (*see also* codification *and* indigenous knowledge)
  great versus little traditions of healing, 95
  great scholarly ways of knowing and traditions of healing, 94–95, 106–107, 112, 238
  holistic, 80
  lexical, 127, 183
  local, 76–77 (*see also* folk knowledge)
  local versus universal, 238
  loss, 183
  as performance, 91
  rediscovery by doing, 184
  representational, 127
  sharing, 80, 126, 163–64
  social differentiation of, 80
  specialist, 80
  substantive versus lexical, 127, 164, 187
  symbolic versus technical (mundane), 121–22, 124–25, 220
  theoretical, 79, 106
  traditional (*see* indigenous knowledge)
  transmission and acquisition, 4–25, 27, 105, 131, 183–84, 195–96 (*see also* learning)
  variation,164
  Western, 88
Kocher-Schmid, C., 47–48, 52n3
Koentjaraningrat, 57
Koerner, L., 131, 134n2, 231
Kohn, E., 6–7, 10, 14–17, 19
Kopnina, H., 3
Kouranko, 89
Kropotkin, P., 30
Kuhn, D., 113, 117–18, 123, 130–31
Kuikuru, 161
Kull, K., 9
Kung! San, 36
Kuper, A., 51
Kuznar, L.A., 133
Kwakiutl, 32

Laidlaw, J., 8
Lakatos, I., 113
land
  conflict, 22, 58
  sale, 57–58, 66, 72
landscape, 41–42, 49, 161
  and biography, 43–44
  cultural density of, 156, 175
language, 15, 20, 51, 124
  learning, 117
Lapps, 107–108, 124, 134n2, 231
Latin, 83, 124
Latinis, D.K., 64, 152
Latour, B., 3, 5, 7,10, 225, 232
Laudan, L., 133
Leach, E.R., 8, 209–10, 215
Leach, M., 88, 93, 151, 158, 211
learning
  institutional context of, 196–96
  role of artwork in acquiring skills, 185
  See also language learning
Lecuyer, J., 81

Leibnitz, G.W., 114
Leiden, 83
Lemonnier, P., 102n8, 195–96
Leeuwenhoek, A. van, 110, 129–30, 231
Leroi-Gourhan, A., 194–95
Lévi-Strauss, C., 8, 12, 18, 46, 51, 209, 215, 223n2, 230
Lévy-Bruhl, L., 17
Lewis-Jones, K.E., 236
lexicalisation, 163, 177–78, 181–82
   degrees of, 162
   of implicit knowledge, 127, 131, 156
Lezaun, J., 27, 242
Li, T.M., 97
Lieberman, P., 117
life, concept of, 7, 10, 15, 25, 27
   'life-like', 216
   as a matter of degree, 219, 221
   peripheral or liminal biological, 200, 209, 217–18
   as a taxonomic category, 208–11
   See also living matter and living things
Linares, O.F., 155
Lincoln, R.J., 160n1
linear-sentential
   fallacy, 179
   mode, 128
Linnaean grid, 129, 237
Linnaeus, C., 25–26, 82, 85, 107–110, 124–25, 131, 134n2, 212, 230–31, 237
   deification of, 125, 231
Lio, 48
lists, 231
literacy, 104, 124, 128, 158, 234
living matter and living things
   boundary issues, 217
   as a category, 25, 199–223
   morphological resemblance between, 220
Lloyd, G.E.R., 118–19, 128
logging, 22, 41, 53, 55–56, 59, 68, 70–72, 74, 152, 166
long fallow systems. *See* swiddening
Lourie, J.A., 196

Lubbock, J., 31
Lukes, S., 100
Lundayeh, 180–81
Luzon, 31
Lyotard, J., 80

Maasai, 37
Mabey, R., 189
machines, 201–208, 219, 222
Magnani, N., 241
Makushi, 138, 163–64, 179, 181, 220
malaria, 233–34, 240
Malay, 84
Malaysia, 17, 59, 98, 151, 157, 240
Malinowski, B., 102n7
Maloney, B.K., 59, 151
Maluku. *See* Moluccas
Manokaran, N., 228
Manusela National Park, 141, 143, 145, 148, 218
Maori, 226
map-making, 137, 157–58, 160n1, 174
   ground truthing, 159
   participatory, 156, 159, 174
   problems of official ignorance, 158
Marchand, T.H.J., 184
Martin, G.J., 137
Martin, M., 161
Marxism, 29
Maschio, T., 43
Masipiqueña, A., 97
'masyarakat terasing', 57–58, 66
material culture, 184, 195, 235
materialities, including plant, 7, 225, 234–35
mathematics, 119, 129
Matses, 162
Matsigenka, 161–64, 177, 182, 182n1
Matsuzama, T., 185
Mauss, M., 121, 194–95, 215, 220
Mbuti, 33, 36
MacAndrews, C., 56
McCormack, C., 9, 45
McKey, D., 238, 240
McKibben, W., 3
medical anthropology, 233

Meilleur, B.A., 161–62
Melanesia, 21–22, 40–52
meme, 116
memory
　episodic, 11
　externalization, 123–24
　semantic, 11
Mende, 186
Meratus, 228–29
metaphor, 17
methodology, 100, 113, 119. *See also* plot surveys and methodologies
Meyer, R., 239
micro-ecology, 194–95, 197
Micronesia, 20, 120
microscopy, 130, 231
Miller, D., 208
Miller, T.L., 224, 230
Milton, K., 101
Mindanao, 31
mining, 43
Mithen, S., 9, 115, 216
Mnong-Gar, 48
models
　instituted, 126
　multi-dimensionality, 135, 162–63, 165, 179, 182, 238
modernism, 105, 112
'modern synthesis' of botanical science, 230
modularity
　limits of, 214–16
　as model of mind, 9, 115
Moerman, D.E., 115
Moluccas, 15, 48–51, 53–54 60, 65, 67, 84, 93, 95, 137–38, 141–42, 145, 164, 204, 207
Mongolia, 238
Moniaga, S., 56
Moore, J., 82
Moran, E., F., 159
Morgan, C., 52n2
Morris, B., 19
motion, 216, 217–23
　independent, 220–21
　physical, 201

motors, outboard, 200–201, 205–207, 218
movement. *See* motion
Mpembe effect, 119
multisensorality, 216, 222. *See also* synaesthesia
Muraille, B., 135
museums of economic botany, 236
　and ethnography compared, 234–35
mutualism
　of social and natural concepts, 121, 215–16, 223
　of tool and organism concepts, 222
Muyuw, 41–42

Nader, L., 104
Namibia, 158
naming of plants, 183
Napier, J.R., 189–90
narrativity, 48, 119, 122
Native Americans, 29, 32
natural history knowledge and intelligence, 46, 104, 115–16, 134n3
　European, 211
natural kinds
　concept, 9
　minerals as, 211–12
natural resource management, 137
natural selection, 107
naturalism, 8, 10–12, 16, 18–20, 26, 201, 227, 242
naturalisation of society, 40
nature
　anthropogenic, 42
　cognitive versus social theories of, 44–45
　as essence, otherness and things, 9, 46 (*see also* thingification)
nature concepts, 2–5, 18, 20–21, 27, 40, 51, 61, 64, 72, 100, 119–21
　changing, 70–71
　cognitive aspects of, 41, 45–48, 51, 61, 101, 107, 120–21
　English folk classification and, 209–10
　and the gradient of agricultural intensification, 49–50

cultural and social construction of, 41, 225
as 'other', 47
deconstruction of, 2, 7–10, 45
in relation to grain and seed cultures, 49–50
as relational constructs, 225
renegotiation of, 61–67
and scale, 2
socialisation of, 40
vegetative versus seed propagation influencing, 49–50, 62–63
Western, 58–59, 61
nature-culture distinction and opposition, 45, 209, 215, 225
nature-cultures, 3, 10
nature, end of, 3, 5
nature-like concepts, 4–5, 45–46
navigation, 120
Needham, J., 100
neem, 8
Neihardt, J.O., 29
Nelson, B.W., 136
Neolithic, 185
neo-paganism, 28
networks of understanding, 118
neurophysiology, 104
New Britain, 41, 43
New Guinea, 22, 31, 33, 35, 41, 43–44, 46, 50, 60, 136, 143, 148, 161, 186, 204
Newton, I., 110, 114, 120, 231
physics of, 20
Ngaju, 228
Nida-Conklin hypothesis, 178
Nigeria, 91, 134n3
nitrogen fixation, 115
'Noble Savage', 28
Non-governmental Organizations (NGOs), 22, 76, 78, 89, 94–98
indigenous, 89
North Borneo. See Sabah
Nuaulu, 6, 13–14, 22–25, 36–37, 48–51, 53–76, 135–40, 142, 144–45, 147–48, 152–54, 156, 158–59, 161, 163–72, 174–77, 179–82, 186–88, 200–208, 212–13, 215, 217–19, 221–22, 226, 228–29, 232, 234–36, 240–41, 243
classification of vegetation types, 143–151
Ethnobotanical Database (NED), 142, 165–66, 176
ethnoecological classification of forest, 165–77
Nuer, 17

Oatley, K.G., 112–13, 119–20, 126, 130
Ohmagari, K., 183
Ohnuki-Tierney, E., 121
Ojibwa, 10–11, 17, 20, 211
Oksapmin, 52n2
Ok Tedi, 42–43, 50
Olson, D.R., 128
omniscient speaker-hearer, 124
ontological
friction, 242
paradox, 19
turn, 1–2, 6–8, 10, 16, 18, 20–21, 25–26, 201, 242
ontological interfaces
between local functional domains, 227, 241–42
created by plant and knowledge movement, 227, 238–41
ecological versus phylogenetic, 227, 236–38
museum versus lived practice, 227, 234–36
scientific phytomedicine versus medical anthropology, 227, 232–34
pre-Linnaean natural history versus science, 227, 230–32
taxonomic orthodoxy versus local folk classification, 227–30
translation between, 226
ontology, 6–13, 15–18, 20–21, 26–27, 98, 201, 207–208, 211, 213–14, 220, 243
early modern naturalist, 231
flexible, 231
and plant knowledge systems, 224–43
oral transmission of knowledge, 79, 81

orality, 104, 106, 124
organomorphism, 215–16
'Original Affluent Society', 36
Orta, G. da, 83–84, 102n3, 107
Osseweijer, M., 96
Overing, J., 100

Padoch, C., 59, 151
Paijmans, K., 148
Pakistan, 98
palms
    folk classification of, 228–29
    psychoactivity of fruit, 228
Pálsson, G., 5, 9, 82
Parfionovitch, D., 239
Parker, E., 161
Parkes, P., 96–97
Parkin, D., 61
participatory methods, 141
pastoralism,14, 32
Patalima-Patasiwa distinction, 15
Pedersen, M.A., 7, 13–15
Peeters, A., 84
Peluso, N.L., 59, 137, 151
Penan, 98, 138, 161, 180
Pepys, S., 192
person, concept, 15, 17, 19
personification, 41, 215, 220
Persoon, G.A., 57, 97, 136
perspectivism, 7, 13–16, 215
Peru, 162
pest control, 119
Peters, C., 151
Pfaffenburger, B., 112
pharmaceutical industry, 96
pharmacology, 83
physics, 119–20, 129. *See also* Newton
phytomorphism, 215, 220
phytotherapy, 236
Pierce, C.S., 130
Pina-Cabral, J. de, 6
Pires, J.M., 151
plants
    breeding, 119
    as cultural objects, 236
    ecology, 162
    measures of diversity, 150–51
    toxicity in phytomedicine, 238
Plantades, F., 110
Platten, S., 184
Pleistocene megafauna, 33
Pliny the Elder, 211
plot surveys and methodologies, 137–42, 144–46, 148, 152, 164, 166, 169–73, 175–77, 237
pollution, 31
polythesis, 200, 216, 221
Popper, K., 112–13
Portugal, 83
Posey, D.A., 59, 78, 96, 151
post-modernism, 100, 103, 105, 114
posture, 192
potlatch, 32
Poulsen, A.D., 148
Powell, J., 242
Praet, I., 221
Prance, G.T., 59, 151
pre-adaptation, 185
prehension, 179, 227, 229
primitive
    ecological wisdom (*see* indigenous ecological wisdom)
    society concept, 28–32, 34
printing, 84, 196
Proctor, J., 148
psychology
    child, 214
    cognitive, 46, 113, 117, 208
    developmental, 214
Pujol, R., 81
Puri, R.K., 138, 151, 161, 180

Radermacher, J.C.M., 85
rainforest, tropical, 162–63, 185. *See also* forest
    ecology, 157
    lowland, 143–51
    modelling, 158
    patchiness (mosaic) of, 135, 150–51, 158–60, 162, 164, 166, 171, 177
Rambo, A.T., 59, 151
Ranger, T., 79

rank concept, 223n2, 227, 229
Rapoport, A., 32
Rappaport, R.A., 4, 35, 51, 186
rationality
    and relativism debate, 100
    spheres of, 122
rattan, 152, 172, 228, 241
Rauto, 43
Raven, P.H., 46, 162
Rayner, S., 5
recursiveness, 7, 16–18, 20
reductionism as a response to increased knowledge of diversity, 237
redundancy and repetition in knowledge storage, 79
Redford, K.H., 59, 151
Reed, E.S., 218
regimes of function compared with regimes of making, 241
relationality, 11, 27
relativism, cultural, 103, 133, 233
remote sensing, 135, 158
reproduction, inference of, 217
resin extraction, 74n3, 139, 152, 154, 167, 241
Rheede tot Drakenstein, H. von, 83–84, 107
Rhoades, R., 99
rice, 182n1, 186
Richards, P., 86, 89, 91, 117, 119, 124, 186
Richards, P.W., 137, 148, 154
Rival, L.M., 48, 202, 220–21, 223n3, 240
Robbins, J., 43–44
Robertson, R., 101
Rodman, M.C., 42, 44
Roepstorff, A., 9
Romans, 29
Ross, N., 161
Roszak, T., 28
routinised experience, convenience of, 195
Roxburgh, W., 85
rubber, 97, 240

Rumphius, G.E., 54, 84–85, 107, 110–11, 211–12, 230–32, 234
Runa, 15–17, 20

Saami. *See* Lapps
Sabah, 157, 180
sago, 37, 49, 57, 59–60, 62–63, 65–67, 69–70, 138, 151, 156, 164, 168, 170, 172–74, 228, 240
    processing apparatus, 200–205, 207, 218–19, 222
Sahel, 33
Sahlins, M., 26, 36
Sahul, 143
Salick, J., 138
Sapir-Whorf hypothesis, 178
sasi, 93–95
Sausdal, D.B., 17
Schieffelin, E., 43
Schmid, J., 47, 52n3
Schmink, M., 59, 151
Schreer, V., 228
science
    abstraction in, 129, 131
    as argumentative reasoning, 130
    artwork in, 129
    boundary maintenance, 124–25, 133
    as cognition, 127, 131
    concept of, 9–10, 12, 19, 23, 27, 76–77, 80–83, 85–89, 99, 103–34, 123, 126, 130, 132
    and counter-intuitivity, 100, 118–19
    as a culture, 123
    definition, 103, 107, 113, 133
    ethnocentrism of, 86
    and ethnoscience, 117
    folk, 119 (*see also* ethnoscience)
    globally instituted, 126–32
    history of, 103
    as an instituted mode, 122–26
    institutionalisation of, 128
    material culture (instrumentation) in, 129–30
    programmatic theories of, 112–13
    proto-science, 107–108, 230
    pseudo-science, 133

as routinisation of intense criticism, 130–31
simplification in, 129
social production, 126
as specialist knowledge, 116–19
as 'sufficient precision', 133
theories of, 104, 112–14, 118, 129–30
uncertainty in, 130
'science-like' thinking' as a universal, 114–16
'Science Wars', 103–104
'scientific' anthropology, 133
Scoones, I., 80, 90
Scott, J.C., 23, 136
Scott, M.W., 6, 13, 18, 26, 225
Scribner, S., 128
secondary biodiversity
    folk classification of, 161–62, 182 (*see also* classification *and* forest types)
    folk systematics not a good guide to, 165, 178, 182
Secord, J., 82
Semalai, 241
Seram, 36–37, 48, 53–55, 57, 59–60, 64, 66, 137–39, 143, 145, 148–49, 151–54, 157, 164, 179, 205–206, 228, 241
Shakespeare, W., 31
shamanism, 14, 101
Shepard, G.H., 136, 162–63, 181
Sierra Leone, 186
shifting cultivation. *See* swiddening
Shiva, V., 86
Shore, B., 123
Sigaut, F., 192, 195
Sillitoe, P., 44, 46, 50–51, 136, 138, 154, 161, 178, 182n1, 186
Singer, C., 110
Sioux, 34
situated practice, 227
Sivaramakrishnan, K., 137, 159
SKEPHI (Sekretariat Kerjasama Pelestarian Hutan Indonesia), 56
skewers, meat, 200–203, 218–19
slash-and-burn, 56
Slikkerveer, L.J., 88, 90, 92, 99, 102n2

smell, sense of, 216
Smith, J., 223n2
sociality, 219, 235, 238, 243
sociobiology, 29
sociology of science, strong theory, 114, 233
Soedjito, H., 74n3
Soemarwoto, R., 182n1
Soleri, D., 119
somatic practices, moral enforcement of, 195
Soselisa, H.L., 240
sound (acoustics), 216
    ecology, 41, 43, 50–51
Southeast Asia, 24, 60, 84, 97, 136, 141, 161, 180–81
space-time, 47
species
    concept, 9
    density of useful, 176
    keystone, 228
    richness, 146, 148, 176
    transformation, 110
Spencer, J.E., 150
Sperber, D., 118, 134n3
spermatozoa, 110
spice trade, 53–54, 65
spirits, 25, 200, 202–203, 205, 207, 211–12, 220, 222
    as pseudo-organisms, 212
spontaneous generation of living matter, 110
Spradley, J.P., 21
Spretnak, C., 28
Sprugel, D.G., 151
Staal, F., 100
stable equilibrium models, 150
Stark, K., 64
Steward, J., 4
Stewart, P.J., 52n2
Strathern, A., 52n2
Strathern, M., 7, 9, 21, 42, 44–45, 51, 61, 100–101
Street, B., 28–29
Strodtbeck, F.L., 31
Stross, B., 183

Sturtevant, W.C., 234
Suharno, D.M., 148, 180
Suharto, 159
Sunda, 143
Sundar, N., 97
Survival International, 30, 78
suspension of belief, 117–18, 122
sustainability, ecological, 21, 34, 37, 56, 59, 70–71, 76, 151
Sutisna, U., 142
swiddening, 49, 56, 59–60, 66, 86, 136, 138, 151, 154, 161–62, 164, 172, 181, 185–87, 241
  cycle, 168
Swift, J., 33
syllogism, 129, 211
Sylvan, R., 28
synaesthesia, 50, 184, 188, 216, 222. *See also* multisensoriality
synecology, folk, 238
systematics, folk, 162
systems approaches, 4

taboo, 16
Tacitus, 29
tactility, 216
Tantra, I.G.M, 142
Taoism, 31, 34
Tasaday, 31
taskonomy, 187, 194, 197
taskscape, 187, 193–94
taxonomy (including folk taxonomy), 9, 13, 24–25, 79, 82, 107, 116, 124, 134–35, 143, 162, 165, 178, 200, 208–14, 216, 218, 227, 234–35, 237
Taylor, P.M., 207–209
Telefomin, 43, 47
textualisation of lexical knowledge, 128–29, 131
Theophrastus, 212
thingification, 9, 46, 215
Thomas, E., 183
Thomas, K., 35, 44
Thompson, J., 80, 90
Through the Looking Glass, 1–2
Tibetan medicine, 106, 129, 238–39

time-space compression, 101
Timor, 54
Tobelo, 207–209
Tönnies, F., 31
tools, 25, 192–93, 199–208, 215, 218–19, 221
  animation of, 199
  classification of, 212–13
  in motion, 199
  taxonomy, 213
  tool-body arrangement, 193
toponymy and toponymic grid, 155–58, 164–65, 167, 174–75, 177
Torquebiau, E.F., 151
Torres-Cuderos, M., 161
totemism, 12, 15–16, 32–33, 46, 201, 204, 242
transitivity, 214, 227
trans-local generalization, 131
transmigration, 22, 53, 56–57, 68, 70–71, 164, 166
Traube, E.G., 48
tree
  management, 89
  naming and identification skills, 161, 164, 166, 175
Trobriand Islands, 122
Truswell, A.S., 36
Tsembaga Maring, 35, 186
Tsing, A., 3, 228–29, 231–32
Turnbull, C., 33, 36
Turnbull, D., 112–13

Uexküll, J. von, 7
Ulijaszek, S., 196
Umeda, 43
Urapmin, 43–44, 52n2
usefulness, as a classificatory device, 236

Valencia, R., 137, 141
Valentijn, F., 110–11, 231
Valeri, V., 49, 62, 74n4
Vandergeest, P., 137
Vanuatu, 42, 44
Vayda, A.P., 4

Vesalius, A., 129
Vienna, 83
Vigh, H.E., 17
Vilaça, A., 7, 17
Vitebsky, P., 101
Viveiros de Castro, E., 7, 14–16, 20, 27, 215
Vygotsky, L.S., 126

Wagner, R., 42, 44
Walden, 28
Waldstein, A., 232
Walker, D.H., 115
Wallacea, 143
Wallace's Line, 139
Warren, D.M., 88, 90, 92, 99, 102n2
Wastell, S., 26, 242
Watt, G., 85
Wear, A., 81
'web of life', 237
Weckerle, C., 237
weeds and weeding, 25, 183–98
  as an anthropological category, 185–87
  as a cultural domain, 187–88
  'cyborg' weeding, 197–98
  deskilling, 198
  identifying weeds, 188–89
  learning how to weed, 184–98
  material culture regarding, 191–94
  as a relational practice, 194
  as sociocultural activity, 194–96
Weiner, J., 40

Weiner, J.S., 196
Wellman, H.M., 118
WEIRD people, 17
White Jnr, L., 34
Whitmore, T.C., 141–42, 148
Wiersum, K.F., 159
wilderness concept, 42, 185
Wilkin, P.J., 241
Wilson, B.R., 100
Wit, de, H.C.D., 111
witchcraft, 16
Wola, 50, 161, 182n1, 186
Wolff, X.Y., 180
Wolpert, L., 100, 113, 118, 133
Woolgar, S., 27, 242
world system, 30, 54–56
writing, 79, 94, 106, 131, 179
Wulandari, A.P., 240

yams, 185–86, 240
Yearly, S., 89
Yekuana, 161
Yopno, 48
Yu, D.W., 136

Zafimaniry, 207
Zande, 16
Zapotec, 210
Zarger, R.K., 183
Zeitlyn, D., 19
Zerner, C., 56, 93, 95
Zimmerman, F., 82, 84, 102n6, 233
zoomorphism, 215, 220

www.ingramcontent.com/pod-product-compliance
Lightning Source LLC
Chambersburg PA
CBHW051529020426
42333CB00016B/1841